Two vols., crown 8vo, cloth, gilt top, price $5.

CORRESPONDENCE

OF

WAGNER AND LISZT

FROM

1841 to 1861.

TRANSLATED INTO ENGLISH WITH A PREFACE BY
DR. FRANCIS HUEFFER.

"These letters may, without hesitation, be classed among the most important documents of musical biography in existence."—*Times.*

"This correspondence is a weighty contribution to the store of valuable literature, dealing with what is,¡beyond all comparison, the most pregnant and important period in the development of musical art. Nothing more instructive with regard to the real character and relations of Liszt and Wagner has been published. Seldom has the force and fervour of Wagner's German been rendered with such accuracy and character in a strange tongue."—*Manchester Guardian.*

"These volumes, valuable as they are in illustrating the art philosophy of Wagner, contain many references to contemporary musicians and musical critics, practical hints as to the manner in which Wagner's masterpieces should be performed, and much other matter of supreme interest to musicians."—*The Scotsman.*

NEW YORK : SCRIBNER & WELFORD.

RICHARD WAGNER'S
LETTERS
TO HIS
DRESDEN FRIENDS.

Richard Wagner

Taken from a portrait
painted in 1842

RICHARD WAGNER'S
LETTERS

TO HIS

DRESDEN FRIENDS,

**THEODOR UHLIG, WILHELM FISCHER, AND
FERDINAND HEINE.**

TRANSLATED INTO ENGLISH, WITH A PREFACE

BY

J. S. SHEDLOCK.

AND AN ETCHING OF WAGNER BY C. W. SHERBORN.

NEW YORK:
SCRIBNER AND WELFORD.
1890.

PREFACE.

THE correspondence of Wagner and Liszt commenced in 1841 and closed in 1861; in this volume the letters extend from 1841 to 1868. Of early letters there are only a few; and setting aside these and the last written to Heine from Munich in 1868, the series may be said to begin in 1849 and to close in 1860. This represents the period of exile at Zurich; and amid much that is familiar we come across much that is new. Of the eventful visit to Paris in 1850, there is the briefest possible mention in a letter from Wagner to Liszt; but here in letters to Uhlig and Heine he pours out his whole soul, and tells of his sorrows, his anger, and his despair. The picture which he draws of himself is indeed a striking one. The Paris failure, however, as Wagner himself fully acknowledges, resulted in good. He returned to Switzerland, and soon the whole plan of the *Ring des Nibelungen* was conceived. The letter in which he describes his ambitious scheme to Liszt bears the date November 20th, 1851; but he had already written on the same

subject to Uhlig a week before.   Then, again, there
is the unfortunate visit to London in 1855.   The
five letters addressed to Fischer are full of characteristic details.   These subjects, and others connected
with Wagner's literary works, are naturally to be
found in both correspondences ; and it may be that
here and there we are reminded even of the phrase-
ology of the letters to Liszt.   But the differences are
greater than the resemblances.   Liszt showed great
sympathy for Wagner as a man, and extraordinary
enthusiasm for his art-work ; and this sympathy and
enthusiasm proved indeed powerful bonds of union
between the two.   But Liszt was a famous man,
and Wagner comparatively unknown ; and the friendship was not of that intimate kind which is so
clearly displayed to us in the letters to Uhlig, Fischer,
and in particular to Heine.   And in other important
matters Wagner himself tells Uhlig how Liszt
" stands apart from me in his life and mode of
thought."   But his Dresden friends were all in a
comparatively humble station of life, and in " modes
of thought " one with him.   The letter to Wilhelm
Fischer, dated November 20th, 1849, shows clearly
how strong was the bond of friendship between the
four men.   In many small, and perhaps in themselves unimportant details, we feel the difference in
the style of writing.   Here there are colloquialisms,
strong expressions, jokes, etc., such as are not to

be found in the letters to Liszt. There are details
with regard to Wagner himself, to his wife, his
home-life, his bird, and his dog which tell their own
story. To mention only one small instance. To
Liszt he writes two lines about the death of his " dear
little parrot ; " but to Uhlig a whole letter. I
would specially ask readers of these letters not to
forget their specially private character ; the bitter
remarks about certain musicians of note, the violent
denunciations of men standing in high places, and
the liberty of speech in which he occasionally
indulges must all be considered privileged. They
evidently were never intended for the public eye. In
a certain degree, one may regret the publication of
such letters ; there is a tendency to pick out what
is objectionable for condemnation, if not ridicule.
The good and the bad must, however, be taken
together. To have both put before us is in one
respect a great advantage ; we have the *whole* man,
and no one-sided representation.

A few particulars respecting the three friends
to whom these letters are addressed may perhaps
prove welcome.

Theodor Uhlig, who began at an early age to
take interest in music, studied composition under
Fr. Schneider, from 1837 to 1840. In 1841 he
became a member of the Royal Orchestra at
Dresden, and in 1852 leader of the same. He

was an accomplished musician, and composed overtures, quartets, trios, songs, etc.   He, of course,
became acquainted with *Rienzi*, *Flying Dutchman*,
and *Tannhäuser*, produced at Dresden under
Wagner's direction : however, up to the year 1847,
he was not in sympathy either with him or with his
art-views.   But an attentive perusal of the composer's "Programme" to the Choral Symphony, and
a careful examination of the score of *Tannhäuser*
lent to him, at his own request, by Wagner, brought
about a revolution.   Uhlig became a zealous disciple
and firm friend of the master's ; and from that
time down to his last day (he was snatched away
by death on January 3rd, 1853, in the thirty-first
year of his age) he devoted to him his time and his
talents.   Like Liszt, Uhlig found Wagner at times
difficult to get on with ; and in the letters before
us we find that on one or two occasions a rupture
seemed imminent.   In one letter Wagner writes :
" Truly, in our intercourse, if one of us two need
to make apology, it is I, once and always.   Pay
no attention, if now and then something in my
letters vexes you.   Unfortunately, I am often in
such bitter humour, that it almost affords me a cruel
relief to offend some one ; this is a calamity which
only makes *me* the more deserving of pity."   Uhlig,
like Liszt, made allowances for genius.   We learn
from a letter written by Wagner to Liszt, dated

July 11th, 1851, how much he valued the friendship of Uhlig. Speaking of him he says: "Thus I gained a friend, who subsequently from a distance made it the task of his life, as far as his power extended, to serve me in a manner which—the inclination being equal in both cases—has been surpassed only by your brilliant genius." After Uhlig had become acquainted with Wagner, he abandoned composition and took to literary work. He was one of the most industrious contributors to the *Neue Zeitschrift für Musik ;* and the obituary notice by J. Rühlmann in 1853 shows how highly his services were valued. Besides articles on Wagner's operas and pamphlets, he wrote a series of articles on the Beethoven Symphonies, and another series entitled *Lesefrüchte auf dem Felde der musikalischen Literatur.*

Wilhelm Fischer, who was born about the year 1790, was connected with the opera at Magdeburg and Leipzig ; in the latter city he appeared as a *buffo* bass singer. He went to Dresden in 1831, and became stage-manager and chorus-master at the theatre. In December 1840, Wagner, who was in Paris, sent the score of *Rienzi* to Herr v. Lüttichau, the Intendant. The first of the letters to Fischer is dated September 7th, 1841, and refers to the acceptance of that opera by the management. From that letter it appears that Wagner was not

personally known to him then. They met in the
following year ; and from that time down to Fischer's
death in November 1859 they were on excellent
terms.   In an obituary notice of his old friend,
Wagner speaks of the consolation of knowing that
such beings exist, of the happiness of meeting such
a man on one's path.

Ferdinand Heine was a comedian engaged at the
Dresden Court Theatre, and also a designer of the
costumes.   The first letter addressed to him by
Wagner is dated 1841, and the last 1868.   In this
collection there are only twenty-six ; so that it is
natural to suppose that many have got lost.   The
" highly honoured Herr Heine " changed to " dear old
friend " soon after they came to know each other, and
then he was addressed as *Heinemännel, Nante*, etc.
In his third letter Wagner claims the right of family
friendship, in that Heine was a friend of his father's.
In the letters there are many references to Wilhelm
Heine, the son, and to America and Japan.   This
talented son, born in 1827, went to New York in
1849, and became known there as a painter.   He
was artist of the expedition of the American squadron
to the China Seas and Japan during the years 1852,
1853, and 1854, under the command of Commodore
Perry, and he is twice mentioned in the official
narrative of the expedition.   In 1856 he published
his *Reise um die Erde nach Japan*, and between

1873 and 1880 his great work *Japan, Beiträge zur Kenntnis des Landes und seiner Bewohner.* Wilhelm Heine died in 1885.

The hurried and at times careless manner in which many of these letters were written, sentences apparently having been put on paper as fast as pen could write ; the constant references to persons and things which, with time, have lost their meaning; the fact that there are no answers to the letters, as in the Wagner-Liszt correspondence, to throw a light on questions or doubtful passages ; and the colloquialisms so plentifully scattered through the letters,—all these things have rendered the translator's task one of exceptional difficulty ; and as Wagner asked of Fischer with regard to *Rienzi,* so I too would ask of my readers—indulgence and patience. An attempt has been made to reproduce the style of the original ; and the question is not how far it reads as clear or good English, but how far it preserves the spirit of the original. I beg publicly to express my thanks to Messrs. Grevel & Co., the publishers, for their assistance with regard to the Saxon idioms and even slang, and to Mr. W. Ashton Ellis (editor of the Wagnerian quarterly, *The Meister*), for valuable aid and many useful suggestions, as well as for the preparation of a comprehensive Index.

J. S. SHEDLOCK.

LETTERS

TO

THEODOR UHLIG,

1849—1853.

LETTERS TO THEODOR UHLIG.
1849—1853.

DEAR FRIEND,

Every now and then I feel anxious about you :
how are you, are you well, and have you experienced
no reactionary unpleasantnesses ? There are some
friends, very few, for whose sake I often think of
Dresden : among other things I have a warm remembrance of a passionate Beethoven Symphony, and then
I am transported with delight and affection back again,
in thought, amongst the Royal Musicians ; yet I must
frankly confess that the freedom which I here inhale in
fresh Alpine draughts is intensely pleasing to me. What
is the ordinary care about the so-called future of
citizen life compared with the feeling that we are not
tyrannized over in our noblest aims ? How few men
care more for themselves than for their stomachs !
Now I have made my choice, and am spared the trouble
of choosing ; so I feel free in my innermost soul, and
can despise what torments me from without ; no one
can withdraw himself from the evil influences of the
civilized barbarism of our time, but all can so manage
that they do not rule over our better self.

I

My friend Liszt, with devilish impetuosity, wishes me to write an opera for Paris : I have been there and arranged with a certain poet to furnish him with the complete sketch of an opera libretto, while he undertakes the execution of the same in French, and to see about a commission for me from the Grand Opera to write the music (excuse me, I have not expressed myself very clearly). Now, besides my *Siegfried*, I have in my head two tragic and two comic subjects, but not one of them would suit the French stage : I have also a fifth, and I care not in what language it is presented to the world—*Jesus of Nazareth*. I think of offering this subject to the Frenchman, and hope thus to be rid of the whole matter, for I can guess the dismay which this poem will cause to my *associé*. If he have the courage to hold up against the thousand conflicts which the proposition to treat such a subject for the theatre will cause, I shall look upon it as fate and set to work. If he abandon me, all the better : I am then freed from all temptation to work in the hateful jabbering language ; for with my disposition, you can easily imagine that only with the greatest repugnance should I set to work on such a mishmash : if I do, it will be out of consideration for my creditors, to whom I should make over the French fees.

Into what good humour the sight of the Parisian art-economy has put me again, you will shortly see in an important article of mine in the *National*, " Art and Revolution," which I believe will appear in German at Wigand's in Leipzig. I am living here—helped in communistic fashion by Liszt—in good spirits, and I may say prosperously, according to my best nature : my only and great anxiety is about my poor wife, whom I am expecting here very shortly. To my very great astonishment, I find that I am a celebrity here ; made so indeed, by means of the piano scores of all my operas, out of which whole acts are repeatedly performed at concerts and at choral unions. At the beginning of the winter I shall go again to Paris to have something performed and to put my opera matter into order. You cannot imagine what joy one finds in frugality if one knows that thereby the noblest thing, freedom, is assured You know how long I was brewing in my blood the Dresden catastrophe, only I had no presentiment of the exact hurricane which would drive me thence; but you are thoroughly convinced that all the amnesties and restitutions in the world would not induce me to become again what, to my greatest sorrow, I was in Dresden. I have just a last remnant of curiosity, however, and you would give me much pleasure in letting me know how matters stand with you. My wife has never found leisure to give me news of Dresden, the theatre, and the band. Do relieve this last Dresden longing. Do you happen to know anything definite about the state of the police inquiry ? The fate of Heubner, Röckel, and Bakunin, troubles me much. Anyhow, *these* persons ought not to be imprisoned. But don't let me speak of it ! In this matter one can only judge justly and adequately if one looks at the period from a lofty point of view. Woe to him who acts with sublime purpose, and then, for his deeds, is judged by the police ! It is a grief and a shame which only our times can show.

Yesterday, at length, I received my scores : I looked through a little of *Lohengrin* at the piano, and cannot describe to you what a powerful effect this my work produced on me! Now I come to a favour which I have to ask of you. At my request you at once undertook to prepare, at your leisure, the piano score of this opera. To you, and especially to me, it must be most unpleasant to find that this work is interrupted. If you are still of the same mind, and are willing to continue to place me under obligation (always on the understanding that you will be compensated for your trouble by the future publisher of the opera), I beg you to get the score from the Dresden theatre in order to continue the piano version. Ask the chorus master, Fischer, in my name, to apply for the score for himself, in order to hand it over to you. For that purpose I enclose a few lines to Fischer, which I beg you will forward to him at once.

Now farewell, and let's hope we shall meet once again. If I should hear of any post likely to suit you in Switzerland, shall I tell you of it? This Switzerland, with its nature, its air, makes the most miserable man well and happy. I should like to bestow it on every one whom I love, even upon L.

Salute the few friends in the band who are yet willing to receive a salutation from me: among them I may probably reckon Horack. Salute Müller and H., also young Fürstenau. I rejoice that on that most fatal Tuesday evening, when I came once more to the Town Hall, it was in my power to render a good service to Fürstenau: probably he is not aware that without me it would have fared badly with him.

Tell Eisold I cannot come again to-morrow to the rehearsal of *Martha;* he should engage Röckel in my place. I am curious to know in what way Tietze will manage to reconcile me with the Princess A.; but I do not despair of his genius yet succeeding; on this, indeed, rests my whole hope for this life. But the man was an excellent double-bass player.

Again greetings in my name; for example, to Schlick. But, above all, delight me by sending a really long letter.

Once more farewell, and remain good to me.

Your
RICHARD WAGNER.

ZURICH, *August 9th,* '49.

Address to Mr. Alexander Müller, Professor of Music at Zurich.

2.

MOST WORTHY FRIEND, AND STILL ROYAL
CHAMBER MUSICIAN!

First of all receive this flattering title as a fiery coal for the depressing " Ex-*Kapell-Meister.*"

Then let me thank you for your excellent letter. I am also indebted to you, namely, for the uncommon amount of time which you must have withdrawn from your deep speculations about the nature of three-four time. You hold to me with a faith and devotion, of which, for state reasons, high traitors are unworthy. Though you try to reconcile this with your royal Saxon conscience, my human political phantasy declares you free from fault, and so praises you heartily.

I have read through the letter several times, and your true nature, as therein revealed, has afforded me special joy. Ponder over your character, your knowledge, painfully acquired, yet, on that account, more solid, your capabilities, and your powers of performance, etc., and compare them with your position and employment, etc. Do, I say, ponder over the legitimate condition of our art and life relationships; and then, without attending university lectures, you will sufficiently recognize that the good God of the existing Christian and political social organization is a grand affair, but that royal bands are not bad either.

Your letter is so full that I cannot possibly answer it; I therefore write you, for reply, a new, if shorter one. God knows how it is that I cannot become quite sad. As my wife is now with me, and as for the coming months I can be without anxiety as to my means of existence, I feel as jolly and as comfortably disposed as a dog who has got over a whipping. But I have not yet got back into working order. Next week we shall go into a small house in which I shall have a special room for work: up to now I have only been able to sit down and scribble in a coffee-room, and this circumstance explains how I have been able to satisfy your request, and get my Wibelistic article ready for publication. While copying I re-wrote much, so that you may find it interesting to compare the enclosed manuscript with the old version; and I would specially call your attention to the third section of the *Wibelungen*, and then also to the twelfth, dealing with "real property," in which you will meet with a rich use of the material.

I send you this little work with the request to

forward it with enclosed letter to the publisher Wigand in Leipzig : the expense of sending it will, I hope, not be ruinous, yet I advise you, in case of necessity, to arrange for a subscription from the radical members of the band.

Wigand is already publishing a pamphlet of mine, *Art and Revolution :* of its French fate in the *National,* I have, as yet, learnt nothing. Get this little work as soon as it appears : it will be only a precursor—as soon as I set to work again I shall follow it up by one of greater detail, *The Art-work of the Future ;* to which, afterwards a third, *The Artists of the Future,* will form the conclusion. I will not give you at random a notice of the contents of these writings ; it must not be done in a rough, but in a really complete, way.

It is most essential that I should accomplish this work and send it into the world before going on with my immediate artistic productions. I must come myself, and those who are interested in my artistic being must come with me to a clear understanding ; else shall we for ever grope about in hateful twilight, which is worse than absolute darkness in which one sees nothing and only religiously clutches hold of the old-accustomed balustrade.

If I accomplish this to my satisfaction, I shall then set to work at the music of my *Siegfried ;* for that is what I yearn after, with all my soul's sincerity. Equally sincerely do I desire to escape from the Parisian opera scheme into which I so unwillingly entered. Compelled from the commencement to think of gain, I naturally entertained the idea, and let events take their course. And so now, as I have already told you, I

am placed in the droll dilemma of deciding between
Parisian help really offered, and my inmost aversion.
The report that I am writing an opera for Paris does
not make my decision a matter of difficulty, although,
not to appear a bragger, I should certainly like to confirm it; but consideration for my wife, who really is
somewhat of a bragger, and against whose practical
common sense I may have to fight hard, if I have to tell
her the plain truth, viz., that I will not write an opera for
Paris.   Were this matter not in many ways connected
with my prospects of subsistence, she would shake her
head, but give way.   There's the critical knot, which I
can only cut through with great pain.   Already my wife
is ashamed of our stay in Zurich, and thinks we ought
to make every one believe that we are in Paris.

You see, dear friend, it is such trifles as conventional fame-seeking and anxiety for daily bread which
threaten to exert—and in a decisive manner—their
august modern, sovereignty over the true, free sphere
of man's art.   But can there be a choice here?   Certainly
not, not even if persons like you begin to be prudent
and practical.   I will be happy, and a man can only be
that if he is free; but that man only is free who is what
he can, and therefore must be.   Whoever, therefore,
satisfies the inner necessity of his being, is free;
because he feels himself at one with himself, because
everything which he does answers to his nature, to his
true needs.   Whoever follows a necessity, not from
within but from without, is subject to compulsion; he is
not free, but an unfortunate slave.   The free man laughs
at oppression from without if only inner necessity be
not sacrificed to it: it can cause only fly-stings, not

heart-wounds. ✓ I don't care what happens to me, if only I become what, according to my nature, I ought to become. So shall I be right, even if no idler take notice of me.

Apropos ! If you know any persons who would give me as much per year as would satisfy my wants, in exchange for all that I may do during my life, in the way of writing poetry and music, please give them my address. Without this help I can do nothing.

I have scarcely anything more to write to you, for I have already chattered the best part; so I will finish, at any rate, about myself.

✓ The little troop of my Dresden friends, of whom you send me news, gives me endless joy. How far above difference of character, capability, order and prospects of life is the one sure feeling of love, which all government and society are giving themselves so much trouble to root out ! It makes me happy, and I can love not only this man, but all men, if even the roughest fellow salutes me in a friendly way—as my wife says to me.

Salute, from the bottom of my heart, the friends whom you have named to me, and do not forget X.

But say specially to H., from me, that if I do not write specially to him this time, this among other things may make him disposed to excuse me—that I presume you will let him see this letter. I am also superhumanly indebted to him in that he behaves in so silent, tender, and noble a manner with regard to a loan, which sum I formerly spent in publishing my operas ; and which, considering his modest means, was not so easy for him to dispense with. Thank him for it in my name. A thing of this kind is of great value, and truly I don't ignore it.

Farewell! Salute my friends once more, and let me soon have fresh news. Write often to me, and do not trouble about the postage : I will make up for it out of something else ! I shall soon have your article here to read. Adieu !

Your
RICHARD WAGNER.

ZURICH, *September* 16*th*, '49.

My address is always :—" Alexander Müller, Prof. d. Musik."

I have requested Wigand, in the enclosed letter, if he does not print the *Wibelungen* MS., or give it to another publisher, to send it back to you to Dresden. In case you get it back I would trouble you to get as good a publisher as possible.

Please see the enclosed letter through the town post, pre-paid.

September 19*th*.

After further inquiry I learn now that this packet— originally the *Wibelungen* MS. which I intended sending by parcel post—must contain no real letter. I therefore give you the enclosed letters unclosed and unsealed, with the request that you will close and seal them for me, so that each one may think he is receiving an absolute secret. For the money spent on sealing-wax or wafers kindly reimburse yourself out of the proceeds of the enclosed waste-paper, as well as from the fuel of the enclosed conductor's stick, of the Spontini kind, which you might perhaps even sell to Engelmann as a truncheon for the commander in Don Juan.

3.

DEAR FRIEND,

You cause me great anxiety! First of all you send me an immense letter to open, which must have cost you at least the half of your month's salary; and then you give me such unheard-of things to read about as the story of the piano score of *Lohengrin!* Seriously—at least in what concerns this last miracle—I beg of you for no one's sake, not even mine, to expose yourself to such enormous fatigues; for such forced undertakings are of this kind, and health has to pay a heavy penalty. At the present moment I can confirm this in a striking manner. For the last fortnight, *i.e.*, since I have settled down quietly in my home, I have been seized with a furious desire to produce a new literary composition, *The Art-work of the Future;* and to so great an extent, that even to-day I grudge the time to write in an orderly way to you or to my other Dresden friends, although I have much to say.

Already, on receipt of your last letter, I did not care to write again until I had quite finished with my new work, which I should then have sent with my answer : a notice which I give you, but not as a letter—which I still owe you—but only as a notice.

Through you I learn that Wigand has written to me. I point out to you thereupon that I have not caught sight of a line from him, not even a copy of my pamphlet, which I had begged of him. As, therefore, I do not know how it will fare with my letter to Wigand —which I send direct to Leipzig, as I did a fortnight ago—I prefer to entreat you to tell Wigand that I have received no letter from him; and therefore I would request him, if he desires to send me news with safety, to do it through you or Heine.; as, up to now, I have always received my letters from Dresden. You yourself please address letters to me for the future in the following way :—

an Fräulein Natalie Planer,
am Zeltwege, in den hinteren Escherhäusern,
No. 182 parterre,
Hottingen, bei Zurich.

The person addressed is, in fact, my sister-in-law, who, with my wife, lives here. I hope this name will appear innocent to the police, although, through violation of letter secrecy, we have only to fear delay and uncertainty ; but in no way the discovery of God knows what conspiracy !

In my new work I have had to express my thoughts in an exhaustive manner, but the subject having once been broached in my pamphlet, this could not well be helped. Nevertheless it leaves, for example to you, still an enormous lot to do ; as I, in grasping the theme which I placed before myself, could only draw in very broad strokes. Wigand must really publish this little work for me. I hoped to be able to send it off by the end of November. Anyhow, it is getting almost three times as thick as the first pamphlet, but I confidently hope that the interest which it will create will not be that of a passing day, but a lasting interest, substantial and suggestive. How shall I set to work to get him to pay me properly for it ?

My head is all a-fire from dealing with so many principles of art—it is impossible to write any more to-day ! So please don't be angry with me.

As soon as I have quite finished, I will write proper letters again—even such as Fürstenau wishes, whom I beg you to greet heartily and to thank.

Kindly see to enclosed, about which I am also anxious.

In short, accept my best thanks for your last excellent letter, and for the fresh proof of friendship towards me contained in it ! I shall shortly have much to write in reply.

Salute also young R. from me, if he happen to be in Dresden !

But come, farewell ! I am done up, and must get into the open air : Peps won't leave me any more in peace ! Farewell, dear Uhlig.

ZURICH, *October 26th,* '49.

4.

DEAR FRIEND,

Here follows once more a whole load. Don't be angry if it overburdens you. I thought you would like to look through my new work before it came, in ceremonious fashion, before the world : so read it and communicate with Heine, so that we may lose as little time as possible with it : you might read half and communicate to Heine the first half read, while you go on with the second. Then I beg you to send the manuscript to young R. at Leipzig : he might read it quickly through and afterwards deliver it, with the letter, to Wigand. The treatise, as you see, has become somewhat bulky : if on certain points I have not been concise, on the other hand I have been compelled to leave much unnoticed—I hope, however, only what is not of characteristic importance. Now you have it in your hand ; read it, and you will see best for yourself ! I am not inclined to make any changes. One must not question a thing once out : excellencies and defects, for the most part, stand in proper relationship to one another.

As in this writing I communicate to you my whole history up to the present day, I find it almost unnecessary to write much besides to you. But I consider it specially necessary to thank you heartily for your letters ; in respect to which, however, I always regret that your money-bag is really becoming the victim of enormous postages—as, for example, the time before last. Do be more prudent. From your last letter I perceive particularly your anxiety to obtain favourable notices of my literary works. Do not trouble so much about them. Only one thing is important—that they be read as much as possible ; and what will tend to this pleases me. That they should be attacked is quite natural, and a matter of indifference to me. I bring no reconciliation to worthlessness, but war to the knife. Now as our public life is full of worthlessness, and specially so with regard to professional artists and literary men, I can in this present time only find friends among those who are quite removed from this ruling publicity. Here there is nothing to convince, to win over : extermination is the only cure. To accomplish this in time, we shall receive the necessary strength if, as disciples of a new religion, we learn to know ourselves, and by mutual love strengthen our faith. Let us stick fast to youth ; let old age kick the bucket, there is nothing to be got from it.

This will have been my last literary work. There

would be much to look over again, as I, for the most part, only traced general outlines. If I had to do this alone, it would only be a proof that I had not discovered the right. If that be so, nothing further is of any avail ; but if I have been understood, and if I have convinced others—even if few in number—others must and will make everything complete in the matter. That is the work of many, not of one. I count particularly on you.

I have not yet received anything from Wigand. I have not yet been able to get even a copy of my pamphlet : yet at the bookseller's shop I am assured that a parcel for me has been advised. Only I happened once to turn over the leaves of somebody else's copy of *Art and Revolution*, and soon found, to my distress, many misprints. Conformably to our pedantic custom, I have written certain words in my new manuscript in capital letters, in order—especially in the philosophical part—to avoid compositors' mistakes : but I beg Wigand, nevertheless, perhaps to send it to you for correction, and I am sure, with your great conscientiousness, to be well guarded against misprints.

Your news always interests me ; but in order to spare you, and to draw your attention only to what appears most important to you, I let you know that through the papers we get pretty exact news of political events in our dear home. Not so about the everlasting art-movement : but even newspapers I intentionally seldom read. These things become to me more foreign and indifferent every day.

I ought long ago to have received the musical paper : the person who promised it continues to dilly-dally. I will very soon add fuel to flame.

I am not in such good humour as last summer ;
autumn and winter are not my friends.   Besides, there
are the cares of life—this is the name, you know, for
money worries.   I cannot think of earnings, and I have
lost all hope of support.   Something of mine will be
played at Paris, at a *Conservatoire* concert.   Even if I
fix my eyes on Paris, I must not think for a long time
of success and fees.   Besides, I have now a strong
desire to really begin an artistic work, and to be able
to stick to it : how, under the circumstances, I can
satisfy that desire, I know not.   So I hang between
heaven and hell ; and besides, I have a strong
inclination to cast myself into hell, where, at least
during the winter, I should be warm.   I feel very
lonely !

I wished to write to Fürstenau ; or rather, as he
wished, to my artistic friends in the band and theatre
at Dresden.   I rejoice at the thought of doing it, but
put it off to another time in order to do it better than I
possibly could to-day.   Give my best salutations to all,
and communicate to them my design with regard to
them.   Hähnel has not yet come : I should be delighted
to see him, and I thank you for the information.   Dear
friend—I promised you a proper letter : this time accept my precious manuscript in its place.   Of matters
personal there is not much to say, and general matters
are touched upon in the manuscript.   Besides, I am
weary of work, and somewhat melancholy.   What good
can come of it ?   Do not answer evil with evil ; and rest
assured that I love you heartily, and am truly glad
to have won you from your coyness to be one of my
friends.

Farewell, and expect soon something better from me than I give to-day.

Your
RICHARD WAGNER.

November, '49.

N.B.—Were it possible to start a newspaper, perhaps under the title *For Art and Life,* I would willingly contribute to it, in order to help to propagate the new principles far and wide. One day I must say more about this matter.

5.

DEAR FRIEND,

I have kept on fancying that I had still to receive a letter from you, or from one of you, my friends, and that —if I wrote—I answered that at the same time. Probably you have for the moment nothing special to communicate to me, as you know that in one important point I am cared for. The news from X. has deeply touched and affected me, and truly in more than one respect! With women's hearts it has always gone well with my art; and probably, because amid all ruling vulgarity, it is always most difficult for women to let their souls become as thoroughly hardened as has been so completely the case with our political men-folk. Women are indeed the music of life: they receive everything in a more open and unlimited manner that they may enrich it with their sympathy. While I was expecting news I was surprised by a remittance of money from Dresden, through Herr P.; I at once wrote back, as well as I was able, and described the feelings prompted by these proofs of love and sympathy on the part of persons whom I scarcely knew. If such experiences render every man good, noble, and cheerful, at the present moment they have quite a blissful effect on me. I have never felt the consciousness of freedom so beneficent as now, nor have I ever been so convinced that only a loving communion with others procures freedom. If, through the assistance of X., I should be enabled to look firmly at the immediate future without any necessity to earn a living, those years would be the most decisive of my life, and especially of my artistic career; for now I could look at Paris with calmness and dignity; whereas, before, the fear of being compelled by outward necessity to make concessions made every step which I took for Paris a false one. Now it would stand otherwise. Formerly it was thus: Disown thyself, become another, become Parisian in order to win for yourself Paris. Now I would say: Remain just as thou art, show to the Parisians what thou art willing and able to produce from within; give them an idea of it, and in order that they may comprehend thee, speak to them so that they may understand thee; for thy aim is just this—to be understood by them as that which thou art. I hope you agree with this.

So on January 16th, 1850, I go to Paris; a couple of overtures will at once be put into practice; and I shall take my completed opera scheme: it is *Wiland der Schmied*. First of all I attack the five-act opera form, then the statute according to which in every great opera there must be a special *ballet*. If I can only inspire Gustave Vaez, and impart to him the understanding of my intention, and the will to carry it through with me, well and good; if not, I'll seek till I find the right poet. For every difficulty standing in the way of the undertaking I, and the subject connected with me, are attacked by the press; and if it is a question of clearing away without mercy the whole rubbish, and cleansing with fresh water—in that matter I am in my right element, for my aim is to create revolution whithersoever I come. If I succumb—well, the defeat is more honourable than a triumph in the opposite direction; even without personal victory I am, in any case, useful to the cause. In this matter victory will only be really assured by endurance; who holds out wins absolutely and holding out with me means—for I am in no way in doubt about my force of will—to have enough money to strike hard and without intermission, and not to worry about my own means of living. If I have enough money, I must at once see about getting my pamphlets on art translated and circulated. Well, that will be seen when I am on the spot, and I shall decide according to the means at my disposal. If my money comes to an end too soon, I confidently hope for help from another quarter—*i.e.*, from the social republic, which sooner or later must inevitably be established in France. If it come about—well, here I am ready for it, and, in the matter of art, I have solidly prepared the way for it. It will not happen exactly as my good-natured friends wish, according to their predilection for the evil present time, but quite otherwise, and, with good fortune, in a far better way—for, as they wish, I only serve myself—but as I wish I serve all.

Don't make such a fuss about my last work! But I

should be a fool were I to deny how pleased I am that
it has taken hold of you. From Wigand I know
nothing about it; certainly ten louis d'or have been
sent to me from Leipzig for my first pamphlets, but no
news besides. I hope, however, it is printed? The
misprints in the first works were cruel, and often quite
distorted the sense. Do please correct the new one!
I have also begged Wigand to see to it. After this
piece of writing I was so determined to do no more
literary work of that kind that now I must laugh at
myself; from all sides necessity urges me to put pen
to paper again. If we are quite candid, we must
also truly confess that it is the only thing which has
sense and aim; the real art-work cannot be created
now, but only prepared for; yes, by revolutionary
means, by destroying and beating down all that deserves
to be destroyed and beaten down. That is our work,
and quite other people than ourselves will be the first
true creative artists. Only in this sense do I conceive
my impending activity in Paris: even a work that I
may write and produce there can only be a momentum
of revolution, an affirmation sign of destruction. Only
destruction is now necessary—to build up can only
for the present be caprice. I have still very much to
say to those before whom I place my *Art-work of the
Future;* therefore I made inquiries respecting a newspaper, in order—even if only in outline—to be able to
utter my thoughts aphoristically about certain matters.
Now my wish is that a sheet should appear once
a week, or two to three sheets a fortnight. Such
a periodical must in every number contain a full
cannon charge, to be sent against any rotten tower;

that overthrown, next time another would be attacked, and so on. The cannonade would last as long as there was ammunition. That would be noble and useful, and were I in Germany I could attend to such periodicals all by myself—perhaps this even would be possible from abroad. Now if you wish to start a paper, I beg you to get rid of all that smells of "musical paper:" always conceive the undertaking from a general standpoint— Art and Life, and truly, according to their core and essence, not according to the husk—under which, on the one hand, I understand politics, etc., and on the other, modern "art criticism." With that we could not even entice a cat from behind the stove: to such stuff men have for a long time, unfortunately, been accustomed, and thus their sight has been darkened for the kernel of the matter. I have been written to from Stuttgart about a "monthly paper," in the programme of which "Art and Life" also figures: I have promised to take interest in it, and also have recommended you; but when it comes to the upshot there is far too much "politics" and other conventional stuff in it, German "patriotism" and similar nonsense, the contents of which are too familiar to us. However, I must send something: probably an article on "Genius." Do get your articles out soon? Make haste—for sometimes it seems to me as if everything would be too late—yet one thing consoles me, that what is really good cannot be either late or early. If my *Art-work of the Future* should soon appear, please send me here at once a copy "in wrapper" per post, at my expense, of course.

Everything can be addressed to me here up to

January 16th : afterwards—Paris, Mr. Albert Franck, libraire, rue Richelieu.

(This last notice is specially for Wigand, if he will send me a few more copies of the work about which I am asking.)   I still cannot get a sight of the *Zeitung für Musik* here.

What is my dear little Heinemann doing ?   Has he recovered from the trouble, the anxiety, and fright of which I was the cause ?   I hope my last letter has calmed him, and heartily wish he would testify the same to me by writing.   In any case the best comfort for you all is the knowledge that I am so thoroughly helped: yes, I confess, in every way that is a consolation. I always expect every day to receive a letter from you ; Fischer also owes me one : still I will send this off to-day, even if you gather little more from it than that I live and—thanks to my friends—am courageous and full of spirits.   Also, under such money-shower-conditions, my wife ought not any more to show a sceptical, anxious face : I hope also to have convinced her that whoever helps me intends only in my person to help art and the holy cause for which I fight.

Affectionate greeting to Frau R. and Herr P. from me !   I shall soon have much to write to K. : but do see if he has anything of a voice !   Were I now of his age, and what he is, and had I as much voice as I had formerly, I should without hesitation become an actor : as actor, and poet, and musician at the same time, I would—even at dead calm—revolutionise the whole drama ; for who but the actor could have the practical force for it ?   Think, dear friend, if Tichatschek had, in addition, my resources, or I his voice, how would it stand with the theatre nowadays? Our cursed writing of abstract poetry and music is the very devil to get on with : we have the will and not the power. Well, more on that matter! But first I should like to know how it stands with K.'s voice. Early in the year I expect to be in Zurich again, to get to work : he must then come to me ; he could live with us, and thus I could see and show him what he should do.

Adieu! Write soon to me and don't pre-pay any more letters *now*.

I will write again before I go away.

Farewell, dear friend, and don't delay the Vespers to-day.

Your
RICHARD WAGNER.

ZURICH *December 27th*, '49.

6.

[PREFACE.—Don't be alarmed at the "thou,"* and look upon its spontaneous use in these lines as a reactionary outbreak of nature against our wretched etiquette. Let's hope thou wilt answer in like reactionary manner.]

DEAR FRIEND,

In any case I should have written to you to-day, to let you have a short notice ; now I receive your letter, which requires a longer answer. Yet I am anxious that you should receive news quickly, and therefore,

---

* This preface notwithstanding, we shall keep to the "you" in the letter.—TR.

in order to post the letter to-day I make it only so long
as time will permit.

The news is this : I shall not be ready to start on
the 16th. If anything should happen of special importance which you should wish to communicate, address
here still. Eight days before my definite departure I
will let you know.

In no way has any change in my plan been made, so
far as it depends upon myself, but only a delay in
carrying it out so far as it depends on others. The
unexpected remittance from Dresden (of about five
hundred thalers) I have set apart entirely for the purpose
of satisfying this immediate instinct, that of providing
for the barest necessities of my own and my wife's
support. The sum notified by you to me I had intended
for the furtherance of my Parisian plan. As I have
no news thence, it has occurred to me that the remittance received from Dresden (through Herr P.), perhaps
included the sum intended for me by X. I should, in
this case, not be less thankful for the sympathy shown
to me, but it would necessitate a change in my arrangements. Paris for me, without guarantee for my holding
out as long as possible, is quite another matter. However, the first thing is to gain certain information. At
the end of the year I wrote to X., which I should even
have done without the news from you, as a letter was
owing from me ; naturally, I said nothing in it about
that communication. In any case, I shall probably
receive an answer within a few days. On your side,
perhaps you could find out from Herr P., in a suitable
manner, whether there is any ground for my supposition
with regard to the participation of X. in the remittance

sent from him to me, and let me know quickly. I hope
I shall not appear brazen-faced and greedy to you; I
submit to everything, and thank for everything, as soon
as I know for certain.

Besides, I have been ailing, and am still not quite well.
My familiar winter complaint has set in even here—
rheumatism, which caused me much anxiety, as it went
towards the heart. I had lost all inclination for work;
I have not even yet been able to put on paper my
opera plan, I felt so oppressed; and I only consoled
myself with an expression of Feuerbach's: "He who
has never called out, 'My God, why hast Thou for-
saken me?' that man has never had God in him." But
I can write down that opera plan in a few days, if only
fresh air blow again through my brain.

I had so much to write to you, also so much to
answer in your letter, that I should consider it wrong
and unseemly to do it now at a rush. But I fear, were
I to-day to express myself only briefly, I should chip
off the point of the matter, and never be able to return
to it in minute detail. Only this much: if on reading over again my *Art-work of the Future*, you do not
clearly perceive my plan, I must have expounded it
badly. The genetic origin of our mutilated modern art
from collective Grecian art, could only be made clear
by showing in a precise manner the important moment
when this art passed from direct representation into
indirect representation; from Tragedy into the so-called
plastic art. Perhaps you may have understood my
argument as if I had wished only to notice and compare
one by one the different kinds of art; in that case you
have misunderstood me, or I have not expressed myself

clearly. I so grouped all the arts, according to their
nature, as to be able specially to show by them the
development of all art, up to our modern art ideas, in
common with the development of the whole being of
man. Here in the allotment of space it was right to
act in a thoroughly impartial manner; and I felt therefore compelled, in a note, to make excuse for my long
dwelling (proportionately) on music.

But if I wish to show that plastic art, being artificial—only an art abstracted from true art—must cease
entirely in the future; if to this plastic art,—painting
and sculpture,—claiming nowadays to be principal
art, I deny a life in the future, you will allow that this
should not, and could not be done with two strokes of
the pen. Now you must write to me about this when
you have looked through the treatise again. I quite
understand, too, that you take chief interest in music;
perhaps I shall return to it at greater length at some
future opportunity.

Now for to-day : Conclusion !

It has touched and rejoiced me that you have often
thought you could not hold out. Despair, disgust, and
fiercest wrath—that is the water for the baptism of our
new life. But from my inmost soul I have been forced to
laugh heartily at your lack of liking for what is French,
and at your recollection of the cobbler in *Lumpaci Vaga-
bundus*. For so is it with many ; and then I always
think of the cobbler, this very cobbler. Enough! With
so much to tell you to-day, I ought not to unbosom
myself so hastily. You must not give up, but write
much to me. With that you quiet one of my needs.

The Music Society here has for a long time asked me

to study with them—or rather with their orchestra—a Beethoven Symphony. Now I have twice drummed through the A Major Symphony with them. There is a rehearsal again to-day. At first I lost all inclination, but gradually it begins to amuse me; and in any case I hope to establish something solid, especially if I set aside all pride. I think I shall bring a little feeling of shame and disgrace to the (very) rich merchants here, and induce them to open their gold-bags in order to do something descnt towards a good orchestra; if I succeed, I shall think of you for its head.

You write me nothing concerning K.: I am most anxious to know if he has a voice. I take lively interest in him, not only because I like him, but because I like the future as much as I hate the present; and to this future would willingly bring thoroughpaced artists.

Good-bye for to-day! Hearty good wishes to your new-born child!

I have forgotten nothing in this letter, but intentionally have only mentioned certain things. Good-bye. Salute my friends. Soon more from

Your
RICHARD WAGNER.

ZURICH, *January 12th*, '50.

Hottingen is a parish—a *faubourg*, really, of Zurich. Zurich itself consists of many separate parishes, of which each has its special name.

7.

DEAR FRIEND,

    I am glad your letter has already reached me, for

I start early to-morrow in order—if all goes well—to arrive in Paris by the 1st of February.

I have at last decided to start under all circumstances, and specially from dietary reasons. I am somewhat knocked up, and am suffering from extreme nervous exhaustion. The last eight days have convinced me that here, in uneasiness, wanting to work and not being able, I shall not get better. So I snatch at a somewhat desperate means—a by no means trifling journey—in the hope that it will refresh me and strengthen my nerves, as one often experiences this by travel and change of scene.

My opera scheme for Paris is, nevertheless, ready; only I have still to translate it. How do I feel with all this? Fearfully stupid; for I seek continually to belie myself on behalf of my friends.

I shall spend the first days in Paris very quietly, and be purely concerned about restoring my much-impaired health. Wigand's honorarium—which, according to your news, I am to find in Paris—I have reckoned upon for my expenses there : may I not be deceived.—I hope Wigand will send me some copies of my new pamphlet : he or you might send me at once a first copy in a wrapper (at my cost). For the present the old address holds good :—Mr. Albert Franck, libraire, rue Richelieu.

I must write to K. in detail, and in a decisive manner ; besides, I want to know if he has a voice. He will soon hear from me. Salute the whole R. family, with all the strength which in this present exhaustion is still at my command. I can't write any more to you to-day. I am about to start. More from

Paris. Salute dear good Heine : I thank him a thousand times for his letter. Farewell.

Your

RICHARD WAGNER.

ZURICH, *January* 28*th*, '50

8.

[Address without Christian name :—Monsieur Wagner, 59, rue de Provence.]

DEAR UHLIG,

That the thicker letter comes as an enclosure, you must attribute to the fact that I do not exactly know K.'s address.

From this letter you will get an idea of my health.— Splendid—feeble, full of pain, and unable to sleep ! Think to what a point I have come. Last night a wretched joke on your Christian name came into my head (Louisd'or instead of Theod'or), and, like a ghost, it scared away all possibility of sleep from me. I cannot yet write you a letter, but I expect news from you daily. I am also expecting my book. Here I have been able to do nothing but move out of one dwelling into another. I have met Semper. No money order from Wigand as yet. To the March number of the *Deutsche Monatsschrift* (Stuttgart), I have promised to contribute an article, " Art and Climate." The good friend in the *Allgemeine Zeitung* has determined me to expose the lazy, cowardly, preposterous objection of " climate " in all its emptiness. In any case, I am resolved to publish

Papers for Art and Life entirely on my own account;
perhaps fortnightly. If the *Art-work of the Future*
attracts any notice, I shall hope to win Wigand for my
undertaking. Tell me what you think of him, and of
the matter itself.

I have made a mistake in the *Wibelungen*; not,
however, in the title, but in publishing it in pamphlet
form : it ought to have come out in a monthly journal :
make my excuses to Wigand on that account, and
salute him.

I have not written to the king, and yet there appears
to me some truth in the report. At the beginning of
June last year Semper told me in Paris that Heubner
was condemned to death, and that the execution would
soon be carried out. That made my heart jump to my
mouth. From the country I wrote at once to F. v. L.
(naturally without saying a word about myself), telling
her to go to the king and caution him against carrying out the sentence (in case it had really been
pronounced). I spoke in praise of Heubner, and
explained how the king would not only have done
better if—as he first intended—he had called him to
the Ministry ; but that now he could not do better
than learn to know Heubner and make a friend of
him. Naturally L. did nothing, as the whole thing was
only a rumour ; but now, sentence having really been
passed, she has probably come forward with a letter.
So what has come to your ears may quiet you. But
now I intend to write to my three friends at the *König-
stein*, and shall forward the letter to the commander of
the fortress for inspection. I have at heart to send an
energetic brotherly greeting to them. Your last letter

I have already read twice through here in Paris : we have no further details from Dresden.

Farewell, my faithful, dear brother ! Soon more from
Your

RICHARD W.

PARIS, *February 8th*, '50.

Salute Heine. I shall write to him shortly.

9.

[It is too late to pre-pay the letter ; don't pre-pay yours, and we shall be quits.]

Really this only was wanting to me, that Wigand should leave me in the lurch with regard to the honorarium. I have so much amusement in Paris that only this joy of daily useless waiting was necessary to render it complete. As Wigand had already sent word to Zurich that he would send me money to Paris, I only took from my wife—whom I wished to leave fully provided with money against all conceivable circumstances—as much as I thought I should require here in addition to the honorarium : necessary expense in the matter of dress has exhausted my supply sooner than I expected, and I should already have written to my wife to send more money had I not every day thought I could count on Wigand's sending the sum. As my wife, in case of necessity, has enough money for me, the matter, fortunately, is of small moment: but it is annoying, because from day to day I have not know precisely in what state I am, and therefore have delayed to take the necessary steps at the right time with my

wife.   I wish Wigand would send me a bill of exchange
direct to my address.

It is quite splendid here in Paris, dear friend, and
in your last letter you thoroughly foresaw how much
good it does me to refresh body and soul here.   In
one point only are you mistaken, and not to appear
quite unthankful I must set this right: the complaint
about the feeling of loneliness which I once expressed
in a letter to Heine did not in any way relate to
Zurich and my friends there, but merely to my position
in general, and particularly also a wee bit to my good
friend Heine, with his ideal of Parisian success.   I
was fortunate enough not to have this ideal looked upon
by my Zurich friends as the one allotted to me : they
were so thoroughly agreed to leave me to my nature,
and to take me, in all I undertake, just as I am and
just as I do, that this thoroughly sound expression of
the simple Swiss intelligence of my friends contributed
not a little to make me feel by no means alone in their
company, whenever I turned away my eyes from the
greater world.   Feeling deeply the necessity of this
justification, I must tell you in a few words who these
friends are.   My nearest are two, through whose support,
offered in the most generous and tender manner, I and
my family were kept during three months : one is
Wilhelm Baumgartner, pianoforte teacher, a solid, clear
head, a cheerful, uncommonly good-natured and studious
man ; and the other Jacob Sulzer, town-clerk (next to the
burgo-master) of the canton, a philosophical, well-trained
mind, a noble, firm, far-seeing radical.   Both are still in
the twenties.   In the second rank stand : Spyri, a young
advocate, open-hearted, very receptive, enthusiastic,

devoted; Hagenbusch, second town-clerk of the canton, an energetic, fine young man, bright intellect, sound heart, sprightly manners: both likewise still in the twenties. My old friend, Alexander Müller, from Erfurth, and settled for the last eighteen years in Zurich as music-teacher, is a first-rate musician, a trusty and very devoted friend to me: unfortunately, through too much teaching and through irritating illness, he has become somewhat inaccessible to new ideas. To these intimate friends may be added a number of more distant, but very pleasant, acquaintances. In their circle I have often found myself stirred up and roused almost more than was good for me.

Here in Paris people have an immense lot to do, but merely with themselves or with paltry matters. I do not know any artists: even Berlioz—whose eccentricities I would willingly forgive—cannot, as body-guard of Meyerbeer, attract me. The only man who interests me here is Liszt's secretary, Belloni, appointed to look after my business affairs and intrigues: but he has not yet arrived in Paris. Through an extremely fortunate misunderstanding and inexactness on his part I have arrived in Paris four weeks too soon. The copying out of the parts of my overtures seemed so expensive here—as I have at length discovered after being in Paris ten days—that I have had to write to Liszt about it, and so await the parts, at least of the *Tannhäuser* overture, which have been printed.

Meanwhile I have seen *Le Prophète* for the first time in my life, and on the very evening before I received your last letter with the book, for which please accept my best thanks. During the last act I was unfortunately disturbed by a banker, who was talking at the top of his voice in his box. However, I have become convinced, and in fact at this forty-seventh performance of the opera, that the work has won from the Parisian public an undeniably great and lasting success: the house is always full to overflowing, and the applause more enthusiastic than I have ever found it here before.

I am glad to be able to tell you that I have discovered the nature of my illness : it was, to a great extent, melancholy ; at any rate a strained state of mind has brought my constitution into the present dangerous and excited condition. Just lately, in a detailed letter to F. L., the contents of which will be communicated to you, I have thoroughly explained the motives which have decided me under no condition whatever to write an opera for Paris ; at most I would agree to give *Lohengrin*, a work which I have completed, and which has become indifferent to me, to be plucked to pieces and woven into the wreath of honour of the great Parisian opera-house : as, however, I am not so childish as to believe that this gift would be found suitable ; and as, besides, it is quite impossible for me to help with even a stroke of the pen towards such an offering of my wares, I imagine that my dear friends, Heine and Fischer (to whom, indeed, I do not yet venture to communicate this), will not have the pleasure of seeing a Wagnerian Swan-knight swim across the Rhine. Already—and this was a great boon to me—I felt better after sending off that letter, an improvement which became more marked when yesterday I received the answer, which brought hearty congratulations on my resolve. Not to be looked upon altogether as a fool, I will wait here for the production of my *Tannhäuser* overture, and then, by means of a journey southwards, try and fully recover my health. Thus, dear friend, a horse in the desert cures itself by biting open a vein; the vein with me is: Parisian Opera. I feel happy as this unhealthy, stagnant blood passes from me.

Perhaps it is possible to get my *Art-work of the Future* translated into French for this place. When it appears it will be well to have left behind me all French mountains, otherwise I should be unconditionally expelled. I have had to give up my plan of working, not for present but for future Paris: apart from the unfortunate circumstance that I have only German, not French instinct, my articles would only be accepted by socialistic papers; the first would no sooner have appeared than I, under the conditions known to me at present, should receive notice to quit Paris within twenty-four hours.

Paris and the French know their own business, and no one need tell it them first in translated jargon. To you I say only this much: the cobbler in *Lumpacivagabundus* is right! The sparrows on the roofs sing his song here, and the roofs and the houses mournfully repeat it. Should I not live to witness the fulfilment of the prophecy of the star-wise cobbler, grant me a human death in that Alpine valley, but do not compel me to die like a rat in the great sweet-smelling drain. From the Alps I will write you a German *Wiland*, spick and span, which the people will some day understand. *Siegfried* and *Achilles*, for which the interpreters are not yet born, I will bequeath, printed— black upon white—to a more fortunate posterity.

Since yesterday I have been writing at the article for the March number of the *Deutsche Monatsschrift*—" Art and Climate."

Never fear about my new home in Switzerland! To the Swiss authorities I am no exile ; my expulsion would have to be specially demanded by the Holy Alliance, in which case, by means of citizenship, quickly to be obtained, I should be safe. So K. can come without any fear.

Good-bye, dear friend! To-day is the 24th of February. I will go and walk about a little in the *Champs Élysées !* Salute my friends, and especially my dear Ritters.

Farewell !

Your
RICHARD WAGNER.

59, RUE DE PROVENCE

(Wonderful misprints again in my book ! for example, *unmenschlich* instead of *urmenschlich !*)

10.

DEAR FRIEND,

That you are all dead and buried I will not believe, for even the Krebs-fever does not bring about death so speedily ; that *you* have suddenly given me up, after being convinced that nothing could be done with me, I will not fear, for I should, in any case, have expected from your fine sense of decorum, that you would have given me knightly warning of the termination of our friendship. Long before now, also, I had expected a letter from K., at any rate, as a polite answer to mine, sent to him four weeks ago. I am astonished! I can only think of one cause of hindrance. I told you to write directly to me here, under my own name. Has it appeared necessary to the authorities to open and keep back your letters? It is possible; and for that reason I write to you to-day, so as to get an explanation. Awaiting this, I will make use of these lines to tell you something really good about myself.

What appears to us as chance—and what, after all, in relation to us personally is only chance—often shapes itself in a wonderfully coherent manner, and often stirs and completes to an extraordinary degree our inner being. So is it with the chances of my present stay in Paris. I had never conquered my very deep aversion to a Parisian opera-expedition. Yet you know from my last Zurich letters the view which I at last took of the matter, and which decided me for a time to think with enthusiasm of my projected Parisian activity. Oh what joy is it now to me to perceive how my better nature, and everything outwardly connected with it, revolted in so commanding a manner against these bungling plans, that its decisive victory has preserved me from endless bitter consequences, annoyance, and trouble of all sorts! Its first veto was declared by my illness, which was, for the most part, the result of melancholy. Just as I am fresh and eager for all undertakings into which I can throw my whole soul, so was I sad and slow when Paris was the subject. Nothing would succeed with me. With endless trouble I forced myself to my Wiland; it always sounded to me like "*comment vous portez-vous?*"—the ink wouldn't flow, the pen scratched: without was bad dull weather. Think of me arriving at Paris in this state of mind. Paris would never have come into my head again had it not been for Liszt's secretary, Belloni, who undertook to look after all squabbles and pettifogging affairs, for which naturally he was to have some day his share of profit. In November of last year this Belloni asks me for the scores of the *Rienzi* and *Tannhäuser* overtures : in obedient fashion I send them. At the beginning of December he informs me that these overtures are taken up by a new concert society—*Union Musicale*—in competition with the mouldering *Conservatoire* concerts—and that they are to be performed in the course of the winter ; he would let me know the dates. At the same time he announces to me that he means to go, towards the end of December, to Liszt, at Weimar, but that he will be back again in Paris by the 15th of January. So I, of course, calculated the time of my journey to be at latest the end of January. I announced this to you, and fixed my departure. In the middle of January I receive a letter from Liszt, in which he summons me, in the most glowing terms and with confidence of victory, to start for Paris : he certainly did not mention Belloni, but I had a right to suppose that his sudden impulse to write to me had been arranged by agreement with Belloni, who I thought was with him—or, rather, on his road back to Paris. Good ! I arrive in Paris, and the first thing I learn is, that Belloni had *just* started off for Weimar, but that Liszt had known nothing of this projected visit of his secretary. If in all this Parisian business, as poet and composer, I was to be the head, so was my skilful, indefatigably able and experienced Belloni, to be the whole rest of the body. Well, this amiable Belloni *has not yet returned to Paris.* I beg you will realize the meaning of this communication ! Never mind ! I was in such an excellent frame of mind, and was so burning with desire to celebrate my heart-nuptials with Paris, that I thought of my projected literary writing for Paris : the possibility of finding no translator who would venture to reproduce my things in French, did not deter me—my desire was too great, for I knew my Dresden friends were watching with eager delight for my first Paris scandal, with which they might be able to box the ears of my Dresden enemies, to their own great personal satisfaction, and as an excuse for their lasting friendship towards me.—Then one morning an agent of the Ministry of the Interior walked into my room. For full an hour he took down what I had to say about my aims in Paris, and when he was quite convinced that I only intended writing music of the most innocent kind—according to use and custom, *pas de deux*, and the like—he gave me his blessing, encouraged me to devote myself with true zeal to art, and—as he was indeed in a paternal mood—he whispered in my ear some patriarchal warnings closely connected with the packing up of my trunk. I learned later that this well-meaning man was an enthusiastic admirer of Meyerbeer. At that time I saw, too, for the first time, *Le Prophète*— the prophet of the new world. I felt happy and exalted ; cast aside all rummaging plans, which seemed profane to me ; as, indeed, the pure, noble, most holy Truth together with divine Humanity already lives so directly and warmly in the blessed present. Do not blame me for this change of opinion. He who strives for the cause alone, should hold fast to no prejudice, but willingly let go all false principles as soon as he perceives that they were suggested to him only through personal vanity. When genius comes and drives us into other paths, an enthusiast willingly yields, even though he feel himself incapable of accomplishing anything in these paths. I see, I become a fanatic when I recall that evening of revelation. Forgive me !

From the only other quarter whence I learn something about you, I have just received a letter which has completely cut me short. The beautiful state of transport into which I had fallen has passed away ; and, sobered down, I proceed, in order quickly to close (why ? you will hear).

So, my Parisian art-wallowings are given up since I recognized their profane character. Heavens, how Fischer will rejoice when he hears I have become a man of order ! Everything strengthened me in my ardent desire for renunciation. After endless waiting, I at last receive the orchestral parts of my *Tannhäuser* overture, and pay with pleasure fifteen francs' carriage for them. I then find that the parts have arrived much too soon, for the *Union Musicale* has time for everything except for the rehearsal of my overtures. I am, however, told that there may be rehearsals at the end of this month, and actually under a conductor who, in all the performances given under his direction, carries out the happy idea of indicating *tempi*, *nuances*, style in a manner quite different from that intended by the composer ; and, with passionate conscientiousness, insists on studying and conducting himself without ever allowing the composer to expound his confused views about his own work. Rocked in blissful dreams, I receive at last a letter of

Heine's, with an enclosure from Wigand—namely, a money-order for ten louis d'or, which, from your letter, I had unfortunately expected would come to twenty louis d'or.

In short, early to-morrow morning (at eight o'clock) I start off with the intention of being back here at the end of the month, for the possible rehearsals of my overture.

I am sorry for Heine and Fischer. Poor fellows! they picture me floating along on a sea of Parisian hopes; they will be greatly and painfully undeceived. Salute and console them. When my cursed ill-humour of to-day has passed away, I will write to Heine. To his fidelity must I present an earnest face. A thousand greetings to my dear R.'s, from whom I should so much have liked to receive a line. The merchant M., of Dresden, will bring you something from me when he returns from his great Parisian business trip; a good daguerreotype copy from an excellent portrait, which my friend Kietz has taken of me here.

What more shall I write? I am all confusion about my hasty departure. I have now only to write the verses to my Wiland; otherwise the whole poem is finished—German, German! How my pen flew along! This Wiland will carry you all away on its wings, even your friendly Parisian hopes. If K. does not write soon, I shall presume that he is raving too madly about Krebs. Krebs is clever—so is Michalesi—what more do you want? But K. should restrain himself, and not give himself away so much as he does, as with me! Farewell! Another time you will receive a more sensible letter, with a list of misprints in my last book. If people do not comprehend me, even after this work, if I am charged with improprieties, I clearly see the reason : one cannot understand my writings for the misprints.   To my joy, some one is playing the piano overhead; but no melody, only accompaniment, which has a charm for me, in that I can practise myself in the art of finding melodies— *Adieu ! Bon jour ! Comment vous portez-vous ? Agréez l'assurance de la plus haute considération, avec laquelle j'ai l'honneur d'être*

Votre tout devoué serviteur,
RICHARD VANIER.

PARIS, *March* 13*th*, '59.

" Kunst und Klima " appears in the Stuttgart *Deutsche Monatsschrift*, in the March, or, at latest, in the April number.   The article is important.

II.

DEAR FRIEND THEODOR,
Your last letter to Paris I received yesterday— your last of all to-day.

All that I like so much in your letters—especially the earlier one—which from the bottom of my heart rejoices me, and to which, indeed, I can only answer with my warmest love, I will not notice in detail, for it concerns you in your whole character as a man ; and for that I should need much, very much time, and especially also inclination, to arrange my answer with pen, ink, and paper.   Now I will at once tell you what I don't like in your letter, or better still, *write it ;* for it can be done briefly, and perhaps better by writing than by word of mouth.   So listen !

You are not yet perfect, *i.e.*, the royal chamber-musician still sticks in your body,—that same chapel-musician who performs his duties, who is chosen on widows' fund committees, and who seeks to come to terms with Müller about the " Modality" of this or that passage. Your care for the better payment of supernumeraries was noble and kind; but that in all men you only see supernumeraries, that in your care for me you place this care for salary so much in the forefront, and only allow place for my nature and my resolves after you feel yourself rid of this care—that has made me downright vexed with you. Your joy, when you at last learn that I have a yearly maintenance—this joy which first gives you courage to let me be what I am—all this has seemed to me very unworthy of you; for I allow you all joys, only not those of the Philistine ; for you are my brother. As I read your last, enclosed, letter by the fireside, I got so fearfully out of temper, that I threw the letter of my best friend—I repeat, embittered and angered by this your unworthy joy at my "mainten-ance,"—I threw this letter into the bright chimney-fire ! Rejoice now, my dear brother, at this my deed ! By this expiatory death are you absolved ! This letter, engendered by your last remains of a royal chamber-musician, this letter is resolved into the elements ; and as I know that this letter was the last deed, the last vital spark of this chapel-musician, so I hope that this no longer exists, at least no longer in the soul of my brother Theodor !

What placed this letter of yours in so clear and hateful a light was, that it came as enclosure in a letter from E., which I read just before yours. Ask E. what I mean by that, and in two words she will make it clear to

you ; for, believe me, this maiden is far ahead of you—
and why ? By birth, because she is a woman. She was
born human ;—you and every man nowadays are born
Philistines, and slowly and painfully do we, poorest of
creatures, succeed in becoming human. Only women,
who have remained what they were at their birth, can
instruct us ; and if they did not exist, we men, in our
paper swathings, would go to the ground past praying for.
Would E. have taken seriously the passage in one of
my letters in which, in reply to your strongly expressed
belief on the matter, I affirm that Paris is refreshing and
rejoicing me to a high degree, that it is magnificent, etc.?
I scarcely think so, and imagine she must have understood the irony better than the royal *Kammer-musikus*.

To touch upon one more practical point. As I have
still to do with the member of the widows' committee,
so I tell you that, in regard to the Wigand affair, I am
not so insolently at ease as to be able to do without the
two hundred francs, for I quite counted on them when
I calculated my expenses. Misled by the prospect of
twenty louis d'or, I ordered clothes in Paris, which I
much needed. Now I see myself compelled to give a bill
to my tailor. In order to pay this, Wigand's louis d'or
are absolutely essential. Can he send them by return
to Paris ? If so, write this by return to the address :—
" *Albert Franck, libraire, rue Richelieu,* 69." If not, I
shall expect the money at Zurich, old address, or Orell
and Füssli. I am borrowing it now from my Zurich
friends. Or do you imagine, because you think me
in clover (oh, you bad chamber-musician !), that I
would also expose all my affairs with my tailor before
the world ?

It is impossible for me to conduct my overture my-self in Paris, for this reason, *that it will not be performed there at all*, as there was not proper time for rehearsal—perhaps "next year." I received this answer on the eve of my departure from Paris, and truly in a very pleasant quarter. I think I never laughed so loud and so from the bottom of my heart as on that evening and in that place.

* * * * * *

Enough! I have nicely washed your head; and now I will smear a little pomatum on it! Are you glad to learn that I am a happy man? If you wish me to be happy so long as I live, do not measure me this life by its length, but by its contents. Time is the absolute Nothing: only that which makes one forget it, that which annihilates it, is Something. Do you desire a life only black and white, you can have it as long as you like: if you want true colour in it, don't trouble any more about its length. If I die soon, I have done and completed what I could do and complete, for I can only accomplish what is possible to my nature; if, at last, it wears out, it has performed what it could, and what it never could perform except by continually consuming itself.—

So, *I am happy;* if you are sensible, you will all be so. In Zurich I have already a lady violin-pupil for you; she wishes to be a member of our orchestra. But more about that another time. Much is happening. Be sensible, and if you no longer play the chamber-musician, we can all be happy before the world attains to like happiness.

Farewell! Everything must have an end. So also this letter! Greetings to Elsa Marie!

Your

RICHARD W.

March 26th, '50.

12.

DEAR THEODOR,

Two words as postscript to my last letter. If you should receive an honorarium for *Siegfried*, do enclose the money—in case you get it by the end of this month —to Sulzer, with the remark that I had myself intended it to discharge a debt to Sulzer. If you can only get it later, or if it is promised to you, do let Sulzer know that you are expecting money from me ; that you will shortly see about the settlement of a debt to him in my name.

Frau R. will give you one hundred thalers for my wife. One more important thing.

Ask Wigand to send me the complete works of Feuerbach to Berne, and write and tell me at what bookseller's I shall find them. Farewell.

Your

R. W.

June '50.

If you write only to me, address to K., Berne, *poste-restante.*

13.

(TO A MUTUAL FRIEND.)

DEAR FRIEND,

Here you have the manuscript ; give it to Uhlig if he is coming to Weimar. If he does not come, send it to him as soon as possible, wherever he is staying. I have, as you will see, put in much colour in copying.

Now my wishes with regard to its appearance.

The article, according to its plan, is intended for Brendel's *Neue Zeitschrift für Musik*. Whether Brendel will have the courage to grapple with the consequences of its appearance in his paper, I know not ; but if he will, he must give the article in one number, *all and complete*. He might, if necessary, give a quarter of a sheet to it.

If this is too much out of his usual course, I should be most loth to allow it to appear in two numbers ; *but that would be the utmost:* I entirely forbid further cutting up. If Brendel will not do this, the article might be printed as an extra supplement—just as is done with paid loose insertions—and given with the next number. For this I will see to the costs.

If he won't do anything with it, Uhlig must try to bring it out as a special pamphlet. In this case, some change must be made at the beginning of the article.

The name "R. Freigedank" must pass muster. That all the world will guess I have written the article does not matter ; yet by an assumed name I avoid useless scandal, which would inevitably occur if I put my own name as signature. If the Jews should happen unfortunately to treat it as a personal matter, they would come very badly off; for I am not in the least afraid, even if M. should get me upbraided with his former favours, which, in such a case, I should expose in their true light. But, as said, I do not wish to bring about a scandal.

I ask for six copies. About the matter itself no more correspondence ; choose one of the ways indicated, so or so, according to Uhlig's judgment.

Farewell, and do not fall among cheats, especially if your people should not come to W———. The day after to-morrow I go up the Rigi. Peps is barking loudly.

Your

R. W.

ZURICH, *August 24th*, '50.

14.

At last, best friend, I can write to you. I have been intending to do so for the last eight days, but the non-arrival of the longer letter, which you said was coming, kept me from doing so. The letter, in spite of all my efforts to get it sooner, only reached me yester-day evening. My impatience was great, for I knew that your letter would put an end to my indecision with regard to many matters ; the news which it contained did so in the way I foresaw.

I presume that through Frau R. you have been informed of the change in my affairs ; let me, then, be silent about the immediate past, and only briefly tell you this much, that I have got a new wife. Though, speaking generally, she is the old one, yet now I know that, happen what may to me, she will stand by my side until death. For my part, I certainly was not thinking of trying her in any way ; but, as circumstances have turned out, she has passed through a fiery ordeal, which, indeed, all must endure who nowadays consciously wish to stand by the side of those who recognize the future, and steer towards it. My friends here have proved their mettle splendidly.—I have aged much, and I now know for certain that I have entered on the second half of my life, and have left all hopes of great things behind me.

Strange that a friend, who in many important matters

stands apart from me in his life and mode of thought, should take such interest in my whole being, should show such staunch fidelity, such active care. I mean Liszt. He does not understand my way of thinking ; my mode of action is thoroughly opposed to his ; yet he respects all my thoughts and deeds, refrains most carefully from everything which might in any way offend me, and appears to devote himself with his whole soul to one thing only—to be useful to me and to spread abroad my works. With the most detailed—I might say refined—care, he is now seeing to the production of my *Lohengrin*, at Weimar, and from all that he has communicated to me, I am almost certain that it will succeed. He therefore begs me to support him in his efforts to get the opera likewise performed at Leipzig and at Hamburg. I have been compelled to reply to him that I could take no pleasure in such performances, because they would only prove failures. Wherever I offer myself, there I lose all influence. I have explained to him that I feel perfectly satisfied with regard to the Weimar production, because I know that he is there at the head of an enthusiastic and uncommonly willing *personnel*. Liszt, besides, informs me that there is some talk, should *Lohengrin* succeed, of commissioning me to compose my *Siegfried* for Weimar ; for which purpose an honorarium would be paid to me in advance, sufficiently large to enable me to live undisturbed until the completion of the work. Thereupon I have answered that I would never have composed *Siegfried* as a castle in the air ; but if *Lohengrin* turned out thoroughly satis-factory, I presumed that actors would thereby be trained for me at Weimar who, with proper zeal and earnestness, would be able to bring *Siegfried* to life in the best possible way. For the Weimar company, I would therefore specially get the *Siegfried* music ready for performance. Already I have procured music-paper, and a Dresden music-pen, but whether I can still compose, God only knows! Perhaps I can get into the way again.

You see, things having so shaped themselves outwardly, a great change has also come over me. The moment one feels connected with others one becomes much more settled, calmer, and freer, than if left entirely to one's own choice, which makes one not free, but only confused. So now the choice as to what I should do next tortured me : was it to be a poem, a book, or an essay? I seemed to myself so capricious, and all my doings so unprofitable and unnecessary. If, even by means of this indecision, I became clear, and through this clearness seemed miserable, I only received fresh confirmation when I came to see the effect produced by my writings. I anticipated that, in general, no further notice would be taken of them ; but, only with a deep sigh, do I at last perceive that even by the few of our own party who took notice of them, they were quite misunderstood. Prejudice has such a firm hold, that only life itself can break it. Only a true artist—and he must be a man as well as artist—can understand the matter under discussion ; but no other, not even if he have the best will thereto. Who, for instance, amid our artificial-egoistic handicraft-copyings, can possibly grasp the natural attitude of plastic art to direct, pure, human art? I entirely set aside what a statue-sculptor, or a history-painter, would say to this ; but that even a writer on the æsthetics of art, in other respects well disposed—who is not working for his daily bread, like the one in the *Deutsche Monatsschrift*— should display such absolute want of thought; that on this subject he should fall into such nonsensical babbling about art as he has done, that is sad. Well, I read the notice of my last work. Then I went home with K., read clearly to him and to myself the section relating to the arts of sculpture and of painting; and, although thoroughly disposed to question, we both found the turning-point of all human history and art so clearly expressed, and intentionally developed at length, with special emphasis in the section dealing with sculpture, that we were compelled to decide that these critics—who had not even noticed this *important argument*, but only seemed to assume that I, through ignorance, and because I wished to say something about these other kinds of art, had fallen into vagueness and uncertainty—that these critics had misunderstood the whole book, since they looked upon the chief point, insisted on with energy—the downfall of the egoistic-*monumental* in favour of the communistic-*present* with all *its* movement only as a secondary aberration.— At such moments one's hands fall, and one becomes convinced that all talking and writing on the matter is vain and unprofitable. When it really comes to pass, the public will quite understand; at present he alone understands it who is urged to it by necessity—that is, only one who is an artist, and, as an artist, has become human. I do not boast of the loneliness in which I find myself, but with all my soul could wish to lose myself among a million of persons of like deep experience and need. It was this, and no other impulse, which led me to write that essay; but I see now, clearer than ever, that the man who does not learn by himself, and by his own experience, will surely not get understanding from without.   I had intended to set to work at another book —*The Redemption of Genius*—which should cover the whole ground.   Feeling the uselessness of this book, I determined to content myself with two little essays: first, *The Monumental;* then, *The Unbeauty of Civilisation*, deducing the conditions of the beautiful from the life of the future.   But what should I effect by that? Fresh confusion—and nothing else!   But above all—no notice would be taken of it.   So already the poem of *Achilles* haunted me: I wanted to get it ready for publication.   Now you say Wigand will not even print *Siegfried*.   God be praised!   He has more sense than I.   Then comes Liszt and orders *Siegfried* for performance at Weimar.   *That's the right thing*—if at Weimar they make *Siegfried* only half-understood, that will be the most important thing of all for me: what people see they believe; and if they be but a few, they are certainly more than I could hope to win over and convince by writing.   So, for the present, good-bye, author. Let alone the publication of *Siegfried:* it could only lead to confusion.   Keep the manuscript!

Had I made these observations only to myself, perhaps I should have remained embarrassed; but now I have made them to you, and sympathy for you has quickly helped me.   Since my return to Zurich I have procured all the numbers of the first half year of the *Neue Zeitschrift für Musik*, and I have read not only *all your* articles, *but* nearly all the rest.   First I read only your articles; they rejoiced me beyond expression, and, more than that, I *learnt* much from them. I thank you very much. In your own line you are a master : I cannot say more. Your thoroughness is crushing, and no one who has any brains in his head would venture to discuss with, but only to be taught by, you. Your two articles on the Beethoven Symphonies are of decisive importance, and it quite delighted me to see how the power of truth overswayed you in your view of things, so that in favour of this truth you cast to the winds your own former art-nature—yes, you, as if animated by love, annihilate the whole Beethoven who has touched us in so deep and sympathetic a manner, in order to see rise from these noble ruins the one, true, eternal art—the common good of *all* men ; just as we recognized that Beethoven, in order to rise to the universality of a higher life, even annihilated his own most personal nature. In the individual this great process of self-annihilation only takes place unconsciously ; but if we must annihilate this individual so beloved by us, this can only be done consciously, and whoever so compels his free will to do this, that man stands, in the history of human development, on a higher plane than the self-annihilator. So it is : you express what exists ; we can do nothing else ; it is the highest, and until we have declared this we are not earnest helpers in the work of the future. But I know what a mighty effort it must have cost you so to annihilate in yourself the egoism of your special form of art. I look all around, yet see no one whom I can compare with you ; for just the fact that you were so definite, so absolute a musician distinguishes you. That man alone is capable of attaining to overpowering, strong, human love who has first felt

love with fullest force in perfect individual, personal
relationship ; to destroy this power means then only
infinitely to widen and extend it ; you have been able
to get so far for this very reason that you were so
positively, thoroughly, entirely a musician.—What is
now your position ? Look into the *Neue Zeitschrift
für Musik*, and to your disgust you will recognize
it ! Your articles are not even *read* by those who
write *with* you in the same newspaper, else would the
Schumannist, at least, have *waged war* against you.
Now, who has *understood* you ?—Dearest, confess that
we are both crazy ! I cannot see the absolute necessity
for one and the same journal to contain at the same
time the highest and the lowest, and I am therefore of
opinion that you should look about for another paper ;
but when I perceive where, and among whom I stand
with my solitary pamphlets, I entertain strong doubts
as to whether you will be better off anywhere else.—
Hear now, what I advise ! Give yourself up entirely to
humour ; develop your excellent capabilities for it more
and more, and in a more definite manner. Write no
longer seriously, and laugh incessantly ; that is the only
way in which one can preserve life and continue to be
useful. Ah ! how I have chuckled over the "*Reflexionär*"
and the "*Baron von Lorenz*," etc. Suddenly everything
seemed good. Wit only is still fruitful.

Besides, Kolatschek—who is here in Zurich, as he was
in danger of being shoved from Würtemberg to Austria
—told me your articles have given him enormous pleasure,
and that in any case he will print them in the *Monatsschrift*, only he must wait a little, so that what is purely
artistic may not appear too early in a paper which has

only touched upon art in the most general manner. The *Monatsschrift*, however, is getting on and will prosper.—

Now to another matter.

Dear brother, something must be done with you; you cannot stop in the Dresden band-mire. You are no giant in health, and your liveliness, your great diligence in intellectual pursuits, must pull you down, so long as you continue your orchestra-fiddling, physically of so absorbing a nature. You know the family R. is thinking of migrating to Switzerland next spring; you ought to come with them. As what ? First of all, as a sensible man, who takes life easily, spares his health, prepares himself for future fitting activity, and already now is of as much service on all sides as he can be to intelligent and sympathetic men. You will do here all you do in Dresden, only not the one thing which you ought not to do, *i.e.*, you will no longer go fiddling in the orchestra. On the contrary, you and K., perhaps also S., will be engaged in giving concerts ; in winter especially you could give public quartet-performances. I will guarantee you a good subscription list. How stand matters now ? Have you any means ? If not, can you, to begin with, raise a small sum ?—If you, the R's., and we, instead of three or four homes, were to have one, do you not think, provided each one were to act, work, and assist to the best of his power, that we should live better and cheaper than if separated ?—I merely throw out the suggestion, for I have no intimate knowledge of your situation. I only know that the Ritters are very fond of you, and would willingly have you with us. Take counsel with yourself ; look upon it as the most important decision of your life, be merciless to all obstacles ;

and talk over the matter with Frau R. It can and must be done!

I feel very well again just now in Zurich, and I would choose to live here rather than anywhere else in the whole wide world. We have a most delightful dwelling by the lake, with the most magnificent views, garden, etc. In an old coat I go down to the lake to bathe; a boat is there which we row ourselves. Besides, an excellent race of men, and whichever way we turn sympathy, politeness, and the most touching readiness to do service: yea, more, and more trusty, friends than I could ever find in beautiful, big Dresden. All are glad to see me; of Philistines here I only know the Saxon exiles. Ah, how unfortunate and worthy of pity you seem to me there!

K. gives me much pleasure, and I am pleased to see that he does what is sensible of his own accord. His capacity is extraordinary; he understands with marvellous quickness. When he is walking out alone with me, he expresses the most amiable confidence; at such moments he can talk your head off, but always with charm and animation. To the astonishment of all, he lately gave a piece of his mind to a parson, in an inn, so that the latter stood perfectly aghast. I should like, for practice' sake, to make him music director of the Winter Theatre show here; perhaps I can manage it. Meantime, he is learning Scandinavian. Curiously enough, he spurred me on to *Siegfried*, even before Liszt's incentive.

Listen! Cannot you come at once to us? Be assured you will not in any way repent of it, and you will only experience one sorrow—not to have done it sooner.

Now—farewell for to-day! I hear you are at the baths

with Kummer ! May you both prosper ! I shall also rejoice heartily if Kummer comes. My health is better ; however, as yet I have no real strength, and feel, for the most part, very tired ; but the nervous complaint has much abated. Ah ! let us above all things get healthy. If we have it in our power, we are not deserving of life if we avoid any sacrifice whatever on that account.

Farewell ! Write soon, and give me a favourable decision.

Your
RICHARD W.

I must, after all, write to Feuerbach. Make inquiries about the place where he lives, and send him the enclosed letter. Whether I shall really get his works in this manner, according to Wigand's intimation, "he may ask for them himself," is a matter on which I must still reflect.

15.

(TO A FRIEND AT HOME.)

I can offer no objection now to having my scheme, formed over two years ago, for the institution of a national theatre for the kingdom of Saxony, printed and circulated. It has now no practical meaning, since all the conditions under which it might possibly be carried out have disappeared ; nor do I feel moved by the wish of some friends who, by making known my projects, would like to refute the statement of many a critic of my writings on art—the statement,

namely, that I was incapable of proposing anything
capable of being worked out in a practical manner. Far
more am I induced to show, by a clear example, how
in our circumstances all effort to *reform* is altogether
without prospect of result; while, on the contrary, the
complete undoing of those bad and unnatural circumstances has become the only possible solution.

Who, in the spring of the year 1848, was not filled
with *hope?* The leathern armour against which we
previously struck whenever we attempted to obtain
relief from existing grievances, seemed, before the
rays of the March sun, to expand into yielding, soft
human flesh, through which we even seemed to feel the
beating of the heart. How unnecessarily cruel did it
appear to us to aim with deadly dart at this heart
almost laid bare, and, as if in duty bound, murderously
to pierce through that flesh. Mummies for us had
become men ; as men we wished to speak to them, and
with them to plan and establish what is human and
reasonable. *Reform and Constitution ;* those were our
watchwords, the standards under which we hoped to
conquer and to become happy. It seemed so natural to
us merely to make our wishes fully harmonise with
those of our surrounding and of the community of
our comrades to proclaim the wish of the corporation,
as its need, to bring this need into necessary unison
with the great common state interest, and then to place
for examination and acceptance what had been thus
finished, proved, and clearly formulated, before the State
authorities, whom we ventured to think desirous of more
exact knowledge, so that at last we might quickly see
brought about the inauguration of that which would be

to the mutual advantage of all parties. Thus the attainment of the good seemed to depend upon our own wills, and each one who was strongly sensible of such will, ventured to feel himself called upon to collect his experiences and opinions, and to make well-founded proposals to the competent authority.

It was in that spring, rich in hopes, that I drew up my plan for the reform of the Royal Court Theatre and of the orchestra at Dresden, which naturally went so far as to propose the erection of a national Art Institute for our very small fatherland. A special circumstance prompted me to hasten on with the production of my plan. On all sides was the rumour confirmed that the *General-director* of that royal institution would resign on the approaching twenty-fifth anniversary of his administration. Now if I hurried on with my proposal, it was with the intention, before the place was filled up, of making him who had to dispose of it acquainted, through the responsible Minister of State, with the high tendency and significance which might be given to that splendid art-institute ; and as hereby only a standard for regulating the future was suggested, I had the comfort of being able to do something generally useful, yet without injury to that person who—if he had intended remaining at his post—would, in any case, have been a hindrance to the general good, and hence, though contrary to my personal wish, would have been attacked by me.

I placed my plan before the Ministers of the Interior and of Public Worship. The enthusiasm with which the first, Martin Oberländer, agreed to my propositions, after he had made himself thoroughly acquainted with them, delighted me all the more, as formerly I had found him generally prejudiced against the theatre. Such is always the case with honest men who trouble themselves to remove real distress from a suffering people, and, on the other hand, naturally will not understand how an institution which in its present condition and influence seems only to serve for amusement and for the gratification of luxury, can claim their attention to an equal or even a similar degree. Oberländer's warm sympathy for my proposals consequently seemed to me a first triumph ; for if, on the one hand, I wished to withdraw such precious means as were at the disposal of the royal band and theatre at Dresden, from the hurtful influence of inartistic guidance and expenditure, on the other hand I was not less concerned to dispel the fore-mentioned ill-feeling which—as well as from the Minister of the Interior—I had also to expect from a great number of the deputies at the expected Diet ; and, by demonstrating how, with suitable employment of those means, even the grounds of their dissatisfaction with the influence of the theatre would vanish, to induce them to take an interest in the institution in question, rather than by withdrawal of the means—a thing easily to be feared—utterly to crush it. How unnecessary was my trouble ! how unnecessary my anxiety !

The Minister confessed to me that he could not venture to promise success in the matter, if I persisted in my desire to have it taken up by the King himself and placed as a government proposal before the deputies of the Diet, and, indeed, for the simple reason, that from his observations hitherto he could not expect to find the King favourably disposed towards such energetic plans.

If, as in the present case, it were held as a privilege,

inherited by birth and by divine right, that only a courtier of ancient nobility could be director of a royal art institution, not only whether or not he understood anything about the nature of art, but (to quote the saying of a monarch possessed of artistic tastes) just because he understood nothing—then this particular supposition, as soon as, by its very nature, it affected the interest of a personage, could only, in cases like the one in question, lead to something like the following phenomena :—

A royal band and a court theatre exist : the monarch does not trouble himself much about their activity, because he runs after other less noisy amusements ; nevertheless he likes, now and then, to see something good brought to light as a result of their activity, and he enjoys nothing but these good things ; only all dealing with the economical management of the institution is painful, because it always costs more than it ought to cost, and his intendant assures him that it would cost much more still if good things only were performed. Vexed at this, the thought enters into the king's head, whether it would not be better to give over the direction of the institution into the hands of a practical, experienced man of business, who for a fixed sum would undertake to supply the art needs of the court and of the capital. He could almost make up his mind to adopt this measure, for after all, by its means, there would only be a lowering of art, but in no way a detraction from the dignity of the throne. But now a proposition is made to him, not directly in the interests of economy, but in the interest of art, to place that institution on a thoroughly new footing, on a truly higher and

more worthy one; but this can only be done if, among
other equally stringent conditions, *not* a courtier
ignorant of art, but an experienced artist be entrusted
with the direction.   Everything dealing with principle
naturally excites closer attention than that which
deals with mere occasion: let it in any way concern—
if only in appearance—limitation of power, and the
matter will be closely examined in order to find out
what can lie hidden under aims apparently worthy and
calculated to benefit all.   This mistrust dulls the
sight even of the sovereign, who, in the present case,
was generally well disposed, even not to overlook,
from lack of sympathy, the interests of art: his
troubled look, his involuntarily biassed judgment, are
directed to the one thing which can give a firm and
tangible hold, and this is again here the personality,
the personality of the courtier, who if not perhaps
in his individual inclination, yet in his position of
honour, as member of a privileged corporation, feels
himself aggrieved by that proposition.   This courtier
may have thought of resigning his position in the
art institution, but feels compelled, by remaining in
it, to offer himself as a sacrifice, so soon as he
reflects that he, as a personage, is expected to give
way, not to another personage equally qualified, but
to the deliberate dictum that all personages of his
rank are incapable.

But to the sovereign it must appear doubly hazardous by a definite act to place in doubt what belongs
by birth and arbitrary destiny to the courtier—the
capability of doing anything for which hitherto he has
been judged capable.   To what indeed—in Heaven's

name—would it lead, if the destiny, fixed by birth, that is by the grace of God, of certain special men to exercise any one privilege should be called in question ? Well considered, everything is possible to the sovereign, short of the disowning of his courtier ; so this one thing is settled—*the courtier must remain.* What ought to be done now to further, in spite of all, the interests of art ? Mark you—*nothing !* Now, as there is nothing to be done, it becomes clearer than ever that from the very beginning there was really nothing to do—that restless heads only hatched chimeras, gave themselves up to fantastic humours ; yes, rightly considered, therein only pursued quite personal interests, as, for example, to become intendants themselves. Now, God's name be praised ! the tricks of this vanity and boundless selfishness have been found out, the mask of love for art has been torn down, and it is now quite clear that the enthusiastic reformer only wished to receive an increase of salary ! *Things remain on their old footing.* Whither am I losing myself, best friend ! I seemed suddenly as if clothed again in my court uniform, and that happened to me in sight of the bare, free Alps ! Now, this court uniform is pulled off : one arm was still sticking in it when I drew up that paper on reform, and that I was not clear of the whole thing at that time is the principal fault in the paper : the stiff embroidery got in my way when writing. I felt like our constitutional members, who, if it came into their heads to construct a pianoforte, would not trouble two straws as to whether the keys could be pressed down or the chords made to sound, so long as the constitutional pegs were firmly hammered in due row, and tightened according to rule.   How these childish maniacs rejoice again in these days, when in Electoral Hesse the pegs stand gloriously firm, like German oaks, although keys and chords, prince and people of the electorate, are running away from each other !   My constitutional proposal of reform is just such a row of pegs : as a curiosity I merrily fling them over to you, and trust to the sound of the beautiful human voice, which, without keys, chords, or pegs, will begin to sound if one no longer hammers on rattling pianos.

You know that I no longer think of reform ; but that certain persons may clearly see why, it would perhaps be advisable for them carefully to read and examine that document.   They will then recognize what inconceivable trouble he, who as a revolutionist, is now a horror to them, gave himself, in order, while public, and specially art affairs, were in the worst possible state, to achieve the possible in a peaceful way—that is the essential in its mildest form—so as to bring about a prosperous working of art for itself, and in connection with citizen life.   All errors which are to be found in my document proceed from the fact that I really desired the impossible ; the impossible, namely, in the sense disclosed by the result.   When our court actors petitioned His Majesty for a continuation of the present conditions of the Court theatre, this, on the whole, did not much mislead me : I only recognized clearly to what pitiableness that state of things which I was attacking had reduced my companions, and I could only hope to see them raised to more human and art-like dignity as soon as the state of things had been brought to pass in which, by their pitiableness, they could only do harm to one another. But when I saw how that expansion of the leathern armour, of which I spoke to you above, was only a movement of anxiety, how that suppressed throb of the heart was only the life of fear; when anxiety and fear had again tightly drawn this armour into an iron harness, when these lowest of all sensations turned the most soft-hearted and most good-natured men behind that harness into cold cruel beasts, then, at any rate, I had opportunity to reflect in detail on the nature of things, which in their endlessly ramified loathsome connection constitute the essence of the present time; and, among other effects, were also the cause why my well-intentioned document on reform slumbered peacefully in the desk of a simple ex-March-minister. May this then be placed as a piece of literature before the reading-loving public: as a document forming part of the history of our most noble constitutionalism (what a grand word this is!) it may not play altogether a bad *rôle*. To my practical opponents it may serve to show that now I am much more practically disposed, in no longer adhering to plans which at first sight may not perhaps appear to them so unpractical as my present disbelief in all reforms, and my belief only in revolution.

RICHARD WAGNER.

ZURICH, *September* 18*th*, '50.

16.

BEST AND DEAREST FRIEND AND COMRADE,

I have long been waiting for a letter from you, and yet always in vain. Therefore I think it best to write what I have fresh to tell you, so that—in case your letter still fails to come—you may receive this for the present.   So I go at once to the "business"!   Formerly Heine asked me to allow my paper on the reform of the Dresden theatre and band to be printed.   Now I have read your mention of the same in the notice of my writings in the *Zeitschrift für Musik.*   Lively recollections of that former time came to me making clear the point of view of our constitutional reformers, whose partial, and quite possible, conversion is occasionally a point of honour with me, good-gatured devil as I am! Well, I thought that the appearance of my plan of reform, together with the story of its fate, might perhaps not have a bad effect on them, and so, within the last few days, I have drawn up—in form of a letter to a Dresden friend—a preface to the intended publication of my paper, which possibly may have somewhat of a spicy flavour.   I now send you this preface, and at the same time a letter of Oberländer's, who will hand over the manuscript to you.   Reflect carefully over the matter, and then if you think it suitable to bring the matter to light, inquire at the publishers whether this can be done decently.   If you wish to set Wigand entirely aside, inquire in my name at J. J. Weber's in Leipzig (the publisher of Devrient's book, which did well) ; if he won't, then perhaps at Kori's, in Dresden, etc.   Anyhow, I leave everything to you, on the understanding, of course, that you are willing to trouble about the matter. If it were possible to obtain any honorarium for me, I should much like it ; my state of finance is rather wretched.   Liszt spoke to me previously about an honorarium of thirty louis d'or for *Lohengrin*—instead of which I had altogether only 130 thalers. Further, he announced to me that I should receive a commission to write *Siegfried* for Weimar, and be paid beforehand enough to keep me alive undisturbed until the work was finished. Until now, they preserve there the most stubborn silence. Whether I should give *Siegfried* to Weimar, intending it to be produced there, is after all a question which, as matters now stand, I could probably only answer with an unqualified No! I need not begin to assure you that I really *abandoned Lohengrin* when I permitted its production at Weimar. I certainly received a letter yesterday from Zigesar, which informed me that the second performance— given, through somewhat energetic remonstrance on my part, only after most careful rehearsals, and without cuts—was a wonder of success and of effect on the public, and that it was perfectly clear that it was and would remain a " draw." Yet I need not give you my further reasons when I declare that I should like to send *Siegfried* into the world in different fashion from that which would be possible to the good people there. With regard to this, I am busy with wishes and plans which, at first look, seem chimerical, yet these alone give me the heart to finish *Siegfried*. To realize the best, the most decisive, the most important work which, under the present circumstances, I can produce—in short, the accomplishment of the conscious mission of my life—needs a matter of perhaps 10,000 thalers. If I could ever command such a sum I would arrange thus :—here, where I happen to be, and where many a thing is far from bad—I would erect, after my own plans, in a beautiful field near the town, a rough theatre

of planks and beams, and merely furnish it with the
decorations and machinery necessary for the production
of *Siegfried.* Then I would select the best singers to be
found anywhere, and invite them for six weeks to Zurich.
I would try to form a chorus here consisting, for the
most part, of amateurs ; there are splendid voices here,
and strong, healthy people. I should invite in the same
way my orchestra. At the new year, announcements and
invitations to all the friends of the musical drama would
appear in all the German newspapers, with a call to visit
the proposed dramatic musical festival. Any one giving
notice, and travelling for this purpose to Zurich, would
receive a certain *entrée*—naturally, like all the *entrées,*
gratis. Besides, I should invite to a performance the
young people here, the university, the choral unions.
When everything was in order I should arrange, under
these circumstances, for three performances of *Siegfried*
in one week. After the third the theatre would be pulled
down, and my score burnt. To those persons who had
been pleased with the thing I should then say, " Now
do likewise." But if they wanted to hear something new
from me, I should say, " *You* get the money ! " Well,
do I seem quite mad to you ? It may be so, but I
assure you to attain this end is the hope of my life,
the prospect which alone can tempt me to take in
hand a work of art. So—get me 10,000 thalers—
that's all !

—But now let us turn from fiction to fact. I do not
think that I could seriously set to work at the music of
Siegfried this winter. First of all, winter in itself is
my deadly enemy ; secondly, I shall probably have
many not very elevating hindrances. You know that I

have become surety for X.'s music-directorship at the theatre here ; I am therefore compelled to trouble about the theatre all through the winter. Besides, I have set on foot a special fund for the establishment of a better orchestra, and should—if this answer expectation —feel compelled to trouble about the matter. So I reckon not to be able to attack my important artistic work before the spring. (In the spring of 1852, perhaps with a rush, the performance might take place, if some rich man or other, between this and then, has made me a present of the 10,000 thalers.) I am therefore thinking, this autumn and winter, of doing some literary work. All generalities in art are, for the moment, repugnant to me ; no one understands them until his nose is driven into particulars. Now my particular work would be music, and, above all, opera. Brendel, so I hear, is printing *Das Judenthum*, and places his paper at my disposal. Through you and K. he has hinted something about an honorarium ; I see well I must be satisfied with what he gives me, and my great wish is that he give something. Will he pay me a fee for *Das Judenthum?* Forgive me this Jewish question, but it is the very fault of the Jews that I have to think of every farthing profit. In any case, I will send you shortly rather a long article on modern opera,—about Rossini and Meyerbeer.—

Within the past few days, I have had a great joy. Feuerbach wrote to me, and once more I have had the good fortune to experience what it is to have to do with a *really genuine* fellow. There is no "however," and "but;" he says straight out, plain and plump, what he had already written to Wigand at Leipzig—

who, by the way, told me nothing about it—namely, "that he failed to understand how there could be *two* opinions about my book; that he had read it with enthusiasm, with rapture, and must assure me of his deepest sympathy and warmest thanks." I asked Kolatschek why on earth then he should have had my book reviewed by an ass.

One thing more! The *Zeitschrift für Musik* always comes here very late (by carrier), and irregularly. Your excellent—not because it is of use to me, but indeed to the asses—article on my writings up to the notice of *Kunst und Revolution,* has only just come into my hands. *Do* see that Brendel sends me a copy directly *through the post.* I will pay the postage—that is, of course, understood!—

So! Now I have chatted out what concerns me; about what concerns you I intentionally say nothing to-day, for I must first hear all about it *from you yourself.* I am anxiously awaiting this letter from you about yourself; then more on the subject!—Go and see our good Frau R., and tell her something about me. In any case, I will soon write to her myself. In advance, I already regret that I shall have nothing suitable to write to her; in fact, nothing suitable in what concerns her and her family, for it really seems as if for a long time to come I shall have to *write* to her. I have really no clear insight into her situation, and can, therefore, in what concerns her, only fumble about in a superficial manner, which often gives me a painful impression, as though I were troubling her with my wishes and propositions. I salute her with my whole heart.

If I have forgotten anything to-day, I will set it right when I answer your next letter.

So farewell, dear, dear fellow, and keep me in friendly remembrance.

Your
RICHARD WAGNER.

September 20th, '50.

K. no longer lives with me. Address (for prudence' sake) again to "Fräulein Natalie Planer (bei Frau Hirzel), Sternengasse in Enge, Zurich."

I am deeply moved at your journey to Weimar, and also very glad that K. has found you well.

Not to be overlooked :—

When you are arranging about the printing of the manuscript on Theatre Reform, one condition must be thoroughly fulfilled for me—I must receive here, in convenient time, a complete proof for correction. It is *most essential* that I should be able to look once through the whole before it comes out, to be able to make, perhaps, even small alterations—perhaps only to indicate something to be omitted. You yourself might even make one change in the manuscript before it is printed, namely, towards the end, in which mention is made of the order of installation. I have, I believe, left in this manuscript the provision that the conductor should be appointed by the ministry. If it had come to the point I should have reserved to myself the right of insisting *that he should also be chosen by the corporation.* —So change !—You will find marginal queries, which I have also answered in the margin. Well, all this naturally will be left out. For printing it would per- haps be economical if, in the reform of the orchestra, those rather long sections which contain no specialities or calculations, were printed *in smaller type*.

Title.

Plan for the institution of a National Theatre for the Kingdom of Saxony,

Delivered in the spring of the year 1848, to the Saxon Ministers of the Interior and of Public Worship, by Richard Wagner.

And one thing more !—

Can you tell me offhand of any poor devils in Dresden, whom God in His righteous anger against the human race has made *players on stringed instru- ments*, and who, to stave off this anger from them through a winter—five to six months—travelling money being allowed and a monthly salary of forty Swiss francs, *i.e.*, fifteen thalers (which, through extra receipts—concerts—might amount to twenty thalers), would come here ? If you do, *let me know at once.*

17.

DEAREST,

I write to you to-day only hastily ! I intended doing so in greater detail in a few days ; but Kolatschek gave me to-day a commission for you which must be attended to now.

That is, Kolatschek begs you to prepare as quickly as possible a thoroughly representative article on my operas (*i.e.*, specially Lohengrin) for the *Deutsche*

Monatsschrift. It ought to appear in the last number of October, and you must therefore see that it is in Stuttgart by October 20th. Moreover, notice of it is sent from here to the publishing-house (Hoffmann's in Stuttgart), and you would have to send your article there, when ready, *by letter-post,* and simply, by letter, to refer to Kolatschek's order. I think you will be able to knock up an article by October 20th. So much, for the present, about the commission. I was opposed to it : but Kolatschek proved to me that in the interest of our party it would be inexcusable if the *Deutsche Monatsschrift* did not just come out with something substantial about the matter in hand, and only re-gretted that it could not have been done sooner. So he particularly begs you, even without being specially prompted by him to inform the *Deutsche Monatsschrift* of anything that appears to you worthy of mention, and to do this as often as a suitable opportunity pre-sents itself. You have only each time to send a short notice, something to this effect :—In so many days I shall forward a notice of so and so—whereupon Kolat-schek will send instructions to Stuttgart ; you would only have each time to send directly to that place.

Already Kolatschek wished to fix upon one of your old articles for the number of the 1st of November (from now the *Monatsschrift* will appear in fortnightly numbers) ; consequently he had scarcely any desire to put your article again into your hands for revision. Anyhow he will yield to your wishes, and in any case write to you.—With regard to the non-appearance hitherto of the article he begs—and is—to be excused. As we have got on to the subject of literary work, listen

to the following :—Give up the attempt to publish my
article on reform! that means this much : I have determined to let the document rest as it is and not to make
it public. (1) I could not do this *without* the preface,
which I lately sent you ; now I fear no one in the world,
but I would willingly spare the feelings of any one who
wishes me well, even though he be narrow-minded. My
friendly intendant at Weimar (a thoroughly good soul)
would just now feel unhappy at my description of the
courtier. I should be sorry just now to cut him to
the heart ! (2) The document, after all, has no further
interest ! You can show the manuscript to any one in
Dresden who takes an interest in it. (3) J. J. Weber at
Leipzig who would be most likely to take it, must shortly
do me other service.—My would-be article on opera is
becoming rather a voluminous piece of writing, and
will perhaps not be much less in size than the *Kunstwerk der Zukunft.* I have decided to offer this writing
under the title, "*Das Wesen der Oper*," to J. J. Weber ;
so we will not use up the man.—I have only finished
the first half ; unfortunately I am now quite hindered
from continuing the work. Every day I must hold
rehearsals, and, besides, conduct the orchestra myself,
as X. is not getting on very quickly. In a month I
hope to be able gradually to withdraw myself from the
theatre. For a wonder, this time we have got very
good singers !—

Stop ! I must come to an end ! They are already
waiting for me—so you must be satisfied for to-day.
Shortly I will write more, especially about your water-
opinions ! I only drink water when I thirst after it,
and yet I am far less sanguine than you. What do

you expect then ? Be true, mercilessly true ; rejoice in truth for its own sake ; thus will you have enough for the present ! We shall not set matters right, but what of it ? Shall we, too, on that account, begin to tell lies ? How I rejoice now that the hollowness and nothingness of political life and art-doings are ever becoming more evident ! All men know now that they are thoroughly contemptible !

Is that not then enough for the present ? Only think that a few years ago no one had any suspicion of it ! To the Dresden journalist I can only say : " Fellow, you lie and deceive ! " Well, more soon. Also to Frau R. Farewell, you water-man !

Your

RICHARD W.

ZURICH, *October 9th*, '50.

18.

DEAREST BROTHER,

I break in upon a morning, at this time most precious to me in my literary work, in order to write to you.

In the first place, Kolatschek begs you, since you could not get the article in question ready for the second October number, at least to finish it in time for the first November number. For this purpose you must, in any case, send it to Stuttgart by the 8th of November. If by any chance this is impossible, you are requested to let Kolatschek know so that he may have time to write to Stuttgart and make other arrangements.

Liszt will send me shortly a copy of his big article on

Lohengrin for the *Journal des Débats*, so that a good translation of it may be made under my supervision, and this he will have printed in several numbers of the Augsburger *Allgemeine Zeitung*, as compensation for the Dingelstedt nonsense. This restless striving of Liszt to kindle with devilish power the fire of my fame touches me deeply. The Weimar people think by their cunning care to be able to open up a path for me to the great public : three performances of Lohengrin have taken place, and in consequence of the success the intendant there joyfully expresses to me his conviction, that quite the same popularity is assured to this opera in Weimar as *Tannhäuser* has won. They therefore all believe, that only small concessions on my part and zealous propagation on theirs are necessary soon to place the whole German opera-public at my disposal. I presume that I appear to them stark mad, if in return for such announcements I obstinately assure them that they are in *error about something which appears to me quite impossible.*

—I must take this opportunity of telling you that Lüttichau has demanded back from Weimar the score of *Lohengrin*, which he pretends he has only lent to them, but certainly did not sell. I am racking my brain to know what that means ; perhaps you will be able to explain the matter to me.

Last week I could not get hold of the *Neue Zeitschrift für Musik*, so do not know the replies about which you write. In any case I have no inclination to go in for much scribbling about the matter ; on the contrary, I have a damned short answer all ready—in fact, out of the New Testament, which I know well by heart.—

Also I have not yet seen the continuation of your
Lohengrin article.—

I cannot remember at all what I may have once told
you about Otto's continuing to compose. With regard
to Hiller's *Konradin* I recall the following circumstance. After I had offered thoroughly well-grounded
criticisms to Hiller with regard to the choice of poem in
his *Traum in der Christnacht*, and after he had confessed
that these criticisms were just, he begged me to help
him with my advice in the choice of a new subject.
When I learnt later on that he was pondering over
Konradin with Reinecke, I expressed in a general way
to him my doubts as to this subject, but remarked, that
in any case very much would depend upon the manner
in which it was conceived and developed as a poem ;
wherefore I offered to give further opinion as soon as
he confided the sketch to me. I remained a long time
without learning anything, until at last I heard that
the verses were written, and that Hiller was at work
setting them to music. I presumed that I was mis-
trusted, and mixed no more in the matter, until finally
Hiller, of his own accord, candidly confessed that he
feared the poem would not please me, and that I might
probably raise such solid objections as to take away
from him all inclination to compose if he came to know
them ; he therefore held it better to remain in conscious
error about his project, so that, at any rate, he might
succeed in writing an opera, which might be deferred—
Heaven knows how long—were he to wait for a poem
which appeared to him perfectly worth setting to music.
—That is the Hiller story.—

I send you herewith an explanation of mine out of

the papers here, which will make clear to you my position with regard to the theatre ; perhaps you can make some use of it.   Strange to say, the interest I have taken in the opera here has in any case resulted in something quite different from that which I first intended. You know X. wished to become musical director ; he paid no heed to my remonstrances, and I wrote to the manager of the theatre.   He at once offered me two hundred francs a month if I would undertake the direction of the music myself, with liberty to call in the assistance of X. at my pleasure.   I declined the offer.   I regarded the whole theatre business merely as a scratch affair, enabling X. to learn how to conduct.   At the first rehearsal I was struck with the singers ; a tenor, in my opinion, next to Tichatschek, the best in all Germany, and of whom I know with certainty that he would be receiving very high terms from the great theatres, if their stupid managers had sought him out, instead of waiting, as they are known to do, until the pigeons fall ready roasted into their jaws.   He lacks the mellowness of Tichatschek's voice, but makes up for this by a noble manly presence, and a pleasant, safe manner on the stage.   In his style of singing, which is at the same time energetic, brilliant, and agreeable, I have only to regret the drawbacks which of necessity have become common amongst us through the singing of the translated foreign operas.

In addition to this tenor I found a very good, highly gifted lady vocalist, with a full sounding voice of extended compass, and with sound style ; and, besides these two, a baritone with a fine voice, energetic acting, and most characteristic, noble facial expression.   Everything else quite tolerable at a pinch, the orchestra—recently engaged—very good and in tune, only unduly weak in the matter of strings. In short, I could not leave it to X.'s nervousness to introduce these artists to the public : I conducted myself, and again did so at a second performance. By this the affairs of the theatre took quite a different turn. The theatre having formerly been so bad, persons *of rank* had quite given up the habit of attending, so that, for the present, they cannot be reckoned on. On the other hand, my recommendation has drawn to the theatre a section of the public which everywhere scarcely gives any heed now to the theatre, and they are the only ones who are of moment to persons like ourselves nowadays, namely, the *really* cultivated, not the plutocracy. It has delighted me with slender outward means to bring about all results solely by the delicate and the drastic effect of genuine representation, and that was naturally something quite new. To be brief, let me tell you, that quite imperceptibly the show has become an institution in which my public seeks nothing but real art-enjoyment, and I find myself in the droll dilemma how to get quite clear of the matter and yet respond to the good feeling aroused. I am uncommonly loath to withdraw from the direction, as unfortunately the attention of the public is too much occupied with my action in the matter ; and, under existing circumstances, I cannot leave the performance to the director appointed by myself, until I can assure myself, the artists, and the public that he has grown fully equal to his task.

But I must withdraw, because with the best will in the world I do not see how a *répertoire* can be kept up which should prevent that being pulled down on the one side, which I am building up on the other. Up to now I have chosen only operas which I know could be properly performed, not by luxurious means—which are wanting here—but only by that which is to hand; such as *Freischütz* and *La Dame blanche*. Then there remain three Mozart operas—perhaps Euryanthe—and the few operas of the French school up to Boildieu, *i.e.*, by Méhul, Cherubini, etc. The principal misfortune of our theatre is just this, that year after year performances are continually being given; so that not the cause itself, but custom is thought of, and the institution which can only be maintained in this manner. If the public—which I certainly hope—encourage the theatre, I shall always take a leading interest in it.

I say nothing here about all æsthetic scruples excited in you and in others by my declarations and works on art, as in my *Wesen der Oper*—which I hope to be able to send you in a month's time—I intend to discuss everything thoroughly and exhaustively. I shall even be compelled to pass judgment on my former operas. The book is becoming somewhat bulky. I cannot tell you more about it to-day.

But let me say something about your water-cure! First of all, I acknowledge, that you are wise in your diet, and that I am indescribably glad that it suits your constitution so well: it is most certain that only radical water-cure can help us out of the most unnatural state of bodily health. Want of sound nourishment on the one hand, excess of luxurious enjoyment on the other hand, but especially a mode of living quite contrary to nature, have brought us into a degenerate condition which can only be got rid of by entire renovation of our deformed organism. Superfluity and privation : these are the two destroying enemies of our present humanity. Give yourself the trouble first of all thoroughly to seek out what we have to understand by superfluity, and you will certainly find that everything is superfluous which the walls of a town surround, and truly, not only that which swallows up the superfluity, but also that which produces it. All we who live in a town are condemned to the most cheerless suicide. How is it then with the inhabitants of our villages ? Among them is not all striving from deprivation to superfluity ? Excessive work corrupts men here just as well as in towns, and to such a degree that they cherish the same longing for superfluity which makes idle rest—the only contrast to excessive work which they are capable of comprehending—seem to them worthy to be desired. Only a universal activity is a pleasure thoroughly satisfying in and for itself ; but by *the laws relating to property* we are all bound to a special activity, to an activity which only discharges itself in the direction of one craft, absorbing one of our powers only, and *this one* to so high a degree, that our total capacity is consumed in it ; and so in this one daily occupation we perceive our physical ruin, our moral annihilation, and treat as our enemy the distasteful, loathsome, bitter work, which we end by confusing with activity in general, and therefore only venture to wish for unconditional idle rest in exchange.

In the country this work is all the more repulsive, since being concerned *purely and exclu-*

sively with cattle and filth, it turns men into filthy cattle!

Whithersoever we look in the civilized world we recognize the degeneration of man from the causes here assigned. With good reason, however, we can only despair of this world, if we regard these *causes* as necessarily eternal.

Now, as we need a water-cure in order to make our bodies sound, so do we need another cure to heal, *i.e.,* to annihilate the conditions surrounding our disease. Do we then wish to return to a state of nature, do we wish to be able like human animals to attain to the age of two hundred years? God forbid! Man is a social, all-powerful being only through *culture*. Let us not forget that culture alone can enable us so to enjoy as man in his highest fulness can enjoy. But true enjoyment consists in compressing what is generally worthy of enjoyment into something concise and particular, so that, in a moment, we can receive what time and the elements offer to us in widely ramified connection. Who, in the moment of enjoyment, thinks of the duration of this enjoyment? As soon as we think about duration it is all over with happiness. If we fill our lives with true contents, if we rejoice in our activity, whether it be the activity of giving or of receiving enjoyment, we shall never have to fear an end of this activity, but it will itself again become an action. Whether we live one hundred or only thirty years, what does it matter, if we only live enjoying? Life in itself is only *abstract;* but active enjoyment *is something*. Believe me—through water we become healthy; but we *are* first really healthy when we are also able to drink wine in moderation!

My companions are coming: I must now close! Probably you have enough for this time! Farewell, and do not play antics with your light, lest you set fire to your bed!

Farewell, heartiest greetings from your,

R. W.

Zurich, *October 22nd, '50.*

19.

Dearest Brother,

What a dreadful fuss you are making about me! If you were a Jew one would think that you had so much per cent. for it. If I now speak about myself, it must be in more modest terms, and certainly not from affectation.

I ought not to write to you just now, when I am somewhat unstrung. I would rather have communicated my thoughts to you, if only briefly, when in a more sanguine condition. I need scarcely tell you that you make a great impression on me, that through the *rôle* which you assign to me, I see myself, not so much rewarded by comfortable ease, as kindled and spurred on to activity; this I mention to you particularly, to quiet you in regard to myself. When the looking-glass of one's will is thus held before one, one feels more prompted to acquire the power of doing; and, indeed, I believe I can only hope to reach this power by gaining myself companions in order, together with them, to attain to true art, a thing most certainly impossible to the solitary worker. You would not believe what trouble I give myself with this object, to call forth full understanding from all those who only half understand; yes, even to make myself intelligible to my enemies who do not, or will not understand me; and lastly, I rejoice merely because I am always myself coming to a better understanding. My book, which now is to be called *Oper und Drama*, is not yet ready; it will be at least twice as big as the *Kunstwerk der Zukunft*. I have still the whole of December to devote to the conclusion, and then certainly the whole of January for copying and revising. In advance I can only give you the outline. (1) Exposition of the nature of opera up to our time, with the conclusion, "Music is a reproductive organism" (Beethoven has used it, as it were, to give birth to melody)—therefore a female one." (2) Exposition of the nature of the drama from Shakespeare up to the present day; conclusion— "the poetical sense is a procreative organism, and the poetical purpose the fertilising seed which only comes with the ardour of love, and is the stimulus to the fructification of the female organism which must beget the seed received in love." (3) (Here *only* I begin.) "Exposition of the act of reproducing the poetical purpose by means of perfected tone-speech." Ah! Would that I had said nothing to you—for I see after all I have really said nothing to you. Only this, in addition; I have spared no pains to be exact and complete; for this reason I at once made up my mind not to hurry, so as not to be superficial. I will still add a diagram; I am not sure whether I shall put it into my book.

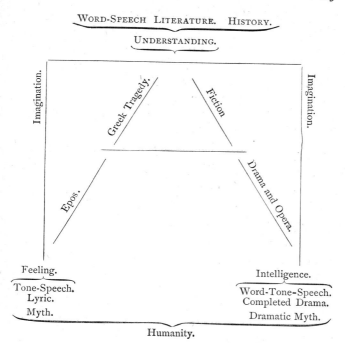

WORD-SPEECH LITERATURE. HISTORY.

UNDERSTANDING.

Imagination.

Greek Tragedy.

Fiction

Imagination.

Epos.

Drama and Opera.

Feeling.

Tone-Speech.
Lyric.
Myth.

Intelligence.

Word-Tone-Speech.
Completed Drama.
Dramatic Myth.

Humanity.

Now to yourself! I share your probable anger against Kolatschek for splitting up the article. I have not yet caught sight of him so as to take him to task about it. Concerning your other articles, you can give yourself the answer beforehand, and indeed to this effect, that they will not appear in December. Hence about my operas I only know half your opinion. If I were to say, "I thank you," I should be afraid of making myself ridiculous; but if I were not once to say, "I am glad," I should rightly appear an ass to you. Besides, I really don't know what you dislike in your *Lohengrin* article in the *Zeitschrift für Musik*. There was one thing which seemed to me perhaps not to have satisfied you, and this was, at most, the pragmatic presentation of the plot ; for the rest you have said much that is new to me, or, at least, shown what was known to me in a new, in your own particular light, so that I can only thank you heartily for it. You must know well that I have learnt ever so much from you ; in my new work I have had occasion to quote you once. Rejoice at yourself !—

I hear you are again unwell ! Yes; water can perhaps help you from within ; but does a man only live from within, not also from without ? And how is it there with you ? Well, I am also going through some sort of a water-cure ; besides baths of a morning, I drink cold water in bed. Now to-day let me just hastily throw out a suggestion to you. You cannot come and settle in Zurich, but if you made a real effort might it not be possible for you to pay me a visit in the summer ? You could live and take your meals with me ; the journey and leave of absence you could perhaps manage.

Farewell for to-day. I am not a Swiss citizen, but only a resident in the community ; the withdrawal of the character of exile only depended upon that. Get Frau R. to tell you about my affairs with the theatre.

Farewell ! Salute wife and child from your

R. W.

(My wife has made me a very comfortable new dressing-gown. This by way of news to yours.)
December '50.

20.

BEST FRIEND,

How angry you will be with me for not having written at once—as you wished—immediately after receipt of the last number of the *Monatsschrift!* How it happened I really don't know. I only remember one thing, that I worked the whole forenoon with fanatic diligence, and in my lonely walk after dinner, I conversed so constantly and in so lively a manner with you, that when evening came it no longer appeared necessary to write to you; and I set to work again. At last I was seized with a furious fit to finish my book, so as not to write to you until I could send you a part of it in a tidy copy; this resolution was conceived and carried out. I send you to-day the first of three parts, and intend to send the second as soon as I have a tidy copy ready, and in like manner the third, so that you may not have all on your hands at once, and that your head may not get confused with hasty reading. You will thus be able to look at my stuff at your leisure, and you might give it to the R.'s to read, without causing any delay in the publication. The first part is the shortest and easiest, perhaps also the most interesting; the second goes deeper, and the third—is a piece of work which—goes to the bottom of the matter. The whole will be a book of from four to five hundred pages. I will communicate with you later on about the publisher; I think we'll try J. J. Weber at Leipzig; X. would, after all, not take it; besides he is now—as I already wrote you—in bad odour : no one will have anything to do with him.

Well, that is one thing settled ! Now about your

article in the *Monatsschrift!* I must tell you quite
briefly that it has given me great pleasure, and I thank
you for it. You are of immense service to me—or if you
prefer it—to the cause, by the sobriety of your conception and by your mode of presenting it; and I know
this sobriety demands more strength and greater mastery
of the subject than the fireworks which, for instance,
Biedenfeld has let off in the *Europa* about me. I am
really delighted at your articles which are to appear in
the next number of the *Monatsschrift*. Only be firm
and indefatigable; there is a fearful lot still to do!

The greatest joy that you have caused me is, however, the clear prospect which you hold out of paying
me a visit this coming summer. You see, flesh
and blood is still the all-important thing. As I told
you, I have, up to now, always taken my walks here
with you. Everything is settled; you take the train
here as far as the Lake of Constance (it doesn't cost
much). On Swiss ground, on the other bank of the lake
I will await your arrival in the steamer; then we shall
drive over St. Gall to Wattwyl, there we get out, and
go on foot through the Toggenburg country (heavenly!)
to the Zurich lake; from Schmerikon the steamer takes
us to Zurich to the "Villa Rienzi," as the country-house
in which I live, close to the lake, is called by all my
friends. I am curious to see if you will miss Pillnitz and
Saxon Switzerland.—Then we shall take a Swiss friend
with us and go for a week among the Alps. You can
return home *via* Strasburg and Frankfort :—all the way
by rail.—I think you can manage with 100 thalers: if
you have more, all the better—if not, you have enough.
Well, it will be a happy time.

I have now also become half a water-man ; I have at once followed your advice about the Neptune girdle : I hope it will do me good. Altogether I feel that I am much better than last year : I work hard—*i.e.*, for a long time at a stretch, and do not appear the worse for it ; it is also an advantage to be somewhat quieter in my home—*i.e.*, clearer, more discreet, more intelligent—or whatever you like to call it.

Apropos ! Have you already heard of the Brussels affair ? Think of my surprise when I received a most cordial invitation from Brussels to have my *Lohengrin* translated and performed there. I felt as if I had fallen out of the clouds. Anyhow the offer gives me great joy, even if nothing comes of the matter ; first of all, the translation must be entirely according to my wishes ; and secondly, I must be sure about the singers, before I definitely give my consent. Liszt has already sent in these conditions for me ; in order to inspect and hear the singers, I should naturally have to go myself to Brussels. Well, we shall see ! Anyhow, the people there deserve praise, for they don't make a leap in the dark, but the conductor there, "Hanssen," *knows* my operas.

But no one will find fault with me now for being cautious ; I have just had a nice lesson from Paris ! You have perhaps read about the *Tannhäuser*-overture-stories there ! Would I had only done as I wanted when I learnt they wished to give it there ! I wanted at once to have the parts taken away, because I foresaw everything as it has happened ! But—they say there that I am stubborn and *over-excitable !*—Well, I am in for it, and now people are making merry over me : it is quite delightful! Enjoy the joke, and read the *feuilleton* in the *National* about this concert.—You will see!—Well, Paris is, after all, indifferent to me—and so not much harm is done!

Now, farewell, my dear, old friend! Write to me soon again, and make proper preparations for the Swiss journey!

Salute old Fischer, and tell him that I thank him much for his letter. I will soon write again to him!

Farewell, heartiest greetings to wife and children from your

R. W.

ENGE, ZURICH, *January 20th,* '51.

(You can confidently write to me to my own address.)

21.

BEST FRIEND,—

Here you receive the second part. The third will, I think, follow in a fortnight. I should really like, before sending this off to-day, to have known whether you received the first part properly. The inscription "printing matter" always makes me suspicious as to whether it is opened, etc.

So as not to forget it, I at once mention a mistake in writing, which I beg you to correct. In speaking of "historic" music, I make a play upon words, and call it "hysteric." I have written this word incorrectly thus, "histeric;" do restore the *y*. Writing now weakens me so, that I always write with trembling, confused hand.

Now I must say what I think about the matter of publication. This time I must go prudently to work, for I *must* be fairly well paid for this book. I am now without any money-source, and at any rate, for my own negligence I ought no longer to be a burden to others. Nevertheless, I confess I cherish the bold thought of not selling my book for less than sixty louis d'or. It has cost me four months' incessant work ; and besides, it is a thick volume.—Naturally it is merely a question how we shall set about the matter. If we could only really learn from Wigand how the *Kunstwerk der Zukunft* sold, we should know better what to ask.—I told you I had J. J. Weber at Leipzig in my mind. I fixed on him because Liszt wrote to me that he was thinking of offering his pamphlet on *Lohengrin* to him, and hoped he would publish it. Then I noticed that Eduard Devrient's theatrical writings appeared there ; and, besides, that he had done good business with Laube's plays. Now, as I have also the thoughts of publishing my three opera poems with a long preface, so J. J. Weber appeared to me to be the right man to whom I could offer both these works. Just now by chance J. J. Weber's *Illustrirter Volkskalender* has fallen into my hands, and I see that with this publisher I have fallen into the primeval quagmire of reaction.

That has made me more than doubtful. Firstly, will he, after all, accept a writing specially directed against the state ? Secondly, is it advisable to offer it to him ? On the last point my friends wished to quiet me; they altogether refused to attach any importance to the sentiments of a bookseller.

Enough : Kolatschek offered of his own accord to open

up communication with the publisher of the *Deutsche Monatsschrift* (now Kühtmann at Bremen) respecting my book. I accepted, so as in any case to have a choice. If I came to an understanding with Kühtmann some sections of the book would first have to appear as special articles in the *Monatsschrift*. This certainly will not in any case do harm, for it attracts and excites attention. (It would of course be mentioned that these articles were fragments of a larger work about to appear; in any case the publisher must first be found and made to agree to this.) In the accompanying manuscript you will already find three articles marked with pencil. When everything is in order, you might pick out something for the *Neue Zeitschrift für Musik*; or I myself would indicate what should be selected.

Now let me know whether you had any other publisher in your mind.—I will, however, enclose a small letter,—as a preliminary inquiry,—to J. J. Weber. If you have no valid objection against it, see that it is sent to Leipzig. So much for to-day about this matter.

Your "Instrumental music" has given me great pleasure. You are quite right in saying "that men are not to be made artistic, but that art is to be made human." Now I am curious about the second article, which I shall probably have to quote in my third part. Generally speaking, I don't like citation; there is something pedantic about it. What has once been openly said is common property, and no longer does it belong to him who has said it. In this sense I would forgive myself all plagiarism, for I should not count it as such.

You are right in publishing certain things from my

organization manuscript. I am curious to see what you will get out of it. Ought not the church music to be included ?—

Was the new year's leading article really yours ? Surely not. The *premature* science made me laugh heartily. Even now must I learn that I should not have discovered the most important conditions for the form of the drama of the future had I not, as artist, lighted quite unconsciously upon them in my Siegfried. I have a great mind to write an open letter to Brendel for his paper.

I am somewhat out of sorts. In a fortnight I will lounge about a bit, as well as I am able. I have had to lay aside for a time my Neptune girdle, on the advice of a first-rate physician, who is in favour of water-cure. Farewell ! Greet wife and child.

R. W.

I feel inclined to dedicate my book " To thinking musicians and—poets." What's your opinion ? Would not the poets cry out that I am madly arrogant ? *Greetings to the Ritters.*

Beginning of February '51.

22.

DEAR FRIEND,

Here you have my will; now I can die—what I could still accomplish seems to me useless luxury !— The last pages of this copy I have written in a state of mind that I cannot describe clearly to any one.

Our parrot—the most aimiable creature, and most tenderly attached to me, the little talking, singing, whistling good spirit of my secluded little home—was of

late often unwell; I had to get a veterinary surgeon, and
then it gradually improved; I set to my work with such
diligence that I forgot everything. On the day before
the copy was finished, the poor thing so longed to come
out to me that my wife could not resist, and brought it
to me on my writing-table; it wished to sit at the
window through which the sun was shining.—I closed
the curtains in order to be able to work: altogether it
fidgeted me, and my wife had to take it away again:
—then it uttered that sad cry so well known to me.
Afterwards it was agreed—that really ought to send
for the surgeon. I said—it won't be anything serious
—and thought to myself: to-morrow you will finish
your work,—then you will go. Early the next morning
it was suddenly—dead.

Ah!—if I could say to you what has died for me in
this dear creature!!

It matters nothing to me whether I am laughed at for
this. What I feel, I cannot help feeling; and I have no
longer any inclination to do violence to my feelings;
anyhow, I should have to write volumes to make clear
to those disposed to laugh at me, what such a small
creature is and can become to a man who in everything
is guided *only by phantasy*. Three days have passed,
and still nothing can quiet me; and so it is with my
wife:—the bird was something indispensable between
us and for us.

Dearest friend,—I write briefly to you to-day! To
be plain, I only wish the hateful manuscript out of my
hands.—I thank you heartily for your letter, which at
first rather upset me. Do in everything what seems
good to you! I am only concerned to get at least

some money for this work, as I—*am still alive.*—By all means send the letter to Weber—it does not matter. I have as yet no further news.—Do what you think fit, and I will thank you for everything.

If I could only take pleasure in life ; pleasure in art is not possible to me ; be true and agree with me. In the whole wide world I have not *an inch of ground* on which I can present myself just as I am. Confound this quaver-life !—All that I could expect from art-work seems to me just such phantastic self-quieting as that with which I used to silence myself in company with the little dead friend.—I have nothing left to do but to vainly deceive myself.

—Farewell—for to-day.—Do what you think right.— I thank you for everything !—

Farewell ! Don't forget R.'s ! and greet your wife from me !

There will still be many faults in the manuscript.—I have only been able to glance through it once.

The little pet had only just lately picked this up, and with unspeakable joy used to whistle it at me when I came home.

Middle of February '51.

23.

Dearest Friend,

I had written to Weber asking him to answer me direct, but I have heard nothing from him up to the present. Only Liszt writes me that he proposes to send one of these days to Weber for the *Illustrirte Zeitung*, rather a good-sized manuscript on *Lohengrin*, which he originally intended to publish as a separate pamphlet. To get clear of all this uncertainty, I enclose here a couple of lines to my brother-in-law A., likewise a publisher at Leipzig, asking him to confer with Weber, and in any case then to give you news. A. will in any case assist us with his advice, and—should nothing be arranged with Weber—name the other publishers to whom one could turn.

If A. asks you for the manuscript merely send it to him, as he would have full power from me to do so. But first strike out a whole passage—you will find it just on the first page of the preface—from *Der dieses Narrenhaus jetzt mit so wahnsinniger Emsigkeit,* and so on, to *über unsren Irrthum klar zu werden.*—I wrote this preface when I still thought of turning the whole into a series of musical newspaper articles ; now, as an introduction to a somewhat large book, this tone may perhaps have a too snappy, perhaps paltry, effect on the reader. It would be terrible if the book should come to be looked upon simply as an attack on Meyerbeer. I wished I could withdraw still much of this kind. When I read it, the mockery never sounds venomous—but if others read it I may often seem to them a passionate, sour-minded individual, and this I would not appear to be, even to my enemies.

On this occasion I would give you a piece of advice : lay aside henceforth a certain taint of polemics. When necessary, one must strike heartily, for dear life, and with all the strength of which one is capable ; but then there must be an end.

Constant bickering and taunting make a highly unfavourable impression on the spectator, whom after all
one wishes to win over, namely, that of the incapacity
of both opponents to fight. See, I am no longer capable
of setting right even the grossest misunderstandings
about my article on the Jews ; if no one is found to
undertake such correction—*whenever it is of importance*
—well, in this cause I have gained the victory over no
one ; or if the correction is not of importance, I should
only spoil for myself the public avowal of victory. In
your present literary works I have one thing to find fault
with : you allow your own light to shine too little ; my
writings have somewhat estranged you from your own
peculiar method. That which I perceive from a more
general standpoint you are well qualified to look at
from a more special standpoint. You have already done
this exceedingly well, and you will certainly do it well
again ; only take care not to show yourself to your
opponent in a state of dependence which he cannot fail
to perceive by the outer garment which—out of love to
me—you too frequently hang around yourself. I have
at last managed to see the *Rheinische Musikzeitung.* I
do not care a bit for this paper ; it is the old style of
musical newspaper, which in its uselessness and un-
fruitfulness will last as long as our modern music lasts.
But this paper is consistent : if any one wishes to edit a
special musical paper, this represents the extreme liberal
standpoint ; if he goes a step beyond, he disowns our
whole musical conditions as incapable of further development,—and of what use is then the musical paper ?—
Or he says yes to-day and no to-morrow merely for
the sake of prolonging its existence, and thus becomes

7

despicable.   The editorship of the *Rheinische Zeitung* is
either so inextricably mixed up with our musical doings
that it maintains with an honourable conscience the
standpoint which it takes up, or it is sufficiently intelligent and prudent to see, that in order to keep
the paper going such a standpoint must be taken up.
Even in this—somewhat jesuitical case—it extricates
itself from the affair with a good grace, and anyhow,
in a better and more respectable manner than the other
paper, for which I cannot find any one term of contempt strong enough to express my disgust.   Stupidity,
cowardice, and vulgarity, will do, however, as a multiple
epithet. Curiously enough the *Rheinische Zeitung* was the
only paper which gave an intelligent and well-intentioned
notice about the performance of my *Tannhäuser* overture
in Paris ; the *Rheinische Zeitung* is, in fact—a musical
paper of the day.—I understand that you must now
continue to write in a musical paper, but—please only
write good articles in it, such as you can write ; and,
for Heaven's sake, don't carry on any more warfare in
this periodical !—

How I feel now ?   Yes, if I could only describe it !
The one thing I could now set to work at with an appearance of usefulness would be writing about art ; and
that is just what no one wants.   You will see that only
with great trouble can I find an editor ;—as to being
paid, I can scarcely think of such a thing.—Would it be
better for me to set to work and compose another opera
for myself?—It's enough to make one die of laughing !—

Consider again the matter of extracts from my manuscript for Brendel's paper.—O, happy time in which
I did not understand why I should ever look at a

musical paper! How rich was I then, how beggarly poor am I now!—

I think, dearest—there will soon be an end of me, soon—altogether. If I trouble now about a publisher and things of that sort, I am guided purely by the instinct to earn money. If any one were to give me a little farm I might become a plain, simple *man*, and certainly not think any more of writing about art. —

Many thanks for your last letter! Farewell, and greetings at home.

Your

R. W.

March 10*th*, '51.

24.

DEAREST,

Do not be astonished that I have not answered you for so long a time! I did not like to write again while in my former humour, which, besides, must have distressed you, and therefore wished to wait until I had inwardly recovered. This, to a certain degree, has taken place, and I am again in better spirits. Outward circumstances have contributed thereto ; first of all Frau R. again supplied me with money, also I have found a publisher for my book. Liszt's article on *Lohengrin* in the *Illustrirte Zeitung*, which I lately read through, warmed and most thoroughly comforted me and excited me anew to artistic activity. And it happens also now that Breitkopf and Härtel promise to print the pianoforte score of *Lohengrin*. I have just received their letter, which prompts me to write to you quickly and briefly.   Unfortunately it does not mean money for me, because I have an old debt with Härtels which the honorarium will just wipe off.   However, I am highly pleased with the affair.   Now attention !   Send off your pianoforte score, forthwith, to Härtels with the enclosed letter to the firm : I mention to them that, as yet, you have received no honorarium for it, and that they would have to settle with you for your work.   Write to them in the same sense.   Whether they will pay you much for such a desperately hopeless undertaking is not to be thought of, and scarcely to be demanded.—Why do you have anything to do with *me ?*

One thing you must at once change in the pianoforte score ; the second part of Lohengrin's narration in the last act must be taken out. I have for good reasons cut it for performance, and for the same good reasons it must not be printed.   This cut and a small change in the interlude immediately following (three bars instead of the incorrect two bars) you must manage thus :—

Sein Ritter ich   bin Lo - hen-grin   ge - nannt

(Please arrange it in your own way!)

One thing more:—I really wanted Härtels to show themselves generous and to have the score engraved. To that they have not given a positive refusal, only they wished to wait for a more favourable turn of things with regard to me, and so on, before they entered upon so costly an undertaking. Anyhow, they want a copy of the score from me. I cannot at all manage this at my own expense, and I should be loth to part altogether with my autograph score, the only tiny possession remaining to me of my work. I wonder whether old Fischer (ask him!) could get the copy which Lüttichau possesses for the price he paid for it (36 thalers)?—Are you marking the instrumentation here and there in characteristic places?—Do take care that the scenic remarks are the same in the pianoforte as in the full score!—

Well. There's a piece of business again.—

—J. J. Weber at last wrote to me that he would pay

me an honorarium of 100 thalers for my book. Being
in want of money I was about to accept, when my
brother-in-law A. offered, besides the 100 thalers, to pay
me another 75 thalers after the sale of 400 copies ; also
concerning the rights of further editions I shall come
more promptly to an understanding with him. So he
will print it. But,—if I were compelled to live by my
pen ! ! !—

K. will—I believe—soon return to Dresden, in order
to have active influence on the future movements of his
family, in so far as it stands within his power. I am, as
one might well imagine, thoroughly safe *here*. You must
not ponder much more over my remarks about yourself ; you must already have understood my brotherly
hint. Your article on the Mangold Opera has pleased
me *very much*—not so your great attack on Bischof—it
was too much spun out, and the catchwords repeated
to weariness. The bit about Krebs was very amusing ;
but will it do you any good ? After looking into
the Hamburg article on *Meyerbeeriana*, together with
the energetic editorial remarks, as well as the notice of
Schumann's Genoveva, with the somewhat vulgar attack
on me, etc., etc., you will probably not insist on my
withdrawing my opinion.

Besides, I have already cooked a private little dish
for this place. Soon a pamphlet of mine will appear
here, "A Theatre in Zurich," in which I show in a
very practical manner the possibility of a theatre here
which should be all the more distinctive in that it could
and ought to be an *original theatre*. I cannot count
on an immediate success, but, with good fortune, on a
gradual one. I base all my courage only on the hope

of practical realization.—You shall have the pamphlet as soon as it is out.—

Excuse my horrid scribbling ; I *had* to write to you, and *could* do no better.—

Salute the R.'s a thousand times ! Greetings to your wife and children, and farewell—but do come soon !

Your

R. W.

ZURICH, *April 19th*, '51.

25.

DEAR FRIEND,

The delay is most unpleasant to me, also that you did not see at once about my letter to Härtels : it contains a business memorandum which had nothing to do with the sending of the pianoforte score. Despatch the letter at once, and explain to Härtels the delay in the forwarding of the same.

—I can have nothing to do with L. ; however un-willingly I part with everything out of this opera, still I would rather send off the whole score to put an end to formalities. Keep it by you till the pianoforte score is finished, and then await further instructions from me.— Send the finished first act of the pianoforte score at once to Härtels, so that they can begin to print ; tell them at the same time when they are likely to receive the second act, and so on. Write to Härtels that I should be pleased if they commenced printing at once.—

—Who is Riccius ?—I wish that any one knowing up to now so little about me, as for instance not even to have seen the score of *Tannhäuser*, would write nothing about me ; under the most favourable circum-stances he will write in a confused and uncertain manner.

Do try and persuade the man *to wait until my new book appears :* it will, I think, soon be out.

To-day is the great Zurich festival :—I am going to the banquet, and have to make haste.—

Adieu !   Greetings to your family.

R. W.

May 1st, '51.

26.

DEAR FRIEND,

I write a couple of lines out of my turn, *i.e.,* without first waiting for news from you.

Your article on the *Tannhäuser* overture, with which you have truly surprised me and touched me to the heart, specially prompts me to do so.   But quite apart from the effect which it must make upon me so far as I am personally concerned (you must take flattered vanity as little as possible into account), the article is excellent—and truly in every respect—and though the contents are ideal, it is at the same time practical to a degree beyond anything within my knowledge.   I congratulate you on it, and strongly beg you to let me have a copy for my house archives !—I have long been wishing to ask you about another matter, but it has hitherto escaped my memory, and so I at once touch upon it.   You wrote to me once that you had received news of Röckel through Dr. Fl. Schulze ; I would thank you to go to the same source to find out if by chance I could write to him, and to whom and how I should have to address for that purpose.   You told me R. had received writings, *i.e.,* pamphlets of mine.   Has he also received my *Kunstwerk der Zukunft,* and would it be possible to send him *Oper und Drama ?*

There have been some strange goings on as regards this book. After I had promised A., and broken off with Weber, I received from the latter at last another letter, in which he proposes in return for the manuscript, to pay me down twenty louis d'ors at once, and again the same sum after the sale of the edition of 500 copies. Naturally I had to close with him. But how the whole thing has been delayed.

Next week I shall be able to send you my pamphlet published here, " Ein Theater in Zürich." Don't be astonished if I send it to you unfranked : I have a reason for doing so.

Offers have been made to me from Weimar for a new opera. I should have to deliver it by 1st July, 1852, and up to then, and during that time, I should be paid altogether 500 thalers. Now I have come to a new determination with regard to the subject I ought to take in hand. If I settled on *Siegfried's Death* with the serious view to performance next year in Weimar, the whole thing would appear to me a perfect impossibility. Whence should I get actors and a public ? All the winter through I have been tormented by an idea, which of late has so completely taken hold of me, that I will now realize it. Did I not once write to you about a genial subject ? It was that of the youth who sets out " in order to learn fear," and who is so stupid as never to be able to learn it. Think of my alarm when I suddenly discover that this youth is no other than the young Siegfried, who wins the hoard and awakes Brünnhilde. The scheme is now ready. I am for the moment collecting my strength so as to be able next month to write the poem of

Young Siegfried. In July I set to work at the music ; and I have such bold confidence in the warmth of the subject and in my powers of endurance, that I think, by next year, I shall start with undiminished strength the composition of *Siegfried's Death. Young Siegfried* has the decided advantage that it presents the important myth in the form of a play to the public, just as a fairy tale is presented to a child. Here everything makes a plastic effect by means of sharp sensuous impressions, here everything is understood at once,—and then if the serious *Siegfried's Death* follows, the public knows all which has there to be presupposed or even only hinted at, and—my game is won,—all the more as by my *Young Siegfried*, which throughout appeals far more to the popular conscience, and which is less heroic than filled with the gladsome mirth of young manhood, the *actors* are practically exercised and prepared to solve the more important task of *Siegfried's Death.* But each will in itself be an independent piece. They are only to be presented to the public in succession the first time ; afterwards each, according to taste or means, can be given quite by itself. Besides, I have no longer a general, abstract public in my mind, but a special one, to which I purpose to address myself (*mittheilen*), so that by it I may be understood.

Now farewell ! Don't sweat too much over the pianoforte score. Write to me soon how you are, and *when you are coming* (*the chief thing*).

Greetings at home, and to the R.'s from your

R. W.

May 10th, '51.

27.

This time I am quite distressed at being so long without any letter from you. Were not the contents of our letters always so innocent, I should feel disposed to think something had, for once, been confiscated. Have you received the score of *Lohengrin*, which I sent from here on May 1st? Have you received a second letter from me in which, among other things, I asked for a copy of your article on the *Tannhäuser* overture? Have you not written to me since then?—And have you received through the R.'s a copy of my " Theater in Zürich"?

Is the pianoforte score giving you so much trouble that you can't get away from it? I have no further news from Härtels. What are they about? Are they already engraving? When you are seeing to the proofs I would like first to look through them before they are struck off; perhaps here and there an idea may occur to me. *Do* arrange with Härtels that you send me each time the revise, and I will return it to Härtels without delay. One thing more! I was informed lately that to make things easily practicable you had so transcribed the orchestral parts, as to present the theme alone in the various registers of the pianoforte score. My friends, however, think that, in order to preserve, or at least to indicate, the full framework with its harmonic upper-voices, a somewhat more complex arrangement would not only be possible, but having regard to the *technique* of the present day, quite practicable. If that were quite out of the question it would, after all, be better to arrange it for four hands. I am less in favour of the four-hand arrangement—but would prefer perhaps small notes. Have you, perchance, conferred with Liszt on this matter? I am really anxious to see something, and especially to have some news.

I am fairly well. However, I am tormented with a complaint which my doctor looks upon as a favourable crisis in my state of health generally:—it does nct trouble me in my work.

Now do say when you think of coming to see me. The weather will soon be favourable. In the summer my wife must go to the baths at Graubündten.—

You already know that Weber, after all, prints my book. Lately I received four sheets to correct. To my astonishment I see that he is going to publish it in three volumes, small octavo, wide-spread—in fact, noble print. So he will increase the selling price. Oh, you booksellers!—

Greetings at home and to the R.'s.

Farewell. Write soon to me, and give me plenty of news. Also get ready to start, so that we may soon see each other again. Farewell. I will not pay the postage of this letter, for I shall only send it off after I have made fruitless inquiry at the post for a letter from you. I can only get information about seven o'clock, and then it will be too late to pay the postage. Do the same with your letter,—and in general! — —

June 3rd, '51.

28.

DEAR FRIEND,

It is quite time that I should be heard again. Our last letters have crossed; no matter. As the

time of your departure from Dresden is approaching, I
have nothing further to communicate to you by writing,
excepting what concerns your journey. I think you
ought to travel here by the Bavarian railway ; that
route will bring you here quickest. Travel *viâ Ulm*
to *Friedrichshafen* on the Lake of Constance ; from that
place you cross over in the steamer to Romanshorn, and
there will I wait for you, unless something—Heaven
knows what—goes wrong with me. So tell me exactly
when you start, and when you reach *Romanshorn.* One
thing more. As you wish to return by the *shortest*
route, you would, after all, do better to come here *viâ*
Frankfurt and Basle, for the other way is, as I have
said, the shorter. You would then have the advantage
of seeing the Rhine. If you should come this way, I
of course would not come to meet you, for the road from
Basle to here presents no attractions. I would then wait
for you here, and change the territory of arrival into
one of departure, inasmuch as I would, when you go
away, accompany you to the Lake of Constance, and
that would make a very pleasant walking expedition for
us. So please say exactly what you will do ?

Now what more should I write to you to-day ? I
think I will reserve it. I have still no news from
Härtels. Anyhow, they must wait for all corrections
until you return to Dresden. It will be late before it
comes out ; also my book at Weber's progresses at a
very slow pace.—

(My "lectures" here consisted of certain passages
out of *Oper und Drama*, which I read quite in private
to a number of acquaintances and friends here.)

Now the rest by word of mouth. That is the most

sensible of all, and I rejoice at it with all my heart. (I commenced *Young Siegfried* on the 3rd June, and I shall have finished it in a week.)

Farewell! *Au revoir!*

R. W.

June 18th, '51.

29.

Dear Friend,

Again to-day a word or two about your last inquiries. I will answer them in the most concise manner. Come *viâ* Kempten and Lindau; from Lindau you take the steamer direct to

Rohrschach,

there, in Rohrschach, I will meet you. So write exactly *when you will be there*, or at least *when you will be in Lindau*.

For the rest only this by letter:—bring with you the score of *Lohengrin*. In case Härtels might want it, I have offered it to them; so, in passing through Leipzig, offer it to Härtels; but *only in this case*. If they do not want it for the moment, I should be delighted if, for the present, you would bring it to me; perhaps we could do something with it. On your return you can, after all, carry it back, partly for correction, partly for Härtels, if they want it.—

Do bring also with you the copy of *Siegfried's Death*. What else might I want?—I know of nothing of importance. A thousand greetings to the R.'s from me! Say to them that early *to-day* my *Young Siegfried* came into the world ready and well-rhymed. Your wife must not be angry that I so disturb her! Greetings

to her.   Let Brendel be Brendel, and—get ready to
come.   Yours,

R. W.

June 24th, '51.

30.

O, you bad man ! homo malus ! How long have
you made me wait for a letter !   Had you heard my
cursing and swearing during the last eight days it
would have quite alarmed you.   I thought I should at
least receive a letter of four sheets ; instead of that
comes a miserable mutilated sheet of note paper, so
that it truly excites my pity.   Oh, how quickly are you
degenerating in Saxony !   Rascal ! — —

I set hard to work after your departure.   It exhausts me very much, but when at last I wish to
recruit myself, I really do not know how to manage it.
The worst times are those in which I wish to refresh,
distract myself.   Only then do I become fully aware
how matters stand with me.   I have first to strike
every spark of joy out of a whole heap of flint
stones.   So long as I work I can *deceive* myself, but
so soon as I wish to unbend my mind I can no longer
deceive myself ; and then I am, on that account, terribly
miserable.   My only escape is always to be thinking of
fresh work, and my only joy is to commence to cripple
my strength.   Magnificent kind of art that.   Gladly
would I throw it away for one single week's life ?   I
am terribly without nourishment from my surroundings.
I cannot get on at all with men.   At such times I feel
a truly ardent craving for something, no matter what, to
come into my hands from the outer world.   From earliest
morn my only distraction is the hope of receiving a

letter—a token of love. Well, midday comes—nothing
arrives.—The whole day passes for me in unsatisfied
hunger, and I gnaw into myself afresh.— —But why
should other people exist merely for the purpose of
giving me nourishment ?—I know each one has enough
to do to think for himself, and at last I shall be reckoned
an insatiable ! — — — —

My *Mittheilung* was ready soon after you left. What
you do *not* know is actually the most important part.
This is a decisive work !—The copying took me over
a week ; but last Saturday week everything went off to
Härtels, also the explanation about the " score." I am
expecting an answer in a few days. I should be glad if
(the *full* score of—Tr.) *Lohengrin* also were engraved ;
after all, there may be some theatres which would give
the opera. Copying is a tedious, formal, uncertain, and
expensive matter. I can scarcely think Härtels will
decide for both scores; anyhow, they have not expressed
the wish. I have nothing to say against a performance
of *Lohengrin* at Leipzig ; only I wish they would lead
up to it in a more systematic way, *i.e.*, first give the
Dutchman, then *Tannhäuser*, and—only then, *Lohengrin*.
I will write as much to Härtels. Wherever I can exert
any influence, I would propose this plan ; at least, that
they should give *Tannhäuser* first. Altogether, I get
rid a little of my repugnance to the production of my
operas. When a theatre suddenly wishes to give one
of my works, I have surely a right to presume that
there are special reasons, and generally—or rather
most certainly—that an enthusiast is at the bottom of
it, who is anxious to gain the cause acceptance. If I
can influence conductor and actors by letter, I see a

possible guarantee before me; but where such is not
the case, as in Dresden (so far, at any rate, as the
conductor is concerned)—I let the thing go.

Lately I received from "Bote and Bock," in Berlin,
a request to state my terms for *Tannhäuser*, which the
Schwerin Theatre wishes to give; at the same time,
they would like to have a copy for themselves, with
performing rights. I was quite astonished, and thought
at once—"in return for a modest honorarium," etc. I
could not get Schwerin out of my head, when suddenly
I remembered that Röckel's sister, Madame Moritz (a
highly talented actress and singer), is there: she has
seen *Tannhäuser* at Weimar. You see things often
happen thus. On this occasion I have an immediate
request to make to you. Do go with enclosed letter
to X., and get him to hand over to you twelve scores
of *Tannhäuser*. Fischer tells me that there is no score
of *Tannhäuser* among the music I left behind. Should
demands increase, it is as well you should have a supply
of copies, of which I could at once dispose. I would,
therefore, beg you always to keep in readiness one or
two *complete* copies, namely, with the *new* ending (Fischer
would let you have the theatre score at any time, and
you could get this copied in by Wölfel),—and also with
the *cuts* and small *changes* (also with regard to the Introduction to the third act), which you will likewise get from
the theatre score. Ask, too, for a dozen books of words.
In case X. should hesitate to part with the scores, let
me give you this bit of information. I had one hundred
copies of this score struck off by F.; I defrayed the
cost out of the money then paid to me in advance
from the theatre. For this indeed, the king himself

8

strictly speaking would be my creditor, and no one else.
Now I do not know exactly how many copies I kept
for myself; many of them I gave away here and there.
As there are none to be found, I presume that, originally,
I cannot have had more than thirty. I gave all the
others to X.—at least sixty copies—but about this I
won't dispute—X. himself will know best. X. was to
try and sell these copies through the music trade, and
we fixed the price at ten thalers. As his business was
in want of funds, I consented that X. should make use
of any money which might come in from sale of the scores.
Now I don't know how many he sold, but the number
on hand must still be very large. If X. hesitates to
give the twelve copies wanted, he might be answered
thus : " You are keeping back more copies than you
will probably require for the music trade, but you
cannot sell them to a theatre with permission to perform. Now if you prevent Wagner from selling his
work to theatres, you are standing in your own light
with regard to the music business, for then no one will
buy the pianoforte scores. If, by keeping back the
scores, you wish to compel Wagner to give the theatre
honoraria to the music business, that would be a piece
of villainy towards him—whose means of living is not
secured by any rights—which he would answer by not
having his operas performed at all."—Should X. insist
that for every copy sold to a theatre he should receive
the music trade price of ten thalers, you must finally yield
in the matter, and give a guarantee for the same. I speak
here merely of *possible*, not *likely* eventualities : I do not
expect them from X. Will you always reckon up the
expenses to Wölfel, and I will at once settle with you ?

There's a lot of business!—Now something different!
—I have seen about a copy of my new "comic opera
libretto" for Liszt, but I am not sure whether I shall send
it to him now.—I am going to set to work at the music,
and expect to have a really pleasant time. You perhaps cannot imagine it, but everything comes quite
naturally. The musical phrases fit themselves on to
the verses and periods without any trouble on my
part; everything grows as if wild from the ground. I
have already the beginning in my head; also some
plastic motives, like the Fafner one. I am delighted at
the thought of giving myself up wholly to it.— —

But one thing more. Since eight days I am under strict
water diet, and it suits me thoroughly. I have not read
much of Rausse, but so much I know already, namely—
no wine, no beer, no coffee—only water and cold milk.
No soup, but everything cool or tepid. Early in bed,
three or four glasses of cold water; then rubbing down
—midday, a bath in the lake, or a hip-bath. My stomach,
which was altogether out of order, is in a good state, and
I feel easy in the abdomen. During the day I continually drink much water; after a meal I go out for half
an hour, and so on. My head is much lighter, only often
somewhat giddy; probably this is the immediate effect.
I shall *go on* unconditionally in this way, for I feel how
much good it is doing me. I do it, too, with goodwill,
and with water and milk, I have a relish for food and a
good appetite. At the end I shall have more health than
I know what to do with. Tell me, what shall I do with
it?—Greetings at home, and also to Julia, who is now
the only one of the R.'s left in Dresden!—K. is in
Stuttgart.—The letter to Röckel is insipid, and written

under compulsion ; but see to it through Schulze (who, indeed, can address the envelope). After I have received a letter from Röckel I can write better to him.—

Adieu, you dear, good man ! Thanks for your love and faithfulness.

Your
R. W.

Upon my word the article from London signed "Butterbrodt," on the Thalbergian opera (in the *Signale*), was excellent. It made me go into fits of laughter !— I have not properly read Krüger : I shall get to know all about it from your replies. Minna sends best greetings. She is concerned about your hollow cheeks, and begs you will return with better looks next year !—

I beg X. to put the new ending in the second edition of *Tannhäuser*. If he will pay the costs, would you be so good as to arrange the piece ? For Heaven's sake do leave out the *preliminary remarks* of the Weimar book of words (concerning Master Wolfram) in the pianoforte score of *Lohengrin*. They are not *mine*, and are *worthless !*—

31.

DEAREST FRIEND,

I am going to the hydropathic establishment.— I am just back from Albisbrunn, where I have had a consultation with the doctor, and have fixed my removal for Monday, the 15th.—

I cannot suffer things by halves : mere dieting has done me no good. But were I, in my present state, to set to work at *Young Siegfried*, by next spring I should probably be incurable. Now I have a strong desire to do the thing thoroughly ; for the thought of becoming perfectly well is quite a new one for me, and plans and propositions of the highest importance are connected with it. Thus can I still be of some real use.—Besides, were I to roam about in my languid state of health I should be acting against all my convictions and principles. But the idea of setting to work at *Siegfried* in perfect health has about it a something which I may call—joyful solemnity. So—it is fixed—I go through the whole water-cure.

Now I have a fresh request to make. There are still about twelve sheets of *Oper und Drama* to correct. I wrote to-day to Weber asking him to send them to *you*, together *with the manuscript*. You must see to them for me. I have already given orders to Härtels—who, by the way, have not yet answered me—that you will undertake the correction of my *Mittheilung*, etc. Don't be angry with me for disposing thus of your time : when I am well again I will in turn *correct your* articles for Brendel.

From now address me as follows :—

> " Albisbrunn bei Hausen,
>   im Kanton Zürich."

One thing more ! My wife maintains that some of my scores, and in particular of *Tannhäuser*, were lying about in the rooms of our former house-neighbour, Madame P. So get them. The lady lives where we last lived in Dresden, on the same floor.—

Farewell ! Let me soon hear from you, and remain good to me.

Your

R. W.

ZURICH, *September 8th*, '51.

32.

BEST FRIEND,

Before I go to Albisbrunn—that is to-morrow—
I will quickly answer one point in your letter of
yesterday, and so settle this much.

In two successive letters you bring before me X.'s
complaints. What effect do you wish to produce on me
by this ? Do you wish to determine me to think about
help for X. ? In that case you ought to have stated to
me *how* I could procure help. So far as I can now see
I can only help him by being less scrupulous with regard
to intended performances of my operas than, according
to my principles, I ought to be. To spread them about
among the theatres would bring good business to X.,
and with it freedom from his cares. You know that
even for Leipzig I have in mind to get my two other
operas produced before *Lohengrin*. I have sold *Tannhäuser* to Schwerin. Would you have me hand over to
him forsooth this, and perhaps other honoraria which
may follow ? Who would justify me in disposing of
these small and chance receipts otherwise than for my
own wants, so long as I am indebted for the supply of
these to the real sacrifice of one single family ? Even
in this very year I was in the deepest need of money,
and in pitiful manner was forced to seek help through
friends. I am using the Schwerin honorarium for my
water-cure. Up to now I have no sure prospect of
receipts from any other quarter. Well, just say what
I could do *now*, when X. is pressed, though only for
the moment—for his receipts *are* standing (if *only*) on
paper ? If I can give him something—before the paper
is turned into money—then I'll do it.—Besides, if I cause

X. trouble, I have the strongest reason for considering it my greatest misfortune that formerly I went to him. Of all persons in the world, he is the least fit for such a business. During the last years in Dresden this man tormented the very life out of me. I can truly say that the greater part of all the martyrdom which I have ever suffered bears the name "X." But now he is utterly incompetent to manage his own business. Only here in Zurich have I really received the clearest proofs how injurious he has been to the sale of my operas. If any one asked to have music on approval, he explained that he could only give it for cash down, or on account; and such conduct is outrageous. By this means he has prevented musicians who wished to get my things put before their pupils from doing so. Of similar nonsensicalities I have had endless cases mentioned to me—and from other sources.—In short, our sorrows are decidedly mutual ; and I confess that I have become somewhat hardened against his lamentations. Also, rest assured, it is not always so bad as he makes out.— —There's a tale— —

R.'s letters have filled me with melancholy and grief : everything is sad, very sad, and I can take no pleasure in R.'s good humour. Could not Schulz procure for him Feuerbach's lectures on the nature of religion ? More about this another time !—

One other request. Let me know exactly the state of the *Lohengrin* business at Dresden. I will *not* allow the opera to be produced there, even if I provoke public scandal over the matter. I should like to see if the people will be able to avoid knowing *who I am !*—

Unfortunately I have no answer yet from Härtels. If they ask you again for the score, give it at once.

If they mean to engrave it, the Wölfel copy will thereby become useless : whatever Wölfel has written could go at once to Härtels ; and the copy could be finished at leisure in Leipzig.   I think that, should they wish to have the score in any case, even if they do *not* engrave it, they can have it copied just as well there (and this would be of advantage to them for the purpose of circulation)— and so in the principal matter they get *their* way.

You have not grasped the right meaning of the ending of *Tannhäuser*.   This ending is no *alteration*, but a *rectification*, which, unfortunately, I could only make after seeing the work on the stage, when I became convinced that the former ending only gave a *hint* of what had actually to be communicated to the *senses*.   I understand that slaves of custom prefer the first (because accustomed) ending—and all the more as the rectification in Dresden was insufficiently carried out so far as stage management was concerned.   But in a certain sense I am ashamed of the first working of the end, which, in truth, is only a sketch : it should therefore cease to be known, and of course disappear *entirely* from the piano-forte score.   (An "ossia" is the very deuce!)   The only practical objection would be want of money to engrave it ; so if X. will not give it, I'll find it !   You must pay the costs ; I'll send them to you !   So that's settled !—

Your fresh emaciation causes me truly deep anxiety.   If you do the right thing you will join me at the colony :— I stick to that.   I cannot see why from some citizen-like feeling of honour you should go on fiddling yourself to death in Dresden.—Farewell !   I'm off early to-morrow morning to Albisbrunn.   Truly your

R. W.

That *Figaro* affair was most ingenious : I laughed right out !—One thing more !—Send me scalding hot all the numbers of the Brendel newspaper which contain articles of yours—in wrappers and unfranked (! ! !)—to Albisbrunn. Don't forget this ! (*Every one* of your articles.) You have my address. (I have not yet seen your reply to Kr. !)

P.S.—I am just in receipt of your last letter. I have nothing fresh to announce to you. I have already spoken to you about the *Tannhäuser* ending. (In this matter I am somewhat surprised at you.) I will write out the certificate, and will have it witnessed. If it does not go to-day, it will be sent on to-morrow. As a matter of course the portraits are already on the way.

September 15*th*, '51.

33.

MOST AMIABLE MAN ! (*Homo amabilissimus.*— Lin. II. 73).

This letter will not be up to much, as I write it lying down.

For the rest—water-cure : to be brief. Have read likewise Rausse on "Mistakes." Weather bad. October better. Not alone. Lieutenant Müller taking the waters with me. Still much excitement ; busied myself with too much theory. Your letter great joy ; best thanks— go on—Härtels respectable : having sent ten louis d'or. Ought to engrave the score of *Lohengrin* at once. Härtels are right. Shall find a way for *Siegfried* ; will first finish it. (Please make a fuss about Härtels' graciousness with regard to engraving a score of mine ! ! !) (*Musik. Zeitung*). Want your exact, honest, individual opinion about Dresden : not caring a rap for my "friends" ; why the

Court and L. ? *If*—well, only on one condition—Eduard
Devrient getting it up for the stage, *you* authorized by
L.   If not the devil take them.—Härtels write, Piano-
forte score ready—only to be corrected (?).   Thousand
thanks.   You doing much for me !   Another time *I !*
Carl greeting.—Grand letter : be satisfied.—

Soon write again.—Hearty greeting.

Your
R. W.

ALBISBRUNN (not knowing the day).

34.

DEAR GOOD FELLOW,

You are really the only one with whom one can
get on.   Many thanks for the letter received to-day :
it was the first and only one which I received since
your last, although many others were due.   My last
lines to you from Albisbrunn you probably received the
day after you sent off the letter just to hand.—I can
only say, " I thank you heartily for your love."—

You already know that Müller is here.   Albisbrunn
suits me to perfection.   For the last three days my
bodily health has so improved, that I often feel in the
highest spirits : it is the light healthy blood which is
now filling my veins.   Besides, fine weather has set
in with the new moon.   I often feel at times like
these as if I were gently and pleasantly intoxicated.
Oh ! what is all wine intoxication compared with this
feeling of most joyful ease, which often has no moral
foundation.   It is extraordinary how at first I was
worried by theory and abstraction ; it was like a
disease of the brain—an eternal cross-volley of abstract
thoughts on the theory of art, which I would willingly

at once have communicated to you to work out, if only to be rid of them. Still I felt that I should have minutely to describe them even to you, and that would have made matters worse. Now a grey cloud seems to be passing from my brain. I have had a beneficial mucous discharge through the nose, and my senses are gradually taking pleasure in their immediate surroundings. So I think I shall soon be restored to health and happiness, and I will communicate to you another time my thoughts on art, provided indeed they are of any importance.—Under these circumstances I am satisfied with my doctor; he is considerate, and takes pains to understand my constitution. Ah! were you here! When the air is clear, one is lost in wonder at the prospect. And—you must really come for good and bring your children with you!

I will not write any more now. Klemenz is already waiting with the damp cloth to give me my mid-day washing.

I am bestowing the greatest attention on your notices (on *all*, indeed), even if I do not answer them; once more, very great and best thanks! Go on, and rest assured that you do me good through and through by your thoroughness.

Farewell, greet wife and children.

Your
RICHARD W.

ALBISBRUNN, *September 30th*, 1851.

(I have no news from Liszt.) B. has not *sent anything yet* to me!

35.

DEAR FRIEND,

Your letter of yesterday found me indisposed.

I am in a somewhat serious mood, and just in a state
to see clearly through all delusions.   As I am exhausted,
I can only reply briefly.—

You might well have spared me X. all over again ; I
thought I had told you enough about this matter.
Concerning *him*, he is piqued about the R.'s inheritance,
and hence suddenly the violent lamentation ; that he
does not possess sufficient sense of propriety to feel that
the R.'s are not in the world solely for his sake, need
not cause any surprise ; but I hope you will perceive
what a difference there is between R.'s sympathy for
my future and X.'s peddling business.   So far as *I* am
concerned, I consider this speculative meddling in so
delicate a relationship as mine to R.'s, revolting.   If it
continue I shall most probably energetically and entirely
abandon all claim to R.'s sympathy for me.   I wish
some people would do me the favour of considering me
dead.   Really and in truth I am so for all that officious
crew.   I am dead, and X. may act as fancy, or rather
as his stupidity, prompts; in fact, as he has been inspired
by it up to now.   Let him bring out a second edition of
Tannhäuser or not : *to me* it is absolutely indifferent, if
he is so stupid as not to see *now* that every tolerable
man of business can transact business with me at this
very moment.   But if such a man as X. is not even a *man
of business*, I would certainly like to know in what capacity
he could appear to me worthy of regard, so that I should
trouble about him.   Let him go, and tell me no more
about him.   Be silent about him to me as if I were *dead*.

Through Liszt's friendship I have been again drawn
into a half-and-half world in which I begin to feel myself
deeply and painfully moved.   For the moment I know

not what to do to get right out from it. Only one thing is clear—that I do nothing further. No more *Illustrirte Zeitung;* at least, certainly no more with my help. I do not intend in any way to become celebrated ; at least, I will not help to make myself famous. Leave the rubbish alone, dearest Uhlig ! With respect to the present world, can one have any other pleasure than, at best, to deal a blow according to one's whim and fancy ? How impure and tainted is all other dealing with it. Let men do as they like : they must leave me out of account,—I am *dead* for *this* world.

All this recent *desire* to perform my operas is, after all, most disgusting. I make myself—as I see more and more clearly—only ridiculous, by defending myself against a wish that cannot will. Have Härtels not written to you about the score ? It seems to me as if it would be more prudent for them also not to go beyond wishing. If they print the score, they will only cause me fresh perplexity.—

Concerning my " Preface "—this my *last* word—I have still a request to make. As soon as you send back the last sheet of this *preface* to Härtels, ask them, by writing, in my name, to send a corrected proof of the whole preface at once to Liszt ; and—as soon as this is *done*—to notify the same to you, so that I may at once know it. Only *then* will I send off *Young Siegfried* to Liszt; and I shall have to declare to him my intention to finish the composition, although I cannot let the whole be produced at Weimar, *unless I am there myself.* This will naturally give quite a new turn to the whole matter, which must inevitably result in my deciding to render void the whole Weimar covenant. I anticipated this, and made up my mind from the beginning not to touch the Weimar subsidies, so as to be able, should circumstances arise, to be quickly rid of the matter. But, unfortunately, I was forced to touch and spend the first hundred thalers which I received from Weimar in July, and how I shall be able, just now, to put aside the November remittance I cannot imagine; for with the R.'s pecuniary help alone, I have hitherto not been able to make both ends meet. With this I have involuntarily answered a question which—in the form in which you put it—really vexed me. I do not like answering such singular questions, even when I think they are put with the best intentions. Only the supposition that there may have been some gossip, determines me to answer in a more definite manner—namely: last winter I was obliged to borrow money of my friends here; but I consider—or rather, according to those friends, I am justified in considering—this in no way a case of debt. Since February I had no longer occasion to borrow. In March Liszt sent me one hundred thalers—at the same time the R.'s sent theirs; and in July the Weimar intendant did the same—so from that time I managed all right, with one exception, when, counting on the twenty louis d'ors from Schwerin, I took the waters. This money, still failing to come, leaves me in want, and I must borrow. Why the deuce are you suddenly concerned about my money-affairs? I have become somewhat long-winded, and must now conclude. To clear matters I answer briefly some queries.

"Libretto of Hoffmann for you!" I do not remember. Mistake (perhaps "die Bergwerke zu Falun"?—not worth the trouble). "Trautmann and *Tannhäuser* score." As Meser likes; he can also give one to Heidenreich. All the same to me. Am anxious about you, as it is so long since you wrote. More of this another time.—

Remind Weber in my name about the correction.— " The critical friend of *Lohengrin*," Dr. H. Franck.— Your articles keep up even to Pabst's opera. Rare wit and excellent ideas. If I write nothing specially about them, always understand that I agree.

With Brendel—all right !—

From the *Gegenwart*.—

See to it at your leisure. But why ?—

I want a small house, with meadow and a little garden ! —To work with zest and joy,—but not for the present time. Besides *Siegfried* still some big plans in my head ; three dramas, with a three-act *Vorspiel*.—If all German theatres tumble down, I will erect a new one on the banks of the Rhine, gather every one together, and produce the whole in the course of a week.—Rest ! rest ! rest !—Country ! country ! a cow, a goat, etc. Then — health — happiness — hope !—Else, everything lost. I can no more. *You must* come here !—

Your

R. W.

I remain at least four weeks in Albisbrunn.—Müller sends greetings.—Don't be anxious about me ; I shall be better by-and-by.—

Don't refer to X. again. If your conscience moves you, act for yourself, but not for *me*.

36.

By the way ! a correction in post-haste—a defect to which you call my attention at the right moment.

In the text, and in the pianoforte score of *Tannhäuser*

(if a new edition is to appear) the end must be rectified thus :—

1. Text :

Tannhäuser.

" Heilige Elisabeth ! bitte für mich ! " (He dies)

The younger Pilgrims (entering from the front of the Scene ; while the sun is rising)

Heil ! Heil ! Der Gnade Wunder Heil !

Erlösung ward der Welt zu Theil !

Es gab in nächtlich heil' ger Stund'.

etc.

Landgraf, Ritter, Singers and older Pilgrims.

Der Gnade Heil ist dem Büsser beschieden,

Er geht nun ein in der Seeligen Frieden !

(Finis.)

I beg you will fill in the necessary scenic remarks from the old and new books (neither of which I have at hand).

If Härtels have not got on very far with the printing, you might send on this insertion ; otherwise you can attend to it in correcting.

2. (Pianoforte score) from :

" Heilige Elisabeth ! bitte für mich ! ", go on just as it stands in the old pianoforte score—quaver triplets and chorus of younger pilgrims—in full, right to the end. Only where the great Pilgrim theme (formerly only in the orchestra—trombones and trumpets) comes in, put the voice parts as they are in the altered score—in unison :—

The younger pilgrims (soprano and alto) continue here, as formerly, with the " Halleluja."—

You quite understand me, do you not ? The miracle only hinted at in the altered form must be completely restored; the "er ist erlöst! er ist erlöst!" etc., naturally comes out.—Thus is everything consistent, and the idea completely developed.

The reason for leaving out the announcement of the miracle, in the Dresden change, was quite a local one: the chorus was always bad, flat, and uninteresting; also an imposing scenic effect—a splendid, gradual sunrise—was wanting.—But here, where I wish to express my idea to the full, that consideration has no longer any weight with me.

So change this *in the book and in the pianoforte score.*

Farewell for to-day, and thanks for everything!—I am not well. This cursed *Tannhäuser* affair prevented me from sleeping all night. That's my way.—

Adieu!

The affair with R., etc., in W., is really terrible.

37.

DEAREST FRIEND,

Best thanks for your letter! I answer it at once, because I want another one from you soon. But I must be brief, otherwise I cannot write at all.

The R.'s are a new world for me. Between us everything is readily understood. We rejoice mutually, and everything which the one does pleases the other. There is no talk of *thanks* between us.—And could I be indifferent if I had to fear that a set of fault-finders would suddenly mix in this noble relationship, people who can neither understand nor love me,—who, merely for the sake of slander, and to a certain extent of dishonour, would cause me——? O, for shame! Think over the

last years of my life; then look at the others, and look
at the R.'s, and I hope you will understand why I was
in such a state when that suspicion, that presentiment,
arose in me.   Good heavens! to preach is always a hard
task !—Must I then really preach ?—

As yet I have no news from Liszt; only B. wrote to
me that on the 3rd of this month Liszt had not yet
returned.—

Extraordinary that I cannot get hold of the *Musik
Zeitung*.   Brendel sent me a few old numbers, and then
nothing more.   So, though I pay, it is impossible for
me to receive the wished-for numbers through the post
as soon as they are out.   Funny !   Brendel seems to do
strange things.   For goodness' sake, why do you not send
them ?   Cannot you get a second copy of your articles ?—

I must pull up.—

I have been packed up in a wet cloth for three weeks,
and shall continue in the same fashion.   For a time I
had to discontinue on account of too great exhaustion.
I am now much excited ; but—I live in hope.   My
appetite is always excellent.—

To Weber :

OPER UND DRAMA,

von

Richard Wagner.

Voilà tout !   Do write that to him !

Now Uli ! Uli ! man of fair complexion ! write and
tell me whether Elsa is well again.—Greetings to your
people and to the R.'s.—Emilie is coming to Albisbrunn.
Farewell, and——

Your

R. W.

ALBISBRUNN, *October 20th*, '51.

38.

DEAR FELLOW,

I do not see why I should not write to you to-day, even if it be but little. We are surrounded by a thick cloud. I have just come down from the Albis heights, where I have had the most magnificent view since I stood on a certain " Kreuzthurm." The whole chain of the Alps, from Säntis to the Bernese Oberland, in the clearest sunlight, and a thick sea of cloud spread over all the depths, from which the awful world of islands stands out nobly. I wonder what it is like on the Räcknitzer heights now ?—

Emilie wrote the day before yesterday. She is coming to us here at Albisbrunn. We can always make something of *her !*

If you hear anything of Liszt's doings at Weimar, please let me know. Your news about Moscheles gave me much matter for reflection. Ah ! if I could only draw Liszt away from his illusions, it would be grand. It has much to do with my works. My Weimar *Siegfried* becomes more and more problematical,—but not *Siegfried* itself. For this much is certain—I only work for art, for nothing else, unless it be for a little decided humanity.—

I am getting more and more to believe in my cure ; anyhow, my condition was and is now of a critical nature : were it not for my wife, I should remain here the whole winter.

Please send me the exact title of Rausse's writings on hydropathic treatment. I shall order them, in any case, for myself. You would probably also like soon to have your Rausse back again ?—

One thing more. I beg of you to get from Fischer

the following scores of mine which are in his possession, to make a pile of them, to pack them up, and send them to me the first chance you get.   Could not Emilie bring them ?   Otherwise, perhaps by parcel-post—or, in the worst case, by carrier.

The things are :—

1. *Die Feen* Opera.   Three vols., original MS.
2. *Das Liebesverbot oder die Novize von Palermo.*   Two vols., ditto.
3. *Rienzi.*   Four vols., ditto.
4. *Der fliegende Holländer.*   One vol., ditto.
5. *Der fliegende Holländer.*   Lithograph score, in handsome binding, with leather back.
6. Beethoven.   Ninth Symphony.   Engraved score.
7. Beethoven.   Pastoral Symphony.   ,,
8. Bach.   Motetts.
9. Schumann.   Symphony.

And the rest of the engraved music; only not the arrangements of *Rienzi*, etc.   These I present to the gods.—

See how you can get all that for me.—

Do you really think that, in consequence of the forthcoming historical concert, I might be called back to Dresden ?   Ah, that would be too grand !—

Yesterday I wrote a few lines to Emilie.   With regard to the miserable business I referred her to my last letter to you.

May heaven keep and preserve you in its incomprehensible love and foresight !   Also may it grant you black hair and a good corporation !

Write soon, do you hear ?

How is Elsa ?   Your

ALBISBRUNN, *October 22nd*, '51.   R. W.

P.S.—If you have any fancy for keeping the printed music of No. 6 and onwards, pray do so.   I really don't want it.—

39.

DEAREST FRIEND,

Only a line or two.

K. will willingly assist Brendel; only he must first get well: for the present he neither reads nor writes. Perhaps one day *I* shall air another of my fads in B.'s paper.

I am extremely glad that Härtels have behaved in a becoming manner towards you; but why anything short of one hundred thalers? Truly I reproach myself now for loading you so with my affairs: do not be angry with me on that account! Manage so that one day I may be able to repay your kindness.

I am writing to Härtels about the title: exactly as you propose. The remark must be left out.

Still no news from Liszt.—

My cure is going on all right; it is easy to trace the healthier blood. But I shall still remain.—My wife is just now on a visit here. She sends hearty greetings to you and yours. May your sick baby rapidly improve!!!

Hope you will soon write again. In a few days I will also put my pen to paper again. Greetings to the R.'s. Farewell!

Your
R. WAGNER.

ALBISBRUNN, *October 28th*, '51.

40.

DEAR FELLOW AND FRIEND,

I will write to you, but I don't know exactly what.—Yes—that I am more than grieved to have loaded you with so much work on my account. I

seem—as if I were ruining you.   Quiet me, if you can
honestly do so.—

My wife has been here on a visit for the last four
days, and only went away early this morning.   I shall
certainly remain here another fortnight.   Minna has
made a good joke ; she called our doctor a water-Jew !
Capital !   Well, but he does me no harm !   I already
know myself what is good for me.   He is also somewhat
rough and unsympathetic,—a money-speculator—rather
than charlatan.   He is no longer actually a physician,
and that is good ; twelve years' practice have, however,
given him the necessary experience.   I consider and
feel myself quite on the road to recovery : my strict diet
helps me most of all ; for example, of an evening nothing
except a piece of dry bread and—water.   Milk only of
a morning—no butter at all.   Thus I am making good
blood.

X. wrote in detail to me yesterday.   He sends me a
copy of an article from a very well-known—but preferring
to remain unknown—musician, which—it seems—you
have not yet read.   It is a phenomenon of interest,
and you must try and get it.   You will find it in the
Fueilleton der neuen Oderzeitung, 28th, 30th, or 31st
July : "A letter about Richard Wagner."

X. is righteously wroth about the mutilations of
Tannhäuser at Weimar.   It must be restored.   In
short, I beg you (listen, another request !) to send off
at once to Weimar a copy of the *Tannhäuser* score
arranged like those which I begged you to have in
readiness.   Besides the new ending—the second finale
(as we gave it last in Dresden), the retouched introduction to the third Act, etc., are of importance.

Have you yet seen Frau P. ?—

I have received no fresh numbers of the *Musik. Zeitung.* When I am back in Zurich, I will become a subscriber through the post ; then, perhaps, things will be in order.

(Please let me know what you have expended for the *Tannhäuser* scores ?)

Härtels have not yet written to Liszt ; they certainly seem to have stuffed their ears with wool !—

—Isn't it strange that the most important articles on my works are never in musical, but in other—for the most part political—papers ?—

Enjoy this beautifully coherent letter as best you may. It pleases me so little that I will close and send it off.—How is *Elsa* going on ? Farewell, best friend !

Always your
R. W.

Albisbrunn, *October* 30*th*, '51.

(Still no news from the R.'s.)

41.

Well !—Härtels have only just read the " *Vorwort*," and will not venture to publish it. I have written to A. that he or another may undertake the matter.

I have just written to the R.'s.—

You will receive, according to my instructions to Weber, two copies of *Oper und Drama :* one is for Rühlemann : best greetings to him from me. Heartiest wishes for Elsa's recovery !—I have no fresh news.—

I quite understood your joke—very good ! Your

"Confessions" *excellent*. I congratulate you! Likewise the remarks about Sattler. You are the right sort of chap! Good-bye, old fellow!

Your
R. W.

November 1st, '51.

42.

A couple of lines in great haste, so that you may get an answer to-day. After all, there is not much to answer. Only about one thing don't be anxious; your letters have all reached me, and in proper time. I wrote my last letter but one about an hour before yours arrived.—

I am going on fairly well. Besides the water business, I am busy building a house on paper—with a pair of compasses and ruler. Later on I shall construct it in cardboard. I shall still remain here a fortnight—in the snow and cold; but 'tis no matter.

I have already written you about the affair with Härtels; I am now expecting an answer from A. I think the matter will be arranged. But how the whole thing drags.—

I have received the *Musikalische Zeitung*. But this you know: I have already complimented you. During the winter, on principle, I shall idle myself into health, and only sketch just as fancy takes me. I am planning three dramas (the second and third of which are the two *Siegfrieds*) and a big *Vorspiel*. When all is ready, I think of carrying it out in my own manner.

Poor, poor fellow! To transcribe X. is truly a heavy

job. Best thanks for it. It's just possible I may get hold of his book ; but whether I shall read it——?

I have written to Härtels about the copy for X. If it must be—greet him from me. But surely I shall not have to write to him ?—

Take care of little Elsa ; it's a good thing the illness is over.

Well, good-bye ! Write soon again, will you not ? I will not fail to do so ; if only I had as much matter as inclination to write to you.—Best greetings.

Your

R. W.

November 3rd, '51.

43.

I write to you again to-day, so as not to forget something important.—

Already in Dresden I tried my hardest to buy a book, which, however, was long out of print. I found it at last at the royal library. It is a thin little volume, small octavo, or even duodecimo, and is called "*Die Wöl-sungasaga,*" translated from the old Norse by *H. van der Hagen.* It forms part, I believe, of the old northern *Ritterromane,* which Hagen—if I mistake not—published in Breslau between 1812 and 1816. I now want to look through this book again. There is no means of getting it here. There is therefore no help for it, best friend ; you will have to be good enough to borrow this book from the royal library for yourself, and then send it to me here for a short time. You might, perhaps, pack it up with something (*Figaro ?*), and I will then send it you back—at latest in a fortnight—with your *Rausse* books. Of course, everything through the post.—My music—when you have done looking through it—could very well be sent by carrier. I think you have nothing to risk with the book ; for—in the worst case, should it be lost, or should there be a question of breach of trust, you would only have to make good this loss to the library—*i.e.*, pay the price of the book. But it won't come to that.

For the moment, I can only tell you a little about the intended completion of the great dramatic poem which I have now in hand. Just reflect that—before I wrote the poem *Siegfried's Death*, I sketched out the whole myth in all its gigantic sequence ; and that poem was the attempt—which, with regard to our theatre, appeared possible to me—to give one chief catastrophe of the myth, together with an *indication* of that sequence. Now, when I set to work to write out the music in full, still keeping our modern theatre firmly in mind, I felt how incomplete the proposed undertaking would be ; the vast train of events, which first gives to the characters their immense and striking significance, would be presented to the mind merely by means of epic narrative. So to make *Siegfried's Death* possible, I wrote *Young Siegfried;* but the more the whole took shape, the more did I perceive, while developing the scenes and music of *Young Siegfried*, that I had only increased the necessity for a clearer presentation of the whole story *to the senses*. I now see that, in order to become intelligible on the stage, I must work out the whole myth in plastic style. It was not this consideration alone which impelled me to my new plan, but especially the overpowering impressiveness of the subject-matter which I thus acquire for presentation, and which supplies me with a wealth of material for artistic fashioning which it would be a sin to leave unused. Think of the contents of the narrative of Brünnhilde, in the last scene of *Young Siegfried*— the fate of Siegmund and Sieglind ; the struggle of Wodan with his desire and with custom (Fricka) ; the noble defiance of the Walküre ; the tragic anger of Wodan in punishing this defiance. Think of this from *my* point of view, with the extraordinary wealth of situations brought together in one coherent drama, and you have a tragedy of most moving effect ; one which clearly presents to the senses all that my public needs to have taken in, in order easily to understand—in their widest meaning— *Young Siegfried* and the *Death*. These three dramas will be preceded by a grand introductory play, which will be produced by itself on a special opening festival day. It begins with Alberich, who pursues the three water-witches of the Rhine with his lust for love, is rejected with merry fooling by one after the other, and, mad with rage, at last steals the Rhine gold from them. This gold in itself is only a shining ornament in the depth of the waves (*Siegfried's Death*, Act iii., Sc. 1), but it possesses another power, which *only he who renounces love* can succeed in drawing from it. (Here you have the plasmic motive up to Siegfried's death. Think of all its pregnant consequences.) The capture of Alberich ; the dividing of the gold between the two giant brothers ; the speedy fulfilment of Alberich's curse on these two, the one of whom immediately slays the other,—all this is the theme of this introductory play.—But I have already chattered too much, and even that is too little to give you a clear idea of the vast wealth of the subject-matter.

I should much like to have that *Wölsungasaga* once

more; not to take it as a model,—you will soon find out what relation *my* poem holds to this saga,—but to recall exactly to my memory everything which I had once conceived of the individual details.—

But one *other* thing determined me to develop this plan—viz., the impossibility which I felt of producing *Young Siegfried* in anything like a suitable manner either at Weimar—or anywhere else. I cannot and will not endure any more the martyrdom of things done *by halves*. With this my new conception I withdraw *entirely* from all connection with our theatre and public of to-day; I break decisively and for ever with the formal present. Do you now ask me what I propose to do with my scheme?—First of all, to *carry it out*, so far as my poetical and musical powers will allow. This will occupy me at least three *full years*. And so I place my future quite in R.'s hands; God grant *that they may remain unfalteringly true to me!*—

I can only think of a *performance* under quite other conditions. I shall erect a theatre on the banks of the Rhine, and issue invitations to a great dramatic festival. After a year's preparation, I shall produce my complete work in a series of *four days*.

However extravagant this plan may be, it is nevertheless the only one to which I can devote my life and labours. If I live to see it accomplished, I have lived gloriously; if not, I die for something grand. Only this can still give me any pleasure. Farewell!

Your
R. W.

ALBISBRUNN, *November 12th,* '51.

Still no news to-day from A. Would you be kind

enough to write to A., and also to *Härteis?* They might let me know how matters stand! I almost believe they do not get my letters!

44.

It is again long since I had news. For the last five days I have been expecting an answer from A. concerning the publication of the three *opera poems.* I am out of all patience that just this *preface*, the conclusion of which—as regards Weimar—no longer agrees with my latest decision, appears much too late. Now I shall be almost compelled to let Liszt have earlier warning that our opera compact is at an end, for by that " Mittheilung " he will see that it really was my honourable intention to work for Weimar. Now, to my great disgust, I must still read the insipid announcement of a " **Jung** *Siegfried.*" (Pfugh! how affected!) It is really too ridiculous and vexatious.—As soon as I have written to Liszt, I will beg you to see about a new notice for the musical papers, in which the matter can be explained. By the way, try and induce Brendel *in my name,* not to accept anything more from H. "*aus Zürich.*" I am sufficiently vexed that we sent the stuff the first time. Brendel may, after all, have thought that he was obliging me in accepting it. Let him accept any trash he will, but —if he really wishes to oblige me—nothing more from H. *aus Zürich.* Quite apart from the utterly disgraceful insipidity of these communications, they cause such stupid confusion here ; and, at last, people will think *I* am at the bottom of it. So, do not forget!—

Last Friday evening, just as I had left my hip-bath,

the postmaster of Hausen rushed, all out of breath, into my room, and showed me Friday's Zurich paper, in which was written :—

" Richard Wagner, at present living in Zurich, has received full pardon from the king of Saxony. (He had been condemned to a long term of imprisonment for participation in the May revolution.)"

To the astonishment of my good postmaster, I remained terribly indifferent. Since then I have received no confirmation of the news ; so probably it is not correct. If indeed there were any truth in the report, the only thing I could do would be to ask to be denationalized from Saxony, in order to become a citizen here. With a Swiss pass, I could then travel wherever I liked, but I certainly would not come to Germany. However, for the present it is all talk, and I will not swagger and make myself ridiculous. Let me add only this—*my* pardon would be a striking evidence of arbitrariness.— —

Now something about my cure. For my wife's sake, I have now settled to go home again on Sunday, November 23rd ; the 24th is our fifteenth wedding anniversary. For the moment, this is how I spend my day :— 1. Early, at half-past five, wrapping up in a wet sheet till seven o'clock ; then cold tub and a walk. Eight o'clock, breakfast : dry bread and milk, or water. 2. Again a short walk ; then a cold compress. 3. About twelve o'clock, rubbing down with damp towels; a short walk; another compress. Then dinner in my room, to avoid indigestion. An hour's idleness ; a stiff walk of two hours—alone. 4. About five o'clock, rubbing down inaga and a short walk. 5. About six o'clock a hip-bath, lasting a quarter of an hour, followed by a walk to promote circulation. Another compress. Supper about seven o'clock : dry bread and water. 6. Then at six o'clock a whist party until nine, after which another compress, and then about ten o'clock to bed. I bear this *régime* very well now ; perhaps I shall still increase it. For four weeks I have sweated sulphur, and then my wet cloth has become reddish : I am assured that this proceeds from the mercury. A great deal of perspiration, with body at high temperature. My eruption came out again ; now it is gradually disappearing.—When I am back in Zurich, I shall continue the cure. I shall do little work ; only plan and sketch from time to time. If necessary, my wife will have to see to my wet-packing. Very severe diet ; so it would be the very deuce were I not to live a little while yet *in good health*. I shall, I think, one day accomplish something.—What do you think ?— Now I will see if I get a letter from you to-day.—Yes, one has come. For to-day only a short answer. I am greatly astonished that the P. has no scores ; perhaps she has some without knowing it. Natalie made a note of them ; I'll get her to write. Emilie cannot possibly bring the things with her ; of course not ; send them by carrier. That will cost least. But first you can look carefully through everything, just as the fancy takes you. In what you send me, keep only to that which I asked for. The printed things I really do not want ; please accept them as a present from me, if you care for them and they are not in your way. So only my operas, as I mentioned. If X. will spare me, as a gift of honour, a piano score of *Rienzi*, and one of the *new Tannhäuser*, send these also. I have still the piano score of the *Dutchman*, but the rest is missing.—I should like to have all these in the course of the winter.—More shortly. Between the arrival and departure of the post there is here only a cursed short time. If the *Musik. Zeitung* arrives punctually, I shall be delighted ; up to now there are no signs of it.

(Introductory play : *the Rape of the Rhine Gold*. I. Siegmund and Sieglind: the Punishment of the Walküre. II. and III. you know. Adieu for to-day.)

Your
R. W.

45.

I have just made up the packet for Weimar. It contains : 1. A big letter of three sheets to Liszt ; 2. a letter to Ziegesar, with two hundred thalers (which K. has given me) ; and 3. The poem of *Young Siegfried*, which I now send with a light heart to Liszt to read.

The windfall in the R. family just at this moment appears to me almost a dispensation of Providence. The yearly allowance which Frau R. now allots to me will prove a powerful defence against the pressure of compromise and commonness, as well as a mighty weapon against the faint-heartedness of the art-world of to-day. Even without this piece of luck—so far, you know me well—I would not have moved a step out of my path, and the latest crisis in my artistic plans would have come about not one jot otherwise than is now the case. Only I should have had such troubles, anxieties, and struggles, that I must have set to work in sad and bitter mood, and not, as now, in the highest spirits. Say this to my dear friend, Frau R. Tell her that perhaps even she cannot estimate what, by her latest

promise, she has done for me—perhaps for us all.—
But tell her besides, that when, through you, she gave
me the advice not to *break* with Weimar without
necessity, she had no idea of the state of matters. Say
to her that it was not arrogance, obstinacy, or caprice
that made me feel unfriendly towards Weimar; but
that now I have a scheme which—by its very nature
and the manner in which it has taken root in my mind
—quite prevents me from thinking any more about
Weimar. Ought she not to trust me, feeling that, at
least *now*, I should never *change my mind* unless there
were some real occasion for it?

I cannot write much more to you, for it is getting
late.—Do deliver this letter to Frau P.; it will calm the
good woman.—

A.—at last—writes to me that Härtels are quite willing
to keep my book; only I must make a few changes.
If the fools would only send me what I am to alter!—

Why three articles on the first part of *Oper und
Drama*, which really contains little but criticism, and
only two on the third part? Yet this third part is
indeed the most important to bring to a proper understanding, because it goes to the root of the matter. Do
not forget, as centre and axis of the whole, to give
prominence to "*subject-matter*"—second part; for the
important point here is, that I treat *form* purely from
this aspect, whereas others have always dealt with form
quite apart from contents.—

The *Norma Aria* (for Lablache in Paris) is the famous
number alluded to; is it not?

Farewell for to-day! Your

R. W.

10

New address : *am Zeltweg*, Zurich.

No more. I return on Sunday, so write now to Zurich.
November 20th, '51.

46.

Well, what more do you want ? I have just
written a " most complimentary " letter to Brendel, which
is to go off at the same time as this one. I offer, for
the future, to be an occasional contributor to his paper.
Are you satisfied now ?—

I am back again in Zurich since the beginning of the
week. The cure has worked wonders with me ; my
lightness of head and general state of bodily well-being
open up to me a new world. I have done well to discontinue the really severe *régime*. Only think, I bathed
lately in water of only three degrees of heat ! Rest
and attention to diet, rather than any particular treatment, will now do me good. But I do not give up the
bath, only take the chill off up to ten degrees. In other
matters I remain a strict waterman ; dry bread, with milk,
in the morning, but only with water in the evening. For
dinner : English cookery—vegetables cooked in water
and meat roasted on a spit, which my wife had to procure.
Last Monday, in honour of our wedding anniversary,
my Swiss confederates spent the evening at my house.
They boozed, as is their wont ; and my disgust at this
hard drinking, without which these unfortunate fellows
have not a spark of mirth or wit, completely convinced
me of my real cure. I can no longer conceive that
anything could happen, or that I could fall into any
misfortune, which would make me again have recourse
to wine, beer, etc. So I revel in an enjoyment of health

of which—as I now consciously enjoy it—I had no conception. My unimpaired spirits and constant good humour—which, in spite of the weakness resulting from the last severe treatment, have never left me—always afford me a ready answer to stupid scoffings: that I don't, for instance, need wine to be merry, and that I can get on very well without the seedy effects, etc. I now take a childlike interest in things to which already I had become indifferent—*e.g.*, about our new house, which is certainly small, but cosy and quiet. With truly childlike joy, every day I bring in something to make our exile home more complete and comfortable. So now I have had my "complete works" bound in red: there are already five volumes; the three opera poems will make the sixth.

These trifles exercise a beneficent and diverting effect on my over-excited mind, just as a hip-bath soothes the head; and, like this, I intend those to form part of my *régime*. Besides, my artistic plans are spreading out before me, and ever becoming richer, more pleasurable, and more decided; and it is with quite a shiver of delight that I think of soon working them out. Also, my plans have a practical bearing; much I may perhaps make possible which lately seemed beyond me: in this I am specially helped by K.'s noble and clear understanding. So you will still see me accomplish something *real* — — but more about that when my scheme is riper!— —

But I say to you further, that I thoroughly well understand my condition, and do not in the least deceive myself about the fact that, as yet, I am not fully restored to health. I am only on the right road to a complete cure, and this I shall effect in the spring, when I think of returning at the end of March to the hydropathic establishment.

So much about this for to-day !—

So I have received *Oper und Drama.* Weber informs me that you have already three copies. If you can really make good and advantageous use of the third copy, act according to your judgment. If not, send it to me by post ; I shall have it interleaved, so as to be of service in the preparation of a—possible—second edition.

Do not be anxious about the changes in the preface to the three opera poems ! How can you think I had changed anything of vital importance ! Nothing in it could really be altered ; better leave the whole unpublished. No, to people of that kind, in constant fear of the censorship, it is mere secondary matters, single expressions, and strong figures of speech, that are offensive. You will receive the alterations for correction, and by them will see that only what is trivial—or perhaps useless—is left out ; and even of this sort very little.

Lately I have asked Härtels for the last sheets of the preface. Since it has lasted so long, the announcement of my latest works had better be made more in conformity with my latest resolves, *i.e.*, without "Weimar."

Go please once more to Frau P., with friendly greetings to her in my name, and tell her that my wife assures me she had the following scores—which she did not give to Frau H.—stowed away in Frau P.'s attic :— *Rienzi,* six copies ; *Tannhäuser,* five copies ; *Flying Dutchman,* four copies. She had these clearly noted down by Natalie, and a memorandum to this effect now lies before me. So if the scores are not to be found in the attic, Herr Heinrich Brockhaus must have carried them off by mistake with *the books* to Leipzig; and I should then be *much* obliged if Madame P. would claim the same from her brother, and then hand them over to you. The library, which that gentleman has in keeping—as security for a debt—will very shortly be redeemed.

Best greetings to Fischer. I thank him very much for his friendly letter, which I intend very soon to answer. (Though I do not know what I ought to write to him. He writes as if every one in Dresden were so infatuated with *Lohengrin* as to want it put into rehearsal at once, and that really only my obstinacy stood in the way of an immediate performance. I, however, hear from all quarters that the management is of quite another mind : —Is that not ridiculous ?)

Good-bye! good-bye ! for to-day ! Greetings to yours, and especially to my little Elsa—Madame Lohengrin !— give her plenty of water, and not too much medicine !—

Please give friendly greetings also to the R.'s.—Yes, now it's quite another matter with

Your

ZURICH (ZELTWEG), *November 28th*, '51.   R. W.

47.

"*Figaro*" must again perform messenger's service! Already I very much wanted to let you (especially the R.'s) read my last letter to Liszt, because I have most clearly explained in it the motives which led to my latest decision with regard to my future artistic plans. Now you also want the letter concerning the Goethe foundation : then it's time to see about *Figaro.*—If anything of the sort should happen again, the Rausse books will follow.—The horrid manuscript will give you much trouble. It is certainly not intended for everybody, so be careful before you read it to any one. The copies in Liszt's possession are—this I mention incidentally—much more complete.

Many thanks for sending the 764,835th part of the royal Saxon state library.

I will quickly answer one thing to-day, lest it should get forgotten.—The article on Schumann was one of great weight and significance ; if only Brendel knew what he has in you ! The contents of your smallest contribution are great, and are now nearly always most refined and appropriate in expression.—*Roger*—excellent.—

I am expecting a letter from Brendel. Whether he gets anything from me for his new year's number depends upon my humour, which I do not wish to force in any way. Some new arrangement must be made about the sending of the paper, for something stupid is always happening. The last time I had to pay 5½ *batzen,* and what did I receive in return ? Nothing new except your Schumann article ! All the rest were old articles, which I had already received from him. I should have liked always to receive at once, through the post, each fresh number that contains one of your articles. Instead of that, B. waits until there are *several* numbers, so that you write about the appearance of a new article long before I get it ; whereas, in my opinion, I ought to receive the paper at the same time as your letter.—

From the new year I will order a copy for myself, to be sent actually *by post ;* for even if B. were willing to let me have the copy gratis, I am sure it would always be posted too late. A thing of that kind annoys me beyond measure. With all my Leipzig orders it seems as if I put my hand into . . .

My Zurich print-seller seems also to dabble in . . . as you have not yet received any portraits. I will inquire about them again to-day ; but in the meantime, let me know if I may send you direct a number of portraits, which you or some one else would undertake to sell ? In this case, how many ? etc. Besides, as I am far away from Germany, and shall probably remain so for some time, it is quite possible that my friends would be pleased to have before them a good portrait of myself (instead of my very self) ;—and as it further annoys me not to appear before them as I now am, but always as I used to look long ago—allowing for the painstaking violence done me by the lithograph—I have had the extremely vain (be it so !) thought that it would be well if a German music- or print-seller would decide to have a new portrait taken. He would then have to give the order to a portrait painter here, to take me and send the drawing on to him—*voilà tout !*—Perhaps the drawing of Kietz— made in March of last year, and, in my opinion, a very successful one—could at once be used for that purpose. It only comes to finding some one who would take up the matter. I, of course, cannot propose this to any one, but perhaps you or some one else could.—

So much for the portrait business !—Be good enough to write to Härtels somewhat to this effect :—the copyist has finished the score. Do they want it for the purpose of engraving ? If not, you must consider yourself, according to previous agreement, pledged to send it back to me.—They might as well write to me and explain, etc. Stupid nonsense!

To-day I have written to Feuerbach. I am trying, with Herwegh, to get him to pay us a visit here shortly. If we succeed, our circle will become still more attractive and brilliant.

We have a very good orchestra here this winter. The musical director of the theatre, a young man of twenty-two, is thoroughly competent—he has both fire and precision.   I have been again requested to conduct three symphonies: I choose No. 8, the Pastoral, and the C minor. As for other things, I do not allow myself to be worried. My disgust increases. I live only for my health and—for my dramatic plans.—

Apropos! Baumgartner has, at his own expense, had his songs published by Senff. See if you could not take this opportunity to write a really good article on the modern drawing-room song, and—put in a good word for Baumgartner. I should be glad, for the young fellow's sake!—

Adieu for to-day. More shortly. My best greetings to yours and to R.'s!

ZELTWEG, *December 3rd,* '51.

I must soon have both of Liszt's letters returned. *Don't forget this!*

Manage in some way—perhaps the *direct* one would be best—that the spare copy of *Oper und Drama* may reach R. at W.

48.

DEAR FRIEND,

I am expecting a letter from you, but cannot wait for it, as I have to ask you about something

("Keine Ruh bei Tag und Nacht") which must be attended to at once.

In the first place (*en passant*)—there is an inquiry to be made at Leipzig of Heinrich Kirchner, the bookseller's agent, about the portrait. One hundred copies were sent to him some time ago by Fuessli of Zurich (certainly more than will ever be sold, however famous you make me !).

Then I beg you to send me as soon as possible a score of *Tannhäuser* according to the original edition— without any changes—just as you find it. I specially want it—of course nicely bound (that's the main point !) to give for a Christmas present to Baumgartner, as I have learnt that it will afford him great pleasure ;— and besides, he buys all my things out of his hard-earned savings. If you would put me under great obligation, you would send me this—by post, please and, at least *this time*, unpaid—and also half-a-dozen copies of those Palm-Sunday-concert-programmes to which my analysis of the Ninth Symphony is attached. I have always forgotten to ask for them ; this time I made a note of it. If a copy of the new edition of the pianoforte score of *Tannhäuser* can be had already, I should be glad if you would send that too.—

And further !

Get Wölfel likewise to prepare for the private library of my most illustrious self a copy of the *Tannhäuser* full score. Nothing is to be changed from the original score, except the ending of the Third Act and the introduction to the same ! (1) Wölfel must alter the introduction according to the abbreviated form, so that the new manuscript may join on to a corresponding page of the original score ; he must write the new on the same sort of paper, and with the same distribution of space, as in my score. The pagination, which through this will get out of order, he must set right by, for example, doubling or trebling the page number on the new leaves (190 and 191), etc. (2) He must copy the ending as he has already copied it for the score of the Dresden Court Theatre (I mean so far as paper and writing is concerned). I only wish the new ending to be made complete, exactly as I asked you to do for the pianoforte score—*i.e.*, with the song of the younger pilgrims—well, you know; but it will be difficult to make this clear to Wölfel.

In this way I should especially like to possess a score of my *Tannhäuser* which would contain it just as I want it to be. The cuts which I only arranged on account of insufficient means of representation must naturally not be made here. Send this score to me—when it is ready.—

Concerning *Lohengrin*, I am really curious to hear from Härtels, whether they will quickly take the score in hand.—I specially need—and, indeed, very soon—a score for myself. If Härtels are willing at once to engrave it, they shall have—of course—the original score; and in this case I beg that Wölfel's copy—which, I think, must now be ready—be sent quickly on to me. But if Härtels delay, and only want the score for their stupid arrangements, etc.—they must be content with the *copy* (a mistake or two will not matter), and then I beg for the original as soon as possible. So—best of men!—reflect! Why should I want it? I will tell you; I am up to a bit of fun! I should very much like for once to hear the *Vorspiel* well performed by an orchestra. To manage this I must proceed most carefully, and in the following manner, as has been arranged and firmly settled. The theatre here closes at the end of *June*. For the first week in *July* I shall engage the theatre orchestra for an eight-days' rehearsal; for this very time I shall engage (or maybe only invite) the best musicians from Berne, Basle, St. Gall, etc., in order to gather together a good orchestra of from twenty to twenty-four violins, etc. I shall send on the parts beforehand to be studied.—With this orchestra, and a body of singers selected from the best sources here, I shall rehearse for a whole week, morning and evening, so as then to give (*i.e.*, to repeat) on *two* successive evenings the following performance. [N.B.— The costs of this undertaking, to be recouped by raised prices, etc., have been guaranteed to me by *connoisseurs* of this place.]

PROGRAMME.

By way of introduction—
Festal March and Chorus from *Tannhäuser*.

1st Part.
(*The Flying Dutchman.*)
I. (*a*) Ballad.
(*b*) Sailors' chorus.
II. Overture.

2nd Part.
(*Tannhäuser.*)
I. (*a*) Introduction to the third act.
(*b*) Song of the returning pilgrims.
II. Overture.

3rd Part.
(*Lohengrin.*)
I. The great instrumental prelude.
II. (*a*) Scene for chorus from the second act (all the D-major, beginning with the watch-tower song).
(*b*) Wedding music (Introduction to the third act); bridal song; and then wedding music repeated.

This programme pleases me immensely : it presents chronologically the growth of my poetic instinct, in musical—so to say, plastic outline. The ballad from the *Dutchman* at the beginning—the wedding music with the bridal song at the close : from the most visionary longing to the chastest realization ; and everything between these two, just as it follows in the great process of our development. You quite understand my programme, do you not ? It is a musical working-out of my preface to the three opera poems, which I imagine will be read beforehand by all who take an interest in me. In the programme I shall not hesitate, *clearly and directly* to give everything necessary for comprehension ; but I shall put the following explanation at the head :—

If I wished to present myself completely—as a dramatist—I could only do this now in an incomplete appearance : I therefore purposely show myself incompletely, displaying merely *one* side of my nature, so as thus at least to escape appearing full of gaps and void of clearness. If you want the *whole* of me, then do your part to make it possible.—

I will tell you another time how I think it possible to give a performance of those three operas—perhaps in the summer of 1853—in an equally thorough fashion as I am now attempting with these mere musical excerpts.—Anyhow, my friends ought not to sit anxiously by and brood over interest and compound interest. For once, a few wretched shillings capital must be risked.— However, enough of this for to-day !—It will be a pity if I give my whole soul to the matter, and have always to hear a groaning hm ! hm !—

You have probably read Liszt's letter which I sent to Frau R. ; is he not a noble-hearted, unprejudiced fellow ! Even where he does not as yet understand me, he makes up for it by a grand enthusiasm.

K. is back again in Zurich : he will not go on with the cure (and in winter time I think he acts wisely :— I also must seriously break off, as of late I went in for it too eagerly). At the beginning of the spring we are both going to Hahn at Horn. I can no longer trouble about a doctor, and I am bound to have one if I go on with my cure ! End of March, April, May—I think by the beginning of July I shall be all ready for my rehearsals !—

You probably do not expect me to say specially what I think of the latest Paris news ! Are we both agreed that those were in error who wished to give to that circumstance an importance which it could not possibly have ? It was the result of the previous reactionary conditions ; thus, in my opinion, only a chronic symptom of illness, and in no wise a decisive, acute attack. (Are you aware, too, that the socialists did not once come to blows ?)

So—a struggle between two reactionary forces, which rightly (and fortunately) could but end in favour of the open, free force as against intrigue !—

Farewell, good, dear fellow ! Best greetings, and write to me soon !

Your
R. W.

ZURICH, *December* 13*th*, '51.

49.

GOOD PESCHKE !

Is the neck-band ready ? How ever will you

commence with the black *Toupé*?   Whence will you get
your pleasant face?   Whence your bent complimentary
back?—There will be a sad falling off, from Peschke I.
to Peschke II.!   I do not think that you can bow
right and left, with such severe encouragement, whilst
fiddling.   Only one request does my wife make—
that you do not forget, if you wish to show yourself
worthy of your new position, No. 5, out of the green, and
No. 7, out of the red book!   These pieces are to be the
real triumphal marches of Peschke I.   So do not forget.

Dramatic-music-fiddling fellow!   You do well to
accept the position.   I respect all your reasons; only
one thing I make a point of: insist on leave of absence,
otherwise it is all up with you, and I shall become
furiously angry with you.   Put forward the plea of
health!   I can really not give up either wishing or
hoping to see you once every year.   I look upon
the fulfilment of this wish as dependent only upon
the possibility of leave of absence: so far as the rest
is concerned, you must allow me to say a word or two.
For example, I expect you to be present when I give
my great summer concert, in Zurich, next year; I
engage you for that purpose; and some extra receipts
to be made by that time ("together with a fair
honorarium"), shall provide me with the means of
paying your fee.   So make Lüttichau acquainted with
this, and ask for leave of absence for July 1852.

And so with the increase of salary, you receive at the
same time an enormously fat boy, without my knowing
anything beforehand?   Who understands better than
you how to arrange such things!   Everything fits in
admirably, and for the 150 thalers a new mouth is

found to swallow them up. Had you not already named the new son *Siegfried*, I would now counsel you to have him baptized *Peschke*. Perhaps both names suit well together—so salute *Peschkesiegfried!*

Now to business!

I thought you would write to Frau P. in the way indicated: it is to get rid of uncertainty, if only in matters of small moment.

As Härtels are going to engrave the score, it is perhaps best for Wölfel to finish the copy commenced from the theatre score; only there seems to be no hurry in the matter. So send me the copy as far as it is ready, and for the reason which I gave you in my last letter. I hope Wölfel will by this time have got on as far as the beginning of the third act; if not, let him write out quickly the orchestral introduction to this act and the bridal song, so that I may promptly have in my possession all that I shall require for my concert. The rest he can write out at his leisure! For *this* winter no theatre will think of giving the *Lohengrin*, and later on, the printed score will be ready, so that Wölfel's copy has practically become a luxury (even Brussels makes no sign!), and I can only use it privately. So far, good! Now let me proceed!

I have not yet received the pianoforte score: Härtels are sending it by carrier! (It never occurs to such people to send on *one* copy by post.)—I have ordered a copy of the "*three opera poems*" for Rühlemann. Kind greetings to him from me, and give him my best thanks for his letter: he must forgive me if I do not answer it at once.—

What is the meaning of all that you write concerning

the "Critic of the *Gegenwart*"?   I know nothing at all about it.—

Frau R. has now endowed me so liberally with scores and silver plate, that I am devilishly inclined to make my house as comfortable as possible !   Please say to our friend that I am exceedingly thankful to her for her gifts, and especially for her last kind letter : in everything she has given me great, great joy.—

Dear friend, I cannot possibly send anything to X. ! It is not that I lack a general desire, but I am not at present in the humour to write anything for the *Musik. Zeitung.*   I could only bring myself to write spitefully, for nothing else repays one for the trouble !   And my malice would have fallen on X. himself, whom among others I should have had to inform that he makes a great mistake if, for example, he thinks that he has understood me in my *Art and Revolution*, when he bravely waxes wroth at my unjust judgment of the past post-Grecian art periods, and reproaches me for having regarded them only through their modern caricature.   In so doing, he does not reflect that this very caricature is precisely the most obvious, most forcible physiognomy of the real unnaturalness of our whole art-culture, the root of which sticks fast just there, where Brendel thinks he most must riot over it.   How, too, can an "impartial critic" so entirely overlook my main contention, which in my pamphlet is clearly expressed, viz., that the difference between the Grecian and our own art-period consists just in this—that, at that time, Art was in harmony with the *public* conscience, and was cherished by it ; whilst now *true* Art (the actuality of which I *there* assume) must proclaim itself in opposition to our public opinion and customs, and *therefore* (end and conclusion of my whole investigation) be *revolutionary?* How superficial X. is when he becomes profound!

Enough! I could not write anything without expressing my contempt for all our art-doings—and especially for that music, for which in truth a musical paper is solely intended—by such hard-dealt right- and left-handed blows, as to bring Brendel into fresh trouble; for I should not only—as was actually the case in *Judenthum* —attack the abstract species, but give a good sound hiding to individuals themselves. Now that my books are out, however, I can no longer possibly feel any inclination for general reflections. If X. wants something *mild* of mine, let him print my letter to Liszt on the Goethe foundation. You could at once ask Liszt for this letter, stating your purpose, and that I am agreeable. If Liszt wishes to strike out anything relating to himself, he may act according to his judgment. Only *I* do not care to have the letter put before me again, so I place the matter in *your* hands. (One name must be altered: " Schöll " not "Schölcher.")

My dear friend, you will shortly hear of things which will enable you to understand why I have now completely given up every attempt to fight against the reigning stupidity, dulness, and wretchedness: I shall let that which is rotten rot, and shall use my remaining powers in production and enjoyment, and not in distressful, and quite hopeless attempts to galvanize the corpse of European civilization. I have only a mind to live, to enjoy—*i.e.*, to work as an artist, and produce my works: but not for the mud brains of the common herd. —As I cannot here develop my ideas at proper length, I must still keep secret the watch-word of my purpose—and, it is to be hoped, of the purpose common to many—in order not to be misunderstood.   So farewell for to-day !

Your

R. W.

ZURICH, *December* 18*th*, '51.

50.

Yes, best of friends !   You ought to have let me known sooner that you had to return the *Wölsungasaga* by the 25th of December.   If now a little delay occurs, " I really can't help it."   I thought there was no hurry. Besides, I have kept far from me everything which would prompt me to work at my great poem, so as to leave the matter to take its time—especially amid these winter frosts.   Now I have looked quickly through the *Saga*, and found out that it will no longer be of any use to me.   So I send you back to-day—with best thanks for your kindness—the little book, and only with a few lines, as it is already late.

Briefly, therefore :—

Your letter of yesterday informed me of your appointment, and conducting adventure ; news which gave me great pleasure.   For the rest, make no mistake about X. ; if he once intends to serve you out, his liberal opinion of your criticisms will suddenly vanish. People of this sort take everything according as they find it useful.

But—you must get leave of absence (certainly for 1852)—do think " of your *health* " !

Could you not haul X. once more over the coals?   The man really is a bungler at his business !   Baumgartner, wanting it for his choral society, has repeatedly asked through the music-seller Hug, for the Sailors' Chorus from the *Flying Dutchman* (as I expressly arranged it for men's voices *only*). X. doesn't stir (and that has always been his way).

Would it not be possible, just at this moment, when the pianoforte edition of *Tannhäuser* is about to appear, to publish on a whole page of the *Augsburg Allgemeine*, and perhaps, also, of two of the most important political papers, a general advertisement of *all* those of my works which have appeared at Meser's (including the *Tannhäuser* score)? Only so can the business get a fresh start! Of course at the same time a fresh supply of music would have to be sent to the music-sellers. All this is really under the jurisdiction of my creditors; and I have already written to you on the matter.— So—enough for to-day !—

I certainly should not have written my letter to X. if I had first read his article on my writings. Good God, what a weak-minded fool! The man thinks to bring about a better understanding for me by representing everything I say, and on which I lay most stress, as really not a matter for annoyance. That's just what he did in the matter of the *Judenthum*, when he showed that after all I really did not mean the Jews! Splendid! Now I can't in the name of fortune see of what use *he* could be to me. But enough of this !—

The pianoforte score has arrived ; I am chiefly pleased at its great correctness—especially with regard to everything concerning the stage performance. But the very idea of a pianoforte score was altogether so painful to me, that when it arrived, I felt scarcely anything except distress and discontent; and it needed all the assurances of Baumgartner and Müller, that the arrangement was an excellent one, to make me fair in this matter towards you and your careful work. You will excuse formal thanks, if I only simply assure you, that I am highly pleased that this disagreeable work of arranging should happily have fallen into *your* hands, and that you should have attended to it with such great affection! Excellent *homo*, now how about the correcting of the full score? I feel—Heaven knows— quite incapable of undertaking this, and for a hundred thousand reasons which I cannot and, besides, need not, set forth. May I put this burden on *you? Is it really not too bad?* Answer frankly!

The next time I will write more. I am well. Certainly, I was much excited, and then again un- nerved, by the *immediate* result of the severe *régime*. Anyhow, I am only *half* through the cure, and must complete it when spring comes. But I *knew* it would be so, and regret nothing.

Farewell! Greetings at home.

Your

R. W.

I have now become a subscriber through the post- office to the *Neue Zeitschrift für Musik*.

51.

DEAR UHLIG,

Yesterday I received the book: "Three opera poems." The preface had to some extent slipped from my memory, and I formally devoured it in the very neat, noble (and marvellously *correct!*) edition. Heaven knows how it is with others, but this preface has deeply interested *me;* I say this fearlessly. This was really the most important message which I had to deliver, for it was absolutely necessary to complete *Oper und Drama.* Surely I now have the right to think I have done enough with my pen! *What* can I still say if now my friends do not clearly understand, and why should I *now* still worry myself if my friends still keep dust in their eyes! I am now—with regard to what is done—perfectly satisfied with myself, for certainly I have left nothing undone in order to make myself intelligible. Anything further is simply the business of those who take an interest in me!—

Unfortunately, I have forgotten to order a copy of this book for our good R. in W. Could not K. remedy my fault, and get a copy, which you *in your turn* might send off to W.?

Well, I have now read through the letter to Liszt on the Goethe foundation. I look upon the publication of this letter as by no means unimportant, only I cannot for the life of me see why it should be in the *Neue Zeitschrift für Musik!* I feel fresh sympathy for Brendel since he defended me against the *Grenzboten*, and if I am doing him service, and obliging him by giving this letter for his paper, he might show his gratitude by having it also printed separately, as a small pamphlet (and not a shabby-looking one); he might send this out from the publishing-house of his paper and advertise it, so that it might come before those for whom the letter is specially intended, and these are certainly not the musicians, at any rate not exclusively.

On the occasion of the pianoforte score, I have again looked a little at the music of *Lohengrin*. Would it not interest you, since *you* always write things of the kind, to discuss the thematic web, and show how the path I have struck out must lead to ever-fresh developments of form? Amongst other things, this came into my mind in the first scene of the second act. Just at the beginning of the second scene of this act—when Elsa steps on to the balcony—it struck me how in the prelude for wind instruments, in the 7th, 8th, and 9th bars, where Elsa appears by night, a theme is heard for the first time which, later on, when Elsa advances towards the church, in bright daylight and full splendour, is presented in complete development, broad and bright. Thereupon it became evident to me that my themes always originate coherently, and with the character of plastic phenomena. Perhaps you can express this better than I.—

—Have you heard nothing of late about E. D.— whether he reads my writings, and what impression they make on him? I confess that I often think of him quite unawares, and I would much like to know how far a man of this sort remains behind through lack of inward energy and genuine courage, and how far on the other side, he is to be brought forward through his good intelligence and honourable will. Can I not write to him? I should be exceedingly glad—at least it would interest me—were *he* to write to me (besides, he really owes me a letter). How could you get at him? In any case, I should like him to have read the "Preface to three opera poems," before he wrote.

January 1st. I kept back this letter until I got news

from you again : this has happened to-day.—I first
answer some of your questions.—

Send me at once the pianoforte scores of *Rienzi* and
Tannhäuser (at *my* expense, of course), and do the
same with the full scores. So far as the *Lohengrin*
score is concerned, I feel almost inclined to stop the
copying *altogether*—especially as Wölfel is so much
behind. Of what good is this copy, as it will never be
wanted ? And *by* the time it is wanted, the engraved
copies will be also ready. However one may regret
what has already been written, a *part* of this useless
labour will cost less than the *whole*. I shall take out
of it only what is necessary for my concert ; the rest
may be destroyed. I am ever annoyed that I gave the
order for the sake of the Brussels windbags, and caused
unnecessary expense. Wölfel might, therefore, still
copy me quickly the *first* scene of the third act with
the orchestral introduction ; then send me this, the great
Prelude, and the great scene for male chorus from the
second act, so that I may arrange all for the concert.
He can at the same time prepare the *Tannhäuser* score
for me. Be good enough to give me a detailed account
of the expenses.—

You are always writing to me about " the " critic of
the *Gegenwart ;* but I do not know what you mean. I
have read nothing of his ; where shall I find anything ?

Brendel has written to me ; his letter and his latest
explanations in specimen-sheet have somewhat disposed
me in his favour. His recent fervour, nay, enthusiasm,
rejoices me. Now I will again write a letter for his
paper ; perhaps I may still be of use to it, and contribute
in a decisive manner towards making it more useful than

it can possibly be under present circumstances.—The letter concerning the Goethe foundation can appear *later on*, because I wish first to widen the tendency of the paper, so that this very letter will then appear *in it* as something intelligible and suitable. But after that, no one will catch me at such a thing again.

Let me soon know what effect my " Preface " is making; and try and get it well known !—

Yesterday, we had St. Sylvester with present-making; with that our Christmas festival has come to an end. I was able, in fairly good humour, to see the new year in. How are you at home ? All the youngsters well ? You write nothing to me about your leave of absence !

I—shall not get any real rest until I commence my great work ; I don't care for anything else. I must positively prey once more upon myself. Only I shall take care that this does not interfere with my spring cure.—

What do the R.'s think of me ? Have they not had enough of me ?—

Farewell, good, dear friend ! Remain true to me, and let me even to-day assure you that you are a great, great blessing to me ! Minna sends heartiest greetings !

Your
R. W.

The silver plate has delighted my wife in a fabulous manner ; she sends no end of thanks to the R.'s.

I think I shall have the parts for my concert copied in Dresden ; in this place there is not *one* trustworthy copyist, and besides, they are *much* dearer than at

Dresden. But do send the *Lohengrin* things, for I must first arrange them.

52.

Dear Friend,

I have gone back to my old mood, and the devil has hold of me again. No cure in the world can keep me from disagreeable outward impressions: their evil influence must ever trouble the inward spring, and bring it to a painful stand-still. Again am I stranded, with all my wishes and aspirations. Beyond endurance I clearly see—I feel—that all my undertakings must remain unsatisfied and without aim! Alas! alas! wherever I knock, each of my plans becomes a barren grey impossibility! I can no longer in any way deceive myself. I lack the only thing which could keep me in a happy state of illusion—*sympathy*, true, responsive sympathy. All with whom I come into contact hang down the head, sigh, are silent, and relapse after this effort into their old callous state. You are really the only one to whom I can still turn for sympathy, for *you* alone possess the energy at least to answer—although, I cannot help noticing that your letters are written on as small a sheet as possible, with the lines as wide apart as possible. Often, as was the case with your two last letters, I ask myself, "Does he find it so difficult to fill the sheet with strokes of the pen?" Others do not even answer me. I asked Liszt for his medallion for Christmas; no answer.

Under circumstances which I will not enumerate, but which from my mood you will recognize, I cannot exactly make out whether this stop to my well-being really comes

from within or merely from without.   I have nothing
to complain of with regard to my bodily functions : but—
my nerves ! I grant that, of late, I have over-exerted
myself with the cure.   The misfortune was that I had
no doctor in whom I placed confidence : my lively
mood was principally the result of the over-excitement
of my vital powers, for in spite of the liveliness, my
agitation was intense.   Still it was a lively agitation.
Reaction naturally set in ; but, if only some joy, some
outward influence resulting in comfort could happen,
it would assume another character, one of pleasant
repose.   But—great Heaven ! how dull, how tedious,
and how flat, does everything in this outer world drop
loose from me,—so that only the regret remains that I
should ever have counted on what comes from without !
and this repentance is of a terribly painful kind.   Now
I prey again on my vitals, and prey and prey, until to
satisfy my hunger I am utterly consumed !

Really, I have been thus for a long time !   If I look
back on my life I must say to myself that little nourishment came from without to satisfy so needy a soul.
Never, not even for a moment, have I felt tender comfort : only angles to stumble against, only sharp points
to tread on !   And now by way of diversion—I do not
say reward (for here there is nothing to reward)—no !
in order to be giving myself once more the chance of
others preying on me—which for the future can be my
only consolation !—by way of diversion, I only desired
—ah ! why should I repeat it ?—Go to concerts and
to the theatre, and amuse yourself ! !—

Nothing will come of *my* concert : I have given it

up. I can no longer bring myself to undertake any-thing by halves, a patch-work. Its aimlessness and the impossibility of satisfying myself, presented themselves once more before me in all their nakedness. Through the obduracy of my friends all farther plans connected with it were frustrated in advance. If, in the first thought of this concert, I only wished for once to hear the Prelude to *Lohengrin*, I now renounce the luxurious apparatus necessary for the attainment of this wish. Strange that it should be with me as with Beethoven ; he could not hear his music because *he* was *deaf* (nothing else could have prevented *him*). *I* cannot hear mine, because I am more than deaf, because I do not live in the world, because I wander about among you like a ghost, because the whole wide world is full of . . . fools ! Ah, dear friend, at least *write* a lot about me, fill the newspapers, and at least I shall become right *famous ;* then I shall have something for my pains !

Ah ! if I were not to rise from my bed to-morrow, if I were never more to wake to this loathsome life, yes —then I should be even happier than the R.'s, when listening to *Tannhäuser ! ! !* Good-bye for to-day !—

Eleven o'clock past ! again nothing ! Good ! This letter must be sent off to-day ; I cannot allow such unburdening of my mind to lie in the drawer.—

Say, is it not unmanly of me to pour out my complaints thus ? Why, do I not rather imitate my lady S., show a smiling face although I suffer, pretend to have no feeling, *i.e.,* lie and dissimulate, so as to become, if no *true human being*—yet as great a *man* as possible, one who is "superior" to his fate, *i.e.,* plays a part, and would fain be otherwise than as he is; "represent" something—any visionary idea, as, for example, L. Bonaparte represented " society " ?—and all that to please the dear sweet Philistines, so that they may say, "Ah, by Jove! there's a man for you !" No ; all who can take pleasure in my labours, *i.e.*, in my *life* and works, shall know, that their joy comes of my *griefs*, of my *greatest misery !*—

Dear friend ! I often have my own ideas about "art," and, for the most part, I cannot help thinking that if we had *real life*, we should need no *art*. Art begins just there, where real life ends, where there is nothing more before us ; then we cry out to art : "I wish !"—I cannot conceive how a *truly happy* man can ever think of "art." Only in life is *power* to do. Is our "art" anything more than a confession of our impotence ? For sure ; at least *our* art is of this kind, and so is all the art which, in our present dissatisfaction with life, we can imagine. It is nothing more than "desire expressed as clearly as is possible to us." To win back my youth, to possess health, nature, a devoted wife, healthy children—yes ! I would sacrifice *all my art !* Take it ! Give me the other !—Ah ! it would indeed be droll, if all our zest for art were but an empty dream ! Well, farewell for to-day ! You have probably had enough.

Your

R. W.

Zurich, *January 12th*, '52.

53.

Dear Friend,

I answer at once your questions :—

(1) How shall the new pianoforte score of *Tannhäuser* be announced ?   " *Second edition with the third act revised*."

With regard to sending me the pianoforte scores, I beg X. to let me have also the *Flying Dutchman*. In return I would make the opera known as much as possible.   Liszt, too, will give it this year at Weimar ; perhaps I shall have it performed even here in Zurich. The publisher can derive nothing but benefit from this. If he does not see his way to that, he may charge me at bookseller's price—fifty per cent. discount.   So I expect *Rienzi*, *Flying Dutchman*, and *Tannhäuser*.

(2) The "three grand-opera poems" must surely be out in Germany, as they are already to be had here. No doubt you will already have been able to see to Devrient, also to R. ?

(3) I have sent exact instructions to Brendel concerning the *two* letters (to him and to Liszt).   Both must be published together, as a detached pamphlet. But I really do not know if you have yet received the letter from Liszt.   You tell me nothing about it.   If Liszt is dilatory, I'll look after it myself.

(I have given Brendel a good blowing up on account of the fresh notice from " A. H. *aus Zürich*."   However, in defence, he pleads your recommendation of such trivialities.   I have explained to Brendel that *nothing*— no, *nothing* of this kind must ever appear again in his paper.   B. has given his promise to that effect.)

(4) I shall certainly *not* give *the concert*.   It is therefore unnecessary to see about the *Lohengrin* scenes.   I therefore repeat : is it not better now to stop the whole score-scribbling ?   Why increase useless

expenses ?   Whoever cares to have the score completed
for his pleasure, let him do so.   I can no longer make
any use of it; I heartily regret the money already
thrown away on it.   After the long delay of this
copying, I know of nothing better than to make the
useless expenses less.   But will you *not* soon let me
know what the whole damage is ?   On the other hand,
I insist on the *Tannhäuser for myself.*

(5) My admiration for Härtel's courageous devotion
has somewhat diminished since I learnt that they do
not intend, as stated at first, to engrave the score,
but merely to print it.   It is, however, a matter of
indifference to me in what way my *Lohengrin* attains
to its paper monumentality.   If they have such good
readers at Leipzig, we might leave it to be corrected
there.   I can reserve to myself the right of adding,
when the printing is completed, an *errata* list, should
such be necessary.

Now about your godfather affair.   If you think me
good for that purpose—well, take me.   I will willingly
assist, and K. is really the right person to represent
me.   I should like to hear your programme respecting
this boy's education.   Will you inoculate him with the
poison of our bringing up, and so leave it to chance
whether he shall spit out the poison, or whether it shall
bring him to ruin ?   I do not ask this jokingly.   We
have the future in our hands.   Shall we be such abject
cowards as to expose our children to the same fatal
course which (let us be frank) has made *us* incapable,
half-and-half, and bad ?   *We* have only arrived at
truth at a period of our lives, when we have already
become incapable of deriving any profit from it.

Shall this—even supposing the most fortunate case—
also be the lot of our children? I will discuss the
matter more thoroughly another time. I first await—
as I said above—your programme.

That you allow yourself (or rather are driven) not to
give offence to R. in this matter, does not please me. I
should have thought that with K. (in my place), Emilie,
Rühlemann, and a fine lady, the ambition of your wife
would have been satisfied. Here, here, dear friend,
must be shown whether we really wish to be free in
our house and in our family!

The day before yesterday I conducted the Egmont-
music and the 8th Symphony. The performance was
—do not laugh, for I know what I am talking about—
excellent. I suffered, however, from great relaxation
of the nerves. Schöneck, the director of the theatre
here, young, very talented, extremely gifted as a conductor, and an uncommonly lively and fiery fellow, is
worrying me to have the *Flying Dutchman* for his
benefit (in March). I am already almost giving way,
as yesterday I had to confess that the actors were
really good, and that the *Dutchman* himself would
have a really good interpreter. The director promises
to accomplish the most inconceivable things in the
matter of decorations. The orchestra would recruit
itself to a decent size by volunteers. The only thing
in the way is my longing after rest, and my general
aversion to everything connected with our theatre and
public. But I am pressed on all sides, so shall leave
the decision to Heaven.

Hark! See friend Fischer at once; give him best
greetings from me, and ask him if he will venture to

get for himself the loan of the complete parts, etc., of the *Flying Dutchman* for three months from L. I will be responsible for the punctual return of the same, and so on. If Fischer can get the things, and without compromising me as seeking a favour from L., this shall decide the matter. I will not put the people here to expense in having the parts copied; besides, I shall thus hold in my hands the power of withdrawing the opera if I see that it is not going well. This I cannot do if the parts are copied here by order of the management. So let Fischer answer quickly. If he consents, and thus compels me, everything will come in time if sent by express-mail.

But send me quickly through the post the pianoforte scores, etc. I am now so nervously impatient in everything, even in trifling matters, that it is not without intention I make this request.

Herwegh was mad about the last Beethoven performance, and straightway declared that it was *divine*. I recommend to you and to K. my new friend, the English poet Shelley. There exists only one German translation of his works, by Seybt, which you must get. He and his friend Byron together make up one complete and noble man.

You will soon hear that I am hard at work on the *Nibelungen* poem; it is my only salvation. Farewell; greetings at home, and to the R.'s.

Your

R. W.

53 (!) *December*, '51.

(I shall continue in the *coup-d'état* month until the desired 1852 really comes.)

54.

DEAR FRIEND,

I hope that in answering your two last letters I shall not overlook any point in them. Let us see if I succeed.

First of all, I beg your friendly forgiveness for the many commissions with which I coolly load you; I fear I am becoming quite shameless. But I hope there will soon be an end of this. And will your wife please not be angry with me on account of this constant packing?

Once again you have taken too seriously my remarks on the christening ceremony of your youngest son. I beg you, for Heaven's sake, to change nothing in your arrangements, even supposing there were still time. I should really consider myself highly ridiculous and impertinent, if you were to look on me as chief busybody in your family affairs! Pray be assured that you can do or leave undone what you please, without my bearing you a grudge for any one of your actions. Credit me with that much common sense. If I am peevish and fanciful, others should not be so too ; of late I have indeed been peevish !—

Also, I look upon your present position in the band as a change for the better. I perfectly understand that you must feel more comfortable than you did under the former opera *régime*. It is all right about the scores sent back from Brockhaus. How fortunate that in this case I was so obstinate! I am writing to Fischer about the rest of the music I left behind, and I thank you beforehand if you will see to the whole thing.

I have at last written to Weimar about the Goethe-foundation letter, and hope to receive it shortly.   Matters proceed in a nice slow tedious way in your corner of Germany; I can't help saying that.   Even the resolute X. gives another proof of it.   How everything connected with this man sticks and sticks!   Well, out of all this I clearly see that people have something else to do than to busy themselves about me.   I really ought not to be unjust—a resolution which every day I form anew.

I am also expecting an account of moneys paid by you for me.   A small arrangement will have to be made about the (unfortunate!!) copy of the *Lohengrin* score. When I—in the summer of last year!!!—ordered the copy through Fischer, I referred him for payment to Frau R., whom I also requested, by letter, to advance the money and deduct it from my next subsidy.   But as in the November of that year the score was by no means ready, and therefore no request for payment was made, Frau R. sent me the full sum.   Now I must pay the costs of this copy out of my ready money; but as things go, I must consider whether I shall not leave myself very short if I now send those costs from here.   I shall receive more money at the beginning of May; so please ask Wölfel if he could not wait until the end of April for the payment of his miserably delayed score, which in consequence has become quite useless.   As a return, he might keep the copy for himself in remembrance of me.   (No one wants the beggarly thing now!)   If he will wait till then, shortly before the R.'s send money to me I will ask K. or one of them to keep back as much as is due to Wölfel, and give it to you to settle the debt. Well, all this is another specimen of Dresden humbug! Greet the ladies to-day in your heartiest manner.

I have received encouraging news from Schwerin.
Tannhäuser has been well and successfully produced
there. The accounts of those concerned are overflowing with joy at the success of their undertaking.
—What has come of the proposed performance of
Tannhäuser at Dresden, concerning which, it was
already a subject of reproach to me that I could take
no pleasure in it ?

From time to time you shall hear about my small
attempts at conducting here. I may possibly write and
sign a notice of the shortly approaching performance
of the *Coriolan* overture. I may perhaps add to it the
remark that I consider this kind of personal notice the
only fitting one in connection with renderings which,
passing from a purely musical sphere, touch upon a
poetical one, instead of that extravagant praise of
performances which must leave those who were not
present at them quite indifferent. Baumgartner's songs
have long been ordered for you ; a fresh reminder is
now being sent to the publishers. I ought myself to
write something about them for the *confed.* newspaper.
You shall have it as soon as it is printed ; perhaps
you may be able to make use of it. Can you get
my article concerning the poetical contents of the
Eroica from the R.'s ? If you can, let me know
next time.—

Herwegh is worrying me about the performance of
the *Tannhäuser* overture ; I will see if it is possible,
but have my doubts. The *Flying Dutchman* is being
seriously thought of. Already a scene-painter from
Munich has been specially engaged here. It is almost
impossible to find any one here to write out the parts,

but only an ordinary copyist; so I have had to write to Cassel again about the orchestral parts. Still I always hope that something will come in the way, so that I may at least be free for the spring and summer, and, undisturbed, be able to attend to my cure. Herwegh will go with me this time to the hydropathic establishment.

Have I now written enough? What more indeed can I tell you? It could be nothing refreshing. Still, Weber gives me hope of the possibility, in the future, of a second edition of *Oper und Drama*, the sale of which is highly satisfactory. Now and then I become conscious that honest X. is egregiously deceiving me. I read the *Grenzboten* long ago, but not right through, because I found it very tedious. Why do you not send me at once Glasbrenner's *Lustige?* Ah, I am tired! Farewell.

Your
R. W.

(1) I have still kept back this letter on account of the enclosure. Yesterday evening, when my wife had gone off to the ball, I read among other things your last short criticisms in the paper (No. 5); they amused me very much. The style of your brief notices seems to me a kind of *genre* painting, in which you greatly excel. I honestly compliment you on it. But what does our venerable Dotzauer say?——If you still have my *Wiland* sketch, please send it shortly with the score. I am beginning to make my will!

(2) Do you often think of your Adam-like state at the Surene torrent? The next time you are *peschkering*, fancy you are sitting at your desk in that primitive

garb, and wonder at the respect paid to you by the highly-cultured fiddlers !—By the way, greetings from the *Uri-Rothstock*. I saw it yesterday. What shall we plan for this year ?

(3) I enclose my article on Baumgartner, which has just come from the printers. See what use you can make of it ! I do not think I have been prejudiced in any way through my friendly relation to B. What I have said refers, in any case, more to the whole class than to this particular species, which in itself is tolerably innocent. It was more my object to have a slap at the silly young folk here, X. X., etc.

W. B.'s Songs (Wilhelm Baumgartner's Lieder).

The position of the lyrics of the day towards modern life is so artificial and complex, so that one often finds it difficult to define the impression they make upon our feelings. Most difficult of all is this with the poems of our lyric literature, when translated into our art-music. Poems, scarcely even intended for recitation, but rather for silent reading, are set to music in such a fashion that, when sung, they must necessarily appear to the poet who wrote them as something wild and strange. With a poem, which as a literary poem perfectly answered to the poet's intention, and therefore in no way called for musical expression, the musical composition can naturally only be a special tone-poem of the musician's, having often quite an arbitrary, and in the best case, only a general bond of sympathy with the word-poem. Thus, in the case of musical ballad-compositions for our song-playing and singing public, the concern is only whether the music—*i.e.*, the melody—be in itself agreeable and entertaining; the "text" is then only important in so far as it enables the same melody to be sung or played to the different verses. Fashion, together with the ruling fashion of singing, is the only standard whereby the agreeableness of these melodies is measured. This changes for itself alone, and without any relation to any particular poem, just as fashion in dress changes without the slightest consideration for the human figure; so, for instance, the Rossini style of singing ruled at the same time as baggy *gigot*-sleeves, and narrow short skirts, just as to-day the Bellini-Donizetti style, with its affected feeling, comes in with narrow sleeves, and baggy, stiffened, long skirts. I leave to the natural philosopher—in the domain of our civilization—to point out the necessity of these fashions. To become a favourite and fashionable composer of this kind is just as easy as to become a favourite and fashionable tailor. The capability of satisfying the needs of fashion, of which mention has been made, is not in the least connected with genius; and it is only by chance that now and then an individual of this class rises above the mass.

Whoever does not aspire to be a modern popular song-composer in the sense named, but who, as a musician, seeks to express by means of his art the feeling which a poem has called forth from him, so as to communicate it to others, will be compelled to preserve a far more intimate connection with the poem than this. The feeling acquired by him as a musician gives him first of all the tone-picture, in which it expresses itself with satisfying clearness; but he can only succeed in giving the necessary individual shape to that tone-picture by placing its outward form in closest relationship to that of the word-poem. It is on this path, and with this method, that we meet with Wilhelm Baumgartner; this is, without dispute, the only truly artistic direction in which the fashionable musician can move when face to face with the modern poet. Baumgartner's tone-pictures, as they appear in the vocal melody, and in an accompaniment which supports and renders clear this melody, are, in the first place, products of purely musical invention; but it is refreshing also to perceive how these pictures become musical exactly in the degree in which they are prompted by the significant contents of the poem; and this gives us the best proof that the musician's attitude with regard to the poet is the right one. These tone-poems are noble throughout, and in them all influence of modern mannerism disappears in proportion as the sensuous (*sinnlich*) form coincides with that of the poem; the very need of which is felt by the composer whose attitude towards the poet is a natural one. Baumgartner, if he would remain faithful to his sound artistic feeling in this direction, must end by seeking for *the* poet who in his poems no longer leaves anything to the purely musical initiative of the composer, but brings to him the complete sensuous and sentient germ for the blossoming of the melody; in other words, *the* poet who not only stimulates his feeling to musical invention, but whose verse itself supplies the living stuff for the formation of the melody. May B. find this poet in his Swiss countryman and friend Gottfr. Keller, and from the united creative power of both, may the true song, inseparable from the poem as from the melody, blossom forth ; a song which is not to be found in the fashionable productions of the day, and towards which B., in the ballads before us, is aiming with praiseworthy zeal.   To enter into further detail respecting these songs would be beside the aim of this paper, and consequently of my communication. On the other hand, my purpose has been merely to call attention to the characteristic difference between B.'s songs and the fashionable songs of the day, and to direct to them all those to whom so distinct a phenomenon may prove welcome.

55.

DEAR FRIEND,
          I send you herewith my interpretation of the *Coriolanus* overture.   I have given up the idea of noticing the performance myself in the *Zeitung f. Musik* : I shall do well to hold my tongue a bit there now.   But I will tell you in the briefest terms what I would have said, so as to induce you to devote a proper article to the matter in question.

The conductor of compositions such as those of Beethoven has seldom hitherto conceived the special nature of his task.   He should clearly be the channel for their understanding by the laity ; and if, at bottom, this can only be achieved by a completely adequate performance, the question must next be—how is such a performance to be brought about ?   The characteristic of the great compositions of Beethoven is that they are actual poems : that in them it is sought to bring a real subject to representation.   The stumbling-block in the way of their comprehension lies in the difficult task of finding with certainty the subject re-presented. Beethoven was completely possessed by a subject : his most pregnant tone-pictures are indebted almost solely to the individuality of the subject with which he was filled ; in consciousness of this, it appeared to him superfluous to denote his subject otherwise than in the tone-picture itself. Just as our word-poets really address themselves only to other word-poets, so did Beethoven in this unconsciously address himself only to the tone-poets. Even the absolute musician, that is to say, the ringer of the changes of absolute music, could not understand Beethoven, because this absolute musician looks always for the " How " and not the " What." The laity, on the other hand, could but be completely confused by these tone-pictures, and at best be only led to pleasure in *that* which served the tone-poet merely as the material means of his expression.

It is only by absolute musicians that the tone-poems of Beethoven have hitherto been presented to the public ; and it is obvious that such a course could only result in misunderstanding. The only province of the absolute musician was the " How ; " and even this he could not see aright if he did not first under-stand the " What," for which the " How " was only a vehicle. Thus the mutual relationship of the con-ductor and the orchestra remained one of complete misunderstanding ; the conductor laboured only to give voice to musical phrases which he himself did not understand, and had only appropriated to himself as a reciter learns by heart pleasant-sounding verses according to their sound which are composed in a foreign tongue, and one unknown to him. Naturally it is only the sheer externals that can here be seized; the speaker can never deliver and intone with personal conviction—he must slavishly hold fast to the merest outward accident of sound, in the manner in which he has been taught to repeat the phrase by rote. Let us conceive for a moment what measure of understanding a poet would meet with if, by the reciter on the one hand, and the hearer on the other, the word-tones only were reproduced and received; as must be the case were the poem presented in a tongue which neither the declaimer (who had only learnt it by ear) nor the hearer understood. Yet this comparison with the customary performances of Beethoven's works one can only pronounce exaggerated, insomuch as one ascribes to tone-speech, as the more universal, an easier and more immediate comprehensibility than to rational word-speech. But here we find the fallacy to lie in the particular sense in which we use the word "understanding." Provided no special poetic subject is expressed in the tone-speech, it may by all means pass as easily understandable; for there can be no question of real understanding. If, however, the expression of the tone-speech is conditioned by a poetical subject, this speech becomes straightway the least comprehensible of all, if the poetical subject be not at the same time defined by some other means of expression than those of absolute music.

The riddle of the poetical subject of a tone-piece by Beethoven is thus only to be solved by a tone-poet; for, as I remarked before, Beethoven involuntarily appealed only to such, to those who were of like feelings, like culture, nay, well-nigh like capability with himself. Such a man alone can interpret these compositions to the understanding of the laity, and above all by clearly defining the subject of the tone-poem, to the executants as well as to the audience, and thus making good an involuntary error in the technique of the tone-poet, who omitted such denotement. If a right understanding be not effected in such a way, every performance of Beethoven's veritable tone-poems, however technically perfect, must, in a measure, remain misunderstood. The most convincing proof of this we may easily win by accurately gauging the attitude of our modern concert-audience towards Beethoven's creations. Were these really understood by the audience, that is to say, consonantly with their poetical subject, how could this same public tolerate a modern concert-programme ? How were it possible to set before the hearers of a Beethovenian Symphony at the same time a medley of musical compositions utterly lacking in depth of content ? Yet do not our musical conductors and composers themselves, for the same reason, namely, that they have not recognized the poetical basis of these tone-creations, prove by the matter and the manner of what, in spite of Beethoven's warning example, they compose to-day, that they have never rightly understood them ?

Were the confused and erratic instrumental composition-mongering of the day possible, if these people had understood the true essence of Beethoven's tone-poems? This essence of the great works of Beethoven is that they are only in the last place *Music*, but, in the first place, contain a poetic subject. Or shall we be told that this *subject* is only taken from the realm of music ?   Would this not be as much as to say that the poet takes his subject from speech, the painter, his from colour ?   The musical conductor who sees in one of Beethoven's tone-works nothing but the music, is exactly like the reciter who should hold only by the language of a poem, or the explainer of a picture who should see in the painting nothing but its colour.   This, however, is the case with our conductors, even in the best instances—for many do not even so much as understand the music—they understand the key, the theme, the distribution of the voices, the instrumentation, and so on, and think that herewith they understand all the contents of a tone-work.

It is only the non-professional musician who has opened the path to the understanding of Beethoven's works, as involuntarily he longed to know what special thought had influenced the composer in his music.   But here men met their first obstacle.   Imagination, striving for understanding, laid its hand on all kinds of arbitrary conceits, of romantic scenes and picturesque adventure. The grotesqueness, and for the most part triviality, of such interpretations was soon detected and thrust on one side by minds of finer calibre.   As such pictures proved distasteful, folk thought it the best plan to lay aside once for all any kind of explanation.   Yet in the impulse that led to such attempts at interpretation there lay a right sound instinct ; but it was only possible for one completely intimate with the characteristic traits of the tone-work to designate its subject, in such a manner as it had—even though unconsciously— hovered before the vision of the tone-poet himself

Again, the great difficulty of such interpretations lay in the character of the subject itself, which is only presented to us by the tone-poet in his tone-painting ; and only one who had well weighed this difficulty could successfully dare attempt to assist a right understanding in the needful manner. Here you might narrate the history of the performance of the *Ninth Symphony* at Dresden, and above all the remarkable success attained there by this reputedly most difficult of all compositions. Further, you might relate how I never after that consented to a performance of one of Beethoven's compositions without in some way directing myself to the understanding in this fashion, and that I was impelled thereto by the irrepressible feeling of the necessity of such understanding. Most striking in every case was the effect of my method upon the executants themselves. Even the most ordinary dance-musicians I have here in Zurich coached up to performances of which neither the public nor themselves had before the slightest anticipation. (Take this as though it came from a private source, as, for instance, that K. had told you the tale.) You might then adduce my pamphlet, " The Heroic Symphony," and report how great was the effect of its understanding, especially upon the musicians. [I must here note that my chief explanations are given in the rehearsals by word of mouth, and at the appropriate passages.] It was, however, in my " *Coriolan* Overture " that I was able to arrive at the clearest interpretation of the poetical subject. I may say that he who knows accurately my explanation of this subject, and follows its clue from phrase to phrase, must admit that without this explanation he had never understood this most plastic of all tone-works ; unless, indeed, he had from the general title, " Overture to *Coriolan*," felt out for himself the scene just as I did myself. With such an understanding the enjoyment of such a composition is immeasurably enhanced. At present almost all our musicians have . . . etc., etc.

And the goal of this endeavour ?—THE DRAMA ! ! !

Only notices of this kind, best friend, must hence-forth be given in the *Zeitung für Musik*. You see how much there is to say on that point. Let us hold fast to the principle which I laid down in my letter to Brendel : " Ever to raise, strengthen, and advance music, where it is developing itself in the direction of poetical art ; and where this is not the case, to point out the mistake, and condemn what is faulty." Beyond this nothing should be done now. If this is not done— well, I don't care a rap ; for, after all, the happiness of my life does not depend on the *Zeitung für Musik*. Adieu for to-day.

*   *   *   *   *   *

I must hastily add something to what I have said above, viz., that in a certain most weighty, and per-haps the only right sense, Beethoven has hitherto been only understood by *non*-musicians, and by professional musicians not at all.

(You must work all this out in greater detail.)

Mendelssohn's performance of Beethoven's works was always based only upon their purely musical side, and never upon their poetical contents, which he could not grasp at all ; otherwise he would himself have brought far other wares to market. For my own part,

Mendelssohn's conducting, despite its great technical delicacy, always left me unsatisfied as to the root of the matter; it was always as though he could not trust to letting that be said which Beethoven meant, because he was not at one with himself as to whether anything at all was meant, and if so, what? Thus he always held on to the letter with the finest of musical cleverness, and thus was like our philologists, who, in their expositions of Greek poets, must always point out the literal characters, the particles, the various readings, etc., but never the real contents. Mendelssohn's gross errors in the conception of the *tempi* show clearly his failure to comprehend the content of a composition; and this every one will recognize who, for instance, heard his *tempo* for the first movement of the *Ninth Symphony*, which he took *so fast* that the whole movement was distorted to the direct opposite of what it really is. In this he suddenly revealed himself to me as a most ordinary music-maker, and I recognized at once the reason why he himself could never create anything different from what he did create.

Well, enough on this matter.

Please be good enough to see at once to the following with Brendel. For the edition in pamphlet form of my open letter to him, I want added to the note under the text (relating to the *Grenzboten*) something which I had forgotten, but which for clearness' sake ought not to be left forgotten. It should run as follows:—

"That among our critical literary men, etc. From that you see, etc. From the frontier (*Grenze*) line which they have drawn, they send out their runners (*Boten*) right and left, and so know how to manage in any event;

Here comes the new matter. just as lately they denounced me on the left hand to the democrats as a secret aristocrat, and to the centre of our civilization, the Jews, as their bitterest persecutor; so we may be sure that if the Russian police should march in from the right, they would equally hand us over to these, after they had recommended their literary rubbish to their protection. The fear of chastisement," etc.

You see my only purpose in mentioning the *Grenzboten* is to show them up as scoundrels.

Now, only fancy, you must send me another score; and, indeed, of the *Flying Dutchman.* I cannot let the theatre here have my extra copy, as I have retouched the instrumentation, and so intend it to serve as model to the score-copies which may be wanted later on. So as soon as the score which you will send for our theatre has been made like my copy, I shall send the latter first of all to Weimar, so that the score there may likewise be made to correspond, and then have it forwarded to you, so that you may have it at your disposal in case new scores should have to be got ready. So get your good wife again to take up her needle and packing-canvas, and send me a *Dutchman* to Zurich; but don't be angry at my worrying you again.

The censor-gap in your " information " is quite intelligible to me, now that I know what has been struck out. If ever I should wish to bring out a new edition of my old works, " Art and Revolution," etc., I should be prepared for a prohibition. Two years ago they had not plucked up this courage of reaction which they have now acquired. I wonder whether they will pursue us right into the territory of art, so as to suppress all ideas of an innovatory character. They have, in fact, left us a fatal playground, and one day they will understand what dangerous use can be made of it against them. I feel almost inclined to inform against this danger, so as to compel them to place art also under police supervision. I am convinced one might bring them to look upon literature as the most innocent thing of all.

It seems as though the letter I expect from you to-day will not arrive, and so I will close this epistle on art and literature, that you may be able to enjoy it in right time. Yesterday evening I rehearsed the C-minor symphony again; I fancy the performance would not have left you cold. Anyhow, it is far better than the Dresden performance, where, out of respect for you worthy royal-chamber musicians, I had to slur over the best which could have been said. I only wish you could hear the 'cello theme of the second movement played, and compare it with the muffled tone of your famous mechanical players.—

Adieu. Greetings at home and to the R.'s.

Your

R. W.

Sunday, February 15th, '52.

56.

DEAR FRIEND,

I really cannot imagine that you will again have to send packing-canvas to me at Zurich : in all probability the matter is now at an end. But keep the material, nevertheless : perhaps you will soon have

13

to send it off in some other direction for me. The
Leipzig people (in a foolish manner, through Sturm
and Koppe) inquired about the honorarium for
Tannhäuser. I have replied to Rietz, and promised
the score, but only on condition that Rietz would
answer for the quality of the performance.—Within
a very short space of time *Tannhäuser* has been given
four times in succession at Schwerin, the subscription
list being withdrawn, and with crowds from all parts
(even by rail) : the success is so great that they might
soon try *Lohengrin.* Anyhow, they have commenced
well there : for instance, they were very firm with the
singers, who, at first, had to learn all the recitatives in
strict time, and thus find out that they could not
possibly declaim them better than as I had prescribed ;
only after that were they allowed a little liberty, etc.—

Nothing will come of the *Dutchman* here this time :
the manager wished to have the decorations painted
at Munich, and for that it is now too late. Heaven
be praised ! So for the present I am rid of this
martyrdom : Fischer and Tichatschek must hold that
matter of the parts in suspense : after all they might
be wanted.

Make your mind easy about the *Tannhäuser* overture ! The Musical Society will send for the best
fiddlers, etc., from Basle, Aarau, Schaffhausen, etc.,
nearly all of them German-born musical directors. I
shall have eighteen to twenty violins, six violas, and
five 'cellos, including a great virtuoso, Böhm (from the
Hechingen orchestra). And then our little orchestra
has made wonderful progress : the wind-players—
clarinets, oboes, and horn—are first-rate. The Egmont

entr'acte I had practised with the oboist, in my own room, as if he were a lady vocalist : the fellow could not contain himself for joy at what he at last produced.

At the first rehearsal of the *Tannhäuser* overture (which, contrary to all my expectations, went off exceedingly well) the orchestra begged me to give them an explanation of the contents, after the fashion of the *Coriolan* Overture, because then they would be able to "play better." The explanation is ready : I enclose you two copies (one of them for the R.'s). The performance is announced for March 16th ; item, the Pastoral Symphony, as a good contrast.—

I have not kept my Don Juan arrangement (*Bearbeitung*). I had done nothing more than carefully shade the orchestration, translate the dialogue afresh, and condense some of the scenes so as to avoid scene-shifting,—to that end I specially modified the scenes, and finally wrote a recitative for Donna Anna and Octavio, so as to connect the churchyard scene with the Donna Anna Aria, likewise to avoid scene-shifting. After Don Juan and Leporello have gone over the wall, the orchestra softly prolongs the chord of F major ; the two mourners (accompanied by servants with torches) come to place wreaths on the grave of the *Commendatore ;* it is here that a short dialogue commences *mezzo recitativo*, leading directly to the Aria, which latter, when sung in the churchyard, gains a very noble and plaintive colour. Besides certain trifling changes, I did not, for instance, allow the great Quartet to commence with the stupid solo "B flat" in the bass while Elvira softly utters her complaint, but made Elvira sing the introductory words from the preceding recitative, "*Treff ich Dich wieder, treuloser Heuchler,*" accompanied by the full volume of the string quartet, so that the B flat (full chord) is merely the close of that phrase, whereas it is generally placed (in ridiculous fashion) at the commencement.

That's enough about this patch-work! If you wish to give the article prompted by me a title and a name, I cannot—considering the purport of my remarks—I cannot at all see how you could call it, "R. W. on the tone-poet B." I should think the following more suitable: "On the conducting of Beethoven's instrumental works;" or if you wish to honour me also in the title: "R. W. as conductor of Beethoven's instrumental works."—

A subject is here touched upon truly fatal to our post-Beethoven musical doings: in my opinion, nothing less than the proof that Beethoven, in his true essentials, is universally and absolutely *not* understood. I, at least, cannot view the matter otherwise, as I myself have become convinced that *I*, too, have only understood Beethoven since I sought for the poetical subject of his tone utterances, and at last found it: *Coriolan* proves this clearly to me. I maintain that until now people, when they performed the real Beethoven, have only imitated and listened to a language of which they perceived only the outward sound, which indeed they only understood as you perchance understand sonorous Greek verse when you hear it recited; *i.e.*, you take pleasure in the sound,— now soft, now strong, now muffled, now clear,—but you do not perceive the *sense* which is conveyed in this verse. Is it otherwise ? What now is all our idolatry of Beethoven ?—Answer !—

I have already countermanded my order to Brendel about the note (concerning the *Grenzboten*) : it must be *entirely* omitted. They have attacked me with the commonest of critical blackguardism, and I should have had to take notice of Schladebach and company, if I had referred to them. They scent out death, and in dying show their real nature : base churls, that is what they are—F. at the head. If you doubt this, I will prove it you to a hair. So—nothing more of this !—

I do not advise you to take the post of musical director : you would become much more of a slave, and have many more disagreeables, than is now the case. If the post should be offered to you—you will completely crush L. if you tell him this straight out, and such an effect could only be an advantage !—

I am heartily glad that your godfather-and-baptism-business is happily over. Luxurious being ! I have never spent anything for the baptism of a child.

(I have procured four of the Mozart symphonies which I wished to produce at Dresden gradually ; among these, the one in D major.—)

I thank you for your garden-concert propaganda of *Lohengrin :* do as you like in it. Unfortunately all this is quite indifferent to me, especially everything connected with Dresden. That is really the most miserable nest which I have come across on my earthly path.

Do not think it necessary to send me water-warnings :

in Albisbrunn I followed the *cure*, and tried to get quite rid of my eruption. Here I am living according to Rausse's "*Missgriffe*, etc."—

A morning wash of sixteen, now as much as twenty, degrees of heat, comprises all. No compresses whatever.—For the rest I am now passing through a crisis with regard to my future cure-plans, the result of which I shall shortly be able to let you know.—

H. Müller has returned from Paris : he is now trying for a staff-appointment in the confederacy.—

Some new acquaintances have forced themselves on me : the men are highly indifferent to me, the women less so. Thus it is with some Swiss families of the aristocracy here (I refer only to the women !). I am astonished to find so much vivacity and even charm amongst them. On this occasion I take the liberty of advising you : do not be alarmed on my account ! There will be no "scandal" ! I can no longer take pleasure in men, nor even in women : yet this last element is the only one which now and then helps me to an illusion, for concerning men I can no longer cherish any. Thus I often play here with quite brilliant soap-bubbles ; when our soft atmosphere in a moment causes one to burst, it amuses me to send another aloft at once.

—— Besides Zurich is rapidly increasing in size : hundreds of elegant residences are being built this year, on account of the ever-growing crowd of well-bred, well-to-do foreigners who settle down here to escape from the worries of the rest of Europe.—

Farewell for to-day ! What is the matter with your letters ? You dwell at length on trifles, and then when I am expecting something, hey presto ! the paper is at an end !—

Are you again domiciled in Dresden ?—Well, take this not as a reproach, but as a request.—

Greetings at home and to the R.'s ! They need not be anxious, they will not lose *me !*—Adieu !

Your

R. W.

ZURICH, *February 26th,* '52.

I should like to have the *Wiland* for my will : I think daily of death.—

Ask the R.'s to salute the Bayer for me : I have a great liking for her, on account of her courageous behaviour in the eventual theatre conspiracy against E. D.

57.

DEAR FRIEND,

I also recommend to you a choice book,— " *Musical Letters,*" by a well-known man (Riccius), Part I., Letter 25 ; " *Male and Female Vocalists,*" p. 224, and, moreover, Part II., p. 157.—

As motto one might take : " One should be very clear oneself before making an assertion."—

—This book was sent me here from the publishers, and I must confess to you that I was seized with the weakness to do some more scribbling for the papers. I wanted to write an open letter to Riccius for the *Zeitschrift,* give free rein to my humour, and honourably explain that having once set R. awry, and not being able to restore his reason, I now wished to make him thoroughly crazy (*à la* Röckel), etc. That this plan at once filled me with disgust again, I point out to you in the interest of truth, and look upon it as a good sign of my recovery.

You are really very lazy with your paper, and you might be a little quicker to hand with corrections, etc. *Apropos!* is your notice of *Oper und Drama* ready yet ?—

I have not learnt anything very new from Dr. Graban's pamphlet on diet : with his revelations of Rausse's exaggerations the author comes somewhat *post festum.* Any one who has read Rausse's last work, "*Missgriffe*," must find it precious cool of Graban, who has enriched himself in all positive matters at Rausse's expense, to make so much of the mistakes which Rausse himself had already corrected, and from which, by analogy, one may well conclude that Rausse, had he lived longer, would have accomplished far more in the way of correction than Herr Graban will ever succeed in doing. In Rausse the fresh touch of nature specially appealed to me : Graban takes a middle course between what we might be, and what we actually are. He justifies the existence of the medical profession, and in this at least he is right, for we shall stand in need of doctors and the science of medicine so long as we live in our present condition. Graban is often downright trivial. But what interested me most was his confirmation of a matter, which, after discussions with Herwegh and others, had already become quite clear to me, namely the exaggeration, founded on want of knowledge, in Rausse's views on heterogeneous substances, the so-called poisons : I confess that my former firm faith in Rausse had led me in this respect into ridiculous self-tortures and absurd assertions. Well, in that matter you had your good share of blame !—

I will write to you about my state of health and about my future plans of cure as soon as I have come to a decision, the determination of which I am waiting to hear from an uncommonly gifted and (despite his youth) experienced hydropathist, Lindemann by name, now living in exile in Paris. Kietz could never say enough to me about him : by a marvellously mild water regimen he cured him of a very serious complaint. In France he is now making a sensation : his cures, to several of which Müller can testify from personal knowledge, are said to be extraordinary ;—he knows me through my Paris friends and from my writings ; he is very fond of me, and wishes I would consult him. His speciality seems to be nervous complaints. On principle he is opposed to cures in hydropathic establishments ; he shows that everything is done there by the rule of thumb. For me this is of great importance ; for although I have the best will to do everything which will help me to get well, yet I have an equally strong dislike to a prolonged stay in a health-establishment. To my disadvantage I have found out that only very mild treatment is of any avail to me : my cure, therefore, can only be effected very slowly, and can merely consist in suitable dieting. It is quite impossible for me to stay half a year in a hydropathic establishment : to bid farewell to intellectual life and active work is with me the surest source of fresh uneasiness and suffering. I am awaiting Lindemann's advice. If I had the money, I would go straight to Paris and see him. I cannot fully explain to you on what my great faith in Lindemann is founded; it has not sprung up in a night. I have got so far that I place no faith in any *system*, but only in a specially gifted and sound *physician*, in an individual. For such an one I long, not for any fads. Still—you shall soon hear more.—Tell all this to the R.'s, however.

You wrote to me last on February 28th. Since then —on the 29th—you must have received a letter from me. I thought you would have answered this by now, and wait again to-day in vain for it.

I thank you for your communication respecting Gutzkow and D. ; I scarcely know what use I can make of it. Gutzkow is cunning. D. makes a wretched impression on me : he is the very type of a mind fundamentally narrowed by its weakness. Where he cannot comprehend anything beyond his own weak reach, it is so convenient for him to despair, and to console himself with the "imperfection" of all earthly things ! Really the man deserves nothing but contempt. You have attached too much importance to my inquiry concerning him.—

B. writes me that he wishes to publish, through the Härtels, two paraphrases for pianoforte of a March from *Lohengrin*, and of one from *Tannhäuser :* concerning the latter he must first consult X. I naturally give my consent, and X., too, will surely not be so enterprising as to wish to publish the *Tannhäuser* March all by himself : this would certainly not please B., as he would much rather have the two pieces brought out by the same publisher. On the other hand, X. might perhaps make some profit out of the thing, and (in the interest of the creditors) I must leave entirely to X. the answer which he will give to B.—

One thing more!—A. Müller, of this place, who bought a pianoforte edition of *Tannhäuser* when it first came out, would like to have the *new ending*. Many, in fact nearly all, who possess the old pianoforte edition would be of the same mind, and I therefore think it would be quite the right thing for X. to bring out a separate copy of the new ending, from the corresponding page onwards, and offer it for sale as "Supplement to the first edition." He would then have to send this off to those libraries where he originally placed the pianoforte editions. Naturally he should not have too many struck off, at most perhaps fifty; if these should not prove sufficient, it could be easily remedied later on. Only it would have to be properly advertised.—

Up to to-day I have not had any answer from the Leipzig theatre.—Brendel received from me some time ago a notice about my position here, concerning which many false reports are circulated. He was to use it as a note to a report received by him from Lorenz of Winterthur, of a concert performance here. Why is this not done? Remind him of it at your convenience.—

I have now spent five days over this letter: I was always expecting one from you in answer to my last. You seem, however, to have counted on receiving news from me first! So let these lines go off.—

We are having a spell of bright sunshine, and my spirits are improving somewhat.—Ah! if I could only have a pleasant journey this summer—to Italy. I am always devouring capital : how unfitting that, on the other hand, I get foddered with bare interest !!

Farewell.

Your

R. W.

Zurich, *March 11th*, '52.

58.

Dearest Friend,

My wife often does me the wrong of keeping something up her sleeve at convenient seasons, and then bringing it out at an inconvenient one, when she can no longer help herself. Thus lately she informed me that her parents would have to move on the 1st of April, and up to that time would be in urgent need of help. We can just manage here up to May, when I again expect money from R. ; but I can no longer undertake to send money away from here : so I should be right glad if an application were made to me from Leipzig respecting the price of the *Tannhäuser* score ; in a letter to Rietz I asked twenty-five louis d'or. Had they accepted these terms, I meant first of all to let you have this sum, so that you could take from it not only what moneys you have laid out, but also twenty-five thalers for my poor parents-in-law. Unfortunately I have had to wait in vain for an answer from Leipzig, and I must therefore look about for other means of help, in the pressing emergency just mentioned. With regard to my debt to you, I had already determined to

ask the R.'s to send their next remittance *through you*
(to which, indeed, they do not object). You would keep
back what you have spent for me, and we could always
go on thus, for as a rule in every half year you will
have spent money on my account. If you approve
of this, I have only in the present emergency to ask
if you could get me the necessary twenty-five thalers
for my parents-in-law on credit, or lend it yourself?
I really hope that this will be possible to so thoroughly
substantial a man as yourself, and, in this hope, I beg
you to see after my parents-in-law as quickly as
possible; anyhow, before the 1st of April. At the
beginning of May you will then receive from the R.'s
(to which effect I shall write to them at the proper
moment) the half-year's subsidy for me, out of which
you will at once repay yourself.—I should be extremely
glad if the matter could be so arranged; it can be
done, can't it?—

The performance of the *Tannhäuser* overture has
now taken place: it surpassed all my expectations,
for it really went admirably. You can best judge of
this by its effect, which was quite *terrific*. I do not
speak of the burst of applause which immediately
followed it, but of the symptoms of that effect, which
only came gradually to my knowledge. The women,
in particular, were turned inside out; the impression
made on them was so strong that they had to take
refuge in sobs and weeping. Even the rehearsals
were crowded, and marvellous were the accounts given
to me of the first effect, which expressed itself chiefly
as profound sorrowfulness; only after this had found
relief in tears, came the agreeable feeling of the

highest, exuberant joy. Certainly this effect was only
made possible by my explanation of the subject-matter
of the overture; but—though my own work again
made a most powerful impression on me—I was
quite astounded at this unusually drastic operation.
A woman it was who solved the riddle: people look
on me as a merciless preacher against the sin of
hypocrisy.—After what I have accomplished with it
here, I begin to set some store by this piece of music:
I really cannot think of any other tone-poem capable
of exercising a like powerful effect on sensitive, intelligent natures. But .the concert-hall is its place,
and not the theatre, where it is a mere prelude to the
opera. There I should propose only to give the first
tempo of the overture: the rest—in the fortunate
event of its being understood—is too much in front
of the drama; in the opposite event, too little.—

The day after the performance Schmidt wrote to
me from Frankfort that he thought he could venture
Tannhäuser shortly. As a preliminary, he begged
me to let him conduct the Overture and the March
at a grand concert. I at once sent him, for that
purpose, several hundred copies of the explanation.—

It is all right now about the *Flying Dutchman:* it
will be produced here in the second half of April.
I can no longer prevent it: my friends here press
me too much. A scene-painter and machinist have
been specially engaged for the staging of the opera:
for the orchestra, etc., everything possible is to be
done. The singers are well-chosen. And so the
performance will be good—perhaps very good. The
Tannhäuser Overture has given me anew a great

opinion of my talent for making the impossible possible.—Would that the R.'s could be present at the performance here !—

At last I get a post-office slip which promises news from you. I had already ceased trying to imagine what (could) must have happened to you, that you had completely given up writing to me. I shall wait till the packet comes from the post, and then close these lines !—

I have just read your *Figaro* letter, and thank you heartily for it. I will write to you more in detail soon, with a parcel which I have to send you.

How I reproach myself when, through some remark concerning your conduct, I cause you to offer explanations. Truly, in our intercourse, if one of us two need to make apology, it is *I*, once and always. Pay no attention, if now and then something in my letters vexes you. Unfortunately I am often in such bitter humour that it almost affords me a cruel relief to offend some one ; this is a calamity which only makes *me* the more deserving of pity. Only, pay no attention to it ! But be ever assured that I love you from my inmost heart, and that you are often my only consolation.—

I am now again frightfully fagged ; but in the face of spring, and of setting to work at my poem, I take fresh courage. Call me not vain if I confess to you that the wonderful effects which I produce around me restore to me now and then a pleasant consciousness of my existence : again it is always the " ever womanly " (" *Ewig Weibliche* ") which fills me with sweet illusions and warm thrills of life's delight. The moist, shining eye of a woman often saturates me with fresh hope. But you—do not complain if I hide myself from you and hold back !—

Your news about R.—rejoiced me ! In *his* position it is only a question of stoicism, and of showing no weak spot to *his torturers !* May I be *accursed* if ever an *enemy* shall hear me complain : against such we must be bold and hard as stone. If ever I wish to rid me of my life, I know *for what* I will venture it— however, I will not boast.

Farewell for to-day ; greetings to Siegfried !

Your

R. W.

ZURICH, *March 20th*, '52.

Don't let me wait again so long for a letter.

If Brendel wants to have a joke with a portrait of me, he ought not to take the old drawing, which I no longer resemble ; better from a new daguerreotype.

59.

DEAR FELLOW !

Look you ! L. K. is a silly owl ! He only looks at opera- and drama-making as a thing for itself : of the subject from which this is only given off as an external manifestation of its inner essence, of the free man, he has as yet no conception. Whence this enthusiasm is really derived is a mystery to me—an enthusiasm for an artistic form without contents ! Good heavens ! and *such* men are my propagandists ! Well, it does no harm, but neither does it do any good ; especially as the good which could result from such propaganda must be quite an imaginary one. O, ye men! act as ye feel; be free—then shall we feel healthily; produce Art! But whosoever fondly dreams of the conversion of theatre managers and the public, he is really as great a fool as the rest! Never mind! Besides, K. is decidedly more enthusiastic about Brendel than about me.

Yesterday I saw Marschner's *Vampyr*. A new method of cure: "Moonshine does the trick!" I was much amused to find that the public were not at all affected by the loathsomeness of the subject; of course this is only dulness of feeling, which in the contrary case would be equally unconcerned at its tenderness. In an opera children may be slaughtered and eaten, and the public will take no note of what is going on. This time the music *quite* disgusted me: this duet, trio, and quartet, singing and drawling is downright stupid and devoid of taste, as it does not even charm the senses, and so only offers so many notes played and sung. I willingly grant that there are some exceptions to be made; but now first I see how far above this so-called "German" manner *my* operas stand. Heaven knows this is only a German soled-and-heeled Italian music, impotent sophistry; nothing more nor less. The poisoned flute in "*Austin*" amused me much.—

March 25th. Yesterday I received a letter from a lady (of aristocratic birth) who thanks me for my writings: "they have been her salvation;" she declares herself a thorough-paced revolutionary. So it is always women who, with regard to me, have their hearts in the right place, whilst I must almost entirely

14

give up men. If I were to compare this woman with
L . . . . K . . . . ! (A letter has just come from
Fischer which I must read.) 'Twas nothing, only
about seeing to the parts for the *Flying Dutchman*.

I have read your last letter through once more, and
have found nothing special to answer. Only *one* wish
has it strongly called forth—to see you soon again !
That you should not pay me a visit this year pains me
deeply, and all the more as I see how much less happy
you will be during that time in Dresden than you
would if you came here ! In truth I greatly pity you,
and your resignation naturally does not much comfort
me. How merrily and (under certain conditions) how
prosperously could we, who are on intimate terms,
live, if we made trial of an intelligent communism !
If, in leading a modest life of close communion, the
united income of a family were distributed among us,
what sufficiency we all should have to enjoy our little
bit of life without a care ! On what miserable living
is it now expended ! Truly, between theory and
practice, there is an infernal difference !—

Yesterday a portrait painter and lithographer pounced
upon me : he wants to take me entirely on his own
account ; his trial-sketches have much pleased me ; so
at last I am in for it. In connection with this, Brendel
came into my mind. If he means to give me, he
ought not to take the old daub : as it concerns my
physiognomy, I am a little interested in the matter ;
I am tired of that silly dressing-gown portrait. So
beg him the rather not to give my portrait. If
I am taken by the painter here it will naturally
be in large size, and thus it probably will not

do for the newspaper. So—let the matter quite
alone !—

For the moment friend and fiddler Ernst is here :
this G-to-E being was, in a measure, recommended to
me, and so I cannot altogether escape from his
melancholy string-existence. He brought me a
message from Hiller, who, with regard to a remark
in my *Preface*, begs to assure me, that though he
might not always understand me, yet he is not only
my "former" but also my present friend. (People of
this sort are now beginning to feel highly piqued : my
retiring into my shell casts a fatal shadow on their
path.)

No answer yet from Leipzig : Rietz must have taken
fright at me. Only Sturm and Koppe have inquired of
the theatre director here, if he perchance knew why
I had not answered them !—

I now send you to-day a newly arranged score of
the *Flying Dutchman*, with the request that you will
keep it by you once for all, so that in case the score
should ever be asked for, the copy could be made from
it—as in the case of *Tannhäuser*. As Liszt is thinking
of giving this opera in the summer, I particularly beg
you to ask him to return at once the score which he
has there, the one which was sent to him by my wife
in the summer of 1849, so that you may set it right
before the parts are copied out. You would then send
him back the corrected copy.

(Put all this down to our half-yearly account, as I
lately mentioned.)

At first I did not wish to systematically revise this
score : for on closer examination I found that to re-

arrange the instrumentation, in accordance with my
present experience, I should have, for the most part,
to do all the work over again; and, naturally, the
desire for such a task cooled down at once.   In order
to reduce the whole brass, for instance, to reasonable
proportions, I should have had to alter everything
consistently therewith; for the brass was not merely
incidental here, but was determined by the whole
manner not only of the scoring, but of the composition
itself.

This discovery certainly vexed me, but—I would
rather confess the fault than improve it in an unsatisfactory manner.   Only, therefore, where it was purely
superfluous have I struck out some of the brass, here
and there given it a somewhat more human tone, and
only thoroughly overhauled the coda of the overture.
I remember that it was just this coda which always
annoyed me at the performances; now I think it will
answer to my original intention.   The changes must
be clearly indicated in the score, and often it would be
best for them to be written out on fresh sheets of
stout paper: better spend a little money on it than
have anything unclear!—

This work, however, has altogether much interested
me : it has an uncommonly impressive colour, and
indeed, one most definite in character.   It is striking
to see how embarrassed I then was by musical declama-
tion ; and the operatic style of singing (for instance
♩ . . ♪ ♩ . . ♪) still weighed heavily on my imagination.—

Your article on the Schumann symphony was again
wonderfully learned : you are a d——d fine fellow !

I am curious to see what will come of it.—For the rest it does not occur to me to expect anything from the paper for myself!—I know that—in all that concerns the practical present—I speak to the wind, and must wait in vain; but I am content if I prove this in effect, and thus ever reveal anew the necessity for the total overthrow of our modern practice—at any rate, to all thinking minds.

The song did not satisfy me: it were better it had been left out; it is all made bar by bar, and with no grasp of the whole. These eternal harmonic tricks are becoming quite intolerable to me now, and I believe—now that I have my rhythmic verse to hand— that in future I shall be able to proceed quite otherwise with harmony than formerly. By this I do not mean that I should return to patriarchal simplicity: but my harmonies will move in broader expansion—more distinctly, and more definitely. This at least is how my new lyrical element—made possible by means of my new verse—is revealing itself to me.—

With regard to X.'s assurance and your timidity, you have quite the right feeling: you understand what the matter is, but X. and company do not understand it. The K. article really shows me how fearfully far behind they are still, and still more so his pencil lines to Br. For them art is always something cut off from life, something too definitely the master of its own caprice. If one shouts this in their ears as I have done, amongst other places, in the Preface and in the second part of *Oper und Drama*, they well-meaningly close their ears and say: "O yes, those are your exaggerations, but they don't mislead us."

How lucky it is that they cannot be misled! O! the *strong* men! *Weak* women are anyhow easier to mislead.

I send you, together with the score, all that you wished for besides: only I can't find the *Glassbrenner* calendar; I'll send it another time!—

With the advent of spring my great poem takes ever stronger hold of me: I shall soon be at work; the wealth of material grows almost to excess, and I must soon begin, so as to be soon rid of it.

Anyhow—*it will be something*, it will be the best I can do.—

So farewell then for to-day! Unfortunately I have no news yet from my doctor; yet I am resolved not to go to an *establishment* again. I will write shortly to the R.'s (to the mother): greetings to them and at home—also to the two-cans-of-" milk "-measure Siegfried.—

Adieu! hold me in kind remembrance.

Your

R. W.

In the score of the *Dutchman* you will find also the supplementary additions to *Tannhäuser*—written down by Fischer—and with these you can have a new score prepared.

60.

DEAREST FRIEND,

Two hasty lines to you!

You will learn everything from the R.'s except what concerns the Leipzig theatre management; the R.'s must learn that from you! So my conditions for the performance of *Tannhäuser* were too exorbitant? This is too heavenly not to have amused me! Listen!

I was asked through Sturm and Koppe what my demand for honorarium would be. Thereon I wrote to Rietz that on such a matter I could not treat with a business office, as my chief conditions were of an *artistic* nature. From the inquiry, however, I see that there is a movement in favour of a performance of *Tannhäuser;* and as I presume this emanates from Rietz, I perceive in it also the best guarantee for the good artistic character of the proposed performance. *On this assumption* I therefore willingly consented to the performance, and asked twenty-eight louis d'or, to be paid, however, immediately on receipt of the score (on account of the public exchequer); but mentioned that the question of honorarium was not that to which I attached the most importance.—Thereupon I receive *no* news, and now first learn through you that my (probably the artistic) conditions are exorbitant. What is one to say to persons like Rietz, who find it extravagant, if I presume that he will exert himself to secure a good performance? Do let Brendel know this. But perhaps the Leipzig folk will henceforward . . .

(Do come to me! I have such a longing!)

This story has again quite sobered me down. You must keep the description of the *Tannhäuser* Overture, in—case—the overture—should—be—per—formed—anywhere. Then the explanation would be to hand.

What are you doing?—My *Dutchman* flies here on the 20th. Sea and rocks are being painted, and ships hammered together, so that everything is in a hubbub. Once again I shall be beset on all sides.

Lindemann has written. An excellent method of cure ! I remain here, and compose poetry.—

Soon more from your

R. W.

Zurich, *April 4th,* '52.

(If I could only see the Berlin painter from Brunnen once more !)

61.

Dearest Friend,

Many thanks for your last letter. I wrote lately to Frau R. As she is already resigned to Pillnitz, I cannot venture to expect much from her decision.

I enclosed a small letter for you, which gave you an account of the Leipzig *Tannhäuser* affair. Now I have to ask your help again in a new piece of confusion which has arisen. In order to make it clear to you, let me proceed historically.

In the year 1846, Dr. Schmidt, at that time the Leipzig theatre-director, asked me for the score of the *Flying Dutchman* with a view to performance. So— with my *Tannhäuser* experience to hand—I retouched the instrumentation most carefully, and sent the revised copy to Schmidt. The performance—under God's help —came to nothing ; but up to now, when I again began to think of the *Dutchman,* I was too easy-going to inquire after the Leipzig score, which had become of no use ; the rather, I set to work afresh to retouch the instrumentation, but at last lost patience, so that—as you will have perceived—I often, and mostly, contented myself with minor alterations. Then the Dresden orchestral parts arrived, and the musical director, Schöneck, who was to set them right according to my new version, finds, to his astonishment, that these parts have already been most minutely altered according to another and more thoroughly retouched copy. Then only does it occur to me that before I sent off the score retouched for Leipzig, I gave it to our Dresden copying department so as to arrange our own orchestral parts in conformity therewith. Now I am in this fix. The parts do not agree with the score which I have to hand here ; but I will not have them changed, because the former retouching is more thorough ; so I now require that earlier retouched score. I am now pretty certain that I had the *Dresden score* made like the Leipzig one, or rather, that I gave a lithograph copy of the *Dutchman* to the office for that purpose ; so that at the present moment there exist *two* copies of the score in Dresden —the original one, and a new one lithographed and retouched. I should like to receive the second one as speedily as possible ; and I therefore beg you to entreat Fischer, in my name, to get Busch at once to give him the said score also (which will not be a matter of any special difficulty), and then you can send it as soon as possible by post, addressed to the theatre-director Löwe here.

But this affair has further consequences. For the copy which has now to be prepared for Weimar, and perhaps for other copies which may be wanted later on elsewhere, I should like you also to take as model that older version (as it is the more thorough). Nothing beyond the close of the overture should be altered in

accordance with the latest version, the rest according
to the older one, excepting if it should turn out here
and there that I had been more thorough in my recent
than in my former changes.   For this purpose I wish
you would hunt up that Leipzig score, so as to procure
it for yourself.   Unfortunately I do not know whether
Dr. Schmidt is still living in Leipzig : Brendel, however, could obtain information on this point.   Then
one would have to find out whether Schmidt kept the
score for himself, or handed it over with the inventory
to the succeeding management.   No one in Leipzig has
a *right* to the score, as I received no honorarium for it ;
but one hundred thalers were to be paid me after the
performance (which, as you know, did not take place).
If you obtain this score, keep it at your disposal : if
you cannot get it, then the *altered* Dresden score, when
I have sent it back, must serve as model.—

Abominable nuisance !—

We have fabulously fine weather here now.   Good
heavens ! how I should like to fly well away this
summer, as far as Italy !   But, after the Leipzig experiences, I have still less hope of receipts.   I may be
glad if in the course of this whole year something
blossoms out from Weimar for the *Flying Dutchman*.
But for travel I need money ; otherwise I shall not set
out at all.   By May I shall be in the thick of my poem :
already I am making my sketches.—

I wrote to you about a painting animal who wanted
to catch me : it is done.   The first portrait was bad,
because the idiot did not understand me.   Then
Herwegh came to the sittings, and under his minutest
guidance—with his intelligent and practised eye—a

really good portrait has been obtained, which will soon appear here; and yesterday I offered it to Breitkopf and Härtel for publication. But it's no good for Brendel. And what should he want me for? Arrange your present portrait business according to this news.

Ernst is fiddling about in the neighbourhood.—

Why, in the name of fortune, do you want information about my music-making in Zurich? Here the order of the day is "be present," not write and read about it. But why, then, does not Brendel publish the special notice which I sent to him about my position here? I gave it to him with a definite purpose.—

Is your eldest youngster well again? There is always something the matter with children! You must have become beautifully lean again: soon you might wear apostles' costume again, and flit about with me at midday amid flowers by the waterside!

Kind greetings at home. Keep safe and sound, and farewell.

Your
R. W.

Zurich, *April 9th*, '52.

62.

Dear Friend,

I can only write to you to-day if I make up my mind to be *brief*. I am so fearfully overwrought and unnerved that the least bit of writing is a torture to me. Yesterday, the 2nd May, we had the last performance of the *Dutchman*. Within a week it was the *fourth* of the series, all given at considerably raised prices (first tier, five francs), and always to crowded houses. In this you have the full expression of the success. The director much regretted that he had to go off to Geneva to-morrow, because he saw that he could now have given the opera yet another four times. I really think it an unheard-of thing to have been able to give such an opera every second day to so small a public with success. The performances, from the second onward, when the barytone had recovered his voice, were excellent; but naturally only from the "opera" point of view. The first performance showed me clearly that I must give up all illusions about the "drama," and be content to have made the most of the "opera" stuff which still clings to the *Dutchman*. So the result really left me quite indifferent, and my inmost feelings of my relation to our theatre and public have not been thereby changed in the least. But that the *Dutchman* proved effective even as "opera" I can now understand, and I willingly acknowledge that the impression made upon my public was unusual, deep, and serious. The women naturally took the lead again: after the third performance they crowned me with laurel and smothered me in flowers. The opera will certainly please in Weimar also.

Kummer came yesterday to Zurich for the fourth performance. He brought me your bulky letter, for which many thanks. I cannot possibly, as I said, answer it in detail to-day. Only one thing I must mention. Let no one judge of any mode of action unless he thoroughly knows all its bearings. Incomprehensible as my "lavishness" towards the theatre-director here may seem, it will be easily comprehensible to any one who knows exactly the whole situation which prompted my mode of action, with all its accessory circumstances and characteristic moods. He would understand how I came to force upon the theatre-director the payment for deficient receipts, when he would by no means accept the sacrifice from me, but, on the other hand, was not to be induced to give up a performance. In such a case I might certainly have done one thing, viz., give up everything, and withdraw entirely. As, the train of circumstances once started, my sole concern was to give the performance, and properly, so I must needs feel that it was expedient to coax round the director into accepting that arrangement : for it was a question by no means of *him* personally, but of the success of the undertaking. Besides, Löwe had engaged *musicians*—at cheap prices ; but they did not arrive, and wrote to excuse themselves. *He* had done his duty, I could demand nothing further of him, and he told me I must make shift. I, on the contrary, with a single eye to success, did not make shift, but engaged a musical director from Aarau as first violin, whom I certainly had to pay money for lessons lost during ten days. In the same way I was obliged to arrange with a musical director from Burgdorf, and with a 'cellist, Böhm, from Donau-Eschingen. Could I have even asked the director about the matter ? Would he not have thought I was mad ? Were not all *artistic* matters connected with the undertaking my business alone, and, if I gave this up, should I not have had to give up the whole ? Enough !

It is most humiliating for me to have to give these explanations. But how can it come into any one's mind to see in this a false "generosity" on my part? Do you think I boast to any one here, and that I make myself out a man of means? My friends know *exactly* how matters stand with me, and to any stranger I, at least, make it quite clear.

But, kind greetings to R.'s from me. I certainly won't fly any more *Dutchmen*.

Ah! ah! ah! what a wretch I must seem to myself!

In the next few days I will answer you about everything in arrears, and will send you what you want; I cannot pack to-day.

Farewell, dearest and best friend. Heartfelt thanks for your faithfulness.

Your

R. W.

Zurich, *May 3rd*, '52.

Do not forget to let me know your new address. To explain my continued conduct towards the director, I should have, I see, to tell you much more yet, which I hope you will let me off. I need only add—he is a *Jew!*

63.

Dear Uhlig,

Schindelmeisser wrote to me from Wiesbaden about the score of *Tannhäuser:* I have granted it him conditionally, and referred him to you about the copy itself. If he asks for it, send it to him. I am not to have an honorarium, but a *tantième* (royalty), for which, of course, I do not much care—this communication is the reason why I shall again be brief.

Nevertheless the packet shall be sent off to you on this occasion. I cannot pick up again : my nerves are much relaxed, and I suffer from sleeplessness.

Only once again in my life can I sacrifice myself by preparing another performance ; if I ever get so far, it will be with—my *Siegfried*. Till then I must keep away altogether from undertakings of the sort : and *after Siegfried* I shall stop. Adieu, *Capellmeister ! !*—

With regard to the literary *rôle* which I have played during the last years, it begins to annoy me very much. I can only look back to it with pleasure in so far as I feel that by its means I have become quite clear in my own mind. But when I perceive the effect which I have produced on the outside world by my writings, I can only feel in a state of revolt and altogether out of humour. Tell me, among all the voices which have made themselves heard in this question, is there one man of whom one could say that he is in any way capable of comprehending what the matter treated really is ? My opinion of the world of art and literature was certainly a bad one, but I had not suspected such boundless wretchedness ! People have become so fearfully stupid, that they literally—can no longer *read :* am I to begin now to give them first lessons in reading ?——

So far as concerns the trouble you have taken in this direction for my sake, I beg of you—at least do not excite yourself : if you happen to write, make jokes, but never get seriously angry, for by that means we shall become ridiculous. In your articles, which I have read, I find that you—in this sense—go much too far : for God's sake stop your attacks upon Riccius ! and suchlike.

I can only expect to make an impression on young people, because they in general are capable of receiving new impressions. The old man of to-day is quite powerless to escape from routine : he never sees what is new, for which he has deadened all his receptive organs, but only himself and what is old. These people must be abandoned to a death by putrefaction ; but in no wise must one fight with them.—

Most painful of all are those new enthusiasts of mine, *à la* W. and K., who draw a scrupulous line between my extravagances and the sound (*i.e.*, old-conventional) part of my work !—Why should I want to know anything about them ? I go no longer to read the papers at the Museum : the next thing I shall do will be to decline the musical papers. Send me now and then a joke, but never more anything serious ! This intellectual diet may appear very egotistical ; but I hope I have won a right to be egotistical, in that I have hitherto made myself too cheap to the world.

You might let me know what is still not clear to you in Part III. of *Oper und Drama :* is it perhaps the great importance which I claim for alliterative verse ? In my opinion this is the only point about which I have not been able to make myself quite clear to others, because this indeed is only possible by deed. I still owe you *this*, but I hope no further, theoretical explanation. But everything else *must* surely be quite clear to you, for it is certainly no matter of speculation, but in reality a statement of the nature of things and of their proper relation one to another.—

Well, enough of this, and, let me hope, for ever. I already heartily regret my curiosity concerning D.

I see before me the whole labyrinth of dialectics into which this wretched individual would drag me if he should really arouse in me the passion to make myself intelligible to him. Hence I wish he would not write to me, because I know that, even with the most strenuous endeavours on my part, nothing could come of it. In his particular line D. has accomplished much, and that has made him obstinately vain; but with such people their particular line must be wholly overthrown, otherwise one cannot count upon any success; and, after all, this success can only be attained by downright murder. How can a man who is all method understand my inbred anarchy? D. is out and out a despot; he wishes to make people happy by compulsion; in him there is no trace of the revolutionist. He is quite wanting in *naïveté;* he has not a drop of artist's blood in him; but is he really an artist? He proves how much a clear calculating compiler without a spark of productivity may accomplish: the new, the non-arbitrary, must ever remain foreign to him: he has no heart for it—*i.e.,* his heart only reaches as far as the theatre-school, and for anything further he helps himself with the "imperfection of human nature here below, and the necessity for a richer unfolding of the same in some star or other." He is—strictly speaking—silly, densely dull, *bourgeois,* cowardly—even to cruelty—or, to sum up, fearfully weak!—

My intercourse with him—now I remember—was—one long martyrdom.—See here, for instance:—he knows that he might expect something new from me, yet up to now he has not gone so far as to look at

15

my books! What does it mean? Will he read for any
other purpose than to contradict me? Will he have anything but *his* system before his eyes, and not perforce
consider everything which differs from it a want of
clearness on my part? But what have I to do with
such a man, and what sincerity is there in him but his
cowardice?

Well, I have enough here to do with men of this
sort: I don't want any Dresden-court-theatre-deists in
addition!—Away with him!—for now I am all occupied
with my poems!

Unfortunately the *Dutchman* affair quite discomposed
me, and now it will take me some time to get myself
right. I still hope to be able to go to the country
again. My surroundings are ofttimes very painful to
me. Alas! I have again been downright wretched!—
Herwegh, the only one—was silent and suffered with
me: what else could he do?—

Now as regards the success of the *Dutchman* with
the public, it was certainly a great one. X. will now
rejoice at it: the pianoforte scores are selling like
mad; only the day before yesterday an order went off
for six complete pianoforte scores and a lot of detached
numbers, *potpourris*, etc.—

I now come to business, and will dispatch it in a few
words.—

With regard to the arrangement of the score of the
Dutchman I specially commend to your notice the
Dresden-theatre score which I am now sending back;
I formerly retouched it with red ink, and indeed more
thoroughly than in my last version: the brass especially
was much more carefully reduced. Only the overture

—the close—has been lately handled by me in a more thorough manner. Get this Dresden score from Fischer as soon as it has returned. Concerning the Leipzig one I enclose the desired certificate !

Best thanks for the catalogue of my music : however, I shall not require it much ! Ten years ago, when I left Paris I took away with me the *Huguenots* (quartet), *Robert le Diable* (two violins), *la Reine de Chypre,* and *Zanetta,* as I had still to make arrangements from them, for which part of the money had already been paid to me in advance : but, as this work became impossible for me in Germany, I afterwards paid back the money advanced, but kept the musical examples, which may certainly have cruelly troubled your imagination. This much to calm you !—

The K.'s found it too uncomfortable at Elgg—and they were not far wrong—and, as Hahn himself advised, they are now at Zurich, where they are looking for a dwelling, and find it so pleasant that—without any persuasion on my part—they are already thinking of settling here.—

So much for to-day ! If I should have forgotten anything of importance, I will make up for it next time ! Farewell, and remain good to

Your

R. W.

Zurich, *May* '52.

The letter from R.'s sister has deeply moved me, and I am rejoiced at A.'s energy of mind, which, anyhow, the poor girl could not understand. Why should he trouble to ask for my three *opera poems?* Dr. Schulze might, at all events, tell me—indirectly

through wife or sister—how I could send news to him.
Best greetings to Sch.—

64.

DEAREST FRIEND,

I am off to the country to-day, and, while there,
I want to know that any business matters, and especially
vexatious ones, are settled, so that at last I may again
be able to confer with my muse.

To-day I received two letters from you at once, the
one with the money, and the other sent afterwards.

It is remarkable that the K.'s feel themselves irresistibly
drawn towards Zurich.   We have found them a summer
abode on the heights, a quarter of an hour from the
town.   The situation was so beautiful, and I so long
for scenery and fresh air, that I quickly resolved to
lodge in the same inn.   So from to-day we and the K.'s
live on the same plot of ground.   Merely address your
letters to Zurich ; everything is arranged with the
postman.

I do not make any further reply to your letter
to-day : I shall have the opportunity next time.—
Cheer up, that your health is once more improving :
accept my heartiest congratulations.

Farewell, and hold me in kind remembrance !

Your
R. W.

ZURICH, *May 12th*, '52.

65.

DEAR THEODOR,

I have waited too long for a letter from you not
to feel bound to answer immediately on receipt of the
one at length arrived, though this answer may not

contain all which meanwhile has accumulated for communication to you.—First of all, I am sincerely sorry at the great distress which your children cause you: the trouble with the youngest, after what you have passed through with the elder one, is truly affecting. Yes, if I knew *this* kind of trouble, I should be quite another sort of person! I hope Siegfried is now going on more favourably: at least, I gather this from the close of your letter—would my good wishes could help!—

We are alone in the country here with Julia; K. is with Hahn, where he must patiently remain. Hahn considers his case a very bad one. Julia seems to have taken a great fancy to me: anyhow, she does all I tell her.

I have commenced my cure in an orderly manner: it consists, besides dieting—from which a glass of good wine from time to time is not excluded—of a cold bath in the morning and a tepid one (22 degrees), lasting a quarter of an hour, of an evening. This has a soothing and gently bracing effect on me. Above all, the open air, in which I roam about two or three hours of a morning before I settle to work, does me a world of good. I do not work for more than two hours at a stretch; formerly by working for five or six hours I greatly overtaxed my nerves.—Now I have finished the complete sketch of the *Walküre* (I): to-morrow I attack the verses. I am more struck than ever with the broad grandeur and beauty of my subject-matter: my whole manner of viewing the world has found in it its fullest artistic expression. How I wish you were here, that I might oftener impart things to you which I must now save up until I can place the whole complete before you. After this work I shall write no more poetry! Nothing higher and more complete can my powers produce. Once the verses finished, I shall from that moment become entirely musician again, only—at some future time—to become *conductor*. I almost hope that I may win—or preserve the life to do it!—

I had much to tell you, suggested by reading articles about myself; perhaps I'll do it later on. On lately reading over Julius Schäffer's first two articles about myself in the *N. B. M. Z.*, I much regretted that the man had not yet read my *Vorwort*. What, for example, he says about alliterative verse (because he does not find a trace of it in *Lohengrin*) would then have been impossible. What he says about the "dissolution of the individuality of keys" might lead to an instructive article. I have shown in the third volume of *Oper und Drama* that harmony only becomes something *real* (not merely an abstraction) in the polyphonic symphony—*i.e.*, in the orchestra—and thus the imaginary individuality of keys (Hitzschold must excuse) passes over to the real individuality of instruments, of their manifold colouring and finally of the mode of execution. So, by clinging to the "individuality" of keys, one clings to a chimera, which anyhow formerly became as much of a dogma with us as the good God Himself. On the contrary, the keys, like the tones in general, only become characteristic in the instruments, and, finally, in the human voice *with words*. Thus, for example, the characteristic individuality of a key (E major or E flat major) is very prominent in a violin or a wind instrument, and it is, therefore, a piece of slip-shod criticism to consider the key by itself, and the instruments not at all, or else also by themselves. The instrumental musicians of the past century as yet knew this not : they worked from the harmonic dogma ; but let one only compare their instrumentation with Beethoven's or with mine.—Whoever in judging my music divides the harmony from the instrumentation does me as much injustice as he who divides my music from my poetry, my song from the words !—However, in all such things I was wrong to have made known my theoretical views too early ; I am still owing the real matter, the work of art, which was certainly ripe in me before the theory. *Apropos !* do protest against the statement that I am working at an "art work of the future ; " bid the silly folk learn to read before they write !—

In regard to Reissiger's oratorio you were quite wrong to send me explanations : *your word is sufficient,* and I am firmly convinced that the oratorio is of such a nature that you could praise it. Already your praise of a sonata of R.'s induced me—a most exceptional thing—to go through that composition ; so I believe you.—

As a rule, do not take it amiss, if I do not always say something about your articles : they always give me great pleasure. But I surely need not tell you that I do not think much of the rest of the paper : I also believe you that it cannot be otherwise. Yet I cannot see why not one of the important points which I have started should be discussed, instead of continual criticisms of *Trios* and *Etudes.* I was by no means displeased with the notice of *Cellini* : on the contrary, it was very good. But instead of piano rubbish—at any rate, just *now,*

at the turning point of the journal—surely something
different might find a place! How can a man—like
Herwegh, for instance—think of expressing his thoughts
between these "Ops. 6 and 7"? There is so much
purely commercial music that no thought can be taken
of us. Lately I received the poem of the *Pilgrimage of
the Rose*. Why does it occur to no one to grasp by
the root a work like that of Schumann's—*i.e.*, above all
to point out the fearful wretchedness of the poem, and
to ask what sort of a composer he must be who could
feel inspired by such a piece of patchwork to write an
important work, and what such music could possibly
contain?—The same sort of thing should have been
done with the poems for the prize song offered last
year by the Cologne people. But enough of this!—

Liszt conducts *Tannhäuser* to-day (the 31st), in
presence of the Empress of Russia! By no means
bad! The Moritz wishes also to take *Tannhäuser* to
Breslau.—Well! now I have pretty well done, and can
say farewell for to-day! To that I join hearty wishes
for the welfare of my little god-child : may they be of
help!—But to see you right soon again is what I most
long for! I always fear, most excellent young man,
that you will fade away from me; certainly not in spirit,
but in body! What a wretched lot is yours, and what
a thing it is to bear it as you do! Yet it must some
day come to a stop even with you!—Farewell, and
strengthen yourself properly in the fresh air! Kind
greetings to your wife.

Your

R. W.

ZURICH, *May* 31*st*, '52.

Yesterday I wrote to "theatre-master" Hänel. Get to know the contents of the letter; they will interest you, and perhaps you could be of assistance to me in the matter!

I have found the sheet of *Tannhäuser* in Fischer's hand—and you shall have it shortly.

66.

DEAREST FRIEND,

Accept from us all the heartiest congratulations on your child's recovery. Your letter reached me while in the company of the ladies, who, as well as myself, at once anticipated that it could only be about your child, as I had already informed them of its severe illness. We shared your cruel anxiety, and now at last felt with you unspeakable joy at the recovery. If anything can increase your joy, may it be the assurance of our sincere sympathy for all that you have lately gone through.

Heartiest greetings to wife and child from your

R. W.

ZURICH, *June 3rd*, '52.

67.

Uhlig! Uhlig! you are a *Hergottstausendsakra-menter!* You have again kept me waiting a pretty time for a letter. This time I also have not been so quick with an answer, but have first finished my *Walküre*. This was yesterday, after a month's work. If you were here I should read you the piece to-day; but it will be some time before I have a copy to spare, for I am again in a very weak state. I work indeed in too impetuous a manner! Now, indeed, when the whole of the big poem is on the point of completion, I begin to ask myself whether I ought not to wish that my friends should become acquainted with it sooner than they would if I first worked out all the music. I feel as if I could not bear so long to know that the poem had not been communicated to them. I cannot possibly give it yet to the printers. It would seem to be a sin against myself now to put into the desecrating hands of our mud-throwing critics that which, in fact, is only half-finished so long as the composition of the music is incomplete. It is something different with my true friends, who, by their sympathy, can only urge me on and assist me while I am at work. I have, therefore, thought of having twenty-five to thirty copies of the whole poem made in fac-simile reprint, so as to place them, after careful review, before my friends. Unfortunately, there is this inconvenience, that I, poor wretch, should have to play the "generous"—for how could I allow these copies to be paid for? It could only be thought of if I were approached by a number of my friends, who begged me to lend them my manuscript for the purpose of having copies made, and who had subscribed among themselves to defray the printing expenses. Everything is exceptional with an unlucky bungler such as I am.

To-morrow week I must go to Bâle for the choral festival of the Helvetic confederacy, at which I have been appointed umpire! Unfortunately they got round me here just as I was on the point of refusing the invitation. On my return I shall set out about the

middle of July on a real Alpine tour—*i.e.*, I shall visit
the Bernese Oberland, go over the Gries glacier down
a long, magnificent valley as far as Domo d'Ossola
(Sardinia), to the Lago Maggiore, ascend the Lago as
far as Locarno, from there to Lugano (all in the Tessin
canton), where I shall probably stop, for it must be
heavenly. Possibly I may finish the verses of the
grand prologue to my three dramas. This all depends
upon the state of my purse. I have not a farthing as
yet, and I know of no other way to help myself than to
write to Liszt to get the Weimar honorarium for the
Flying Dutchman in advance. I am in daily expectation
of an answer from him. Do you think a single creature
has given me news of the Ballenstädt musical festival ?
The beggarly *rôle* which I play with regard to the rising
generation begins to annoy me.

I shall not have the *Nibelungen* work ready before
the autumn (September, October). I must carefully
retouch the two *Siegfrieds*, especially in everything
which concerns the myth of the gods, for this has now
assumed a much more precise and imposing aspect. I
rejoice greatly at the thought of the music.

Do you know anything about the articles of *Fétis
père* in the *Gazette Musicale* about me ? I was told
about them here, and found at the Museum already
three leading articles, " Richard Wagner," etc., etc.,
with, as it seems, plenty more to follow. In any case
you must try and get them to read. M . . . . is at
last bestirring himself : he fears the propagation of my
opinions in Paris. *What an ass !* The caricature of
myself with which *Fétis* regales the French is complete.
He gives quotations (in the meanest manner) from my

Vorwort, and, with great consistency, represents me as attributing the constant failure of my operas not to any fault of my own, but to the present condition of things ; and says that *that's* the reason I am a revolutionist. A "small protest" against some of the most reckless lies would not be amiss just now. He claims "exact information," and asserts, for example, that my *Tannhäuser* in Dresden had by the *third* performance become such a failure that it could *never* by any possibility be revived. And so on. In this matter R. (whom F visited in Dresden several years ago) played him a nice hoax ; but I fear my own information (in the *Vorwort*) may likewise have misled dullards, as I express dissatisfaction with the success of my operas. By that I naturally do not mean outward success (for should I have demanded more than to be called before the curtain at every performance of *Tannhäuser ?*) but merely the character of the success, which made me see that the *essential* in my work had *not* been grasped, or not grasped in so convincing a manner as must have effectively shown itself in order thoroughly to satisfy me from the one true and decisive point of view. It was just the same here lately with the *Flying Dutchman*. No one who only looked to the outward result understood my deep dissatisfaction, and understood, least of all, that this especially concerned the character of the performance, which seemed to all so excellent, and, indeed, had brought about the success (of the "opera").

This last point reminds me to enclose you the accompanying documents in connection with the newspaper war concerning the *Flying Dutchman*, of which you know something. The rejoinder of the *Züricher* was followed by a bitter, vulgar, insulting answer, which I did not condescend to notice, and which, besides, was only directed against my " panegyrists," while preserving a demure and respectful demeanour toward myself. The old trick !

The *National* newspaper also is said to be handling me roughly at the present moment. I do not read it, because, though I should not intend to reply (and I certainly *will* not any more), yet what is written runs in my head for several days, and that might be occupied with something better. I don't in any way wish to represent myself as more apathetic than I am, and such experiences always make me regret that I ever put pen to paper.

I thank you much for your excellent gathering of literary fruit ; also *zur Kritik des Liedes* pleased me uncommonly. It was, I freely confess, an oasis in the desert to me. It may well be that your paper should best maintain itself by criticisms of all sorts, and that, to satisfy the demands of your public, you must notice everything pell-mell ; and thus not only have to devote your attention to what is unimportant, but are forced to present its " good sides." Only give up all these attempts to make of the paper something different from what it was. I do not complain that it remains what it is, but that Brendel allowed my letter to him to be printed in his paper. He ought to have had the courage to decline its acceptance : that, at any rate, would have been consistent. It grieves me much, however, to have to tell you that the *Musikalische Kladderatatsch* makes me most unhappy. Nothing is more horrid than a " rubric " for jokes. A good joke that comes naturally

is a capital thing, and carries more weight than many
a serious remark. But a weekly register of wit, the
heading of which calls out in advance to the reader,
" Now laugh ! " at once locks fast my laughter-muscles,
and so it is with every man of the least taste. This
Musikalische Kladderatatsch is a mistake, and I tell you
this honestly, even though you should have been the
cause of it. The very form is trivial, because lacking
in originality ; the contents are, for the most part, forced,
devoid of humour ; and, as I have said, inevitably so,
since they appear in this ready-made form. I've had
my say : I heartily wish that you may not be so
deeply concerned in it as to feel really hurt by my
words.

E. D. has also written to me : now I'm in for it.
Fresh trouble ! What shall I do with the man ? To
my horror I discover that the man is far more shallow
and superficial than I had imagined. He *can* only have
read the first part of my *Oper und Drama*, for nearly
his whole letter is a *defence of music* against my
" attacks " on it in this first part.

E. D. *defends music against me.*   Is that not delicious ?
He appeals to " harmonies of the spheres," and " groan-
ings and sighings of the soul ! " Well, I have got a
pretty millstone hung about my neck ; for with all his
stupidity this man, as I perceive, has something respectable and true-hearted about him, and one cannot
but regret that one has to kick him so straight out.
Well, I will write to him ; say that to him with my
provisional greetings. Perhaps at the Lugano lake I
shall be in the mood for a letter to him.

Greetings, too, to Fischer. I received a letter from

him yesterday. As it is impossible for me to answer him to-day, I beg you to set right something mentioned by him in his letter. I wrote to Hähnel about some lithographic sheets to be prepared for the *Tannhäuser* decorations. Through Fischer he replies : "The lithographer asks twelve thalers for every sheet ; so three sheets would cost thirty-six thalers. For that I should receive nine impressions from each sheet (?), but each "single" sheet would cost 'three thalers' (?) ; so for a theatre the designs would be 'nine thalers.'"

Now, with the best will in the world, I cannot clearly make out what is meant. If I pay thirty-six thalers for the whole ('why exactly nine impressions ?), will each theatre *still have nine thalers* to pay for a copy of the three sheets ?

Get an explanation of this for me, so that I can soon decide ; for I shall certainly be pleased if can send the decoration-sketches to the theatres. As for the rest, with regard to the spread of *Tannhäuser*, I have everything to expect. For the moment I only know of Wiesbaden. From Breslau an *inquiry* was addressed to Moritz ; from Leipzig came the *assurance* that the director *intended* shortly to give the opera "in the most complete manner ;" from Munich I have no news. Lately, when—amid storm and rain—I had gone off into the woods, Mantius, from Berlin (the present opera manager), came to pay me a visit, and of course did not find me. He assured my wife, however, that the Berlin management had long been thinking of *Tannhäuser*, only had not been able to find a suitable tenor. Now they thought they had got him in Formes, and so a speedy performance stood in prospect for Berlin.

From Frankfort I have no news.   G. Schmidt has not answered.

I am very glad that you are now living in "Satannes-gasse" (Dresden dialect).   You are in a nice quarter of the town there : "a young lamb white as snow," etc. Have not your children got raven-black hair ?   And Siegfried ?   Good heavens ! if you knew what I have now planned in my mind for him.   How delighted he will be one day when he sees what has been made of him.   I want to see his look of surprise.

Let me know whether you have any "increase"—I mean from Lüttichan.   I hear the favours of his lord-ship have run riot amongst you : Lipinski, a diamond ring ; R., two hundred thalers increase of salary ; gold and silver medals to the members of the band.   Ah ! who would not wish to be there ?   Have you been silvered, gilded, or—good-for-nothing'd ?   With your new dignity the last would be unbecoming treatment. Honour to whom honour is due !

R.—so Fischer writes to me—has expressed himself with all possible enthusiasm about *Oper und Drama*. The good fellow !   I certainly owe that to your notice of his oratorio.—

Well, enough of this scribbling !   I could say with T. U., "the paper comes to an end."   I am, on the whole, in a good humour to-day, for when I have finished such a work as the *Walküre* I always feel as if I had sweated some fearful anxiety out of my body— an anxiety that constantly increases as the work is drawing to a close ; a kind of fear lest I might spoil something.   I write my signature, with the date underneath, in as much haste as if the devil was standing behind me, and wished to prevent me from finishing.

Next week we go back into the town. We had bad weather all through June. My wife sends cordial greetings. Proper greetings to yours from me. Adieu!

Some men are not even sheep's heads, but sheep without heads (Lin. ii. 13).

ZURICH, *July 2nd,* '52.

68.

DEAR FRIEND,

A line or two before my departure, which takes place to-morrow. The director of the Leipzig theatre has just been to see me. The matter is arranged. Send him at once a *score* and a book of words (with the remark that the copies for the booking office are to be procured through X.—at a discount). Further, beg Hähnel in my name to send back at once the designs of the decorations, which he has now at Wiesbaden, and then to lend them to Wirsing in the same way as to Schindelmeisser. Then beg Heine, who has now returned to Dresden, to lend his costume-sketches likewise to Wirsing. He will arrange everything for his theatre according to these patterns. Thank Heine for his letter; I will try and write to him on my journey (?).

I have written to Basle, to decline : I can no longer endure such a fuss. Your letters will be sent on to me, so continue to write without worrying yourself. Still you might address your *next* letter to Lugano, Canton Tessin, *poste restante.*

Farewell.

July 9th, '52.

Your

R. W.

16

69.

Dearest Fellow,

Your little letter reached me yesterday, just as I had come down from the Bernese highlands.

A piece of business information appears important to me, and little as it suits my present surrounding and frame of mind, yet I will give it to you at once!

The *lithographing* of the decorations we will leave alone for the present, and, instead, each theatre must purchase the sketches for nine thalers. I have written in this sense to Schmidt at Frankfort: he must apply to you, and you must be good enough to order the designs through Hähnel (to whom my cordial greetings). The designer could, in order to avoid delay, always hold in readiness one or two copies.

About a second score to Schmidt I know nothing: this is probably one procured formerly through the bookshop.

I have continued to dilly-dally about the few sheets for *Tannhäuser:* do not be angry about it; when I return I will send them on.

I have now been travelling for six days: I can count each day by my treasury, for each one costs me regularly a twenty-franc piece. It is splendid here, and in thought I have travelled much with you. Yesterday I descended from the Faulhorn (8,261 feet). There I had a tremendously grand view of the mountain-, ice-, snow-, and glacier-world of the Bernese Oberland, which lies straight before one, as though one could take it in one's hands.—I walk well, and am sound in my legs; as yet, however, I am not satisfied with my head; the nerves of the brain are terribly strained; excitement and lassitude—never true rest! Shall I really never be much better? No cure in the world is of any avail where only one thing would help —viz., if I were different from what I am. The real cause of my sorrow lies in my exceptional position towards the world and towards my surroundings, which can no longer give me any joy; everything for me is martyrdom and pain—and insufficiency! How again, on this journey amidst wonderful nature, have the human *canaille* annoyed me: continually must I draw back from them in disgust, and yet—I so long after human beings;—but this pack of rogues! Devil take them!!—

There are magnificent women here in the Oberland, but only so to the eye; they are all tainted with rabid vulgarity.—

Liszt has duly sent me one hundred thalers for the *Dutchman* honorarium; these I am now spending in travelling. Every day costs me a Number of the opera.

Farewell, and get your stomach in proper order; I cannot, as a rule, digest milk; it gives me heart-burn.

I shall expect a letter from you at Locarno.

Your
R. W.

Meiringen, *July* 15*th*, '52.

Do read in Prutz's *Deutsche Museum* an article "der Geist in der Musik" by Otto Gumprecht (I think it is in the first June number); among other things you will find in it a heavenly explanation of the A major Symphony, in which everything is frenzy, despair, and

—God knows what else ! There's choice reading for
you ! It is inconceivable what a fine thing absolute
music is !

X. was again glorious with his report. What a deal
of trouble the man takes to prove that he was *always*
an exceedingly clever fellow !

70.

O, you Man ! *Homo terribilis* (Lin. ii. 53).

I really expected to find a good long letter here
from you, as you promised in your last note which
I answered from Meiringen : now I find only a few
lines on business. Well, I will not do much more
than answer your questions, as my head, owing to
the journey—and especially to the heat—is all of a
whirl. So :—

I cannot imagine that they were copies which
Hähnel sent to Schindelmeisser : I thought these were
the original Dresden designs on loan ; so I meant
Hähnel should ask for them back at once, as they
were now wanted in Leipzig. Naturally, if he has
the originals in his possession, there is no further
need of the Wiesbaden copies, and Hähnel may now
see how he can get paid for them there. So to
Leipzig, *new copies* for nine thalers, to be paid by the
director. Full stop !—

The Dresden and Leipzig scores of the *Dutchman*
will probably agree, but if there is a difference anywhere, let the Dresden be followed, with the exception
of what I have lately changed, especially in the overture.
When will Liszt have the score ?

From sheer good-nature I will add a line or two

about my journey. The gem of it all was the march over the Gries glacier, from Wallis, through the Formazza valley to Domodossola, which occupied me two days. The Gries is a magnificently wild glacier pass, a very dangerous one, and traversed at rare intervals by people from the Hasli valley or Wallis, who bring southern goods (rice, etc.) from the Italian valleys. For the first time on my journey there was mist on the glacier heights (over 8,000 feet), so that my guide had difficulty in finding a path over the cold walls of snow and rock. But the descent! leading down gradually from the grisly ice-regions, through many a sloping valley, through all the range of vegetation of northern Europe, into the intense luxuriance of Italy! I was quite intoxicated, and laughed like a child, as I passed out of chestnut groves through meadows, and even cornfields, completely covered with vine trellises (for that is how the vine is generally cultivated in Italy), so that I often wandered under a covering of vine similar to our verandahs, only extended over whole acres, on which, again, everything grows that the soil can produce. And then the ever-enchanting variety of form of mountain and valley, with the most delightful cultivation, charming stone houses, and—all through the valley—a fine race of men. Well, I cannot describe it all, but I promise you to go again over the Gries glacier with you.

My first Italian conversation was grand. I could not, for the life of me, remember what *milk* is called in Italian, because this word, as you know, never occurs in Italian opera, from which I have gathered all my knowledge of the language. Soon I became quite a

Vestri, and if you recall that hot-blooded sun of the south, you will have a good likeness of me. From Domodossola, I went on in the evening by a "return-carriage" to Baveno on Lago Maggiore.

This drive crowned the day. I was in a happy frame of mind when I at last passed out of the wilds into unchequered beauty. Unfortunately the next day those rascals of men (*Menschenkanaille*) disturbed my calm reflections: on the steamer—full of Italian Phili-stines, not bad specimens either—poor fowls and ducks, (which were being transported), were so vilely tortured and left to the most cruel privations, that the revolting unfeelingness of the men who had this sight constantly before their eyes, again filled me with violent anger. To know that one would be merely laughed at if one attempted to interfere ! !

But, dear friend, my opinion of the human race is ever becoming gloomier; I cannot help almost feeling that this species must inevitably go to ruin.

Here in Lugano again it is divine ; but my loneliness torments me frightfully. Herwegh has not come (he is now full of worry), and so I have written to my wife to come with Peps. The Frankfort *Tannhäuser* must provide me the money for this piece of extravagance.

Härtels, to whom I had addressed myself about getting multiple copies of the manuscript of the *Nibelungen* dramas, answered me lately, among other things, definitely declaring that it would afford them the greatest pleasure and honour if I would hand over this work to them for publication when ready ; indeed, that I need not think of any one else but them. Well, there's plenty of time for that !—

I am not thinking for the moment about resuming work : my head, especially with this heat, will not yet bear any continuous strain. One more interesting note : on the Faulhorn I ate roast chamois, but in the Formazza valley roast marmot ; I don't know whether Rausse forbids both. Do look it up !—Greetings at home, and soon write something decent to Zurich ! Farewell.

R. W.

Lugano, *July 22nd*, '52.

71.

O MUCH-WORRIED CHAMBER MUSICIAN !

What a fearful lot of postage I must cost you now ! Well, in return, I send you to-day a really beautiful landscape-painting instead of a letter. But as I must answer a business inquiry, it shall be done with all brevity.

I wrote at once to W. on the receipt of your news : I remonstrated with him for his impudence, and told him plainly that if he was going to behave so shabbily he had better at once give up the performance of *Tannhäuser :* and that, as he had not yet sent the honorarium, he had only in this case to send you back the score. All the same, let the copies ordered be finished : if not for Leipzig, they'll do for some other place. Now that I know the cost of the copies, I will in each case quote people the price in figures. Kind greetings to Heine ; I cannot write to him to-day.

I have had an application from Hildburghausen (as per enclosed) : I find it out of place that *I* should answer these people. Either I shall not answer at all, or *you* might undertake to call their attention to my biography in the *Zeitung für die elegante Welt* (1843), and to my *Vorwort* (as supplement). If you are willing to patch up something yourself, that's your affair. It is not of much importance, and at best is only a means of avoiding, or rather guarding against, silly mistakes.—

You will be astonished at the number of places I have been to. I sent for Minna to come to Lugano : then with her once more Lago Maggiore, over Domodossola, Wallis, Martigny to Chamounix (see the drawing), Mer de Glace, etc.—to Geneva, where I found your last letter. Now we are off home by Lausanne.

For this new journey I had set apart the twenty-five louis d'or of the Frankfort honorarium, advanced to me by Sulzer. I intended the Leipzig honorarium to cover the present deficit—you already know of—in the subvention I receive from the R.'s. And yet I am so daring in my transactions with W. !

I will write *at length* to you from Zurich ! Nothing further to-day, except to say that the journey was a success.

Your
R. W.

Geneva, *August 3rd,* '52.

(With a picture of the Chamounix Valley.)

72.

To-day I will add what may be necessary to the few lines I sent lately : I have not much news.

For nearly four weeks I have been on a journey

towards which I had long looked forward as to the
realization of a beautiful dream. I had many an
impression that was pleasing enough, taken by itself;
but I was always seeking after the right one, and—I
could not find rest. It is all over; I have lost my
youth; *life* no longer stands before me; all my working
and doing is only now a protracted death. I have
learnt much during this journey. But I will spare
you; why describe things which will not bear description ?—

I have returned from my journey with one resolve :
as I can now only lead an artificial life—*i.e.*, a life for
art—I will thoroughly do everything which can keep
me artificially on end. I now so ardently long to have
a little house with a garden, here in the country, far up
on the heights by the lake, to look after my little
property, to surround myself with flowers and animals,
and to set up a cosy nook where friends may visit me,
that I intend to carry this out at any cost. It is an
undertaking which I now feel compelled to carry out,
and when I survey my outward circumstances, I have
reason to hope that it will prove successful. There
is no longer any doubt that in the immediate future
I may look for substantial receipts from my operas.
Were I to wait till I had saved up the sum necessary
to purchase an estate, this—considering the state of
my health—would be folly: the "too late" would, in
my case, prove terribly true; and, besides, there would
be the danger of never being able to collect the entire
sum, as I should probably fritter away the money in
other directions. I am therefore resolved—and have
already spoken on the matter with my Swiss friends

here—to advertise at once for a suitable small estate, the price of which should not exceed 10,000 francs.

As soon as I can pay down a deposit of 2,000 francs the matter can be settled : out of my future receipts I could pay the interest on the sum remaining, and also gradually wipe off the capital debt. In any case, even for the deposit money, I might well count upon the assistance of a friendly hand.—

When I reflect that my wife and I shall one day die childless, and therefore a *heritable* property will be of no value or use to us, I should much prefer if some one could be found who would lend me the whole purchase-money, upon the security of the estate, on the condition that after my and my wife's deaths it should revert to him or his, embellished and enriched by my care and at my cost. I could then employ my expected receipts in a still pleasanter enjoyment of life, in travelling, etc. That such a person could be found is not lightly to be expected, and in any case I will not count upon it.—

(A letter has just come from you : I will read it first.)

Best thanks for this letter, and its good humour in spite of your indisposition ! (What is the matter with you, you waterman, that you become ailing of a sudden ? Set my mind at rest on the matter !) To settle " business," only the following brief lines !—

I do not yet know how matters stand with Berlin : I have demanded an honorarium of 1,000 thalers, assigning good reasons for my demand, and have given them clearly to understand that I will not prostitute myself again for Berlin at such a cheap rate. Probably they will decline : I must risk it. If I accomplish anything, it can only be by terrorism.—Make my excuses to Heine for not writing to him. In order to satisfy him I require to be very expansive ; and my repugnance to all such empty scribbling is now frightful. To D. also it is impossible for me to write just now. Thank Heine in my name for his information : it will probably not prove so incorrect ! If it should still come to a definite acceptance, I will carefully see about the allotment of *rôles*. You will probably hear something definite from W. : do not give him the designs without the money ! S. has kept quite quiet : I have given him a sound scolding and warned him that by the next post I expect either the news that the score has been sent back to you, or the honorarium, with the assurance that the Dresden designs will be procured.—This is my last word ; there is an end to good-nature.—

The Moritz had long since written to me that she was trying to get *Tannhäuser* played in Breslau ; so that I was not surprised at your news about the director there.

You did what was right about the score. So far as I know, Seidelmann is a conscientious man, who certainly had good reasons if he asked to look at the score.

You can also conclude in my name with the director Reimann : I. An honorarium of twenty Friedrich's d'or, to be sent to you or to me *immediately* on the declaration of acceptance : II. An undertaking to arrange the scenery and costumes according to the Dresden designs, which can be had through you for seventeen thalers.

It seems that the Düsseldorfers really have a good orchestra : see if you can get eighteen louis d'or from Kramer, and, if not, let him have the score for ten louis d'or. (But, to be paid *immediately* on receipt of the same—to you or to me—'tis no matter which.) See if you can further manage to make Kramer procure the designs from you : but that must not be made a *sine quâ non.*—

It is possible you may also receive a demand for *Tannhäuser* from Prague : if so, then the same conditions as for Breslau, to which I shall have to keep for all theatres of second rank : I see well that I cannot ask higher.—

There ! you will have your hands full !—

On my return, B.'s paper made me quite sad again.—I wrote at once that Brendel should be asked whether he might not want letters from me on the formation of the Alps. Great heavens ! What articles this paper ought to contain, if there were only a trace of comprehension of the task it had to accomplish ! Your reviews are always excellent, and edify me,—but, good God ! what a heap of work there is to be done, if one would only take in hand the right stuff, which is never once offered, with all this reviewing.

—I wish you would send a line or two to your friends, at your leisure, begging them to be more prudent in lending my manuscript of *Young Siegfried.* I actually read lately in the *Kreuzeitung* a joke about the dragon (*Lindwurm*) Fafner ! Such experiences make me extremely averse to carry out my intention of distributing copies of the whole poem among my friends. When an opportunity offers, *do see* that the

Dresden score goes to Weimar for correction : *this is of the highest importance to me !*—

As regards friendship, I grant you are right, and certainly in the Cause you are right ; I am only sorry that in this matter there is any question of right ! You must not discuss theory with me any more ; it drives me clean crazy to have to do with such matters. The nerves of my brain !—there's the bother ! I have cruelly taxed them : it is possible I may yet one day go mad !—

But one line more, in conclusion : if there is one thing about which I rejoice, it is *your visit* for next year ! See betimes about leave of absence : the rest, I hope, you will leave to my care!

Farewell ! Take care of your health, and hearty thanks for all your friendship ! Best greetings from my wife.

Your
R. W.

ZURICH, *August 9th,* '52.

P.S.—I also have been thinking of the full close of *Tannhäuser* for Berlin : so get Wölfel to add the complete ending with the Pilgrims' song, exactly as you meant.

73.

BEST FRIEND !

A line or two to-day on business matters !

I have just had a letter direct from *Breslau :* I have answered and made the conditions, such as I lately wrote to you. So send thither the corrected score as soon as possible, and order the *designs for costumes and scenery*.

Also, see at once about fresh scores and designs, for I have just been informed that Hanover, too, by special command of the king, is on the way towards *Tannhäuser*. If Wölfel is not enough, you must see about a second copyist.

I have not yet received any money ; what is the state of your fund for expenses ?   Can you wait till the autumn, or do you want money before then ?

Another request : as you have so often to write me on business matters, do not pay the postage any more. Am I to ruin you utterly ?—

I have written to Heine to-day.   My head is not clear enough yet for work.

Farewell, good fellow.

Your
R. W.

ZURICH, *August* 11*th*, '52.

74.

BEST OF MEN !

At the same time as your letter I received a fresh load of trouble for you.   A theatrical agent, Michaelson in Berlin, informs me that no less than *five* theatres have asked for *Tannhäuser* (among them, however, Dusseldorf is included ; besides, Riga, Stettin, Dantzig, and Königsberg).   I think I will have nothing to do with people of this sort, and accept the offered mediation so as to be saved a lot of scribbling.   I only stipulate that the honorarium (after deducting commission) be sent to me *beforehand*.   So get ready, you unlucky fellow, to prepare more scores : if you have not a sufficient supply, claim fresh ones from X. With regard to the outlay, I am awaiting a statement from you, and hold myself ready to provide you with money in case you need it. (I have myself received nothing tangible from any quarter. Please provide yourself with copyists for the re-arranged scores.)

From Berlin I have no answer about my honorarium demand. Leipzig has humbly apologized, and prayed for pardon: again I have enjoined on them the necessity of procuring the designs for the scenery. With regard to Berlin I have written to Heine and Liszt about the transfer of the "alter ego" to them.

—Now something important! As I cannot possibly address myself separately to all the conductors and interpreters *in spe* of *Tannhäuser*, I am busy working at a concise address, respecting the performance and the way in which I wish it carried out. It will contain ample details, and, for many reasons, I think its public appearance will be of advantage.

Hence I intend this *pro memoriâ* for Brendel's journal, where it should appear either as a leading article, or better still, as a special supplement, but in either case in full. Give notice of this to Brendel, who indeed wished to have something of the sort from me, and prevail upon him to keep space open, so that the article may come out *without delay*. Unfortunately I can only work very slowly, as any work now tries my head extremely. Yet I hope to have done in four or five days, at latest ; I will then send the manuscript direct to him (to save time), and stipulate that you correct the proof, whereby you will gain an opportunity of reading it before it appears in print.

Now farewell for to-day! You will soon have more news from me! By the beginning of the winter your trouble will probably be over.

R. W.

August 14th, '52.

75.

DEAR UHLIG,

Again a red—*i.e.*, a business letter. The director, J. A. Stöger, at Prague, wants the score and book of *Tannhäuser*, and so I beg you to let him have them at once. By this time you have probably received the missing "sheet" through my parents-in-law.

From no quarter have I received an honorarium, and I think of soon giving rather a rough reminder to the Leipzig director. No answer from Berlin. The director of the Würzburg Theatre has lately inquired about *Tannhäuser*.

Only to-day have I finished the manuscript of my "address on the performance of *Tannhäuser*." It had to be more detailed than I at first thought, and I am now glad that I hit upon this way of removing a great weight from my mind. I am again much exhausted by the work, and I must now try to thoroughly recover from the effects. After ripe reflection, I found it necessary to give the manuscript at once to be printed here, so as to be able to send as quickly as possible a sufficient quantity of copies to the theatres (*privatim* and *gratis*). I have ordered two hundred, of which I will at once send you a good share, so that you may be able to deliver them to the theatres, to gether with the scores; the number in each case to be determined by me. But in this matter I wish to appeal to the public also, and, as soon as it is ready, will send a copy to Brendel to put in his paper.

Härtels have sent me copies of the score of *Lohengrin*, of which I keep three for presentation. In any case you will receive one (as you seem to have received none from Härtels) ; a second I think of presenting to Robert Franz, and will send it to you to see that he gets it. I have really been intending for a long time to write to Franz. Heaven knows how one always puts off a thing of the sort, however agreeable it may be. Kind greetings to him, and assure him that I place great value on the fact that he—next to you and Liszt—was the first *musician* who showed me any friendship.

I cannot write any more to you to-day. My head is again all confused. Rest ! rest ! (just like Reissiger !)

Farewell, and greetings at home.

Your
R. W.

ZURICH, *August 23rd, '52.*

Keep scores in readiness, for shortly there will have to be a regular hailstorm of them !

Peps keeps on barking. Auerbach was also here ; but he did not bark.

76.

DEAR FRIEND,

With the best will in the world, I was unable yesterday to send off the parcel with the two scores and one hundred copies of the Guide to the performance of *Tannhäuser*, because I had no money for the postage : thus do the shabby directors leave me in the lurch.

Fortunately, I have just received the fifty thalers from
the Würzburg theatre-director, and so for the moment
I am afloat again.   You will have already seen what
cunning means I have hit upon to compel the managers
to pay—of the acceptance-permits (*Zwangspässe*) which
I have given to them.   You will probably have received
two for inspection from Würzburg and from Düsseldorf.
I shall stick to this for the future, and heartily regret
not to have invented this plan at the time when I first
became acquainted with the Leipziger.   Probably the
permits did not come to you unprepared, and you no
doubt had warm rolls to hand to appease the voracity
of the theatres.

If only my head were in a better state !   I have done
for myself again with that cursed pamphlet, which I
rushed through in order to get everything finished in
hot haste.   A sharp knife often cuts into the nerves of
my brain ; besides which I am weak and feverish in all
my limbs.   But if my head recovers, then I feel better
at once.   On it—on this laboratory of the imagination—
everything depends.

The matter with Berlin will be arranged, for I go
back to the *tantième*.   Hülsen means quite honourably,
and is thoroughly well disposed towards *Tannhäuser*.
Under these circumstances I must withdraw my vote
of want of confidence in him.   By the *tantième* I shall,
with luck, gain more than a thousand thalers.   But
more about this later on !—

I cannot decently have any more copies of "On the
Performance," etc., struck off : I should indeed be sorry
for some persons of whom I had to make mention in it
in terms of censure.   But if you care to make an *extract*

from it, and publish this—with a notice of the subject—
this would possibly do much good.   You could quote a
great deal : only certain matters of detail (the scene-
painting, etc.), and those scolding comments, need come
out.   But—you will understand what to do.

If *Tannhäuser* should, after all, be given in Dresden,
hand over to Fischer three or four copies of the
pamphlet, so that he may give them in my name to
v. Lüttichau, whom I beg to direct " specially the conductor and the stage-manager" to pay careful attention
to the communication.   I would ask Fischer kindly to
undertake this.   If I only knew of a way altogether to
put a stop to the Dresden performance !

In the case of future orders I will always let you
know whether and how many copies of the *Address* you
ought to send away with the score.   For this very
purpose I send you half the edition.   The theatres
up to the present I am supplying from here.

Now something of great importance !—

Let X. know exactly the places which now have the
score.   I have stipulated with all the managers that the
books of words are to be had of X.   Now, if he does
not bestir himself, they won't care a fig about asking
for them.   So he must write quickly to Berlin, Leipzig,
Frankfort, Breslau, Prague, Düsseldorf, and Würzburg,
and ask for orders.   He must also commission a business friend there to keep a sharp look-out, so that no
books of words are pirated.   For *Berlin*, if (which you
will learn) they give there the complete ending—with the
Pilgrims' chorus—there must be special copies of the
text printed off, with a *newly arranged* last page,
according to Härtels' edition.   This page could be

likewise stereotyped for any other theatres which may follow the example. How sorry I am that all this should be in the hands of such a glue-boiler!!

I must conclude. The packet is too heavy and expensive for the post, so I am sending it by goods-mail. For you and Fischer (Lüttichau) I therefore only enclose five examples with this letter.

I shall send the Guide from here to Prague, Breslau, Düsseldorf, and Würzburg. The other theatres are already provided for, so I think there is plenty of time for the transmission of the greater bulk.

Farewell! Forgive me the many commissions; but if you do not take a double share off my hands, there will be an end of me. Imagine it, this letter almost kills me!

Send news soon, and remain good to me!

Your

R. W.

ZURICH, *August 30th*, '52.

77.

DEAREST!

I can only tell you in two lines that *Figaro* has again conducted himself admirably, and that I thank him heartily for his performances. Reply I cannot at the moment: I *dare not* write, because I cannot. That's how things stand with me!

For the rest, everything is at a standstill—nothing definite from Berlin yet. No *money* from any quarter, excepting Würzburg. What can I do with the *Leipziger*, who does not even answer my letter of reminder?

Wölfel will have enough copying to do, for I see you are not provided with a sufficient number of *Tannhäuser* scores, as you have had to keep Prague waiting. Do employ two copyists! Let the one write the new ending, and the other all the rest: thus a copy can be finished in half the time (the original can be cut in half).—

But I can no more! Farewell!—the score to J. Schäffer shortly.

Your
R. W.

ZURICH, *September 5th*, '52.

78.

DEAR FRIEND,

A few days ago the highly conscientious Prague director sent me the honorarium even before receiving the score: *I hope* he has got the latter by now?—To-day Breslau also sends its golden tribute. I have lost all patience with Leipzig. Already a few days ago I wrote to Rietz to remind W.; but I presume even that will be of no avail, and I therefore beg you (are you angry?) to carry out the enclosed "commission" through some acquaintance of yours (perhaps the first musician you come across). I am getting in a rage with this director: he does not answer at all.—

To-day I forward you also a score of *Lohengrin*, which I request you to send to Julius Schäffer (whose address I do not know).

This is all I can write to-day! Take it not ill!

Your
R. W.

ZURICH, *September 8th*, '52.

Keep scores still in readiness. I have just received a

letter from Cologne : I have drawn an *acceptance-permit* for ten louis d'or.

79.

BEST FRIEND,

Some business, so that you may not get out of practice !—I enclose the sketch of my last letter to my Berlin brother, from which you will see how it stands with the *Tannhäuser* matter there. Let Heine see this draft at once, and then send it back to me.

As things now are (they have suddenly discovered that *Tannhäuser* cannot be given on any one of the Royal birthdays), it is advisable meanwhile that X. should write about the books of words to Berlin (to the general intendant of the royal theatre). You must compose the letter for him (he is an ass). This is the state of things :—My brother writes : "A family, Jacoby by name, received from the late king, Heaven knows for how long, the privilege of printing and selling all books of words for *all* operas. The family receives therefrom a yearly income of 1,800 thalers : to take away from them the books of words of *Tannhäuser* would result in a law-suit and all kinds of things. However, it could be arranged by means of a discount (25 per cent.) : they would not then need to print them, and could always sell them to advantage. Hülsen will speak to the parties. If the parties are unwilling, nothing can be done."—So far my brother !

I would have you notice that the (wretched) Berlin books of words are always sold for 5 *Silbergroschen,* whereas the price of the *Tannhäuser* books was fixed at 3 *Neugroschen.* X. ought therefore to send to Berlin copies on which the price is not marked, or on which it is marked as 5 *Silbergroschen* (for smaller places the lower price could remain). X. could let the Jacoby family have the copy for 2½ *Silbergroschen*, that is at 50 per cent. discount. Thus the people will be perfectly satisfied, and it will make no difference to our receipts.

Should it be impossible to make an exception in the price, or, for any other reason, to mark it at 5 *Silbergroschen*, and so the 3 *Silbergroschen* have to remain, X. would have to reduce the discount somewhat, perhaps to 35 or 40 per cent., in order to make these people amenable. We shall not let it come to a law-suit; on the other hand, even without gaining much profit, we still preserve our rights over the property.

My head is still bad, and as the result of my continual agitation by the invisible land outside, I am in a very nervous state of health.

Röckel's letter of yesterday caused me great, great joy! He bears himself in first-rate style, staunch, and cheerful.—I shall answer him to-morrow.

The "three opera-poems," which he supposes to be already here from Härtels, he has not yet received, neither has he yet had *Oper und Drama*, about which he has much to say. Now I had begged you to send a copy to Röckel as soon as it appeared, and you also wrote that you had attended to it: could you not inquire through your legal friend in Waldheim? Härtels appears to have paid no attention to the matter, for he is even still asking for the pianoforte score of *Lohengrin*. By his wife I am sending him my last copy (already bound for myself), but will you please inquire about the "three opera-poems"?

You may possibly soon receive an acceptance-permit from Cologne for the *Tannhäuser;* keep scores ready !

Farewell, I must stretch myself on the lazy-couch, in order to close my eyes !

Your

R. W.

ZURICH, *September 11th,* '52.

80.

DEAR UHLIG,

With your letter I received also one from Michaelson, who asks for a book of *Tannhäuser* for Riga, because this must be examined at St. Petersburg by the censor before the director can *buy* the opera. So please send to " Herrmann Michaelson (Theater-kommissionsgeschäft) Leipzigerstrasse 42 in Berlin" half-a-dozen books of words (I suppose X has some in stock ?), and tell him from me that the books of words for the theatre are only to be obtained through X. Besides that he will receive the score through you, but only upon advice from me ; I shall have already communicated to him what he must do to obtain such order (payment in advance).

—I have no money yet from Düsseldorf : I have a presentiment that as you have already sent off the score (you unprincipled man !) there will be no end of trouble about the money.

Mühling (not Schmidt's father-in-law) has left Frankfort, and Hoffmann has taken his place : the latter wishes to give *Tannhäuser* with unheard-of splendour, as his inaugural opera.

Hence the delay. I shall receive money as soon as Hoffmann has arrived in Frankfort.

—I cannot write any more to you to-day: I have already devoted my whole writing power to Röckel, to whom I have just addressed a long letter. I am also sending him a *Lohengrin* score, which had been bound for myself (as duplicate).

You have misunderstood me.

As to the purchase of an estate, I had no one specially in my mind : do you consider me so obstinate in my superstition ?—As Berlin seems to have smashed up, my scheme has again disappeared into the dim distance.—

Now listen :

Man ! man ! man !

Get hold of *Hafis* (" Poems of Hafis," collected by Daumer).

I. At Campe's in Hamburg.

II. Lately issued in Nuremburg.

This Persian Hafis is the *greatest* poet that ever lived and wrote. If you do not get him at once, I shall hold you in thorough contempt : put down the cost to the *Tannhäuser* account.

Only be thankful for this recommendation !

Farewell. Look after wife and child, and do all in your power to stop *Tannhäuser* at Dresden !

Your
R. W.

Zurich, *September 12th,* '52.

81.

Best Friend,

Immediately on receipt of your letter I must devote a little writing power to you : already last Tuesday

I felt moved to thank you for your last "choice reading." Good heavens, how proud you will make me! So I am indeed a "musician"! If you only knew how many things passed through my mind on reading that! Altogether, I could really write sheets full to you every day. There is (unfortunately) a terrible quantity of matter for correspondence : day by day I learn more and more, so that I no longer know what to do! But the cursed writing !! I reserve everything till next summer, when, *in any case*, you will pay me a visit : we will not be lazy then !—

I am not one jot better ; only I accustom myself gradually to a fresh degradation of my state of health ; I am resigned, and manage accordingly : I work now every day *a short hour !*—so, good Heine rejoices at my good spirits ? He is right ; complaints from me shall never more be addressed to friends *such* as he is !—

I wrote (very briefly) to D., just to clear up ! And ought I also to have written to X. ? That cannot be quite a correct story. I presume, however, that he confuses my Berlin brother with myself. *He*, as he announced to me, has written to X. about the books of words. This matter, I hope, is set straight by the last instructions I gave to you—still I should like to hear something about it.—With Berlin I am now also straight : had my brother informed me that this time, by way of exception, Johanna was remaining in Berlin till the end of May, my objection would, naturally, have been removed, and with this news I should have been quite satisfied ; but, over and above, Hülsen assures me by letter, that before the spring he hopes to give the opera more than ten times, and undertakes also to arrange for six performances during the first month. In short, the matter is in order : do tell this also to Heine !—

That Reissiger has at once hit upon the idea of "cuts" is delicious ! If you only knew how indifferent to me is this Dresden performance ! The best means to prevent it would be, if a certain person happened to read my pamphlet : he would probably be offended by it, and my opera would be abandoned. I know the people I have to deal with !—

Has Lüttichau got the copies ?

Why I am so eager after the "wretched" Leipzig honorarium ?—I. Because W. outrageously annoys me. II. Because I am *greatly* in want of money. What do you think ? I owe twenty-six louis d'or to Sulzer for my summer tour : twenty louis d'or to my wife, to cover the deficit in our last year's money. I am much in debt, too, with my new establishment here. Then, lastly : how can you imagine I ever have enough money ? In the dog's life to which I am condemned—I cannot get a scrap of—distraction, well-being, or whatever you like to call it—without money ? It is all very well for you to talk. You have children ! Don't make your hair turn grey over my too much money ! I assure you, on the contrary, that I am possessed of quite a vulgar greed : I am now on the hunt for the *Nibelungen* hoard,—I have given up the Graal. Shall I again write down for you my last recipe ?—

Well, don't think of me as more common than I really am : there are still a few noble sides to my character ! So, for example, be assured that I should gladly have given up Berlin, had not the intendant there shown himself so amiable towards me as he has, etc.

Do you believe it cost me no effort, lately, to refuse *Tannhäuser* to a travelling director in Rudolstadt? I am convinced the man would have paid me four louis d'or. (Do nothing with Cologne without a postal receipt!) They have written to me from Schwerin about *Lohengrin. Tannhäuser* has pleased them: in sc short a time it has drawn nine full houses! Heavens! what more does one want?

If only *Fétis père* knew that!

I have also received the Ballenstädt Musical Festival pamphlet. This work is noble and elevating, only I am terribly annoyed that in it they make me a year older than I am! When will people know once for all that I was born in 1813? I see my friends still do not work sufficiently in my interest!—

Franz has written to me: so, as I have a good pen, I will write to him, and this shall soon be set about. Best greetings to him for to-day from me, if you are writing to him.

What continual delight the *Neue Zeitschrift für Musik* always affords me, when I open my postal copy, and read "Chamber- and Home-music!"— The very title annoys me. When I have got over this annoyance, I naturally go on reading with great pleasure; thus I accustom myself to the ruin of my nerves: one might, however, use them to better purpose!—

You must have *Hafis* and *Rausse* bound together: the *fire-* and the *water-*prophet: won't there be a hissing!—

But—God bless you! To-day is the confederate day of penitence, and during the past week the south wind has been raging in a manner to destroy even the devil's nerves !—

Farewell, you favourite of my wife's ! (No joke !) Greet, think, fiddle, and soon write again to

Your

R. W.

ZURICH, *September* 19*th*.

82.

BEST FELLOW AND FRIEND !

A fair is being held in Zurich, and a foreign linen-merchant brought such excellent and ridiculously cheap linen to market, that the Wagner couple could not resist realizing a wish they had long, but vainly, cherished, to reform their very much-reduced washing. I had already done everything that appeared feasible to get in honoraria in arrears, but I so definitely counted on a prompt settlement on the part of the Leipzig S——, that, unsuspecting man as I am, I not only gave away my whole stock of louis d'or, but also gave my wife permission to spend all her house-keeping money, in order to make thorough use of the really unique opportunity for thoroughly fitting ourselves out with linen at an exceptionally cheap rate. Consider, then, what a crime you have committed by taking the Leipzig affair in so easy-going a manner !

After I had waited a full week for the Leipzig money, amid ever-increasing lamentations on my wife's part over her empty housekeeping purse, there comes at last your letter of yesterday, treating this matter with such cold, calm composure, and opening up the prospect of seeing the matter settled in a week !—Well, heaven will teach me how to bear even *that!* But may it enlighten you, and always keep you in the understanding that in money-matters I only recognize the equation: M. M. $0 = 120$. Besides Leipzig, I now definitely expect money only from Frankfort; excuses have been made to me from there on account of the change of directorship. Dusseldorf, in paying, announced to me, that they had sent the postal receipt to Dresden for your inspection: I therefore held it quite unnecessary to say anything to you about the receipt of this money. Probably Riga also will give an order; Cologne appears unable to raise the ten louis d'or. For the rest, I am of opinion that the score-storm has come to an end for the present. If by Christmas *Tannhäuser* has succeeded in a few places, the opera will probably be wanted for other theatres during the second half of the winter. Previous to that I think you will have a little rest, on which I heartily congratulate you. I am sorry for X.: if I could suppose that my pamphlet had at the same time instructed him, the fright would have been only salutary for him; but as there is not the slightest hope of this, the whole thing must have appeared to him nothing but a humiliation, that I caused him with a certain—and for him useless—cruelty, and for which I cannot for the life of me understand how he will set about forgiving me. *For me,* it was a necessity to protest against the Dresden performance of *Tannhäuser,* and against the opinion that it had satisfied me; this was still tingling in all my limbs.

Concerning Röckel, inquire of Härtels *whether* they have sent to Waldheim the things (three opera-poems, and pianoforte score of *Lohengrin*) ordered or asked for by R.'s sister? If they have, then inquiry would have to be made at W., as to what had become of them; and with this I have already commissioned R.'s wife, so that you would have nothing to do with it. Only if Härtels have not sent, I would ask you to see that Frau Röckel in Weimar receives the "three opera-poems" (for her husband): not the pianoforte edition, for I have already sent the score.

With regard to a notice about Berlin, do be most careful! The very passage from my letter to my brother, of which you wish to make public use, was one which my brother hesitated to communicate to v. Hulsen, through fear of offending him. How surprised would this intendant now be to learn of this suppressed passage through a public paper! It might appear more hostile than I had really meant it to be; I should therefore be glad to hear your notice were not yet printed, and that you could modify it in conformity with my communication.

Your last "Chamber- and Home-music" article I read with much interest: perhaps, though, you might have ventured to show up and call attention to some *more* foolish mannerisms, besides this—certainly most characteristic—cadence—trick (*Schlussmoment*). When you attacked male part-singing, it was a great consolation to me: write something wholesale about it one day, and point out to the cunning blockheads, that in modern male-singing there is revealed no momentum coming from below upwards, but one coming down from above, and indeed "coming down" in every sense of this word. In order to show what one may expect

from this male musical mess, ask that *one member* should
come forward, and sing something : from the faint-
hearted and pitiful bearing of this individual, you
may then conclude with what filth the whole thing
is kneaded together, letting itself have howling *à quatre*
drummed into it by schoolmasters, and thereby developing new art germs for the future !

Pray do this.   In consequence of a chill, I have been
seized with a very bad catarrh : if I could properly
nurse it, I might promise myself some good from it ;
but just now, I am again saddled with a virtuoso,
Vieuxtemps, whom I know and like well of old, and
in his company I must daily spend my time.   With
him is Liszt's agitator, my Parisian acquaintance *Belloni.*
From the latter, I learn for the first time how it
happened that the Parisian newspapers fell upon me
in so solemn and so terrible a way.   Belloni was
ordered to spread broadcast in Paris Liszt's pamphlets
on my operas, and naturally there arose a halloo in
the camp of Israel.   Belloni tells me now that my
name at the present moment is famous in Paris beyond
belief, and that I have only to go there to be certain that
scandal would arise.   I had really already conceived the
idea of taking my wife to Paris this winter—if there
were enough money—for a few weeks' amusement, etc.,
and if I could manage the expense.   I thought of
engaging an orchestra for a while—entirely for myself,
and a few friends—and having some things from *Lohengrin* played over, so that for once, at least, I might hear
something from it.   This fuss naturally makes the plan
a doubtful pleasure.

Yesterday I saw a beautiful little estate : if I only

could have it! Tell that to Lüttichau! I have sent a short answer to Franz. If I could only get a little agreeable rest. Yesterday, a young lady told me *what* would cure me: she was very bold, and was right. Heavens, what a downright stupid fellow I am, to be such a crotchety beast! But so 'tis!—

Farewell for to-day, Siegmund, father of Siegfried! Study Hafis! That is my advice to you!

Adieu.

Your
R. W.

Zurich, *September 27th,* '52.

Here you have a couple of epigrams, *à la* Schiller-Goethe, which might be used as mottoes:

I. This is music to think over. So long as one listens to it, one remains cold as ice; only four or five hours afterwards does it produce the right effect.

II. Superscription for melodies:

"Chill and heartless is the song, but singer and player are politely requested to fill it to the brim with feeling!"

83.

DEAR FRIEND,

Sometimes everything seems bewitched, and I only need desire a moment's luxury to be certain that a box on the ears will at once remind me of my proper place in this world. I wrote to you lately how it was that now, above all times, I was looking anxiously for money: good. To-day W.'s letter arrives, which announces to me, that having taken cognizance of the Guide to the performance of *Tannhäuser*, the Leipzig

18

theatre must give up that opera : that the score had been
sent back to you—good ! Then of a sudden my wife
strikes in with a lament that to-day is already the first of
October, and that she is in despair at not being able to
send the rent-money to her parents ! That, indeed, is
the hardest case of all ; for the moment *I* have no money,
and if Frankfort does not send soon I shall be in a sorry
plight. Now you spoke to me about your children's
money-boxes, of a father-in-law who would help in case
of need, etc. Do say if you could advance me *ten thalers*
until the beginning of November (when you will again
receive R.'s money for me), and give them in my name
to my mother-in-law.—That was the first idea that
occurred to me. If you cannot, perhaps I may light on
another expedient. It is really too absurd that I should
be just now in such a fix : that ridiculously-cheap-linen
affair is the cause of it all. If I could only conquer my
propensity for buying bargains !

The Leipzigers are a nice lot ! Master Rietz has not
managed even to write a single line. Well, they might
all be carried off in a sack, for aught I care ! Good
riddance to them !

Belloni is again giving me plenty to do : he particularly
wants me to go to Paris, where he says people would
now make a mighty fuss about me. As he cannot attain
his end in any other way, he is trying to tempt me with
Tannhäuser in French for the Grand Opera.

Herwegh, who also is much in favour of that, wishes
to make the prose translation. *One* thing sets my blood
a-tingling : Roger (so far as I know him) would be the
only singer who could play *Tannhäuser* to my heart's
content : he is the right sort of man, and, besides, under-

stands German. And Johanna, too, in Paris : you see something is being whispered about—but anyhow I won't give an answer for the present. Keep the whispering all to yourself !

You know that I have renounced belief.—Shall I not soon receive a letter from you again ? Only write some amusing tale, something *real good:* you're a hand at telling fibs. Farewell, and——!

(Peps is now playing the bassoon.)

These are the wishes of

Your affectionate *ami,*

R. W.

October 1st, '52.

84.

MAN AND BENEFACTOR,

 Two lines !

To-day I receive a letter from lawyer Steche in Leipzig, who tells me that W. has also replied to him, that the score has already been sent back ; Steche still has doubts about it, as W. is known to be a liar. You, too, do not write to me ? If you have received the score, well and good : if *not,* let Steche (or Brendel) know at once, so that it may be got in. Sulzer thought W. imagined that I should write to him again, and come down a peg or two : it would be funny if he really expected *that !*— Cologne announces the ten louis d'or for me between the 20th and 24th of October, and requests at the same time to have the score got ready. Good—but *not* without a postal receipt !

I am pleased with Schindelmeisser : now he has read my Guide he will begin the study of *Tannhäuser afresh,* and in the right way.   That sounds quite different from the Leipzig folk !

I am most eager for the continuation of your last " choice reading " : to-day's opening against Hagen has my full sympathy.   I have been amused to find that— in spite of all the blowing-up I gave the departed Müller about careless correction—a fault has so ensconced itself in the *Programme to the 9th Symphony* that even the *Zeitschrift für Musik* reprints it.   The quotation from *Tieck* should be :—

"Bald siegend *aus* den Wogen ruft,"

instead of which the printers jog along with their :—

" Bald siegend den Wogen ruft " (without " aus ").

O you unprincipled brood !

Johanna lately sent me her portrait, which is really excellent !   I am delighted with it !

I hear Schnorr is now painting *you* for a *Nibelungen* sheet ; is that true ?   Have you become a giant ?

I will write nothing to you about my work !   It goes slowly, but well !

Farewell, and healthier than I : I shall soon go mad. Greetings to August Bürck !

Always your celebrated
R. W.

ZURICH, *October 5th,* '52.

85.

BEST FRIEND,

I really do not know how to answer your immense letter in a worthy manner.   The reason why I wrote to you to-day—without pressing occasion—is, after all, this : that I wish to make a determined break in my poetical work, so as not, by uninterrupted toil, to fall again into the fatal condition from the painful effects of which I have scarcely yet recovered a little. But letter-writing thoroughly exhausts me, as I have now found out, and you may consider it a high honour if I even fill this sheet. Were it not for the continued bad weather I should have gone off for a few days' tramp. I had already mapped out a tour to Glarus and Schwyz. However, with this perpetual grey sky and damp atmosphere, I must give up all idea of a pleasure-trip; though, even in the pouring rain, I keep up my midday walk of at most three or four leagues with a sorry sort of enjoyment. Thus I come to the chapter of health, and I must tell you at once that your account of your own condition has really given me no comfort. Believe me, dearest friend, you exact too much from yourself. With your extremely delicate constitution you ought to lead quite a different kind of life and occupation if you would prosper. You "serve" to your own hurt! I get my strongest proof of what suits you from the fact that you were so well last year when you came to Switzerland, and lounged about in proper style. From that you can see what does you good. Your dispassionate temperament preserves you, in the contact with your manner of life and occupation, from violent convulsive attacks, such as I from time to time am subject to; but, instead of that, you pine away, imperceptibly, but chronically. Man cannot live by irony alone; yet in everything which you attempt or do that is the only thing which can help you. You ought to be able to lead a pleasant, easy-going life, entirely according to your inclination. How to accomplish that is a matter for you to study as speedily as possible. How I wish I already had a great practical success, to be able to assist you to that which you cannot afford out of your own means alone! For the present, as I cannot help you, I can only take the next best course, and determine you—formally backed up by medical opinion—to get a change in your appointment, so that you might have (at least) two clear months' leave of absence every summer. If you cannot obtain this, or if an attempt is made to squeeze something out of this minimum, then give up entirely your present position, in which you have the least facility of all for getting away, and become again simple fiddler, yet with the silent resolve to take things easily, as others (*à la* K.) do—*i.e.*, when you find fiddling over-taxes you, or that disgust for it is becoming too strong for you to resist, then get on a loose end for weeks or months, just because you could not endure it any longer. But in summer take three months' leave of absence, and when, finally, people begin to kick a bit—well, get a pension, come to me with your bag and baggage, and we *together*, with your whole family, will manage somehow or other. Surely you will not be so foolish as to be prevented by any feeling of *ambition*. I even hope that in this matter you have no scruples of honour, for these conditions have nothing in common with *honour*. Therefore I urge upon you, give up your *present* position; if you cannot arrange it quite to suit your own ease—and with *it* this is absolutely impossible—then make yourself at ease in whatever service you take, even if your loitering should end in your having a pension thrust upon you. This is the only possible

way of keeping yourself right. Without it, in all probability, you must soon be quite used up. Reflect
whether it can possibly be otherwise. I entreat you to
give up this abject feeling of *duty*. Be *unbeseeming*—
that alone can save you! I am glad to hear that the
wet packing has been of good service for your hoarseness. Take care of yourself! *So long as this hoarseness
lasts, give up* **all official work**. *I bind you to this, if you
have any love for me*. Do it for my sake: go gaily off
till your throat is *perfectly* well again. I know how it
was that some time back Lehrs, one of my dearest
friends in Paris, came to grief. The poor wretch, who
was afflicted in a similar manner, could not stop work
and give himself up to pleasant idlings, when he could
easily have been cured. Do what I tell you! I shall
write no more to you, unless you can announce to me
in your next letter that you have said farewell to *all
service* for the present. Think! this must be done,
whatever happens! Listen to my entreaty!

I much long to go to Paris, to make personal
acquaintance with Lindemann. For the present
Herwegh is my physician. His physical and physio-
logical knowledge is great, and in every respect he is
more sympathetic to me than any doctor. In sufferings such as *ours* none but a *friend* can advise us, and
a physician only if he is this as well.

I also have been in a bad state as regards my
stomach, and this was chiefly the result of that cursed
milk-drinking. I now share the conviction of all who
regard milk diet as *folly*. Milk is the food of *sucklings*,
yes, and drunk warm from the mother's breast; but
every grown-up suckling feeds on developed and

intermediary substances.   No animal drinks *cold* milk,
neither does any natural man.   The cattle in the Alps
eat cheese or a fermented drink prepared from milk.
How can we be so foolish as to offer to the same
stomach which, on the one hand, takes prepared food
(even prepared meat), this other entirely raw substance ?
And we, too, with our terribly intense brain activity,
and the whole manner of our life !   The right thing for
us is—enjoy everything, but within the bounds of moderation, as taught by self-observation and experience.
As coffee (generally) is hurtful to my nerves, I take
roast meat—preferably game—early in the day, with
a draught or two of *good* wine.   Your oatmeal gruel
does not please me : do take game—hare !   Game,
while providing a maximum of nourishment, requires a
minimum of digestive power ; and it is imperative for
you to gain strength through nourishment.

My *warm* baths, of 24°, for half an hour before
going to bed, suit me well now.   It would have been
all up with me but for this bath.   It soothes my nerves,
and always gives me sound sleep.   Lindemann advised
me, if I wished to recover quickly, to take a half-hour's
bath of the same kind in the morning, instead of my
present short bath in water chilled to 20°.   I wet
my head (at every bath) repeatedly with cold water.
Perhaps I may yet have recourse to the full early bath.
Our hydropathic physicians, collectively and indi-
vidually, do not know enough about nervous disorders.
To constitutions like mine warm baths *alone* are of any
use, while cool ones entirely ruin them.   If once I can
get my nerves right, I shall be quite a different man.

Well, enough of this.   It would be enough to fill the

whole sheet, to which, however, I must add one thing more. This very moment the postman interrupted me, and brought me an immense delight—a letter from the Breslau Capellmeister about the extraordinary success which the first performance of *Tannhäuser* has had there. The man writes quite beside himself with joy and satisfaction, and I am so enraptured by it that I cannot write any more to-day to you, as the quiet for that has quite gone from me, and this time in so pleasant a manner.

More to-morrow.

October 11th.

You have probably received the Breslau news direct. How much it rejoiced me I told you yesterday. I will now conclude the letter with a few quasi-business matters.

I had thought by now to receive news from you about the Leipzig matter. Perhaps it may come to-day. I mean whether the score is sent back.

The Dresden *Tannhäuser* is no advertisement for me : they may even do there what they like with the ending ! Dresden can be of no more use to me, as it has never been of use—it has, indeed, harmed me ; but it cannot even do that any more. It can only sink deeper into my indifference. Enough ; the remembrances of the Dresden *Tannhäuser* are a torture to me. Now, with regard to the new performance, I have arrived at a :— — completely. So give yourself no trouble about the ending—at least, not for my sake. If you wish to remonstrate with L. for his insolence to me, let this be a matter quite apart.

I enclose the correction of the "leap" in the vocal part. You will recognize my astounding talent for polyphony

If only Brendel could alter the title: Chamber- and Home-Music! My fate compels me to take into my hand every fresh number of the paper. But this superscription is the ruin of me: it is every time a heavy blow to me!

I have, Heaven knows, nothing more to tell you. So I will wait for the postman: perhaps I may then find something further to say to you.

(Lachner is seen to. J. Schäffer has written to me. When you write to him give best greetings from me, and make excuses for me if I should not answer at once. That kind of letter always exhausts me. Would a score of *Tannhäuser* be of any service to him and to Franz? Copies—old version—have you enough in hand?)

Well, nothing has come; only your fugue. I must carefully study it before I reply to you about it. Heavens! you clever fellow! Fugues and maps! But with your map you will not entrap me home. I am no longer a *kee Saxon!* But I have been nearly everywhere there. I have Lohengrinned at Dittersbach (on Schönhöe).

I should have liked to send a longer answer, but time is up, as in the meantime I had to write to Berlin. Johanna had written a long letter.

Farewell, and soon send me good news about yourself, especially that you will obey me—do you hear?

Good-bye!   Your

October 12th, '52.   R. W.

86.

BEST FRIEND,

You must make much of the fact that I write a few lines to you to-day! I wished to work, but found myself in such a bad state that I was forced to spend the whole of the forenoon on the lazy-couch, half asleep and half awake. A change must be brought about: something must happen to tear me from this mere world of thought! This occupying myself with art *par distance* is death to me. No joy is lasting—not even the Breslau news—for I cannot satisfy myself with mere "news." What the change shall be I cannot conceive, for not at any price would I apply for an amnesty! But this I know, a flying trip to Weimar or Berlin, to hear my operas and do something real for them—that would have a highly beneficial effect on me.

I thank you for seeing to my mother-in-law: let a *Tannhäuser* ticket reward your good wife for her trouble! When you receive the R.'s money for me, take at once twenty thalers from it, and give them to the old Planers. Don't forget this! Don't be uneasy about my present money-wants; but you are squandering a fortune on your letters! Whatever does your wife say to it?

Everything is in the best order with Berlin: they are even thinking of soon following up with *Lohengrin*. The Princess of Prussia saw it again lately (October 2nd) at Weimar, and has probably made things hot for *Hülsen*. You have done well to write to S.: the score must be snatched from the rascal's teeth. I have declared to S. that on no terms do I now give my consent to *Tannhäuser* in Leipzig, so long at least as the present theatrical conditions are in force.

What you write to me about X. again begins to touch me : above all am I affected by the adherence to the new ending, which X. never liked.

Your Miniature choice-reading I have not specially mentioned because I found the matter altogether too trifling and commonplace : I have nothing to say about it.

Liszt sent me lately at my request my *Faust* Overture, with a delicate and intelligent remark, a wish for something lacking in it. Remind me to tell you about this another time ; to-day I feel exhausted.

I much covet your soda-water machine : I will inquire whether I can get one here, if not, you must send me one. We have already made exchanges in matters of medicine and diet. I am very glad that your hoarseness has gone. Now there only remains my last orders about your appointment.

In the abjectness of our life and of our occupation lies *at the present* the determining cause of our prostration. In spite of Schlurk, I will never become acquainted with the " *Ritter vom Geiste*." In that matter I stick to a terribly severe diet ! I have not even read Heine's *Romanzero*. I anticipate my complete ruin if I took to that sort of thing.

My principal care is still the *Nibelungen* poem : this is the only thing that really and powerfully elevates me whenever I give myself up to it. The thought of posterity is repugnant to me, and yet this vain illusion comes before me unawares from time to time, when my poem passes from my soul into the world. All I can and all I have is contained in this one thought : to be able to carry it through and have it performed ! ! !

I have now decided on the titles : *Der Ring des Nibelungen,* a festival play (*Bühnenfestspiel*), to be performed in three days and an introductory evening.— Introductory evening :—*Das Rheingold.* First day :— *Die Walküre.* Second day:—*Der Junge Siegfried.* Third day :—*Siegfried's Tod.* The introductory evening is really a complete drama, fairly rich in action : I have finished quite half of it. The *Walküre*, entirely. The two *Siegfrieds*, however, must still be thoroughly revised, especially Siegfried's Death. But then—*it will be something ! !*

I was fearfully depressed at not being able to work to-day ! How willingly would I have gone off for a few days, but the weather is too bad—quite December 2nd !

If there is anything I have not noticed, or which I have forgotten, please forgive me ! And make my excuses also to J. Schäffer !—

Frau R., of course, had written to me, as always, in the kindest manner. We visited the Kummers at Tiefenau near Elgg, which delighted them : but it is a fearful place. Heaven preserve me from *such* a water-establishment ! I would rather burn away in fire— best of all in that of Hafis. Do study Hafis carefully : he is the greatest and most sublime philosopher. Certainly no other writer has given *the great question* so sure and irrefutable an *answer.* There is only one thing —that which *he* commends : and all beside is not a farthing's worth, however high and noble it may call itself.

Something similar to this will also be shown in my own *Nibelungen.*

Farewell ! Be precious cunning, and take things in a wickedly easy way !

Ever your friend, who truly prizes and honours you,

R. W.

October 14th, '52.

87.

DEAR FRIEND,

You will only get a few lines to-day. After some interruption (through indisposition) I am now bent on devoting all my working power to the completion of the *Rheingold*, and I will not make a break by long letter writing until I have finished : this will happen, however, in the present week, and at the end of it I therefore promise you a real letter. So you must have patience with me.—

So to-day (*after* my working time) only two words !

Health. I am glad that I have alarmed you ; for this was just my aim. More about this shortly.

Business. Send to Michaelson the score for Riga, with four copies of the Guide to performance : they are paid for. If he writes to you about *Rostock* (! !), and encloses a postal certificate, send likewise a score and four pamphlets. He asks me besides for some books of words ; send him half a dozen. Tell X. to be always on the look-out about the books of words ; he ought at once to assert his rights at each theatre. (Has he not done this at Wiesbaden ?)

For Heaven's sake spare me the threatened *vouchers* for your disbursements ! Pedant, what am I think of you ? Also I do not want the Dresden *Tannhäuser* literature.

Neither do I want the machine : there is here an

improvement on it by Liebig. You acted quite
sensibly in keeping part of the money : I had
forgotten it.—

See to *three* tickets, third tier, for the next *Tannhäuser*
performance, for my wife's family.—Your own is to go
to the amphitheatre. Had not a dressmaker's assistant
written at once about it to my wife, I should have
known nothing whatever about the performance.—

Do you feel inclined to make the pianoforte score of
Iphigenia in Aulis from my arrangement (*Bearbeitung*) ?
I have offered it to Härtels.—

Mosevius has written to me in a touching manner ;
under his own name he has also written about *Tannhäuser* in some Breslau paper. Would you like to
have it ?—

Nothing more to-day ! Take for breakfast *Cacoigna*,
cocoa purified from all fat : I do so—most easy to
digest and very nourishing.—

At the end of the week, more details ! Till then,
have good courage, and hold in kind remembrance

Your

R. W.

November 6th, '52.

88.

DEAR FRIEND,

You must lately have definitely expected a big
letter. I could not write it. I certainly had finished
my work by the middle of last week ; yet I was much
exhausted, and as the weather quite unexpectedly turned
fine, I made a three days' excursion among the Alps
with Herwegh and Wille (a Hamburger who has settled
here by the lake) : to Glarus, Glärnisch, also the Klön

valley and the Wallenstadt lake.   Unfortunately I was
the worse for the excursion, as in the first inn where
we spent the night I could not sleep at all, and then
on the following day—in spite of my terrible exhaustion
—for my companions' sake I made a forced journey,
which—like everything forced—quite upset me.   So I
only now set to work to write my "big" letter: it
will probably not be extraordinarily "big," for—I
would rather not force myself once more, and with
my complete lack of life, I have so little worthy of
communication.—

But first of all, the "chapter of health."

Dearest old friend, let us be sensible, and calmly
recognize that each one of us nourishes within himself
the germs of his own death, and knowing this, it is
only a question of warding off, as long as possible, from
the body this certain specific death.   With me, for
example, everything points to a death by wasting
of the nerves : my special and characteristic mode of
life consists, to a certain extent, in avoiding the necessity
of this wasting.   This death—though it finally result
from an apparently remote and secondary fatal illness
—is to me a certainty, as certain as the speciality of
my life ; and the only question is, shall I fall a victim
sooner or later ?   So long as I have still an aim in life,
I wish to keep death from my throat, and therefore
adopt all possible measures to preserve myself.   I
intentionally avoid all over-exertion, go as much as
possible out of the way of over-excitement, seek to
regulate my digestion and nourishment, and, above all,
aim at the utmost comfort, rest, and agreeable impressions—so far as lies in my power.

That I can endure for some time yet, if I stick close to this diet, is what many assure me, and what from analogy seems credible to myself.—Now look at yourself: your whole long and meagre body tells you that you possess very deficient nutrimentary powers : by a foolishly inactive and sedentary mode of life in youth, you have increased that constitutional defect to a degree which is now causing you anxiety.   Realize your condition, and attack it from the right point : if you commence properly, you are just the man to easily succeed—and (owing to your colder temperament) easier than I—in forcing the duration of your life, with a little display of energy, to follow your own will.   Look, above all, to your nourishment !   I am glad that you are already on the right road.   Simple nutrient substances are not for folk of our sort : we require something complex, substances which combine the greatest amount of nutrient matter with the smallest demand on the digestive organs.   Our rule should be to eat *often*, *little*, and *well*, and besides, to avoid every great exertion, even in movement ; while on the other hand studying comfort and agreeable rest. Considering your general state of bad nutrition, it is natural that your *throat* suffers most, for the throat is the weakest, tenderest organ.   You lack (these are Herwegh's words) sufficient fat-formative power, and you should take everything that will help to this, even *cod liver oil*, which in such cases is said to have worked wonders.—So reflect, best friend, that you have your health, your life, entirely in your hands !   But let go *every* consideration which would hinder you from the mode of life which to you is a necessity.   Above all—this I conjure you—take *three months* leave of absence next summer, and spend this time with me (Franz is coming also). Simply get a certificate from the doctor, that you require it : he cannot possibly refuse it, and then the leave of absence cannot possibly be denied you. I must agree with you in your unwillingness to *exchange* your official position : but I can only advise you to *to stick to it*, on the condition that you know how to subdue your official conscience, and can thoroughly make up your mind to take matters easily. Otherwise, if the worst comes to the worst, rely on me, I mean on my future, from the success point of view. With a fair amount of certainty I may venture to assume that I may expect good profits in the course of the next few years : you know the necessities of my life are now ensured, and as for "luxury" I earnestly beg you in advance to consider yourself a sharer in that with me. It would be folly if I were now to fall a-boasting ; but so much you must understand, that even now, as soon as I was forewarned of your exact situation, I could help you right well. Now, I merely mean that in forming a resolution, you must take into consideration this possibility also of providing for your life ! And for the present—enough of this !—

I have not much more to tell you that would need a spun-out tale.—The Dresden "event" has become epecially interesting to me, in that from among all my "friends" I have scarcely received any news about it : with your exception, there was—as I said—only a dress-maker's assistant, who informed my wife ; otherwise, unless I include the horrid correspondence-notes of the Brockhaus newspaper, I had no news from any one ; neither R. nor H., nor F. and so on, has sent me a line.

Well, after all, I do not get much from news of that

sort.—But I think I can explain in quite a way of my own, why F. and H. do not write to me:—the *D. A. Z.* writes definitely about an intended performance of *Lohengrin* at Dresden. Now, these two old fellows know that I will not consent to this performance : and, so that I may not prevent it, they will not write anything about it to me, which they would of course have to do if they wrote to me at all. But I beg of you to tell me exactly what you can learn about it : if it is really so, I am determined to write to Lüttichau himself and enter protest. I will not have the distress of knowing that this opera is maltreated by K. or R. : they shall not do that until *Lohengrin* has been given at other good places, where I can gain an influence over the conductors.—

My " ingratitude " might almost have determined me to draw the pen against a third person on this subject ; in order to ask quite quietly, whether I had not returned " thanks " for " benefits " received, through the simple *service for which* I received them,—through my artistic activity in Dresden : whether this then was a — — ? etc., etc.—

Only I have no inclination any longer for these stale wares : it may be otherwise with those who are in the thick of it ; but then they are merely fine Dresden " friends."—

—Schindelmeisser (who will produce *Tannhäuser* on the 13th November, for the first time) causes me great joy : my Guide has had a splendid effect on him, and I believe his performance will be a really good one. He writes me—that he is " amazed " at this music, and cannot find expressions of "rapture" sufficient to describe the revolution which is taking place in him.

You will have received the Michaelson commissions :
be prepared to receive an order from Freiburg in
Breisgau.   For there are desperate enthusiasts of mine
there.   *Apropos !* If one could keep a strict eye on
the whining X. : from time to time I hear of an already
very wide circulation of my pianoforte scores !   That
the fellow always says he has made no money out of
it, really makes me somewhat suspicious.   My creditors
deserve a good hiding, if they do not keep X. under
control : I can do no more in the matter !—

Brendel's *Zeitschrift* becomes more and more
delightful !   Tell me, how can you get consent to
your articles being always so cut asunder ?   With
the last choice reading it was a regular mess !—How
can anything have effect that way ?   Even the " Programme" article he completely mutilated by this
dividing and interrupting !   I was really sorry that you
did not take Gumbrecht to task for his explanation of
the A-major Symphony.—

—Your " *Characteristik* " has pleased me very much,
although it was in fugue style ; this will set your back
up, for that you make your strong point !   But I no
longer understand anything about fugue : it is no longer
point d'honneur with me, *in itself* it is distasteful to
me.   It was the musical life, the expression itself,
which pleased me most in your composition.   I cannot
say this to you properly.—

Franz has sent me his *Lieder ;* as yet I have not
looked at them, but I am promising myself great
pleasure when I do.—Please give him best greetings
from me when you write.—

It is astonishing to me how quiet Brendel keeps over

the Leipzig *Tannhäuser* affair : yet this is an occasion in which one could thoroughly expose the whole miserable-ness of the Leipzig music-makers' guild. Härtels wrote to me in great concern : the director, etc., had declared that my operas contained insoluble difficulties, and " there were the same complaints " (so said W.) " from most of the theatres."—Nice sort of fellows !— —

Well, my soda-water machine is splendid : so, I am satisfied with it!—With the little estate, it stands so—so ! I am no longer thinking of purchasing (and indeed for many reasons) : but I would willingly take on hire, for a fairly long time, a pretty country house with a nice large garden. I am on the look-out for it, but can't find anything suitable as yet. But I won't give up, and hope next summer to be able to offer good shelter to my guests.

Your packet (the great letter) has just come ; I will send for it to the post-office, and then conclude.

———

I have read your letter, and thank you heartily.

I do not find much to answer, and as it is twelve o'clock, and writing of an afternoon is impossible to me, I will only add a few brief lines by way of close, so that it may go off to-day. The *Alcibiades* I will read through in the evening.—The news about your health is welcome, and welcome as only it can be. Think above all of *leave of absence* and the Swiss journey. Härtels have not yet answered about *Iphigenia* (the revised copy of the score is the one belonging to the Dresden Theatre).—With regard to the *Tannhäuser* news, I begin to be struck with admiration at L.'s revolutionary position : it really needs a sort of—love

of the thing, to oppose such a storm.   That the kernel
of the matter will be brought out on this occasion,
makes this Dresden "event" gradually interesting to
me.   The ways of Providence are indeed wonderful!—
Your vouchers, my good fellow, will not be looked
at!—Farewell!   Greetings to the wife!

Your
R. W.

Zurich, *November* 10*th*, '52.

89.

Dear Friend!

The postman comes every morning about
eleven o'clock; I generally work from nine o'clock
up to this time, and when the letters arrive I am
already somewhat exhausted and in need of rest.
So is it to-day, when I have just received your
last letter.   Now, each time I am placed in the
dilemma, of either not answering at all, or—of doing
this as briefly as possible.   If I put it off, the same
thing occurs each next day; unless I gave up my work
for a whole morning, as happens when I make up my
mind to write a longish letter.   (Only under extreme
necessity do I write a single line between twelve o'clock
and bed-time.)   I explain this to you once for all, so
that you may explain to yourself why I write briefly
to you when I answer by return, which I am always
glad to do, so as to get rid of what requires answering
and to induce you to keep our correspondence going.

Not to forget small matters, I will think of them
at once.   Mosevius sent me his article *cut out* of the
paper, so that I do not know where it really comes
from: he only told me it was in a Breslau *Conservative*

paper. (The article in itself is, after all, of no great importance, but it becomes interesting through bearing the signature of Mosevius.)—Fabulous news has lately reached me from Breslau : Michaelson wrote a little time ago, of eight performances having taken place there to overflowing houses : now Frau Moritz announces to me (from Wiesbaden) that a friend has just written to her from Breslau that in a little over four weeks *Tannhäuser* had been given there twelve times, and always to crowded houses. Is this really *possible ?*

There was a famous success on the 13th inst. at Wiesbaden. Schindelmeisser had already written to me beforehand (at the same time also about *Lohengrin*) that it was no longer possible to repress the enthusiasm of the singers and of the orchestra, at the rehearsals. From all this I gather that Schindelmeisser's study was beyond all praise. Both he and Frau Moritz tell me of an unprecedented *furore* after the performance. (Perhaps you have already read something about it in the Frankfort papers ?) I pass over individual details to which this "*furore*" bears witness : above all I rejoice at Schindelmeisser himself (formerly stirred up against me by R.).

After the success merely of the rehearsals, he had resolved on *Lohengrin*. Frau Moritz assures me the precision was unsurpassable. The railway brought many friends from Cologne (Bischoff !!), Mainz, Frankfort, Darmstadt, etc. The factotum of the Munich Intendant was there, with instructions to at once send home news. In any case Munich will soon give *Tannhäuser.*—

You did quite right about Stuttgart.—*Tannhäuser*

will be given at Frankfort in December : but I have
not yet got the honorarium : I am daily in expectation
of a letter from Hofmann.—

H.'s wrote to me lately (in answer to my offer of the
Iphigenia and the *Faust* Overture for publication): they
were very much out of sorts and discouraged by my
behaviour, as I always made it so difficult and almost
impossible for the theatres to give my operas : my deal-
ings with regard to Leipzig were far too tyrannical, my
demands for mounting the works too inconsiderate, etc.
—Thereupon I spared no pains to put before them in
detail my whole intercourse with W., Rietz, etc.,
and to show them how, on the one hand, W.'s
shabbiness in the matter of payment, on the other
hand Rietz's evident disinclination to submit to my
purely artistic demands, were the sole causes of the
rupture, which for the rest was a *solitary* exception :
whereas even the smallest theatres continued to stand
on the best footing with me, etc., etc., etc. Finally
I said to them that, through the easy credence
which they gave to a man known throughout the town
as a liar, they appeared to have fallen into so fatal
a frame of mind towards my works that I did not
wish to disturb it by any further requests, and therefore
—withdrew my offers. I shall not get very far with
these Philistines : they have no conception whatever
of the position and future of my works. Besides I
have so spoilt them by my—almost no—honorarium-
demands, that they are now naïve enough to imagine
that they would never have anything more to pay me
than, perhaps, a tiny honorarium-pittance !—

I must write to L. about *Lohengrin* as soon as I

know anything definite. (I never *presented* my opera to him : that I never did so, was just what annoyed him, as my policy always consisted in leaving *him* to approach *me*. I only agreed to sell him the copy, should he ever desire to produce *Lohengrin*.) Naturally I have no intention of appealing to the law-courts in this matter.—

Well—I must stop : my head is getting bad.—What I have forgotten I will make up another time. Come, have you not forgotten my admonition respecting the X. publishing affair ? Or ought I no longer to burden you with such matters (owing to your unfortunate state of health) ? Be candid ! But, above all, think about the *long leave of absence* for next summer ! If everything goes well and according to my desire, I can receive you in a magnificent garden and country-house.—

The Musical Society in Utrecht (Holland) has been the first to reply to my last notice in the *Neue Zeitschrift für Musik*.—The article on *Tannhäuser* from Dresden is really good : who then is the writer ?—

I am now working at *Young Siegfried*. I shall soon have finished it. Then I attack *Siegfried's Death*—this will take me longer : I have two scenes in it to write afresh (the Norns and the scene of Brynhilde with the Valkyries), and above all the close : beside these, everything needs most important revision. The whole will then be—out with it ! I am impudent enough to say it—the greatest poem ever written !—

About my health another time : I am obliged to avoid all fatigue, that of excessive walking also : only in luxurious comfort can this artificial man,

myself, now prosper ; who knows—if I completely shift
the saddle, if I quite forswear my youth, and consciously adopt a brand-new rule of life, perhaps I shall
see my way to a little further existence. (Leave
sophistries and polemics alone ! Hope—in me !)
    Good-bye !

Your Nibelungen prince,
ALBERICH.

(I will tell you something amusing about Munich
next time.)

90.

Do you know that the revival of *Tannhäuser* at
Dresden has had quite an uncomfortable effect on me ?
From all my information, I am convinced that *even now
Tannhäuser* has won no right and genuine success in
Dresden. Do you remember that of old *Tannhäuser*
only drew a full house when it had not been given for
some time, whereas the theatre was always but thinly
filled when it was repeated at short intervals ? I then
saw from this that the opera was like an extraordinary
riddle to the public, to the solution of which they felt
impelled by curiosity ; but that it always caused a certain unpleasant effect—which scared them away when,
after renewed attempts, it remained unsolved. The chief
blame for this, I maintain, lies in the defects of the
performance, already censured by me : the *real Tannhäuser* is not made manifest at all, no sympathy is
aroused for it. But if they have a *presentiment* of the
significance of " *Tannhäuser*," our good Dresden folk
find it, of necessity, hazardous to have anything to do

with it.—All this rose up again before me when I learnt from you that the *second* performance was by no means over-crowded. But now I read (by chance) in a notice (certainly unintelligent and unfavourable) in the Hamburg theatrical paper, that the unprecedented interest of the public in the first performance proceeded from the expectation that some scandal might take place : at least this may explain why the succeeding performances were by no means so well attended.—I stick to my opinion : I am right ! This Dresden, had I remained in it, would have become the grave of my art ! What, on the other hand, shall I say about Weimar, Schwerin, Breslau, and Wiesbaden ? Everywhere the *first* performance at once hit home, which has *certainly not* happened in Dresden. Seydelmann wrote to me lately that—in spite of many interruptions through illness—they had, up to the previous Sunday, given *Tannhäuser* eleven times, and always to full houses and with like applause.—This much is certain : I have a presentiment that Dresden will now *do harm* to my *Lohengrin*, if it comes out there : I shall therefore try all means to prevent it, as soon as I hear anything *for certain*.

In general, I begin to be afraid of performances in *chief* towns. I shall never find such goodwill there as in the smaller towns, especially not among self !-opera-composing Capellmeisters. Do you really know what happened with the *Tannhäuser* Overture in Munich ? The applause was " very divided." But I must tell you a joke from there. I had sent the Programme to Lachner, and had received no answer : after I had read about the performance, I reminded him of it. Then I got for answer that they had not ventured to make known

the Programme, but that they had added the following notice to the concert-programme : " Holy, serene
frame of mind! Night draws on—The passions are
aroused—The spirit fights against them—Daybreak—
Final victory over matter—Prayer—Song of triumph,"
consequently—they now say—I can rest assured that
my composition was completely " understood." (Is that
not delicious ?)

Liszt's remark about the " *Faust* Overture " was as
follows : he missed a second theme, which should more
plastically represent " Gretchen," and therefore wished
to see either such an one added, or the second theme
of the overture modified. This was a thoroughly refined
and correct expression of feeling from *him*, to whom
I had submitted the composition as an " Overture to
the first part of Goethe's *Faust*." So I was obliged
to answer him that he had beautifully caught me in
a lie, when (without thought) I tried to make myself
or him believe that I had written such an overture.
But he would quickly understand me if I were to entitle
the composition " *Faust in Solitude*." In fact, with
this tone-poem I only had in my mind the first movement of a *Faust* Symphony : here Faust is the subject,
and *woman* hovers before him only as an indefinite,
shapeless object of his yearning ; as such, intangible
and unattainable. Hence his despair, his curse on
all the torturing semblance of the beautiful, his head-
long plunge into the mad smart of sorcery. The
manifestation of the woman was only to take place in
the second part ; this would have Gretchen for its subject, just as the first part, Faust. Already I had theme
and mood for it :—then—I gave the whole up, and—

true to my nature—set to work at the *Flying Dutchman*, with which I escaped from all the mist of instrumental music, into the clearness of the drama.—However, that composition is still not uninteresting to me ; only, if one day I should publish it, it would have to be under the title : "*Faust in Solitude*," *a tone-poem*. (Curiously enough, I had already resolved upon this "*tone-poem*" when you made so merry over that name—with which, however, I was forced to make shift for this occasion.)

November 27*th*, '52.

December 6*th*.

You see by the accompanying how I waited every day for a letter from you : at last I was in dreadful torment—for naturally I felt obliged to account for everything by an aggravation of your illness. My joy was indescribable on receiving to-day a letter in your handwriting ; but how sad the contents have made me ! Poor friend, you are suffering so much, and I cannot help you at all, nor relieve you in any way ! It was certainly a great strain for you, even to write to me : have you no one near you who would give me more frequent news of your state ? I have already begged Frau R. to do so. I cannot bear that you should in any way be disturbed now about my affairs, and I therefore request you to hand over the whole theatre-score-business to old Fischer. Yet I will not write to him until I know from you that you are willing to give up the matter *for the present :* but if you feel that it is necessary for you to be rid of these cares, only send by hand the *Tannhäuser* and the *Dutchman* to Fischer, and tell him why I (and you) ask him.—

For the moment I know nothing else that I could

consider fitting to write, however great my inclination
to chatter to you.   My inmost sympathy with your
suffering state makes everything beside appear by far
too unessential.   Ah, were I only near you, to see, to
help, or at least to be able to cheer you !   You are
certainly in a terribly critical state, which you can
only make bearable by the best of spirits and complete
tranquillity of mind.

I must keep from all inquiries as to the principal seat
of your malady, and yet I would so like to have a
clear idea about it.   Could you not prevail upon your
physician to give me a friendly word of information ?
Ah God ! the more I write to you the more I feel how
necessary it is above all to learn something further from
you first !   Now, I can only say to you : Keep firm, have
a good courage, and as soon as you are well again take
care not to exert yourself so much, even by running, as
you did last summer : I also must give up everything
forced !   Hold on till next summer : if I once get you
again here we will put you all right again.   Hearty
greetings to wife and children, and especially to our
Siegfried !   Courage ! Courage ! this is the deep, sympathetic cry of

Your friend,
RICHARD.

The *Flying Dutchman* is to be sent to Breslau—that
is, if they *now* ask for it again—for it has my sanction.

91.

MY DEAR OLD FRIEND !

You cause me terrible anxiety, and especially as
I so seldom receive news from you.   Frau R.—whom

I thank most heartily—wrote to me about a fortnight ago in somewhat comforting terms : what would I not have given, not to have been again compelled to wait so long ! Above all, I do not know *whether* and *what* I I ought to write to you. That you are now fearfully weak is too evident : does this weakness only interfere with your writing, or does it fatigue you also if your mind is in any way unsettled by news received from any quarter ? It is just *this* which makes me so uncertain, and makes every encroachment upon you, in your present state, appear almost a crime ; so that I always hesitate when I would fain begin a letter, and prefer to wait until I have received news from you. Now, especially on this point (namely, whether excitement by communication with the outer world, and particularly letters, are hurtful to you ?)—if you yourself are still too weak—let me have definite information through some person or other of your surrounding, perhaps your good wife or Dr. Schulze. With the above-mentioned fear, I feel almost disposed to write you nothing further beyond *this request.*

So you do not appear as yet to have given up business matters ! So then, *I must*—in obedience to your wishes—address myself to *you* with the news that I have written to Weimar, and much wish that, besides the arranged copy of the *Flying Dutchman* to be sent *as soon as possible* to Breslau, a *second* ditto be forwarded to Schwerin.—But I beseech you, if looking after these matters is in the least harmful to you, to give up *everything* at once to old Fischer.—

Try, you good, dear friend, to recover your strength right soon. When you are once more fresh and joyful, you shall rejoice also over *my Siegfried,* for it is now ready.

I am after all fairly well. But you——

Let me quickly have an answer to my question above : otherwise I know not whether with every line I compel you to read I am doing you harm !

I hope you are able to **sleep** now. This is above all the *most heartfelt wish* of your

RICHARD WAGNER.

December 23rd, '52.

92.

MY DEAR FRIEND !

Ascribe it to the too great obstinacy of your friendship, if I must again worry you to-day. The Schwerin Theatre has just written in the most pressing manner for the score of the *Dutchman.* I must therefore implore you, as soon so you have the Weimar music-score, at once to get 2 (two) copies arranged, of which the *first* is naturally to be sent to Breslau, but the second as quickly as possible (without previous notice from me) to Schwerin, addressed to the Court Theatre there.——

You see, dear friend, you have brought this on yourself ! ! ! !

Only rejoice me soon with consoling news of your improvement ! With deepest sympathy,

Your

R. W.

ZURICH, *December 24th,* '52.

LETTERS

WILHELM FISCHER,

1841—1859.

LETTERS

TO

WILHELM FISCHER,

1841—1859.

I.

MOST HONOURED SIR,

I well must doubt, that you will recollect my unimportant self at the time when, as a young man, I first devoted myself with wild enthusiasm to music, but nevertheless had already enough intelligence to be able to appreciate your efforts as choir-master at the Leipzig Theatre. Once since then have I had an opportunity of admiring the fruits of your diligence and of your extraordinary address : this was at a peformance of *La Juive* in Dresden. After that, I heard this opera in Paris, and while noticing the difference between the Dresden and the Paris chorus, I could not help thinking of you ; although it made me sorry for the Paris Opera, which did not show to advantage in this comparison.

Chance and good-fortune have so willed, that I should be placed in the position to lay claim to your valuable services to my own advantage.

The general management of the Dresden Theatre

has lately notified to me the definite acceptance of an opera, *Rienzi*, which I had sent in, and I have been assured that it will be produced as speedily as possible. Through one of my friends I know that you—unsolicited by me—have shown a friendly interest in my plans and wishes, and as I am assured that your own vote was recorded on the question of accepting my opera, so, by the favourable result, I have to flatter myself that your decision was not hostile to me. From all these premisses, I have to esteem myself truly fortunate in now being able with confidence to sue for your kind protection. Although the opera, in whose auspicious "birth" yourself will take so great and important a part, is not my first-fruits; although the style and fashion of its ruling conception of dramatic music I only finally decided on after many an attempt in other fashions; and although I feel compelled to protest against the opinion, naturally prevalent in consequence of the obscurity of my name, that in *Rienzi* I am making my first appearance with a first attempt: still I shall be more than blind and presumptuous, did I not of my own accord call attention, in advance, to the fact that I count first on indulgence in the judgment of my work. In this sense I approach you, most honoured sir, when I declare that, during my five years' practice as music-director, I became most thoroughly convinced of the preponderance that practical knowledge gives to judgment, and therefore confidently place myself in your hands, as your many-sided experience must be acknowledged by all. With regard to the many difficulties which, perhaps not without displeasure, you will have to encounter in rehearsing my opera, be assured beforehand—I implore you—of the fullest and heartiest thanks which any one so convinced as I am of the greatness of the obligation can offer in payment.—My special views with regard to the distribution of the choir in separate divisions, etc., I will communicate to you shortly; you will kindly make use of any suggestions which you find practical, while in everything which runs counter to your own much riper views I, as a matter of course, entirely give way to you.

May I succeed in preserving your interest and gaining your respect! Be assured that neither would be the humblest reward to which, in my present purpose, I eagerly look forward!—

With most sincere respect and devotion,

Your deeply obliged servant,

RICHARD WAGNER.

PARIS, *September 7th,* '41.

2.

MOST HONOURED SIR,

In the hope that the few lines have reached you which I enclosed about a month ago in a letter to Herr Heine, I take the liberty of addressing you again, and this time, indeed, with a more circumstantial request to grant me your kind interest, as well as your powerful assistance. A large portion of my future lies in your hands and in those of Capellmeister Reissiger: they are the best hands, as far as power is concerned, and the only point is to be sure of your good-will: it is my study to woo its very core—but, as in this wooing I cannot possibly rely on merit, I hope to succeed simply by begging you right heartily for indulgence. My request can, therefore, be most briefly expressed— it is : *indulgence and patience.*

—Most honoured sir, I place my whole trust in the high character for truth and uprightness accorded you by all; not because I can venture to count on any recognition of my merit, but because true kindness and *bonhommie* can but be considered inseparable from a character such as yours. If you, therefore, can rest assured that I, for my part, will place implicit trust in you, that with all confidence I look forward to the fulfilment by you of a great part of my best hopes, then I think I may be certain of your kind indulgence and interest. Assuming this, allow me now, once again, to return to the object of my hopes, in greater detail than was last time the case. In a letter from Councillor Winkler I am assured that Herr von Lüttichau has also given his consent to my opera being put in rehearsal immediately after the production of Reissiger's new work.

To my very great joy, I see then in this resolution the earnest determination to carry out the promise given to me, and nothing remains for me but to commend myself and my wishes with regard to the forthcoming performance to those on whom depends its fate. At first I intended to put on paper my wishes and ideas respecting the cast and the settling of some debatable particulars in my opera, so as to place them before you and Herr Capellmeister Reissiger. But I soon found that I should cause you quite unnecessary trouble in asking you to read through this little *Promemoriâ :* since, firstly, through the disadvantage of not being on the spot, I should have been compelled to express my views in a very problematical and uncertain manner ; and, finally, I should only have discussed at length certain things which your insight would be in the position to arrange for the best at the very first glance.

I cannot deny that the difficulties, scenic and musical, connected with the production of my opera are great ; and to my regret I see, most honoured sir, that I am loading you, as stage-manager and chorus-master, with a heavy piece of work. It is, however, my consolation to know with what promptitude and activity you are accustomed to solve problems of perhaps greater difficulty. It, therefore, only comes to this—whether you enter upon the task with pleasure or the reverse. My opera may well be not altogether calculated to give you pleasure ; and that, most esteemed sir, is, therefore, the point where I must exclusively rely on your indulgence. Perhaps, however, the consideration that you have on your hands the work of a composer who is also a countryman of yours may inspire you with some sort of affection for the matter ;—perhaps, too, with your practised eye, you may see here and there many a part which might gain in effect by being duly brought to light, and the pleasure aroused by such an endeavour may gradually waken pleasure in my work itself.

I spoke just now of difficulties. One of the greatest of these I consider to be the skilful division of the male chorus into the separate parties of Nobles and Plebeians. As I do not know the present strength of the Dresden choir, I can make no suggestions in the matter. The task is to make the Nobles—who in the first part of the opening of the First Act are themselves divided into two groups—sufficiently strong, without thereby robbing the People's chorus of its due strength. In this, as in many other similar points, I much prefer to trust entirely to your judgment, and am convinced that that is the best thing I could do.

The choruses which are sung behind the stage—viz., the chorus in the Lateran (First Act), and the small chorus : *Væ tibi maledicto* (Fourth Act)—will probably have to be sung by the *Kreuzschule* choir : at least, in planning these scenes I counted specially on this means for carrying them out, as the first chorus must have an imposing body of voices, which would be quite impossible were the theatre-choir divided.

The great tragic pantomime in the finale of the Second Act presents another difficulty. According to my views, the principal personages of the same—Lucretia, Brutus, Tarquinius, and Collatinus—can only be represented by members of the comedy staff who are accustomed to sustain similar parts in spoken drama. The carrying out of this, my wish, will no doubt encounter difficulties and obstacles—therefore, most honoured sir, I lay this matter to your heart, and earnestly implore you to use all your influence so 'that my request, at any rate in its essentials, may be fulfilled.

From among many other things which might appear to me worthy of further mention, I will refer only to the chorus of the " Messengers of Peace," at the beginning of the Second Act. As this is by no means an easy chorus to sing with pure intonation, naturally only the most musical and the best-voiced members of the female choir ought to be selected. The good repute of the Dresden choir leads me to suppose that their number will not be found too small. Nevertheless, it is scarcely to be expected that an unaccompanied chorus can be sung to the end without falling somewhat in pitch ! It would, therefore, be advisable to take measures to support the tone-pitch now and then from the slips ; and this, in my opinion, could best be done if a skilled accompanist undertook to support the voices from time to time on a chamber-organ placed some little distance back.

Good heavens ! I perceive that if I continue in this manner I shall finally rummage out the whole of my foolish stock of wisdom in bespeaking my whims. But I should necessarily weary you, and of all things in the world I would avoid this, as I have too great need of your good-humour.—If you are disposed to make me supremely happy, you will do me the great kindness to honour me with a few lines very soon ; be assured that I shall know how to value such a mark of distinction most thankfully.

In any event, I commend myself to your kind good-will, and once more to your indulgence, as your most obedient servant,

RICHARD WAGNER,

No. 3, *Avenue de Meudon à Meudon près Paris.*

MEUDON, *October* 14*th*, '41.

P.S.—If your affairs will allow of your writing to me before the 25th of this month, your esteemed letter will reach me addressed as above. *After* that date, however, I would beg you to send it to the following address :—*No.* 14, *Rue Jacob à Paris.*

3.

HIGHLY ESTEEMED SIR,

Yesterday, the 7th inst., I received by post from Nancy your kind letter, which, from its contents, ought to have reached me through Herr Leury : probably this gentleman stopped there, and so posted on the letter.

With this preface I now hasten to offer you my cordial thanks for the great interest and forbearance displayed in your honoured lines. Pray be assured that I have been truly refreshed thereby, and that I clearly perceive how great will be my future obligation to you. The hopeful view which you take of my work gives me immense comfort, and I cling to it with all the greater trust, coming as it does from you, a man universally recognized as honest and outspoken. I am also indebted to you for the careful manner in which you have pointed out the disparities and uncertainties that lie in the way of realizing my purpose : by this I am fully convinced of your sympathy, and assure you that I feel under double obligation to you. As this, however, is the point on which you desire especially—and, indeed, in my own interest—a more circumstantial reply, I permit myself to devote the principal contents of these lines thereto.

I hope that Herr Heine will shortly impart to you several passages from my last letter to him, which were principally intended for you, most honoured sir. They concerned the difference which exists between your estimate of the time which my opera takes in performance, and that which I have arrived at after recent calculations. Herr Heine wrote me that you reckon it at five hours,

while I put it at four.   I much wish that you had known
this before you commenced your letter to me, because it
would naturally have greatly influenced your views as to
the shortening of my opera, and perhaps have effected a
change in them in many respects.   Now, if I set about
writing once more in detail on this point, I am obliged
to place in the forefront this observation of mine concerning the playing length ; for I reckon it a piece of
good-fortune to have won the conviction that you have
been led into a not unimportant, though easily account-
able, error.   For otherwise, should your estimate prove
correct, I should not know how to set about shortening
my opera by a whole hour.

Most honoured sir and well-wisher, if we now *agree*
that a performance of my *Rienzi* (not, of course, counting
entr'actes) in its present form, would last four hours, then
a chief cause of apprehension is at once removed, viz.,
that my opera would play much longer than, among
other works, *Les Huguenots*.   But should we have
succeeded in imparting such interest to the dramatic
progress in the action of my opera, that there were no
danger of the audience becoming weary, I might perhaps
venture to assume that in my *Rienzi* this sympathy with
the progress of the action would outweigh the certainly
somewhat higher artistic interest that, for example, keeps
the public awake in the last Act of *The Huguenots*.   A
glance at the compass of the various Acts of my score
will, however, show you that the last Act—the one
which in long operas is always a source of fear—is
almost disproportionately shorter than the others—a
circumstance which we certainly should take into
account.—(Pray do not think that I mention this because

I am under the foolish illusion that it is here a question of talking you over to my interest; on the contrary, I know how amiably disposed you are towards me, and it can therefore only be my intention to come to a clear understanding of the matter by a mutual exchange of our ideas.—I consider this remark necessary, because I should be most disconcerted if you thought you must attribute so incorrect a motive to my objections—and so I proceed :—)

From the passage in your valued letter in which you say that, feeling the great length of the numbers, you tried to make cuts, but could never find the suitable place where this could be effected, I perceive more than ever that it is not individual lengthiness—too wide expansion—repetitions, or superfluous embellishments, that you complain of in my behalf, but only the excessive length of the whole. While on this point, I must tell you that during composition I found myself compelled, by a survey of the proportions of my subject, to refrain from certain *purely musical* amplifications, even where they would perhaps have been of good effect. To make myself clearer, I instance the first choral passage at the commencement of the first *finale :* " Gegrüsst, sei hoher Tag "; did not the subject here provide a good opportunity for an elaborate chorus of exultation ? In the *finale* of the Second Act, the scene in which sentence is passed on the nobles—what material for a grand *ensemble?* In the Fourth Act, where Rienzi approaches the church, and, amid the muffled chants, perceives the proclamation of excommunication—the conspirators in a state of indecision—Adriano struggling with his better self—the horror-stricken crowd—what use could not I

have made of all this to write one of those grand *finales?*
In fact, it cost me here considerable self-restraint to keep
from broader musical development; and I think you
also will have seen that I never protracted a situation;
that, on the contrary, I the rather felt compelled to pass
swiftly from one to the other. All the more necessary
was it, therefore, for me to express myself in a purely
musical way in those important *finale* sections that were
demanded by the situation; and the two *adagio* movements of the second and third *finales*, as well as the
rushing concluding passages of the same, demanded
throughout a more detailed treatment, in order to
restore the stream of music to its rights.

From that passage in your letter I now conclude that
you have felt with me, that of actual long-windedness
(protractions, and repetitions easy to strike out)—I say
this almost with *regret*—there is not much to be found,—
" with regret," because I see how difficult the business
of shortening is thereby made.—Believe me, I would
far rather you had sternly pointed out to me extensions
and repetitions of this sort, and that I had nothing
further to do than readily to follow your suggestions.

Meanwhile, let us look at the matter for a moment
from the other side. Is a duration of four hours, with
a lively and uninterrupted action, really so unbearable,
especially when there are no spun-out passages to
complain of ?—Still, here and there, there will be something to strike out, and I myself make some proposals
concerning this upon the enclosed sheet;—further, as on
the whole I perceive the pantomime and ballet will have
to be considerably shortened, whereby again some time
will be saved. And then—quite frankly: have your

operas **never** played up to 10.15 or 10.30?? I fancy *La Juive* can scarcely have lasted less time.

Now to something else. My proposals for the dividing of the choir are also to be found on the enclosed sheet. It is a great pity that I counted on the co-operation of the *Kreuzschule* pupils; is there then no other largish choir whose services could be secured, if only for the church-chorus in the First Act? I fancied I had read about such a choral union.

Concerning the pantomime and the ballet, you make me most anxious; at any rate, rather than present both in an utterly inadequate way, it were better to curtail them considerably. Is Dresden then really so badly off in this respect? I keep coming back to *La Juive*, for this is the only modern opera of which I have a distinct remembrance: I saw it there in the summer of 1837, and confess that I found the by no means insignificant ballet anything but bad, whether as regards arrangement or execution. Also in *Les Huguenots*, I hear, one misses nothing, and everything is well cared for.—The pantomime, of course, must be entirely left out, if players of importance do not undertake the three principal *rôles* in it. I will write in a few days to the general management, and see if it be possible by its means to induce the comedians in question to take part in my pantomime. If this cannot be managed, the pantomime, as I said, must be left out, and my suggestions in view of this and other events I have set down on the enclosed *pro memoriâ*.

In calling your attention to this document, I mention here once more, that in it I have indicated everything which could in any case be cut, but that this concerns only short passages, which, in truth, would not much diminish the playing length of my opera. On the other hand, I leave to you and Herr Reissiger to cut out whole-sale whatever may be cut without *decided* injury—*i.e.*, **long-windedness**, wherever you may find it. *I*, for my part, am the most incapable person, and at the same time the most prejudiced in a matter of this kind, and I think I cannot do better than once again lay this matter to your heart.

For the rest, pray do whatever you can to hurry the thing on. Nothing is yet copied out; whenever, then, will it be given out for study? This will certainly take up some time, for I know well how many difficulties there are in my opera! Must it really be put off for so long? As it seems now that *Emma de Vergey* and other Italian operas must be taken up again, cannot *Guitarrero* wait till after *Rienzi?* At all events, get the music copied at once, so that the singers can at least have their parts; long passages need not yet be cut out, and the smaller omissions, which are often settled at the vocal rehearsals, can easily be marked. Well, I trust entirely to your goodness.

The enclosed small sheet contains, then, the little *pro memoriâ* I mentioned: I have written it apart so that you may make use of it at your discretion—*e.g.*, com-municate it to Herr Reissiger. How I wish you would make the sacrifice of writing to me soon again, to say what you think of my proposals and what you have settled in my affair! I earnestly beg, as the whole affair is so entirely in my interest, that you will send your kind letter unfranked; however, that scarcely needs saying.

Once more my heartiest, deepest thanks for your valued letter, for your kindness and friendly intentions : I shall never cease endeavouring to show myself worthy of your notice. With the request that you will give heartiest greetings to Herr Heine from me, and that you will continue to me your invaluable friendship, I commend myself to you with deep respect and thanks, as

Your most devoted servant,

RICHARD WAGNER.

PARIS (14, RUE JACOB), *December 8th*, '41.

1. *Suggestions respecting the Cast.*

Rienzi, Hr. Tichatschek ; *Adriano,* Mad. Schröder-Devrient ; *Irene,* Dlle. Wüst ; *Steffano Colonna*—I should prefer a certain Hr. Zezi for this part (is this feasible ?) ; *Orsini,* Hr. Wächter ; *Cecco del Vecchio,* Hr. Risse ; *Baroncelli,* Hr. Schuster ; *Cardinal* (*Filippo de Gardia*), Hr. Vestri ; *Messenger of Peace,* Mad. Hellwig (I do not, however, know her ; is her voice flexible and fresh ?). It is impossible for me to cast the subordinate parts, as I am at present quite unacquainted with this portion of the *personnel ;* so I leave it entirely to the judgment of the management.—

2. *Suggestions respecting the Distribution of the Choir, etc.*

Act 1. No. 1. *Introduction.*—Followers of Colonna and Orsini, eight singers to each part ; People's chorus, 22 men. Very good !—After the followers of the Nobles have left the stage, they will have plenty of time to change their dress (perhaps by simply throwing on a cloak), and reinforce the chorus of the People, with which the introduction *concludes*, and in which male voices predominate.

No. 4. *Finale.*—If it is impossible to employ a special choir of singers for the chorus in the Lateran Church— " Erwacht, ihr Schläfer "—there are only two ways out of the difficulty. *Either:* The chorus of the People— " Gegrüsst sei, hoher Tag "—must be sung on the stage by only 22 men and 12 women, whereas the crowd of People would have to be considerably reinforced by figurants and supernumeraries. Sixteen men and 10 women would then sing the chorus in the Lateran ; at the passage, " Seht wie er glänzt," where the musical structure of this chorus is divided into two parts, the five voices that enter one after the other as *soli* must be doubled, and the remainder would have to sing the sustained notes. These singers would then, of course, rejoin the choir on the stage as quickly as possible. But as the female voices would be the weaker in number, the singer of the Messenger of Peace, and perhaps one other female soloist not engaged in this opera, might kindly consent to strengthen them.— *Or :* The *whole* choir of male and female singers must first appear on the stage to sing the chorus, " Gegrüsst sei, hoher Tag." Then during the somewhat long organ prelude, 18 men and 18 ladies would withdraw from the stage, to sing the church chorus from behind the scene. Considering the great amount of movement on the stage, this could easily be concealed by imperceptibly replacing the departing men by an equal number of supernumeraries, and the ladies by as many figurants. This might be arranged by any device of suitable grouping (the People here should fall on their knees) ; besides, one could suppose the crowd were moving to and fro, etc. Naturally, the principal thing is for the stage not to be left too empty. In this case I would add a short organ prelude, so that the singers who had gone off would have time to get back to the stage for the choral passage, "Rienzi! Rienzi!" The figurants who had for the time replaced them would still remain on the stage, and, by the advent of the returning choristers, the whole would gain the appearance as if the mass of the people were continually increasing. This way of arranging the matter would be *most to my liking*.

Act 2. No. 6.—*Terzett and Chorus* of Nobles : 16 good singers.

No. 7. *Finale*.—The first chorus is to be sung by the whole *personnel*, with all the reinforcement possible,— the Nobles, of course, not to be placed in the front.

In any case, the *ambassadors* must be represented by figurants. It will be the task of the costume-designer to distinguish each ambassador as much as possible from the rest, by the dress and other insignia. Each of these ambassadors must have a small following of heralds, etc., and their train be made as brilliant as possible ; each of them presents himself to Rienzi, and hands him a scroll ; thereby the march might well be given entire, but if the music is too long, the 24 bars in G-major could be omitted.

If the *pantomime* must be entirely cut out, there would only then remain the Warriors' dance, in F-major 2/4, to be performed in old Roman costume ; the combat of the Cavaliers, in mediæval dress ; the appearance of the Goddess of Peace, accompanied by maidens, some in ancient, some in mediæval attire ; and the last great ballet, as a festival *ensemble*-dance, illustrating the union of ancient and modern Rome, with the final unfurling and blessing of the banners (white and blue, with silver stars). The Warriors' dance, for men only, will cause no difficulty. I remember formerly having seen a similar dance in *Jessonda* performed in excellent style by the soldiers quartered at Dresden. I can wish for nothing better than something like that. The concluding *ensemble*-dance would consist, for the most part, of a sort of chain-dance ; the *première danseuse* would, however, have an opportunity of showing herself.—I should assign to her the passage in 6/8 time G-major, and that in 3/4 time C-major to the two solo dancers.

The bass passage, *Misereat dominum*, can be sung by the Nobles themselves behind the dropped curtain ; for the *Monks* are only seen when they have nothing more to sing, and so can be represented by supernumeraries.

During the *Finale*, 16 Nobles, 22 men for the People, as before.

Act 3. No. 8. *Introduction.*—Full male chorus, with auxiliaries.

No. 10. *Finale. War Hymn.*—The men-at-arms are, for the most part, to be represented by figurants, and perhaps only 22 singers should be employed here, so that at least 16 may remain for the Priests (or, on account of the censorship, aged Citizens past service in the field), who naturally will join in the hymn ; for they accompany the military procession as it leaves the stage, and afterwards return with it, so as to sing with the women the small chorus, " Willkommen, Roms siegreiche

Söhne," in which the Warriors naturally take no part, although it would not be very remarkable even if some out of the military procession were to strengthen the above-named passage.

Act 4. No. 11. *Terzett and Chorus.*—For the Conspirators, the 22 theatre-choristers.

No. 12. *Finale.*—In the procession the men are only to be represented by figurants and supernumeraries. Song of the Priests in the interior of the church, " *Væ, væ, tibi maledicto:* " all the basses of the auxiliary choir. The passage for the Cardinal, " Zurück, dem Reinen nur," to be strengthened by these.

Act. 5. No. 16. *Finale.*—Chorus of the People : the whole of the theatre-choristers, with auxiliaries. The final group of advancing Nobles to be represented only by figurants.

3. *Suggestions for Cuts.*

Act 2. No. 5. *Introduction.*—Prelude to the chorus of the Messengers of Peace :—After the thirtieth bar from the commencement, the next 27 bars can be left out : the song would then only begin with, " Ihr Römer hört die Kunde."—If, on the repetition of this chorus, while the Messengers of Peace are departing, something must be omitted, let it be the eight bars from " in düstre Felsenschluchten " to " denn Friede ist gekommen," although this will not answer very well, on account of the text.

No. 6. *Terzett and Chorus.*—The repeat after the close is to be left out, perhaps also something in the middle of the *ensemble;* but here I must ask Herr Reissiger to make the cut for me, as in that matter I am too preju-

diced to find the right point. I should, least of all, like
the passage for the basses :

"Gesch - woren   ist   ihm   Tod," etc.

to be cut out, as thereby *Adriano* would be made too
insignificant.

No. 7. *Finale.*—In the March of the Ambassadors,
24 bars, G-major, are to be left out.

Should the *pantomime* be performed, the cuts could
best be indicated by whoever arranges it. In this case
the dance of the women, E-flat major 3/4, must naturally
be preserved, though probably as a mere solo dance,
with groupings.—Then the whole 32 bars of A-flat,
and the first 31 bars of the following E-flat, could be
omitted. If the pantomime is entirely done away with,
the ballet would open with the Warriors' dance, F-major
3/4 : in this event, instead of the Herald's recitative, I
must precede it by a short instrumental introduction,
for tonality's sake—at most eight bars. The following
cut is, however, to be made in this ballet-number :—
After the first 96 bars the D-major, B-major, and
F-major are to be left entirely out, and the music
passes at once to the C-major 6/8. If the third ballet-
number—*i.e.*, the final grand *ensemble*-dance—cannot
be performed, then, after the G-major 6/8, the Tempo
I^mo C-major 4/4 is to be left out, and one must proceed
with the E-major 3/4.—*Closing section of the Finale.*
Here again, in spite of the extent of this piece, it is impossible for me to find the proper point for cutting. At
best in the *Presto*, where, after the forty-third bar,

24 bars can be struck out, which, however, does not amount to much, and only robs the close of its force.

Act 3. No. 8. *Introduction.*—At the close of this, the *reprise* of seven bars can be omitted.

No. 10. *Finale. Closing section. Allegro motto : E-flat major.*—After the first 82 bars, eight bars can be struck out ; the next 54 remain, and then again 16 may be skipped. In the *piu mosso*, after the first 16 bars, the next 18 can be left out.

Act 4. No. 11. *Terzett and Chorus.*—In the *ensemble*, the first eight bars from the *piu stretto* onwards can be left out ; in Adriano's part the last bar *before* the *piu stretto* must then be changed, so as to correspond with the eighth of the omitted bars.

No. 12. *Finale.*—The march at the beginning, without repeat.

Act 5. No. 13. *Rienzi's Prayer.*—Here I beg Herr Capellmeister Reissiger to cut as he pleases in the opening and concluding symphonies.

In the introduction of the overture, I can also shorten the solo of the 'cello and double-bass ; but I would prefer not to do that until I have convinced myself at an orchestral rehearsal that the *nuances* of phrasing indicated by me are not sufficient to prevent this passage from being wearisome, which, with a perfectly bald execution, would happen without a doubt.

RICHARD WAGNER.

PARIS, *December 8th,* '41.

4.

MOST HONOURED FRIEND AND WELL-WISHER !

Accept my heartiest thanks for your valued

letter of January 25th. Though the immediate occasion of sending it was far from consoling, and though
this endless putting-off of the first performance of my
opera disturbs all my plans, yet, on the other hand, I
should be very wroth with myself, if I were unwilling
to lend a most attentive ear to the reasons which you
bring forward. *As matters stand,* I must honestly
evince my gratitude that you—from an inclination
towards my work, as I must indeed flatter myself—
have at last definitely declared that my *Rienzi* ought
not to come out under such unfavourable circumstances; and you may rest assured that—even though
it be to my momentary regret—I recognize herein the
most convincing proof of your truly friendly intentions
towards me, and heartily rejoice thereat. For certainly
it is of unspeakble importance to me that, above all,
the first performance of my opera should be as free
from fault and as perfect in all its parts as possible.
I have too long delayed to do anything for my reputa-
tion, and indeed for this single reason, that I could not
but regard a bad performance of my compositions,
such as of necessity must have been their fate at a
provincial theatre, as the decisive death of what was
born of fullest life : aware, as I was, how many a
noteworthy talent had already found its early ruin by
sending its productions into the world disfigured and
past recognition.

For the last eight years—since the time when I
felt myself equipped to appear before the public—
I have therefore maintained unbroken silence, and
have always refused every opportunity of appearing
only in an imperfect manner; so much the more then

must it be my object that this, at last, my first appearance should be as successful as possible. For this reason was I so much rejoiced to see my work accepted for performance on the Court stage of their city through the recommendation of my Dresden friends.

On account of its public, and their more or less determinative opinion, *Dresden* could naturally weigh little with me, or, rather, weigh less than *Berlin* or *Vienna:* still it is of the utmost weight to me on account of the character of its performances, which— I know for certain—*can* nowhere be more complete than at the Court Theatre of that city. With regard to Dresden, therefore, it is almost of less importance to me *how my opera will be received there, than how it will be* **given** *there.* You may guess from these my feelings, whether I know how to value the service you rendered me when you declared that the performance of my opera could not take place just yet.

That you should at last see yourself compelled to make such a declaration, this, I confess, however, rejoices me somewhat less. I perceive by the whole delay, by the complete want of respect with which the general management treated my opera, that I should, perhaps, have been sold and betrayed in Dresden, unless *you alone*—at least amongst the immediate management— had taken interest in my affairs. The vacillating behaviour of the Herr Intendant is quite incomprehensible to me: to accept an opera for performance, not indeed through any personal considerations, but because it was recommended to him as worthy of pro- duction, and afterwards entirely to disregard it, is, in

my opinion of things—supposing there lie at bottom
no other unknown motives for his action—a perfectly
senseless proceeding, however often it may occur in
practice and gain an understanding. The doubt im-
plied in this behaviour ought, of course, to be removed
before a work is accepted. Unfortunately, with my
total want of fame, I cannot complain : on the contrary,
I must regard it as a rare piece of good-fortune to have
at least found in you a warm friend. Yet the tact-
lessness and instability of the German *répertoire* is a
sad truth, which one must recognize with real shame,
as soon as one casts a glance at the management of,
e.g., the French Theatre.—No one, however, can suffer
more under this than persons such as yourself, most
honoured friend; and therefore there can be no
possible necessity for me to express myself at further
length to you under this unsavoury heading. Pity
'tis so.

However—to return to my *Rienzi*. Heaven grant
that it may at least come out by the time you mention.
See to it, please, that after the return of Mad. Devrient
nothing else is studied before my opera, for even if
this is settled, I shall still be constantly exposed to
great uncertainty : how easily might Mad. Devrient
return indisposed—what might not happen to Herr
Tichatschek ? I wrote once last autumn to this
gentleman, but naturally received not a syllable of
answer. What is his opinion ?—does he know his
part ? or do you think this will really suit him ?—You
write to me, that in spite of the long procrastination,
you will be good enough to let the preparatory work
for *Rienzi* proceed slowly ; that is fine, for in this way

we shall not be taken by surprise again! Above all, I presume that my opera has been given out to be copied, and in this case I beg you to have the full score copied first, as my manuscript is the only one, and I shall soon want it, since I have only kept back the rough sketch.

Councillor Winkler writes to me on January 17th about the great splendour with which the general management had resolved to put *Rienzi* on the stage : two scenes were to be quite new, and the costumes were estimated at 537. Well, there is still plenty of time, and we will soon *speak* about it. Though much has changed with me and with my plans, through the fresh putting off of my opera, still I shall not change my travelling plans. First of all, after five years' absence from Germany, I long for my dear fatherland, and then I wish my wife to take the Teplitz mineral waters ; so that I feel sufficiently determined to yield to the further wish of talking over matters in person with you and our friend Herr Heine. I think of starting from here about Easter. Nevertheless, I beg you (however unimportant this may appear to you), for the present, to let my intention of visiting you in Dresden be known only to you and to Herr Heine ; I think I have good reasons for this wish.

Please greet Herr Heine heartily for me ;—you might both, my dear friends, write once more hither, so as to make me quite happy. I should also very much like to know how *little Marie* is.

Farewell, my most honoured friend ; be always well disposed and sympathetic towards me, and rest assured that I shall never forget how much I am indebted to you for your great kindness.

With deepest thanks, I am

Your truly devoted

RICHARD WAGNER.

PARIS, *January* 5*th,* '42 (? *February.*—Tr.), 14, RUE JACOB.

Herr Kratz, who was highly delighted with your greetings, thanks you very much, and sends his kind regards to you!

I had intended to write to Mad. Devrient; but, on reflection, I think I can fairly spare her my letter, and therefore beg you to commend me in the humblest manner to her kindness.

5.

MY MOST ESTEEMED FRIEND AND WELL-WISHER,

As you know me and have already suffered in a most unheard-of manner by my worryings, it will not surprise you if I now again keep you wide awake on the exercise of that most heavenly of virtues, patience. I grant that you are the victim of my fussiness: but reflect, that he who suffers untold sorrows in this world, has to look forward to repayment out of all proportion, by joys in the world to come. And even here below, reward is not entirely forgotten: out of pure sympathy for your sorrows I have, for instance, resolved not to return to Dresden until the end of this month. Understand that thereby the joy is prepared for you of seeing me for three weeks less than, according to my former plan, you had to fear! I am preparing for you the joy of not having anything to do with me personally until the end of this month, so that it ought to appear to you only fair to show me some gratitude, *i.e.*, to allow me to worry you somewhat this time by letter.   Permit me then to-day to ask this question : " Have Mad. Devrient and Herr Tichatschek already arrived in Dresden, and are the parts of my unfortunate opera distributed ? "   In order seriously to make known to you my frame of mind, I must assure you that—if it remains settled that before my opera no other new one is to be put into rehearsal—I would certainly force no one and ask for no hurrying on of the performance (for it is fairly indifferent to me whether it come off a month sooner or later).

Only—since we shall in some measure be forced to be ready at latest by the beginning of September, owing to the unfortunate circumstance that the fortnight's absence of Tichatschek in the latter half of that month would be detrimental to a later rehearsal of my opera—I am so persuaded of the importance to us of a right early and undisturbed commencement of study, that I may be forgiven if I am somewhat anxious about the matter.

Most honoured friend and well-wisher, this time you shall not be troubled with further questions ; my poor understanding feels only too little qualified to give lessons to you, and so I only add one inquiry respecting the health of your good spouse, who was indeed better, but not fully restored, when I left.

It is to be hoped that our excellent friend Herr Heine is quite well : I hope that in return for the forbearance which I show him by not writing to him also, he will be grateful and bestow upon me his fullest protection ; be kind enough to give him heartiest greetings from me.

If Mad. Devrient has already arrived, I ask you likewise to give her my respectful remembrances ; may she be and remain favourably disposed towards me !

From your extraordinary affability, may I venture to expect that you will let me have a line or two to set me at ease ?   I expect this as a fresh proof of the undeserved affection which you have bestowed on me, and for which I am bound to deepest lifelong thanks.   Be assured that at least this feeling will never die within me, even though my power should be too little to thank you in deed.

With the heartiest wishes for the prosperity of yourself and wife, I am ever

Your most grateful and devoted

RICHARD WAGNER.

TEPLITZ, *July 7th,* '42.

" Zur Eiche : " Schönau, near Teplitz.

6.

DEAR FRIEND,

For certain reasons—of which I beg you to give credit above all to *this one*, that in consequence of something which has occurred I am particularly anxious to be free from all duty on the mornings required for rehearsal—I have requested Herr Reissiger to conduct the forthcoming choir-benefit concert in my place, and I have therefore forthwith sent him Händel's score.   Decidedly not the least change will be made in the affair, whether Reissiger or I conduct the orchestra.   Nevertheless, I am anxious that you should not imagine that any sort of discourtesy on my part lurks behind.

—I *am* sure your good opinion of me will protect me from this !

Your

RICHARD WAGNER.

DRESDEN, *November 3rd,* '48.

7.

(Address : *Herrn Alexander Müller, Professor der Musik in Zürich.*)

BEST FRIEND,

Unfortunately I must cause you the sorrow of seeing that I am not yet hanged : on the contrary, I have to assure you that I only feel one honest grief, that of knowing myself separated from the few but dear friends, whom, in spite of my wildness, I won to myself in Dresden. Yes, dear, good old Fischer! I would gladly see you once more, to thank you heartily for your faithful and honourable friendship! Well, I shall see you again some day, even were it for the first performance of a new opera in Paris, whither we should despatch you by steam. Only remain good to me, and always think the best of me : so shall we, though at a distance, remain always together, and gladly meet again one day.

My wife must have given you news of me from time to time : so I tell you nothing further about myself; should indeed not know what to tell, except that I am industrious, and am working for the future, in the best of spirits.

I have only one great request. You can easily imagine that my chief care was anxiety about my poor wife. She has now so far recovered that she at

last can come, and I am in daily expectation of a letter
from her, announcing her immediate arrival. Daily
I wait in vain, and I begin to worry myself as to
whether anything has happened to her?

Dear Fischer, would you be so kind as to inquire
at once whether my wife is still in Dresden, and let me
know at once if perchance she should not be well? If
you find her still there, please tell her that I had not
written again to her because I daily expected the news
of her arrival: otherwise I would have let her know
that my prospects continued to improve, that I had
good news from Weimar, and also that I had seen to
everything here for the immediate future, so that she
need not in any way be anxious; that 300 gulden had
been advanced to me on the score of *Lohengrin;*
besides I have been asked by several admirers to give
a private—but well-paid—reading of my latest opera-
poems in the autumn, and later to give a concert with
selections from my compositions. Thus she will see
that the immediate future is provided for, and by the
winter Liszt will be ready with *that* which has only
been delayed for the present! In short, she must be
in good spirits and come quickly!

Yes, my poor wife is my only care; but this
splendid Switzerland will, I hope, prove on her its
wonder-power.—

Now heartiest greetings to poor Heine from the
bottom of my heart. Shortly—so tell him—I will
write to him: then I will enclose another letter to you
also, dear Fischer. You would much oblige me if you
would send news of yourself and Heine! Ah me!
when I think of you, it gives me deep pain to be so

far from you. Well, let us often think of one and another, and write from time to time! Good-bye, dearest, faithful friend! Be assured for ever of my most grateful remembrance, and do not exclude me from your friendly memory! If anything can make you easy about myself, I repeat once more to you that, once my wife is with me again, I regret nothing, desire back nothing, except the few dear friends, among whom you and Heine—almost alone— are included. For the rest, I am happy and in good spirits, were it only that I am satisfied to have saved my liberty, and that I am no longer compelled to squander my strength in vain, as was formerly the case. I live now entirely for my art. So farewell, be easy about me, and with your health preserve likewise your friendly remembrance of me.

Your
RICHARD WAGNER.

ZURICH, *August* 10*th*, '49.

8.

[In this letter "Du" replaces for the first time the more formal "Sie."—Tr.]

MY DEAR BROTHER FISCHER,

Your heartfelt letter, in which you have made me your *brother*, I ought to have answered at once, in order to express to you my joy thereat ; but was I not right in assuming that I need not assure you of this joy, that your own heart would tell you better than pen, ink, and paper how thankfully and gladly I received your out-pourings, how happy they have made me ? Heine has given you my greetings, embraces, and exclamations, and probably told you generally how I am. You can get quite recent news from him about me, which I have thus no need to repeat here ; I am therefore glad not to have to speak much about myself, and I will instead now sing your song of praise.

How is it that we have held and still hold together, in spite of so many points of difference ? That under other conditions you wish such people as myself to the devil, but me you love, and wish me well ? That I would unmercifully fall tooth and nail upon many a one who in some respects resembled you, yet now desire nothing better than right fervently to embrace your portly body ? I will tell you exactly the reason. It is this : that everything in the one of us which does not please the other is not his inmost being, but only certain peculiarities brought about by our conditions of life, which in our contact with this life now assume this and now that surface which we present outermost as we run against and jostle one another in this world. Now, when a violent collision has taken place, a moment arrives when it must be decided whether or no the one shall break deliberately and completely with the other ; and it must as often have happened to you as to myself, that after one single jostle with certain persons we have found it better to leave them quite alone, recognizing by that occasion that our whole inner being is essentially different, that the one acts from a warm impulse of the heart, the other from consuming egoism. But when we feel inclined to have another bout with one another and send the hair a-flying, it is because we long to see what the man looks like without his hair ; for we know that this man is just of our own kidney, and the hairs which one lets fly are nothing more than outer coverings, which have settled on us from difference of age, of bringing up, mode of life, position, etc., and which in such a violent encounter go off thither whence they came—in a measure to the devil.—

I have often called you a *Philistine;* but then we have also called R., for example, a Philistine. Are you R.'s companion and like to him ? Heaven forfend ! R.'s essential nature is as repulsive to you as to me ; and why ?   Just because the Philistine nature is the essence of his being—because, with all his gifts, he is without character, envious, cowardly, and submissive; because a man of his weakness and want of courage, for love of never a *Cause,* but only of his own dear *Self,* which he does not even know how to defend, would fain have everything maintained just in the way most comfortable to himself and his lukewarmness.   *Adieu!* let such persons flock with birds of their own feather ; but no one else can make common cause with them.—Now, dearest Brother Fischer, that is the very opposite of yourself !   For what has always kept us together, but love of and joy in this our art ?   One of us understood it so, the other so ; but we always understood it from our very hearts ;—for us it was always an end, and not a means.   Your life, your age, and your experiences had placed you there, where confronted with the wretched art-tavernry of our time, you thought but of preserving the good which you have rescued for yourself therefrom : you would leave the scoundrels lying strewn on right and left, and gather the sound thing wherever you might meet with it, so as to refresh yourself therewith—as with a sweet remembrance—and to keep yourself personally

from the general rottenness.   With all your love for the
Cause, you have yet become hereby somewhat of an
egotist.   You think : pshaw ! let the muck remain muck ;
as for me, I shall still hold on to what is good and in-
vigorating to the heart.   You were in danger here of
becoming a downright self-opinionated man, nay, a true
Philistine—had not another, a younger and a wilder
fellow, come—who will not let the muck remain muck,
and seeks with both his hands to sweep it away.   For
the present he is raising a stench about you : you are
annoyed, and want to fall upon the disturber of peace :
now the hairs fly about, you recognize your man, and
at last are driven to take the peace-disturber to your
heart, as affectionately as you have done me.   So it is :
chance things alone divide us, such as age and the
externals of life, perhaps even of our faculties ; but not
that which is indispensable in both of us, and that is
the inner nature.   You love the same thing that I love.
You only see it otherwise than I, because you use quite
a different pair of spectacles : you want, above all things,
rest ; I, above all things, *unrest.*   That you are able to
love me, that saves you from the Philistine egoism into
which the devil would willingly draw you, but from
which your fresh, warm, true heart preserves you.
But for me nothing can be more blessed than to be
beloved by a dear, honourable fellow like you, and from
this you may judge of the degree in which I return
your love.   Get leave of absence, and convince yourself
if you will not believe it.

Heine will tell you how I am.   The earnestness of
life announces itself—*i.e.*, I do not quite know what I
shall really have to live on ; that, indeed, is nowadays

the "earnestness of life," and people understand the
term no other way. Does my Paris opera interest you
so much ? Yes, it is not so bad a scheme, only in the
best case it is not an affair which can be settled quite
so quickly. I cannot write music to the first French
libretto that comes : of my ideas for a text not one is
suitable for Paris—at least, not as it is *now*. If things
there were as they ought to be, and as they very probably soon will be, then I should know what to be
about. You will be alarmed when you hear it, so let
Heine present it to you with a little of his costume-
ornamentation. I have already given up the plan of
taking yourself, as choirmaster, for the subject of an
opera.—If it is possible, *i.e.*, if I have money, I will
travel to Paris in January : there the overture to
Tannhäuser shall be played at a *Conservatoire* concert,
and perhaps on this occasion I shall settle with my
poet on a plan. I have not a great desire for
Paris : reflect a little about it, and you will understand
why.

There is a concert here to-day, in which the great
duet from the Second Act of the *Flying Dutchman* will
be given, also a fantasia for pianoforte and clarinet on
Tannhäuser.—For the rest, I go on living here in my
usual way, *i.e.*, in a homely and retired fashion, and I
am glad that my good wife is with me. My surroundings consist entirely of resident Swiss folk : I scarcely
note that there are German exiles here. It is beautiful
here, and I would work to my heart's content if I were
only a little assured as to my livelihood. I have many
plans in my head, which probably will in time find the
proper way to publicity. I have just finished my *last*

literary work : now my order of the day is, nothing but artistic work.

My wife would not part with your portrait : it hangs before her over the work-table, and rejoices my heart every time I look at it.   Ah me ! what is going to become of our dear Germany ?   I know of nothing that goes on in the world, for I scarcely ever read any newspapers now.   Shall we ever see each other again ?—Let us, at least, hear often from each other : that makes up for it to some extent !

Let us hope !   He who has his heart in the right place, to him belongs the future : he who is faint-hearted, he has his portion, and always carries it about with him—I mean in his heels.   When first I become faint-hearted—then, farewell world !   Better dead than living !—Dear brother, should things remain as they are, and you ever get your pension, come then and settle down with us in Switzerland.—Farewell for to-day !   Receive affectionate embrace, and hold me in kind remembrance, which becomes you thoroughly well, especially in my eyes !   Minna sends quite immense greetings !   Farewell ! and soon send news to your faithful brother,

RICHARD WAGNER.

ZURICH, *November 20th,* '49.

9.

DEAREST OLD FRIEND,

You are probably downright angry with me ? —Heine, at least, has not replied to my last letter : I wrote him with the request to communicate the contents

to you.   I suppose this has been done, and also presume that you know how Paris—and also all who, with
well-meant but badly informed zeal, thrust me towards
Paris—brought me almost to death's door, and in any
case to complete despair.   This was a decisive turning-
point in my life, which now, at least, has turned to
good, in that I have become determined in both my
resignation and my will.—I am looking out how to
support myself, and at the same time only apply myself
to my art in such a way that I may retain my pleasure
in and love for it.   For the rest, I reckon no more on
strokes of good-fortune, and only hope, under the protection of noble and truly sympathetic friends, to
maintain myself in as sound a state as possible, so as
to show myself useful to art according to my strength
and *circumstances*.

It would heartily rejoice me soon again to have some
news of you and Heine : of you I only know that you
were *near* attending a performance of my *Lohengrin* at
Weimar.   Now, in any case, I remain here in Zurich,
where I have found a circle of very dear friends.
When one day you put yourself on the shelf, you ought
really to be so sensible as to do it here.   I have no
words to describe the pleasantness of this place ; in Paris
I was completely Swiss-homesick !   The sturdy, honest
race of men would please you very much, and one can
also live cheaply here.

Next spring I shall set earnestly to work at the
composition of my *Siegfried*, of which, should circumstances prove favourable, I expect quite a special
representation.

Now to a matter of business !

A lawyer, Blechschmidt, in Dresden, has written to me about a singing daughter of his, whom he would like to be trained according to my advice : he says you have been her teacher hitherto. I pray you, what shall I write to the man ? I enclose a short letter, in which I refer him to you, as you indeed ought to give your opinion as to whether she really shows sufficient talent to be in need of exceptional training ; in which case, he ought, in my judgment—if he has enough money for that purpose—to seek out the best teacher he can get, for which I certainly give my vote to Garcia.—Will you arrange the matter with the man ?

One thing more ! An unfortunate Prague composer, H., once, ages ago, sent me an opera of his, which later on he asked to have back again. Some one was to fetch it ; he did not come, and I forgot all about the matter. Now he writes to me here. My wife declares that she gave to you and Albert all music of the kind that she found among the things I left behind me. I presume that whatever my brother received was handed over to you when he left Dresden. Do look one day and see if this c——d opera is amongst the music : it was only a pianoforte score, and—I think—bound in red. If you do not find it, perhaps it is with Professor Hähnel, who would hand it over to you if you showed him this letter.—The unfortunate fellow has not even written me his address, and I am therefore asking him at the same time to send it you exact to Dresden. Then be so good as to send him this opera.

Sweet remembrances !—

So you are all getting on remarkably well at Dresden. I hear much about *Martha*—that the performance is going smoother and better. Ah! how I regret being no longer there!—

Good, affectionate, old, faithful friend! Arrange to spend your old age with us by the Lake of Zurich: you will not regret it! A thousand hearty greetings from myself and wife, who is quite well, and become a regular Swiss! Farewell! and be no more angry

With your thankfully devoted

RICHARD WAGNER.

ZURICH, *November 9th,* '50 (STERNGASSE, ENGE, ZÜRICH).

10.

WELL-BELOVED BROTHER FISCHER,

There has again been a long pause, for which I can scarcely forgive myself, as your last letter indeed caused me very great joy. Well, I had really nothing very pressing to say to you, except to thank you for your letter, and to send heartiest greetings: these I have always sent in my—mostly business—letters to Uhlig, and I hope you have always been duly served with them. Now I have cleared up several—by no means "political" —works: spring is at hand, and with the beautiful month of May I wish to set to the composition of my *Siegfried:* but I will first pay my debts—so far as I can with pen and ink!—and so I am going to write to you and Heine. The most difficult of all was to write intelligently to Heine—poor fellow! So I first commenced with him, and gave him all the news about myself, which I should then have had to repeat to you, had I not hit on the ingenious scheme of sending Heine's letter unclosed to you, so that you might read

it through and then send it on to Heine. Please do
this!—Does Heine still live in the *Jägerstrasse?* You
will write the address, won't you?

Now you have learnt how I am; and if you are
satisfied with that, I must first of all assure you that
nothing in your letter rejoiced me more than your wish
that you might come to me here in Switzerland, when
you receive your pension. That is the most sensible
thing you can do! Believe that, and sleep over it
every night until you come. In spite of all temporary
misère, I feel here the courage of a dog who has
got over a whipping;—by a whipping I mean the
eternal soul-and-body-destroying, aimless, and useless
fight with Impossibility, such as I had to carry on
for six long years in Dresden, in my relations with
ignorance and insolence. Now I only do the possible,
and am therefore in inner harmony with myself, from
which at last something or other shall come forth; for
from here I can exert a far more decisive influence
upon our art-doings than there, where in everything,—
even in my own thoughts—I was fettered. Only wait:
the ice shall yet break. In Dresden I should, as Capellmeister " *loci*," have become thoroughly rusty, because
always spitefully attacked, pulled to pieces, and therefore
rendered powerless.—In my book, *Oper und Drama*,
which will appear shortly, you will, moreover, read to
your comfort, that I do not consider true art possible
until *politics cease to exist.* Won't this make you
smirk?—

I have read your last letter through again, and
perceive that I owe you many thanks for looking after
the matter concerning the Prague composer: with that

you have lifted a weight off my heart, for the Bohemian tone-poet really imagined I wished to commit an artistic theft on him.—With regard to the music I left behind, I think the shortest way would be for you to take the stuff into your own hands. Only, if you did not know what to do with it, and the things were in your way, I should after all be glad if they remained at Professor Hähnel's! But if you really will trouble about it, do whatever you think fit: Hähnel, at any rate, will be only too glad to be rid of the stuff. You will probably not need a special authority: I think it will be sufficient in any emergency to show this letter. Perhaps I may ask you for one or two of the numbers. The whole lot you could place, my good, careful friend, wherever you think fit. If you come to Switzerland, then we will make further arrangements.

The principal thing is for you to gradually train down the Dresden choir to such a pitch of badness, that Krebs will exert all his power to get you pensioned: that settled, you will come to the Lake of Zurich. You will not be the only one of the colony: others are thinking about it. Who knows but what we then may both begin to give rehearsals! In any case, you shall lead a comfortable, independent life here with us. Give greeting from me to the old . . . .—I mean old X. With this poor, careful man I have endured no small trouble.—Oh that I should ever have thought of making anything by my compositions! Anyhow, that kept the pot a-boiling. Yet I hear that the business is not doing so badly after all: if it were indeed to prosper, I should for many reasons be heartily glad. Kind greetings to yours from us, especially to your daughter who is with you. Rejoice us soon with news of your welfare, but, best of all, of your arrival.

Farewell, my good old friend! Remain good to me, and soon get your pension!

Your
RICHARD WAGNER.

Heavens! if I could only see the dear, honourable D. once again. I almost fear you do not greet him from me. I would willingly hear from Ed. D.—Give a right hearty kiss to L. from me; but press R. to your heart for me.

II.

BEST BROTHER FISCHER,

In hot haste to-day before post-time a line or two with a pressing request!—

I am asked for the *Tannhäuser*. Get the theatre score of *Tannhäuser* given to you from the office, and hand it quickly to a good copyist, so that he may copy me the *new ending* of the Third Act, and as speedily as possible. — Then get my music given to you by Hähnel; take from it two copies of the *Tannhäuser* score, pack them up and send them—with the *copied new ending*—by *mail-coach* (at my expense, of course) to me here. You also might have a second copy made of the ending, which you could send to me later on.—If Hähnel gives up the things—*and you are willing to be troubled with them*—take everything to your house, or do what you like with it!—So much, to-day, in haste.—

How your letter (through Uhlig) has rejoiced me! *Of that you can form* no *idea!*—You shall receive an answer ; that I promise you !—Greet also Tichatschek, who has also heartily rejoiced me : he too will soon receive an answer.—Farewell for to-day, and do not be angry with me for giving you such a lot of trouble.

Your
RICHARD WAGNER.

ENGE, NEAR ZURICH, *July* 11*th*, '51.

12.

DEAREST BROTHER FISCHER,

Again a telegraphic despatch ! Do not be angry ! —In Brussels they wish, with the energy of the very devil, to translate and perform my *Lohengrin*. I shall take all precautions that nothing foolish is done with it. Now I want, as quickly as possible, a score. So be kind : go to L. with the enclosed formal letter to you, show him the lines written specially for the purpose, and request him in my name to hand over to you the score of *Lohengrin* under the conditions therein named. When Uhlig once asked him for the score, L. desired something in writing from me to himself. Give him to understand that I had hinted to you that I thought it impossible L. should desire a letter from me *to himself*, as he, as well as I, must surely feel how painful that would be. Then let me know the result of your trouble, so that we may proceed farther. If L. lets you once for all have the score for the copying expenses, thirty-six thalers, you might send it off (naturally unfranked) to the following address. (*Stop, no ! Only let me know, and wait for further instructions from me !*) You ought to receive the money from Frau R., *Waisenhaus-*

strasse, No. 4. If L. will not give up the score entirely, but only lend it for a copy to be made, get Wölfel to attend to this copy as quickly as possible. (With the money the same arrangement holds good !)—

You were right again in your hesitation about *Tann-häuser.* Of course the introduction to the Third Act must be copied from the altered form ; if you will besides mark down the cuts and abbreviations with pencil, you will put me under great obligation.

—Good heavens ! some one is waiting for me ; so I must be brief ! Do not be angry with me for bothering you so ! A hundred thousand greetings to Heine—best thanks for your brotherly care, and farewell for to-day.

Your

RICHARD WAGNER.

ENGE, NEAR ZURICH, *July 22nd,* '51.

(In my official letter to you I treat you according to old custom : I thought you would deem that best.)

13.

[Enclosure to former letter.]

I am asked for the score of my opera *Lohengrin.* I only possess my original score, and a copy of it made here would be very expensive, besides being done badly and slowly. Now, Herr v. Lüttichau possesses a copy of this score, for which, at the time, he paid the expenses of the copying—thirty-six thalers. As I have already ascertained, his Excellence has no intention of keeping this copy as a sort of pledge for what I unfortunately owe to the treasury of the Royal Court Theatre ; but on receiving back what he spent for the copying, he would hand it over to me as my property, as soon as he were thoroughly assured that, at my wish, it would be delivered to me or to my order.

Now, I presume that if this letter is shown to his Excellence, he will be assured on that point, and therefore beg you to betake yourself to Herr v. Lüttichau, and ask in my name and at my request, that the score may be put into my possession in return for the payment of thirty-six thalers ; for this, indeed, is of great importance to me.

I pray you for speedy news about this, and thankfully remain,

Yours most truly,

RICHARD WAGNER.

ENGE, NEAR ZURICH, *July 22nd,* '51.

14.

O YOU MOST EXCELLENT FELLOW, MAN, BROTHER, FRIEND, CHORUS-DIRECTOR AND MUSIC-COPYIST !!!

I have just discovered what a piece of work you have done for me—and indeed without saying a word to me about it ! For only now have I had occasion to open the packet which Heine sent me some time ago, commissioned by you ; and as I now look through the score, I recognize with deep feeling and astonishment that father-brother Fischer has with his own hand undertaken and carried out the copying job, which I thought had been attended to by a certain "Wölfel," and for the finishing of which I expected an account, which, after all, I must now ask from

Wilhelm Fischer, Sen. You are indeed a good fellow !
—What now shall I say ? To have given you so
much trouble ! It is indeed more than touching !—
Well, for the present : best thanks ! If I am able, I
will one day do more, or quite another sort of thing !

The reason why I formerly asked you to see to the
Tannhäuser scores was, that the present Frankfort
Capellmeister, G. Schmid (*i.e.*, Prince Eugen), applied
to me—with an enclosed letter from the management
—and wished to have the opera for Frankfort. I
answered him, that I certainly had no reason to oppose
the performance of my opera, except where I failed to
find either in the artists or in the taste of the public
the conditions for an intelligent and good performance ;
that I had no inclination to be scoffed at ; but, on the
other hand, Frankfort seemed disposed to that. He
must therefore—his hand on his heart—answer this
question : whether he felt capable of maintaining that
earnest mood among the singers which the task demanded, and, on the other hand, of so influencing
the public that this earnest effort would meet with its
reward ? I promised to keep a score in readiness.
Prince Eugen still owes me a reply—and the scores
remained unpacked.—But a short time since, the
Schwerin Court Theatre applied to me : I racked my
brains as to who could have happened on the thought
of *Tannhäuser ;* then it occurred to me that Röckel's
sister, the Frau Moritz, is in Schwerin ; she is a highly
intelligent vocalist and actress, and has certainly
suggested the performance of *Tannhäuser,* an opera
which she knows ; this rejoiced me, and afforded me
a certain guarantee. I consented, and received twenty

louis d'or : then I opened the packet.—They want to give *Loghengrin* at Leipzig : I will see if they agree there to give, first, the *Dutchman*—then the *Tann-häuser*, and only *then* the *Lohengrin ;* for thus only can the public become acquainted with me and learn to understand me. I would rather have nothing to do with *Dresden*. First of all, you have no conductor there who has the requisite intelligence and good-will ; secondly, no lady vocalists such as I require ; and, thirdly, I cannot and will not have anything more to do with the whole Dresden management, from A to Z.

How stood matters formerly, when I was still there —I who had written this opera specially for Dresden, and the then members of the company ? Then folk thought good to chicane me a little : already the orders for scene-painting had been given to young Heine, when it suddenly occurred to L. to countermand every-thing. I was silent at the time : but you did not know how miserably depressed I felt to find myself and my artistic efforts so dependent upon circumstances, that only as a hypocrite and sycophant could I see any prospect for my art. Pish! any one with a grain of honour takes himself off.

Well, these are old tales of the past ; they have become indifferent to me, and lately one has received sufficient absolution ; one has now *the pope* (or even two *popes*) at hand.—

My dear old friend ! Once for all, I am built on different lines from what you all suppose, with your use and wont ; in me you have to reap a new experi-ence, and that is why God sends new blood into the world. They shall not drag me down into the swamp of old tradition and traditional commonplace.

Many disclosures as to myself and the connection between my life and my art will be offered you in a very circumstantial " Address " (*Mittheilung*) that I am drawing up as a Preface to my three older opera-poems, which will soon be issued by Härtels. Your love for me convinces me that this will much interest you. Also *Oper und Drama* will soon appear at J. J. Weber's. —I have just written the poem of a " *Young Siegfried* " (of bright contents), and will now set to work at the music. But I am resolved first to be in thoroughly sound health, so that I may also write good healthy music. For this purpose I am going on the 15th of this month to a hydropathic establishment in the neighbourhood : there will I wash out my body, as now by my literary work I have washed clean my intellect.

In case I should again want a *Tannhäuser* score, I have commissioned Uhlig to get a dozen copies from Meser. So please for the future get him to attend to the scribbling, etc. ; he is able, younger than you, and can better bear my plaguing. But you, my dear old fellow, I wish you had long since tried the water cure ; you would not then have found it necessary to ruin yourself by going to Carlsbad. For these mineral baths do no good : they only weaken one more and more.

With your strong and powerful constitution, I am convinced that even now a water cure would free you from your complaint, at least—that you would be in sounder health instead of getting worse. Listen to my advice !   Get your pension, come here, and try water in the presence of and amid the air of the glorious Alps !

Is there any more honour, joy, enjoyment, to be got out of your surroundings ?   And how long do you people think then that your present state will still go on ?   Truly I trouble myself no more about politics ; but even a blind man—unless he is stuck in the thick of it—can see that the end will be terrible !

(Peps confirms this by a sneeze !)—

Now, do not be angry with me if I spoil the joy which *Lohengrin* in Dresden would certainly have caused you.   But reflect, that nothing any more can cause *me* joy except what is *genuine*.   The whole re-solve of L. is not genuine ; it is a mixture of a thousand " I-could-wishes " and " I-would-likes," but not the firm will of a man who knows *what* he wills and *whom* it concerns.   Or is perhaps R.'s wish to produce my opera genuine ?   Get along with all these . . . and turncoats ; they shall not annoy me one hour longer.—

If I now expect to be able to get quite well, it is because I live as pleasantly as it is possible in my situation and in my relations to our present art-world : I live protected by the true and genuine love of men who know me as I am, and who would not have me a jot otherwise.   I am only to be envied.— —

Now, one thing more.   I intended writing to Heine at the same time as to you.   As I have *not* received *his* letter (the one sent through the *Elberti*), which was to contain fuller details, I could not in the principal matter —*i.e.*, in the communications about myself—write any-thing further than what I have written to you.   Now, to save a duplicate, will you not be so good as to send this letter with the enclosed lines to Heine, for him to look through ?

Do make me happy by writing very soon again : you cannot think how much I am edified by your true and hearty friendship ! Heartiest greetings from Minna and self to you and your daughter. Farewell ! get strong, and always think kindly of me.

Your
RICHARD WAGNER.

If you do not write to me for some little time, my address will be : *Albisbrunn*, near Hausen, in the canton of *Zurich*.

15.

GOOD, DEAR FRIEND !

I have been in debt to you for a long while for your last letter, which I received at the hydropathic establishment. With regard to its principal contents, I never quite knew what to answer you. You reproached me for my behaviour towards the *Dresden* Theatre management, and showed me in detail that it was unwise and ungrateful to oppose their wish to produce *Lohengrin*. Dearest brother, have you not quite misunderstood the real state of this matter ?—I hear that L. intends to give my opera ; as I care little for the mere giving, but only that it shall be given *well*, I take my own measures to guarantee this, and to prevent my work from being presented in a completely unintelligible fashion. At the same time, I naturally presumed that the management really intended to give the opera ; had this been the case, they presumably would really have tried to satisfy my wishes. But what is the real truth ?—They are not thinking seriously of giving the opera at all. There you have the whole story, and I have only made a fool of myself in believing that they were serious in the matter. Have you at present heard anything more about a performance of *Lohengrin* in Dresden ? Certainly not. Well, why all this fuss ? as if I *alone* out of sheer obstinacy prevented everything, when everybody else was all aflame to take up the work. Fiddlesticks ! leave me in peace with your Dresden Theatre rabble.

You have deeply touched me, however, by so cunningly attempting to produce again in public a composition of mine, and I sincerely thank you for this proof of your great love ! By sending me the programme you have caused me great joy,—and—I had to laugh heartily over it. But I hope you thought of no further result.

You see, they have after all given my *Tannhäuser* in Schwerin, and the performance must really have been a good one ; otherwise I cannot comprehend how the success, of which I have received clear proof, could have been so great.

For the rest, even this does not inspire me with any hope that my operas will really spread now : I know these are only quite solitary phenomena, brought about by a few isolated individuals. Our real theatrical market remains *intentionally* stuck in its beloved mire, and therefore I have nothing at all to do with it.

As you already know, the theatre-director Löwe is worrying me here about the *Flying Dutchman*. The

man is ready for sacrifices of all kinds : he wishes to
send specially to Munich for a scene-painter, strengthen
the orchestra, etc., etc. Nevertheless, I am trying to
be rid of the matter ; but this becomes more and more
difficult, owing to the pressure of my friends here.
Fortunately, the musical director Schöneck is a thoroughly capable young fellow, on whom I can rely for
the chief part of the labour. So now it is almost a
mere question how we can borrow the orchestral parts,
for here they understand well enough how to copy parts,
but not how to copy them out from full score. I cannot
apply to L., as you will understand : so it comes to this,
whether you, or perhaps Tichatschek, would ask for the
parts for yourself, and give a guarantee ? The reason
could be assigned that the theatre-director Löwe had
applied to you ; then *he* in his turn would give you
a guarantee. Do see if this can be managed !

Uhlig has now received some scores from me which
were in Brockhaus' hands ; he must keep me scores
ready for any emergency, especially of the *Dutchman*,
of which I have somewhat retouched the instrumentation. He now asks whether it would be more sensible
if he took over everything, even what is in your hands,
so as to keep a proper account of all that I left behind ?
As I am really bound to think that the storage of
my things must only be a worry, and certainly no
pleasure, I almost consider I shall be doing you a good
turn if I get you to deliver everything over to Uhlig.
That, nevertheless, you can do as you like in the matter
need scarcely be said.

For the rest, we are going on tolerably well ; and if I
get quite strong again, which I hope will be this spring,

I cannot, under present circumstances, wish for any better existence than that I now lead. How are you ? Are you still angry with me about the *Lohengrin* affair ? My wife greets you heartily, good friend ! Farewell ! and keep us in kind remembrance.

Your
R. W.

16.

DEAR BROTHER FISCHER,

I could not answer you before now, as the *Flying Dutchman* affair here remained in uncertainty. I always hoped to get clean rid of the matter, and there was, indeed, some prospect of that, as the Munich scene-painter who had to stage the opera here declared that there was not now sufficient time. My joy at this, however, was to be troubled, for the theatre-director here hunted up a wandering scene-painter and machinist, who has had to make sketches for him which certainly show much ability. As besides—and this is the chief reason for me—my friends here, after I had let them hear the *Tannhäuser* Overture (really extremely well done), quite seized me by the throat, insisting on my producing one of my operas : I at last said yes, and can no longer draw back. So the *Flying Dutchman* is to come out in the second half of April, and now for honour's sake I am anxious that the performance shall not be bad. The singers that I required for this opera are really quite good, especially the soprano and the barytone ; whatever else has to be procured will be attended to. So, now I must ask you to see to the orchestral parts. I *enclose* the desired lines to Tichatschek for L., and request that you will see that they are despatched with all haste.

The vocal and chorus parts are already copied out, and rehearsing has commenced; so I only want the orchestral parts. But as it will be impossible to copy the parts by the time the orchestral rehearsals begin, of which I must hold a great number, I beg you also to send the duplicate parts : three first violin, two second, two viola, three 'cello and double bass parts, and all for the wind instruments.

So as not to give you too much trouble, I advise you to get Uhlig to see to the packing and sending off; I know he has a large supply of packing canvas. Anyhow, now that it has got so late, the packet must be sent direct by post and not by carrier, and to the address of theatre-director Löwe in Zurich. So I count on having the parts here *at latest* by the end of this month.

Now, do not be angry with me about this vexation !

But whenever are you coming to us in Switzerland ? My wife and I count for sure on having you here once again with us. Let us know your plans about this ! What great pleasure can you still get from Dresden ? —A nephew of yours is already here, and is now a low-comedian at the theatre. Candidly, I wish him an engagement with a good troupe ; he is excellent, full of talent, and quite a different sort of fellow from your ordinary buffoon. . . . I often go to the theatre when he acts. Tell this to your brother. (The family likeness to yourself has quite touched us !)

I wish Heine would again let me know something about his son's fate : I have nothing interesting to tell

him, but certainly he has to me. Do you know anything about his *Wilhelm?*

Good-bye for to-day, you good old friend! Forgive
me these mere business letters! Soon more from your

RICHARD W.

17.

MY DEAR FRIEND AND BROTHER,

I must heartily thank you for the fresh act of
friendship which you have just shown me by seeing
to the parts of the *Flying Dutchman.* Director Löwe
has assured me that the full score and parts are on their
way to Dresden, addressed to you, and sent by goods-
mail, as I myself advised; for, on the one hand, the
packet could not be addressed to Dresden per post; on
the other hand—as far as I know—there was no special
hurry. You people will probably never want the parts
there again, and thus never settle the debt which
Dresden has to pay me for this opera. For now more
than ever have I recognized how bad was the performance
which Dresden gave of this my work, inasmuch as I
have been forced to recognize—without any illusions—
that even in such a hole-and-corner theatre as the one
here it was possible to bring about a thoroughly efficient,
and therefore effective performance. When I recall
what an extremely clumsy and wooden setting of the
Flying Dutchman the imaginative Dresden machinist
Hänel gave on his magnificent stage, I am seized even
now with an after-attack of rage. Herrn Wächter's
and Risse's genial and energetic efforts are also faithfully stored up in my memory! That during my six
years' Royal Capellmeistership I could not succeed in

again bringing out this opera (with Mitterwurzer, etc.), and getting it respected, can only be realized by one who has some conception of what a Dresden Court Theatre is.

All the more, I must frankly acknowledge it, has the hole-and-corner performance here rejoiced me. Certainly I undertook it only and solely for the sake of some of my friends here, who wished to form their own idea of me; naturally, I was highly indifferent as to the public, success, etc., since I was only concerned to bring the matter to light in as intelligible a way as possible. Now, not only was I successful in this, but I perceive the unusually strong impression which the performance itself made upon the mass of the public; while the singers (especially the representative of the principal *rôle*, the barytone Pichon) I so drew out of themselves, that they not only astonished the public by the novelty of their rendition, but often even gave myself most lively satisfaction. The scenery was naturally poor, coarse, and on a small scale; but yet, in obedience to my suggestions, everything was fully indicated, and carried out in accordance with the aim; so that this performance might well serve as model to the larger stages, which would only have to furnish everything with greater refinement and wealth of detail. The orchestra was reinforced, and was right good, often quite excellent. The chorus, which was reinforced by all the comedians who had any voices, and singers not otherwise engaged, was fresh and full of life. Your nephew played the *Daland*—and, indeed, right well.

Although I had the misfortune at the first performance that the principal singer was hoarse from the very commencement, the opera had, nevertheless, such a success, that in eight days it was given four separate times, to full houses, with subscription-list *suspended*, and the prices raised as never before. The director was quite unhappy that he had already booked the railway-seats for the departure of his company to Geneva, for he could now have counted on giving the opera yet five times more in the following eight days, with the same success throughout.

The trying work has certainly fearfully exhausted me, for naturally this result was only possible by means of the most terrible rehearsals. Still, I think I shall soon get all right again, and shortly set to my new work.—So much, then, for this affair !—

Now, I particularly ask you to give me news of Heine. I hear he has insisted on being pensioned off, and is now returning to Dresden. He might write once more, to give me news of himself, his family, and especially of *Wilhelm*. Please impart to him what I have told you here about myself. I send heartiest greetings to him ; may he always keep me in kind remembrance !

With regard to yourself, I still stick to it that I expect you soon in Switzerland. A male choir of at least two thousand will, I hope, suffice for your activity, and that I can procure for you here. With this decoy-song I will now conclude, and indeed with the very best wishes for your prosperity from Minna and myself ! Thanks for all kindnesses, and ever remain good to

Your

R. W.

Zurich, *March 9th*, '52.

P.S.—Has your Wilhelm *tannhäusered* at Cassel ?
I hope it has gone off well ?   I no longer quite trust
old Spohr to conduct the Overture to T. : let us hope
W. helped him.

18.

DEAREST BROTHER FISCHER,

In the old year I rated you soundly through
Heine : in the new I must, on the other hand, wheedle
you into doing me a kindness.—You know about Uhlig's
illness, and can well understand how painful it is to me
to load him *now* with commissions.   But things have
got into fearful confusion ; at Breslau and Schwerin
they are anxiously waiting for the revised score of the
Flying Dutchman.   For this " revision " two pattern-
scores were necessary ; according to which the new
scores were to be prepared—from the one, the Overture
and the instrumental close of the last Act ; from the
other, all the rest of the instrumentation.   Till now both
the scores were at Weimar, in order that the score there
might be arranged according to them ; when *Uhlig* asked
for them there was some delay, and only a few days ago
Liszt announced to me that they would be sent off. In any
case, I now presume that they have arrived in Dresden.
But in order that the *two* copies required (for Breslau
and Schwerin) may be more quickly arranged, there
occurs to me a score revised by my own hand which—
gratis and of my own accord—I sent to the Dresden Court
Theatre (at the time when this opera **was** to have been
put into rehearsal there).   From this score I conducted
the opera last Easter here in Zurich : the Dresden Court
Theatre can have no earthly claim to it, as it already

possesses an older score of the opera ; the new copy
was merely given by me to the office for the purpose of
having the parts arranged thereby ; moreover, I have
in no way given it into the *possession* of the management. (It would be different if it were *intended* to give
the opera in Dresden : then I should say, "*Arrange
the old Dresden score according to this one!*") So—this
second score belongs to me, and I beg you to make
clear my title to it and demand it back : God willing,
this opera also is likely to be more widely given, and
as I do not possess many copies of the score, this
detention is of special moment. Uhlig could keep
this score to serve as a model for the future, while the
revised copy (which we received back from Leipzig)
could be sent at once to Breslau. Thus it would only be
a case of speedily arranging a copy for Schwerin on the
lines of that obtained back from Dresden. For both
places—Breslau and Schwerin—there will only be *one*
thing further to see to—namely, that the *Overture*, and
the *instrumental close* of the Third Act, should still be
specially revised according to *that* score, which I sent
last year to *Uhlig* from *Zurich*. (Mind, this change is
contained neither in the second Dresden nor in the
Leipzig score.) A correct model copy, as well as a
reserve theatre copy, must be prepared immediately
after this.

N.B.—If L. makes difficulties about giving up the
score, it might be merely *lent* for the while ; if *everything* is granted, then the old theatre score must also be
arranged *at my cost :* more he certainly cannot ask.—

Do be so kind, old sinner ! Look after the forty-
year-old stripling for me ! I cannot now trouble

Uhlig with anything !—You will soon hear further from me. Have you commenced the new year well ? Your " unwise," " unpolitical " friend wishes you much health and happiness.

RICHARD WAGNER.

ZURICH, *January 2nd,* '53.

19.

DEAR FISCHER,

I really thought you could bear a cuff better than your touchy reply seems to show. I am sorry that you took the few words to Heine in a more offensive sense than they were meant. It is self-evident that *we* cannot be of *one* mind in *everything ;* and that you did not understand *my intention* with the Guide to *Tannhäuser,* could not but become clear to me, in that you regarded it altogether as a stupid stroke of work. But what of that ? You are quite right—one single conversation would bring us to a better understanding, even on such matters, than all our occasional scribbling ! There is, however, no doubt between *us* as to the chief matter ! So—forgive me !—

Under the painful impression of the news of Uhlig's death, I cannot say anything more to-day than what I am compelled to from business considerations.

You will have received my lines of January 2nd, and thereby the matter of the scores will have become perfectly clear to you.—I am writing at once to Liszt about the second score, in which last year I *considerably* remodelled the Overture (especially the concluding section), and, in correspondence therewith, the ending of the last *finale.* Meanwhile, it would be well to see if perchance

this score is at Uhlig's.   Moreover, I will send to-day
for the (theatre) score here.   If the change is properly
entered, I will send off *this* copy by post to you this
very day ; so that, if the copy supposed to be at Weimar
(but certainly delayed) does not yet come, the *Overture*
and the *ending of the last Act* can still be set right by
the score from here.   As Breslau has been waiting for
a long time, I advise you, as soon as one score has been
revised *in other respects*, to send it off at once, and at the
same time tell them that all the parts may be copied out
by it, *except* the Overture and the *instrumental postlude* of
the last *finale* (from page 409 and onwards).   Cut both
these out of the score, and then send them on as soon
as they are corrected.   But Schwerin, likewise, must be
attended to very quickly.—That L. . . . . has caused
me terrible confusion ! !—

Further ! !   If you are *willing* to take into *your* hands
all my things now lying in Uhlig's house, and to undertake various commissions for me, respecting revision and
sending off of scores, *nothing* could be more welcome
to *me*.   Formerly, I wished to spare you this.—Heaven
witness ! !—The demand for scores will only last about
a year longer ; then *Lohengrin* will be obtainable through
Härtels.

So if you *will*, receive beforehand my best thanks and
my congratulations on your energy.—I will soon write
more !   To-day— —

Minna sends hearty greetings !   Greetings to Heine,
too, from both of us.   Farewell and—no offence ! !
Your
RICHARD WAGNER.

ZURICH, *January 8th*, '53.

20.

BEST FRIEND,

These lines will probably reach you at the same time as the score I sent off yesterday. I will only add something I omitted. Possibly you have already sent off a score to Breslau : in any case, it is certainly best to have the ending of the *Overture* and of the last *Finale* written *afresh :* it is not much : eight pages in the Overture—from page 43 on—and five pages in the *Finale*—from page 409 on.—But in the case of the Overture detailed instructions for the phrasing also must be added —perhaps in a textual note, indicating page and bar. If you have not already sent off the score, you might do this at once—as soon as the rest is finished—and say that the other would follow.—Good heavens ! I am quite unhappy at the terrible delay through this dilly-dallying : in Breslau the performance was to take place in the middle of this very month, and the fault is owing to *that* alone.

Do write without paying the postage. Good-bye !

Your

R. W.

Mehner (extra musician) is a good and careful copyist. *Make haste about Schwerin too ! !*

21.

DEAR OLD FELLOW,

I was already about to write to you, when I received a letter from Cassel, which doubles my reason for writing. So—Wilhelm has really managed to get me from there an official order for the score of *Tannhäuser.*

(Probably the recent success of the opera at Frankfort lent a helping hand.) Now, I must ask you to send off a *completely revised* score of *Tannhäuser* to the intendant of the Court Theatre at Cassel. There probably is at least one such copy in reserve—inquire of Uhlig's widow in case everything has not been sent to you. Now, you will make a nice grimace ! ! !—for I also ask you to enclose with the score *five* copies of the " Guide to Performance " (pamphlet) : they are to be given to the four principal actors and the stage-manager. (I have never—between ourselves—expected that this Guide would be followed to the letter : but partly it has been and is a *necessity* to me, on such occasions, to express my *full intention;* and, partly, I know that people at least hereby receive a shock, which tears them so much away from their customary humdrum ways, as has been hitherto the case with all the recent performances of *Tannhäuser*—much to the advantage of the latter.)

Be so good as to let X. know about this new order ; this is on account of the books of words !— —

I thank you very much for seeing to the *Dutchman* scores. With regard to this matter, I beg you to have another pattern-score got ready quickly (with everything complete), and to send me back the score which I lately sent direct from here, as it does not belong to me, but to the theatre-director Löwe. I then should like to know how *many* scores of the *Flying Dutchman* you have still in reserve.

Apropos ! Wilhelm writes to me that he has already asked you for the Dresden *scenarium;* so will you be good enough to see to the designs, etc. ?

Probably you will again need a reserve supply of revised *Tannhäuser* scores : Uhlig always insisted on having *two* ready. He sent me an account of the expenses half-yearly. Now, please tell me how you wish to, or can, manage in this matter ? Surely you will prefer that I should give you something in hand for your outlay ? Answer me quite freely on this matter !—

Kr. wrote to me lately ; for the moment, give him kind greetings from me, and thank him for his letter. Tell him, further, that I intend shortly to lay the whole details of my Dresden indebtedness before a lawyer (I think *Schirmer*), and to get him—in the interest of my creditors—to look carefully into the publishing business of my operas. I had already repeatedly asked Uhlig to commission Schirmer to call together my creditors, in order to receive authority from them to supervise the business in their interest. I fear, however, that it was never taken up with the proper energy. Anyhow, X. has not made much by it hitherto, for he has had from time to time to pay the costs of carrying it on out of his own scanty pocket. Now, it would be advisable if my creditors, by their empowered attorney, were to get the business into their own hands, and manage it for themselves. For I feel certain that in time this publishing property would fully satisfy my creditors.

I will then ask P. to withdraw for the present in favour of Kr. : he can best do it, I suppose ?

Farewell for to-day. Hearty thanks. Greet the Heines from us, and remain good to your

R. W.

Zurich, *January* 21*st*, '53.

It is possible that you may shortly receive back the Berlin score of *Tannhäuser;* for I have *demanded it back.*   Instead of *now at last* taking up my opera, they are studying there the *Feensee* and Flotow's *Indra :* this is a downright piece of impudence.   I now prefer to break entirely with them ; for it is then positive that next winter Liszt will receive a commission through the Prince of Prussia to perform *Tannhäuser* and *Lohengrin* in Berlin.   This to comfort Heine ! !

22.

DEAR OLD FELLOW !

A *commission*—(not a *request,* because that, in fine, you would not grant me: whereas I presume that— as my duly appointed manager—you would attend to my "commission"!)

So !—

If by this evening you have not received back the score of *Tannhäuser,* then

I commission you

at once to write to the General-Intendant of the Royal Theatre in Berlin, and request that the said score be forthwith returned, as I have otherwise disposed of it.

But I hope you already have it :—for I now know for certain that in any case the Berlin people would not have given the *Tannhäuser.*

But all this will—probably—turn out well.   Only rely (you and Heine also) upon *Liszt,* as I do.

Good-bye for to-day, you excellent business-manager ! Soon more from your godless

R. WAGNER.

ZURICH, *January 29th,* '53.

23.

DEAR BROTHER!

(In haste!) *Genée* in Dantzig wants *Tannhäuser:*
I have asked ten louis d'or, and referred him to you
about the ordering.   If he writes, you are to send it;
so take the agreed honorarium as a **postal advance** on
the book and score—together with four copies of the
Guide.   Keep as much of the money as you think you
will require for disbursements, and give the rest to my
mother-in-law, Frau Planer (*Herzogin-Garten, No. 7*).

Good-bye!   Soon more and much from your incorrigible but grateful

RICHARD WAGNER.

ZURICH, *February 24th,* '53.

If you receive an order-slip with postal certificate
for ten louis d'or from Freiburg, send off at once a
Tannhäuser score!

24.

Now do say, my dear old freind and brother,
whatever can be amiss between us.   I was surprised
enough to have received no news from you for so long,
but now I am suddenly horrified by receiving a letter
from Dresden, in which, among other things, I am informed that, some one having asked you for my news,
you answered that I (and Heine) did not concern you
any more!—Now, for Heaven's sake, tell me whether
anything has again happened?   Since our last *rencontre*
we had—I thought—got on very well?   You had
written your opinion, I mine, and everything was quite
in order!   Have you meanwhile had a quarrel with

Heine, in which I also am concerned ? If this should be serious, it would indeed be sad ! But it is now some time since I heard from either of you. So please say what is up ? You cannot expect me to rest quiet in such a state of matters ? Or how were it possible that in your old age you should all at once bear me a serious grudge ? I cannot possibly bear you one !

So—write to me at once ! Or else can I no longer hang my opera-concerns about your neck. If you are unwilling to have anything more to do with me, I cannot at least remain any longer a burden to you, and some one else must attend to the business matters.

—But—is it then really so serious ? ? I cannot believe it ! Certainly some bee has again got into your bonnet : how often has each of us spied out such an insect before ! Put me at ease at once, and leave me no longer in this uncertainty.

Hearty greetings from Minna. Your picture is well preserved, and you look down from it far too good-naturedly for me to believe that, blind with rage, and roaring like the lion from the *Midsummer Night's Dream*, you would tear to pieces my portrait, which I now enclose.

Farewell, and set things straight !

Your

RICHARD WAGNER.

ZURICH, *April 12th*, '53.

25.

DEAR FRIEND,

Please pack up quickly *a copy of the Rienzi Overture*, which you will find separate—in very elegant binding—among the music I left at Dresden, and send it to Herr Musikdirektor Edele in Berne. I hope ycu are friendly ? Good-bye.

Your
RICHARD W.

ZURICH, *April* 14*th*, '53.

26.

DEAR OLD FELLOW,

I am sorry that your extreme conscientiousness has caused Michaelson an unmerited delay : anyhow, he was right in deducting one louis d'or. It is naturally difficult to get money from these small theatres, and I have therefore conceded M.'s request for 10 per cent. commission, because (as was the case with Genée) he mostly has to pay down cash, and then wait some while before he can squeeze it back from the management.

I thus have, at all events, the advantage of havirg nothing to do with the pack of ragamuffins, and safely receive my money in advance.—Therefore, another time you may place greater trust in Michaelson : up to now he has always acted fairly with me ; if he ever plays any tricks, it will be all up, and he will receive no more scores. So for the future, even without special directions from me, you can send him what he asks for, as soon as he encloses a postal order for at least nine louis d'or. He must, besides, send *you* the honorarium for Königsberg (ten louis d'or—*without* discount) ; take what you want from it for expenses, and give the rest to Heine, so that he may get a supply of decoration- and costume-sketches (*scenarium*) ready. When they are exhausted (Hamburg has already announced itself), only tell me, so that I may make further arrangements.

Best thanks for your letter : congratulations about Teplitz ! My musical festival was certainly fine ; I have *never* experienced a *purer*, pleasanter impression. (Only think, the expenses amounted to over 9,000 francs !) Wilhelm ought to write to me how things have gone off in Cassel ! I am glad he is with you. You are a devil of a fellow : what stuff there still is in you ! I, also, have hopes of my health : I shall soon compose again.—I think you are making the *Nibelung's* ring your *own*.—

Good-bye, you dear old soul ! I have such a terrible lot of letters to write, that I must really cut it short.

Cordial greetings to Heine and to your people from

Your
R. W.

ZURICH, *June* 15*th*, '53.

27.

DEAREST !

I wrote to you yesterday ! To-day.I answer briefly what is necessary in reply to your letter just received.—

It is all right about Carlsruhe, although E. Devrient may not have said anything yet about the honorarium, which, for the rest, is a subordinate matter here.

Please have some more scores in readiness : you will shortly have to send off a good number again. How are matters with Darmstadt ?—

In Hamburg they wanted the *Tannhäuser* on terms of a royalty : thereupon I asked for fifty louis d'or in advance (because I place no trust in the fellows). They asked me to desist from this demand, whereon I do not intend to answer them at all.

Things are moving too in Austria : for example, Grätz ! (stupid affair !).—I am glad that the royal Saxon police make it impossible for me to attend the representations of my operas, which would only cause me vexation !—

What are we to do with Anton Apt in Prague ? As I am no longer thinking of any performances of *Rienzi*, I fancy we might let him have a score—but only in return for twenty-five thalers (for every copy has cost me about this sum). If he sends the money, give it to my old mother-in-law (Mad. Planer, Herzogin-Garten, No. 7). If the price is too high for him, I will lend him, on my behalf, a copy for a time. Get books of words only from X. : they are quite the same.— Whenever shall I learn something about the state of the business ? ! ! ! That X. still continues to dilly-dally, I see, from the fact that a pianoforte score of the *Flying Dutchman* was lately ordered from here, and though four weeks have passed it has not yet come. Of promptitude he knows nothing—and how important is this for the market !

As soon as the ten louis d'or prove insufficient, let me know ; I will then either forward your money, or direct that the next honorarium-payment be made to you !—

May the all-good God preserve you, you Lion !— When shall I get any more news about Hi—Ha— Heine ? The portrait has turned out very well ; the lady-painter especially is very pleased with it.

I find the eyebrows and the mouth too strongly marked.—Yes—my goodness !—if I had such eyebrows, I should be quite another fellow, a second L. !

Now, enjoy your cray-fish (krebse gut). I am delighted with Wilhelm's letter !

Kindest greetings from both of us !

Your

R. W.

ZURICH, *July 1st,* '53.

Please get the *new ending* done *at once* for Carlsruhe. (See yesterday's letter !)

28.

DEAR OLD FELLOW !

You will shortly receive, through Michaelson of Berlin, an order from Cologne for *Tannhäuser,* with postal certificate for twelve louis d'or. I hope this will not embarrass you.—For the rest, you can always send him scores, if he enclose you a postal receipt for at least nine louis d'or. (He holds out a prospect of Magdeburg and Ravel).—I have just written to *Wurda,* at Hamburg, and sent him a form of order on you, with the stipulation that a postal receipt for fifty louis d'or be added.—So get into harness, and let my friend Mehner set to his copying.

I have just had a wild week's revel with Liszt. On Wednesday there will be a great torchlight procession with music and song, for the presentation of various honorary diplomas.—

At Wiesbaden *Lohengrin* went very well.

—Kind greetings to Heine ! How are his eyes ? Is he working at *Lohengrin ?* It would be a good job if it were finished. But he must not injure himself on that account.—Good-bye !

Your reformed rake,
R. W.

Zurich, *July 11th,* '53.

29.

Dear Old Fellow !

You will receive from the management of the Hamburg Theatre a bill for fifty louis d'or, payable at the end of November of this year, in return for which you have to send off *Tannhäuser* to them. Then send *me* the bill : there is some one from Hamburg here who will buy it.

Nothing about X. and the business ?—X. must really not sell any more *scores;* we shall at last run short of them, for fabulous applications are again pouring in on me.

What is Heine doing ?

I sit here (between ice and bears)—who loves me, will take me away !—Good-bye !

Your
R. W.

St. Moritz (Canton Graub ndten), *July 27th,* '53.

(Up to the 14th August I am still here ; address here direct up to that date.)

30.

O Father, Brother, Friend !

How can you believe that I could ever use strong language when I think of you !

Good gracious ! what bad manners you must now be learning in Dresden.

Best thanks for your dear letter! You ever valiant
fellow. Of your deeds as manager I had already read on
returning from the ice regions, where I had been taking
a mineral water. Heaven knows whether the care will
be of any use to me! Only think that I must give up
snuff; for the last six days I have not taken a single
pinch! The effect for the present is as though I should
go crazy—somewhat thus must X. always feel when
you come near him. Concerning this muddle-headed
fellow, I truly fear he will yet become ripe for the lunatic
asylum. That fear it was that gave me the idea of
writing to Kr. to ask him to take the matter in hand.
Be so good then as to deliver the enclosed little letter to
Kr.—You are indeed right to keep back the score of the
Flying Dutchman: you may at most lend it, but only in
return for a sufficient guarantee, to be invented by you,
that it will be given back in a certain time—say four
weeks. The *Dutchman* will also have its turn (if you
let it alone in Dresden)—they already want it also in
Wiesbaden. *Rienzi* you can always part with to private
individuals for twenty-five thalers—under an agreement
that it will never be used for theatrical performances :
the money—to my mother-in-law! Warn Apt in
Prague that, should he not buy the score, he cannot
keep it over four weeks. So much for that! Full stop!

Stay—I have still something to say about the Ballenstädt fellow! He wrote to me, and I have dissuaded him ;
at least, he must pay me ten louis d'or : should he still
persist in his wish, I will in that case give him a con-
tract-order on you—in the customary way (with the
condition of a postal certificate of receipt for ten louis
d'or). Only in return for such a postal receipt, or for

the said sum itself, can he have the score. In general —I will never refer any one to you without such a written order.—For Olmütz also you may expect a similar form. Moreover, Darmstadt, Hanover, Brunswick, and Stuttgart will shortly fall into your hands.—

Good heavens! there I am again with a shameful digression—out of cursed covetousness—for I intended only speaking to you about your management. I have read grand things about it in connection with *Hans Heiling*, etc. I hope you will soon also produce *Adolph von Nassau*. (This little volume interests me very much on account of Wiesbaden.)

How does it strike that soul of a man, L., when you keep bringing out fresh operas? Does he not often think of me, and how you stuck by me, and how R. drew in his claws and was so energetic that he did not know which way to turn?

Some one has lately told me that you are in excellent trim:—according to that account, you really seem to be leading a very sensible life, in spite of your secret whist parties at A. R.'s with G. (O you secret sinner!)—

I thank Wilhelm very much for his fine description of the Cassel *Tannhäuser;* I will send him a special answer shortly. The *Prophetess* is Heaven knows where; but I think I am on the track: the moment I get hold of her, Wilhelm shall lay hands on her. Kind greetings to him.

Minna is by no means well: she is taking remedies, and is going again to the baths: her blood and nerves are in a state of commotion. Fortunately she can now have her little comforts—for that I have indeed to thank *Tannhäuser*.

I am soon going off on a journey to the Mediterranean. A thousand greetings to Heine ; he ought not to worry himself and his eyes so much.   The principal thing I want is a good, easily comprehensible sketch of the decorations and their manner of setting up.   Good-bye for to-day !

Your most grateful

RICH. W.

ZURICH, *August* 17*th*, '53.

Go on writing to Zurich : all letters will reach me.

31.

DEAR FISCHER,

I write only a few lines to set you at ease, although you will already have received a letter announcing to you the receipt of the Hamburg bill of exchange.   (By the way, it was quite unnecessary for you to specify this bill on the envelope : a bill is never specified ; at most, the letter is registered : mark that, you man grown grey in business, and receive a lesson from your reformed scamp ! !)

Yesterday I received five thalers from the Ballenstädt director, so you will have this order to add to your load.

But all this does not make me soft-hearted enough to give money to X., forsooth, for the new pianoforte scores : what I now receive is once, and not again—I ˋshall never again obtain a regular income—and, with exception of present receipts, I may whistle to the wind.   From the publishing business, however well it may be managed, I shall never draw anything : I assign it wholly and solely to my creditors, so it is for them to take interest in the business on their own account—just

as with the effects of a deceased debtor. If they want
the business to yield income, they must spend the
necessary working capital on it. If they won't do this
—well, they have nothing to expect from me, when I
see that they allow the business—my only real property, which I hand over to them—to go to ruin. I
have already expressed myself so definitely on this
matter, that I have nothing more to say. Perhaps it
will be somewhat better managed : God grant it !—

Go on writing to me to Zurich ; all my letters will
be speedily forwarded.—I am off to-morrow evening : I
hope that the fulfilment of my long-cherished wish (to
see something of Italy) may turn out well : I now am
terribly in need of working power.—

Farewell, best friend ! Greetings to Wilhelm and
the rest of your family.

Your
R. W.

ZURICH, *August 23rd,* '53.

32.

DEAR FRIEND,

     I now hear nothing more of you, so that I am
really becoming anxious ! Some time ago I wrote to
Heine, and sent you greetings. He does not answer,
and, with regard to him, I must unfortunately be
anxious about his health. But with regard to yourself,
I must fear that you are vexed with me ? If neither
supposition is correct, do please write to me ; or, rather,
in any case write to me !

You have now much to do : I know you therefore
cannot do any useless scribbling ; but I should much

like to have a sign of life from you both, my good, my only remaining Dresden friends. For I cannot surely forget everything : when I recall the joys and sorrows of the Dresden Court Theatre and band, naturally my heart can but grow warm as I think of you.

Heine will have told you something about me. I have again become quite the musician, and more than ever. I am now writing the score of the *Rheingold* (first commenced in November). In the summer I go to the *Walküre*, in the spring of 1855 comes the *Yunge Siegfried*, and in the following winter I think to take in hand *Siegfried's Tod*, so that everything will be ready by Easter of 1856. Then comes the impossible : to erect my own theatre, in which I may bring out my work before all Europe as a great dramatic-musical festival. Then—God grant that I may breathe my last sigh !—

You see I am full of plans. In any case, I think no more about " our " theatres. These may drag down my old operas completely into the mire of commonplace :— I have abandoned them, and let myself be satisfied with everything, because I expected nothing good : you know my disgust ! My only interest is in the money which I win from the German theatres by this my prostitution : for the rest—I have——closed the books, and am only astonished when from time to time I hear anything good about the performances.

Have you seen to the *Flying Dutchman* for Wiesbaden ?

What is all this about Pesth ? I read in all the papers that they intend giving *Tannhäuser* in the spring, with Tichatschek : that is all very nice, and for

Tichatschek's sake I am glad ; but I should very much like to know how they are going to come by the score. Do ask Tichatschek, who is, I hope, no longer angry with me : my kind greetings to him !

I have heard nothing at all from Dresden for such an age, that I do not know how your Wilhelm is getting on. Is he satisfied ? Has he any prospects of succeeding in Dresden, of doing honour to himself and art ? I should much like now to see you both. I can picture to myself your smiling glance from the conductor's desk at rehearsals. Hearty greetings to him : I do not know what I should write to him in particular. He has not sent me his opera-book : why not ? I should be pleased if I could be of any service to him.

Now, perhaps you will once again let me hear something of you : do not put it off too long ! I often seem completely abandoned—in spite of all fame.

Farewell ! greetings from me and Minna to Heine and your folk, and be good to your

RICHARD WAGNER.

ZURICH, *February* 15*th*, '54.

Do not let X. sell any more *Tannhäuser* scores : we want them all !—

33.

DEAR OLD FELLOW,

Do not be angry with me, if I do not write to you to-day, but only announce an order to you.

Let the Coburg Court Theatre direction have the *Tannhäuser*, etc., as soon as possible.

In a few days I finish *Das Rheingold,* my first score since ever so long. My zest for work at last became so great that I put off all letter-writing until I had completed it.—So expect shortly—and Heine also—a proper letter (also a money-order). For the present you must pay out! Forgive me!—You understand!

Your

R. W.

ZURICH, *May 27th*, '54.

34.

DEAR OLD FRIEND!

You are certainly right when this time you complain of my procrastination in writing, perhaps louder even than I did last winter, when I wondered at your silence. You answered me at last in detail, and at the same time gave me so strong a proof of your vigilant care, by sending me a catalogue of my Dresden musical effects, that I was almost painfully ashamed. Then I thought I ought in my turn to write you a right substantial letter, but waited until I had finished composing the first part of the *Nibelungen*, with the final result that I was less disposed than ever to write long letters. I get more and more out of the habit of doing this; for one thing, because I lead so retired and exclusively industrious a life, and one with such an absolute dearth of outward events, that I should not really know how to fill a decent letter. Yet I must frankly confess another thing: after your last disclosures I ought again to have sent you money for disbursements; but just now, in fact, since last winter, I have been so infamously hard up that I could not spare anything, and all chance sums received were so needed that I could not think of sending off any.

So then I waited till orders should commence again, so as to be able daily to set aside a little sum for you. Yet up to the present I have waited in vain, and I must now conquer my shame and at last write to you even without money. In the course of this and next month I think something must come in, and then you shall be sufficiently provided for immediately. So do not be angry with me!

Best thanks for the catalogue, but it was really not necessary for you to take all that trouble! If it is not in your way, let everything quietly remain in your place: if I ever want anything, I'll ask you for it. I should much like to have my arrangement of Palestrina's *Stabat Mater*: you might, at your convenience, send it me one day.

For the rest, I get news of you through *Noack*, that you are going on in first-rate style, and that in your theatre management you are swimming along better than ever. Now, that gives me great pleasure; but your pension, which you wished to spend with us in Switzerland, seems a long way off yet.

I heard from Heine that, on the whole, he was in good health: only his good wife was ailing. Dear me! it is a shame that I have not written to Heine either for a long time! But he must not look upon that as any diminution of my love: we often, very often, think about him and his, and, I assure you, always with emotion. Tell him this, and give him a thousand greetings.

About myself—I have nothing to say to you. I live, on the whole, a life full of sorrows, however little it may seem so to many—for I have become silent respecting my inner life. Since last winter, I have returned to my music, and work is the only thing which remains dear to me; therefore I work to excess! To me the whole day only exists for the purpose of setting me in a good mood for as much work as possible.

I have finished the *Rheingold*, and the *Walküre* is already commenced. It too must be completed this year. My wife will travel to Germany next week, to see her old parents once more: she will not, however, go to Dresden, but her parents will meet her at Zwickau; she will also visit Chemnitz, and pass through Leipzig on her way to see a lady friend in Berlin. If you could manage to go and say how do you do to her anywhere, she would be uncommonly pleased!— —

I, for my part, would likewise wish to see my friends again, and especially you; but even that would not tempt me to Germany, and I am really glad not to see all the bad performances of my operas there, which would probably break my heart.

So I will endure and work!

Farewell, dear, good old friend. Ever thanks for your faithful love!

Your
RICHARD WAGNER.

ZURICH, *August 8th,* '54.

35.

DEAREST OLD FELLOW!

You will receive shortly through Walther—the theatre-director here—ten Napoleons d'or for expenses.

To-day I beg you to send off as quickly as possible a corrected copy of *Tannhäuser* to the Intendant of the Court Theatre at Hanover.

How are you? Have you spoken to Tichatschek? Farewell.

Your

R. W.

ZURICH, *October 28th,* '54.

36.

ZURICH, *December 19th,* '54.

DEAR OLD FELLOW!

I can never once manage to write properly to you: I have always so much to answer that it spoils all my inclination for a sensible letter. So to-day I have only to request you to send a *Tannhäuser* as soon as possible to Mannheim (to the theatrical manager). Lachner, the Capellmeister of that place, has been here to settle with me himself about it. (Now that reserve of scores would come in handy!)

My wife, who went to Dresden quite behind my back, was mightily delighted at seeing you. It quite warmed my heart. She sends kind greetings. Give greetings from us to the Heine family also. I will certainly write one day quite intelligently.

You will soon receive my score of the *Rheingold* from Liszt: I beg you to deliver it at once to *Wölfel,* so that he may finish the copy already commenced.—

I am diligent—but not in good-humour! Well, there are reasons for that!

Farewell, dear, good Fischer!

Your

R. W.

37.

DEAR OLD FELLOW,

I hear absolutely nothing more of you :—are
you offended with me ?—

I asked you recently to send a *Tannhäuser* to Mannheim.—They also want to give the *Flying Dutchman*
in Mainz ; if the director, M. Ernst, sends in a postal
receipt for ten louis d'or, you can at once let him have
the score (corrected).—

In conclusion, I have many requests to make to-day.
Among the music I left behind, there are—

1. All the detached numbers from *Rienzi*

2.   „   „   „   „   *Flying Dutchman*

3.   „   „   „   „   *Tannhäuser,*

as they came out at X.'s in their time.   I should much
like to have these sent by return.   If they cannot be
found, please persuade Kr. to have the things presented
to me—from X.'s store of publications.   I am in bad
want of them.

Then—could not the Dresden Court Theatre make
me a present of a good copy of the score of *Iphigenia
in Aulis* as I arranged it, so that I might at all events
have a souvenir of this work ?—

Please see what can be done.—

If L. is unwilling, at least have the overture copied
for me (at my expense), with the ending which I published last year in the *Leipz. Zeitsch. f. Musik.*

Ah me !   I only get snatches of time for writing,
because I have always such an intolerable lot of letters
to get through.

I *heartily* long to see you once again and have a
chat.

At the end of February I go for two months to London, to conduct the concerts of the Philharmonic Society, for which they expressly sent one of their directors here to persuade me. As a rule, that kind of thing does not suit me; and as I am not to get much pay for it, I would scarcely have consented, had I not therein seen a chance of next year bringing together in London—under the protection of the Court—a first-rate German opera company, with which I could give my operas, and at last my *Lohengrin*.

For the rest, I am as stubborn as ever, am working most diligently, and already scoring the *Walküre*.

Has Liszt sent the *Rheingold*? If so, let Wölfel copy quickly, so that, if possible, I may have my score back before I leave for London.—

Now, do please write once more!

A million greetings from me and Minna. Farewell!

Your
RICH. WAG.

ZURICH, *January 21st,* '55.

38.

MYSTERIOUSLY SILENT FRIEND, AND BROTHER IN THE FAITH!

† † †

See at once about *Tannhäuser* being sent to Munich: I have come to an agreement with Dingelstedt. Give them also *six* copies of the pamphlet.

X. ought at once to assert his rights concerning the books of words.—

Concerning *sketches* and *scenarium*, I have referred
them to you.—

O you wicked fellow ! !

Salute Heine !

Your

R. W.

39.

But, dear old friend ! how heavy-hearted you
make me, with your extraordinary sensitiveness ! In
Zurich I could not manage to write to you ; but on my
very first leisure day in Paris I have sat down to give
you somewhat of a scolding, as this time you deserve ;
although, considering your hasty youth, you might be
excused.   Let me just tell you how matters stand with
the score of the *Rheingold*.   I had already promised our
young friend several years back that he should make
the pianoforte score of my *Nibelungen*.   As this time I
was adopting a new method with the instrumentation,
whereby I did not first make a completely developed
preliminary sketch, I felt the want of an arrangement
from which I could play to any one.   I therefore asked
my friend to go on with the pianoforte version, while I
was still writing the score, and so I sent him the detached sections as soon as they were finished.—At the
same time, he was to get Wölfel to make a copy, and so
arrange with him that both could work at the same time.
As soon as the copy and the pianoforte arrangement
should be simultaneously finished in this way, I intended
to gradually distribute both copy and score among my
friends for perusal, and I can assure you that you would.

not have been the last. *Liszt* learnt—as did you—that
his pupil had the score, and showed so much jealousy
that, as the latter would be stopped in his work for
some time by the mere fact of his going away, I commissioned him, when I sent him the remainder of the
score, to send it at once to Liszt, and thus interrupt
Wölfel's copying. At the end of four weeks Liszt was
to send back the score to Dresden, that you might first
get Wölfel to finish the copy, and then the young man
was to receive this copy so as to finish the pianoforte
arrangement. See, dear old fellow, that is how the
matter stands; and you ought to see that there is no
question here of undervaluing your friendship. But
now, unfortunately, as I learn, Liszt has kept the score
an immoderately long time; for he wrote me only lately
that he would now send it off to you. I hope that has
now been done, and I particularly request you to notify
me immediately on the receipt of the same; for I am
really most anxious about this solitary copy!!—So
that I may soon be set at ease, be also good enough to
hurry on Wölfel with the completion of the copy; as
soon as this is finished, I will further ask you to send
the copy to Berlin, but the original score, after you have
satiated yourself with the sight of my beautiful hand-
writing, to me.

Well!—are you still angry??—

As you seem anxious to be rid of the music and the
wilderness of waste-paper, with which I have loaded you
up to the neck, I have made a selection as follows :—
Send the following, at your convenience, by carrier :
1. Bach's eight-part Motets. 2. Beethoven's Ninth
Symphony. 3. Mozart's Third Symphony. 4. Bach's

two *Passions*.   5.   Marx's *Moses*.   6.   Music for a *New Year's Prologue* : score 3/4 C-minor (without orchestral parts).   7.   Three of my Overtures (score).   8.   Libretto of the opera *Die Feen*.   9.   Of the opera *Das Liebesverbot*.   10.   Aria from *Norma (Orovist)*.   11.   Aria from *Mary*, Max and Michel (bass).   12.   *Les Adieux de Marie Stuart*.   13.   *Les Deux Grenadiers*.   14.   Seven compositions for Goethe's *Faust*.   15.   Fantasia for pianoforte.

I beg you further to take into your care and keeping the scores of *Rienzi*, *Flying Dutchman*, and *Tannhäuser*, with the books belonging to them, etc.—All the rest you can destroy, burn, and use up as you like ; thus you will get a little more breathing-space.

For your last parcel my best thanks : I beg you to send to London what has still to be forwarded to me. Has then nothing further appeared of the *Tannhäuser* pianoforte score *without words ?*   I should much like to have what is ready of it.—Altogether, my heart bleeds when I think of this publication business : what could not be got from it, if it were conducted with zeal and prudence !   Unfortunately, I hear nothing at all about it, not even from my creditors, who ought to be interested in the matter.

I shall probably never come back to Germany.   You are all so silent about this, that I must well believe there is no prospect of it.   Well, whatever our noble ministers may determine, I shall accustom myself thereto !   But if you want to see me once more before our end comes, you must undertake a journey to Switzerland.   I shall be back again by the beginning of July.   In London I shall score the *Walküre ;* from there, too, good Heine shall at last receive another letter from me. Heartiest greetings to him.   Greetings also to your people ; and amid all circumstances and doubts, keep in kind remembrance

Your
R. W.

My future address will be : *Ferdinand* Präger, 31, Milton Street, Dorset Square.

40.

Best thanks, dearest old friend, for your letter ! I answer it at once, because you therein send me a piece of news which certainly forces me to haste !

Now, I beg you most earnestly to render me a service of friendship, and rouse yourself at once. Point out in my name the danger in which that business hovers, and say that I have received a confidential hint as to X.'s position, which has determined me to make an immediate and fitting end of that wretched affair. Those to whom I made over the ownership of that copyright, until my debts to them were fully covered, must declare through or by their lawyer whether they wish to protect that right completely and against all circumstances that are threatening it.   Already have I seen with despair how badly the business was conducted under the present so favourable circumstances. As yet the pianoforte score without words of *Tannhäuser* has not appeared, which is an irreparable loss.   Here in London I am informed that the pianoforte score of the *Flying Dutchman* had recently been asked for but not

received, because the old edition was out of print: so
there was no thought of bringing out a new one in
good time! If things go on like this, and if I remain
without a satisfactory answer, I shall have to consider
my own property threatened ; and if my creditors do
not at once assure me through their lawyer, that on
their side everything possible shall be done to secure
the greatest advantage from the rights made over to
them, so that all the good may be got out of the
business which it now can offer, I shall find myself
compelled to employ another lawyer, who for his part
will protect my right, and—though in the first place in
the interest of my creditors—will take over the management of the business, so as to conduct it in the manner
which I may consider the most profitable.—I beg you,
dear old fellow, do me the kindness, and press for an
immediate answer !—

That property is indeed the only thing that can
afford me any profit. I have cast away those operas :
from them I ask for nothing further than—that they
should bring in money.

It is otherwise with the works which I have now in
hand : for their creation I only took heart when I resolved to look away entirely from our theatres for their
performance, and to devote all my life's strength to
producing them one day, under exceptional circumstances, as a dramatic-music festival. If it is granted
to me in the future to acquire the means necessary for
this, well and good. If not, I shall content myself with
this : that I made the effort. But only such a prospect
gives me heart to trouble about my art : for our usual
theatre-repertoire with all its wants (to which Flotow

and Meyerbeer, etc., can best minister) I work no more.—This is my fixed opinion, my firm-set will! This will perhaps explain to you the form and fashion of my present composition : it does not occur to me while working at it to think of any existing theatre, with which from henceforth I have nothing more to do ; for works like my new one shall not be given between *Martha* and the *Prophet*. For the rest, I am surprised that you should consider the mere constitution of the orchestra the principal difficulty ! Nowadays one can have for money as many instrumentalists as one wants, and Meyerbeer for the performance of his *Huguenots* in Paris has seven harps : so make your mind easy on that point. But—singers who are not . . . . like your theatre-rabble ; but true, intelligent, and energetic inter- preters ! That is a much greater difficulty, and it will probably cost me years of preparation before I can train them up for myself from talented young people. How I shall do all this must for the present remain my secret : but though you do not yourself assist in a pro- duction of it at Dresden, I hope, at least, that you will hear it given under my direction—to which performance you are herewith most cordially invited.—Now, con- cerning the score of the *Rheingold*, I beg you to send it at once by goods-post to my address here, together with the copy—so far as Wölfel has got with it. I am too much in need of it to be able to wait any longer : I will have the copy finished in Zurich instead, where I have now hunted up a good copyist. I will settle Wölfel's account with you at once.—So, all that is arranged.

It was a great piece of folly for me to come to London, for which I now atone by enduring until the

last concert.   Not, indeed, that I have to complain of
the public or anything of that sort : that is all just as
it is everywhere else, neither better nor worse ; and,
besides, the public of the Philharmonic Concerts is very
favourably disposed towards me :—but,—it is not in
my line to conduct concerts.   A Beethoven Symphony
certainly gives me great pleasure : but a whole concert
of this kind, with everything which it includes, deeply
disgusts me ; and with great inner vexation, I see
myself compelled to conduct stuff which I thought I
should never have to perform again.   Moreover, I see
that here in England I have no chance of anything,
under never so favourable circumstances.   Even a
German Opera, with my works, would give me no
pleasure ; for no performance could ever be so good as
I should wish, for the reason that very few rehearsals
can be held, because everything is so frightfully dear.
So I only endure here, without joy or hope.   I have
paid a visit to the Ney, and also heard her in *Fidelio*, in
which, however, she did not satisfy me.   To-day she
sings in Verdi's *Trovatore*, in which she is certainly
more at home : I heard from the orchestra that she had
already had an extraordinary success at the rehearsal.
She is not allowed to sing at concerts, so long as she is
engaged at the Opera.

So I am spending my time in somewhat melancholy
fashion, amid people who are foreign and unsympathetic
to me ; and I rejoice at the thought of returning at the
end of July to my dear, glorious Switzerland, which I
hope I shall never leave again.   Before I depart I will
write a thoroughly sensible letter to Heine : tell him that,
and give him a thousand greetings from us.   Also

hearty greetings to yours : thanks for your faithful friendship, and be assured of my constant love.

Farewell.

Your

R. W.

22, PORTLAND TERRACE, REGENT'S PARK, LONDON.

41.

DEAREST OLD FELLOW!

As always, so to-day another request ! When you are buzzing ahead, do go to the cloth-merchant Henniger, in the Old Market, and tell him from me that this autumn he shall receive his money in one lump; but that for the present all my earnings are accounted for. Also it would be very nice of him not to charge me any interest : this eternal paying of debts is the reason that I can never hop upon a green twig.—Please be so kind ! !

Has Liszt yet sent the *Rheingold?* Do let me know ; I so want to have the original score back soon, and indeed in London. You shall hear another time how I am : I have really nothing to do but conduct the concerts of Philharmonic Society : for the rest, London does not exist for me. The orchestra has taken a great liking to me, and the public approves of me. To-day is the second concert : selections from *Lohengrin,* and the Ninth Symphony. Chorus wretched ! If only I had my Dresden Palm-Sunday Choir !—Good-bye for to-day ! Heartiest greetings to Heine and your family from

Your now soon forty-two-year-old

R. W.

22, PORTLAND TERRACE, REGENT'S PARK, LONDON.

42.

DEAREST OLD FELLOW,

I write again at once:

Firstly: to congratulate Ernestine.

Secondly: to ask you to see to the copy of the *Rheingold* being immediately completed, so that I may at last get back the original score. But you must make Wölfel write *post-haste*, so that, if possible, I may have my score here by the end of *May:* I will write to you then about the copy.

Best thanks for *Henniger-Modes.* People think now that I am coining money: ah! if they only knew!—

I endure here, like a passover lamb; but it does not suit me, and I hope this will be the last time I shall come to London. I have nothing to seek here, and the Jews may conduct their silly concerts for them. Besides, much scandal is made of and about me.— I shall see the Ney. Otherwise—everything as before!—

Greetings to Heine and your folk. Keep stout and hearty as ever, you *Herr-Gotts-Tausend-Sakramenter!* I shall not last so well nor so long! Adieu!

Your crazy

R. W.

43.

DEAREST OLD FELLOW!

Cordial thanks for sending my score. I am uneasy at your not enclosing a line, because it makes

me think you are angry with me.   Do assure me soon
to the contrary.

The copy is, after all, so beautiful that I feel inclined
to let Wölfel complete it, and so will send you back
the score from Zurich.   For the present, I really want
it here.

My best thanks to you for fulfilling my large request.
I see there is reason to be very cautious about X.   I
therefore enclose a letter to that gentleman, and beg
you, before you close it and send it to X., to give it
to your friend to read, for it seems important to me
that my creditors should be exactly informed about
my relations to X., so that they may take measures
accordingly.   Cordial greetings to P. also from us, and
thank him for his forbearance, as well as for his
faithful friendship.—

I am now somewhat more cheerful, as my London
visit is drawing to a close.   At the next concert we
are to have the Queen of England : it will be certainly
interesting if I, as a high traitor with a public warrant
out against me, conduct before Her Majesty and the
Court.   One might take a lesson from that.   On the
30th of June I shall be back again in my dear Zurich.

Whenever will you come there, you old theatre-
mate ?

A thousand greetings to the *Heinerei !*

Farewell ! and remain good to your much-afflicted
RICHARD WAGNER.

The Ney sang in one of our concerts, and certainly
her voice and style of singing both surprised and
delighted me.

44.

BEST FRIEND,

Cordial thanks for your kind letter, out of
which for to-day I have only to answer the question
about the result of the concert given in presence of the
Queen.

The false reports about my quarrel with the directors
of the Philharmonic Society here and my consequent
departure from London are based upon the following
incident.

When I went into the cloak-room after the fourth
concert, I there met several friends, whom I made
acquainted with my extreme annoyance and ill-humour
that I should ever have consented to conduct concerts
of such a kind, as it was not at all in my line. These
endless programmes, with their mass of instrumental
and vocal pieces, wearied me and tormented my æsthetic
sense : I was forced to see that the power of established custom rendered it impossible to bring about
any reduction or change whatever; I therefore nourished
a feeling of disquietude, which had more to do with the
fact that I had again embarked on a thing of the sort,
—much less with the conditions here themselves, which
I really knew beforehand,—but least of all with my
public, which always received me with friendliness and
approbation, often indeed with great warmth.

On the other hand, the abuse of the London critics
was a matter of perfect indifference to me, for their
hostility only proved to all the world that I had not
bribed them ; while it gave me, on the contrary, much
satisfaction to watch how they always left the door

open, so that had I made the least approach they would have tuned to a different pitch ; but naturally I thought of nothing of the kind.—

But on that evening I was really in a furious rage, that after the A-major Symphony I should have had to conduct a miserable vocal piece and a trivial Overture of Onslow's ; and, as is my way, in deepest dudgeon I told my friends aloud that I had that day conducted for the last time ; that on the morrow I should send in my resignation, and journey home. By chance a concert-singer, R.—a German Jew-youth—was present : he caught up my words and conveyed them all hot to a newspaper reporter. Ever since then rumours have been flying about in the German papers, which have misled even you. I need scarcely tell you that the representations of my friends, who escorted me home, succeeded in making me withdraw the hasty resolution conceived at a moment of despondency.

Since then we have had the *Tannhäuser* Overture at the fifth concert ; it was very well played, received by the public in a quite friendly manner, but not yet properly understood.

All the more pleased was I, therefore, when the Queen, who had promised (which is a rare event, and does not happen every year) to attend the seventh concert, ordered a repetition of the Overture. Now, if in itself it was extremely gratifying that the Queen should pay no regard to my highly compromised political position (which had been dragged to light with great malignity by the *Times*), and without hesitation assist at a public performance under my direction,

26

then her further behaviour towards me afforded me at last an affecting compensation for all the contrarieties and vulgar animosities which I had here endured.

She and Prince Albert, who both sat immediately facing the orchestra, applauded after the *Tannhäuser* Overture—with which the first part concluded—with graciousness almost amounting to a challenge, so that the public broke out into lively and prolonged applause. During the interval the Queen summoned me to the *salon*, and received me before her Court with the cordial words: "I am delighted to make your acquaintance : your composition has enraptured me !"

In a long conversation, in which Prince Albert also took part, she further inquired about my other works, and asked if it would not be possible to have my operas translated into Italian, so that she might be able to hear them, too, in London ? I was naturally obliged to give a negative answer, and moreover to explain that my visit was only a flying one, as conducting for a concert society—the only thing open to me here—was not at all my affair.—At the end of the concert the Queen and the Prince applauded me again most courteously.—

I relate this to you because it will afford you pleasure ; and I willingly allow you to make further use of this information, as I see how much mistake and malice touching myself and my stay in London has to be set right or defeated. The last concert is on the 25th, and I leave on the 26th, so as to resume in my quiet retreat my sadly interrupted work.

Farewell! Cordial thanks for your friendship, and
greetings to those who share it, from

Your

RICHARD WAGNER.

LONDON, *June* 15*th*, '55.

I will deliver your greetings to the Ney.

45.

DEAR, GOOD FISCHER!

How are you? I am just back from a mountain
health-resort, where my wife (in wretched weather) has
been taking whey. I am only now really home again,
and thinking about work and business. First of all, I
am anxious that the interrupted copy of my *Rheingold*
should be finished, and to-day I send you the remainder
—with the few prepared sheets—troubling you with the
request to hand over the matter to Wölfel as quickly as
possible. I have only one remark to make : Liszt will
pay me a visit in October, and he might like to play
through the score with me ; so Wölfel must have finished
by the end of September, that I may have my score back
by the beginning of October. Otherwise I should have
to interrupt him once again ! Very well !—

Besides this I have nothing new to tell you about
myself—except that the King can't help granting me an
amnesty shortly.

I must one day write a tremendous letter to *Heinemann*, and that's the awkward part of it, and why I
never do it. In fact, I have not much to say to him,
except that I would willingly be with him again and
have a good roast together ; we should find a grand
store, I warrant you.

I must put aside my joking to tell you that my *Peps* died on the tenth day after my return from London; for this event has deeply affected myself and Minna. I weep still when I think of the day the dear beast died.—

Now I will set hard to work again; but not overtask myself. For this year I shall be content to finish completely the *Walküre*. Only in the spring shall I set to work on the *Junge Siegfried*.—

What do the gentlemen in Dresden think when they hear of nothing but the *Tannhäuser* in Munich? Do they rub their hands for joy at preventing me from ever attending such performances? I presume so!—

Now please excuse this confused scrawl: it is the sixth letter I have written to-day!!! A thousand greetings to your family and the *Heinerei*, and remain good to your celebrated brother,

RICHARD WAGNER.

ZURICH, *August* 17*th*, '55.

46.

BEST FRIEND,

Nature has a cure for everything! For several days I have not felt well; I feel heaviness in my limbs; I am disgusted with work, and only with difficulty can I get through a part of my daily task; which again puts me out of humour, because only my work can cheer me. So this morning early, I looked with trouble at my music-sheets; and yet I tried to force myself to work; then comes a bill of exchange from friend X. at Dresden, payable fourteen days after sight—395 thalers. Well, this unforeseen event cured me; it reminded me that I live in a world in which men make other demands on

me than those of art-creations ! I placed my music-
paper on one side ; a good loud sneeze escaped my nose
—and I attended to my "business"; also I have
written to Herr Henniger, as you will see by the enclosure.

Pray say what has suddenly entered into the head of
this unfortunate man X. ? I did not know but what
he was well-disposed towards me. If he found that
inconvenient, he might have said so sooner. Some one
must be specially to blame for this sudden, quite unfore-
warned behaviour towards me. The business must be
in a bad state. Heavens ! how my heart bleeds when I
look on helplessly at this scandal from afar ; nor can it
afford me any consolation to have done everything in
my power to help.—But, for a reason like this, one
does not pounce upon an old friend one had else
treated with consideration. There must be some sort
of gossip at the back of it, and my supposition is surely
correct, that these people think that through my operas
(perhaps also London ? ? ! !) I am up to my ears in gold,
and living in riot and revel ! Well, I have written to
X., to set his mind clear on the matter. These sumptuous receipts are no longer mine ; but I have been
fortunate enough to find a friend to whom I could make
over this most uncertain revenue in return for a small
yearly allowance, which at least makes me certain as to
what I have and what I can spend each year. Still, if
I do not wish to contract fresh debts, I have only enough
to enable me to make both ends meet ; and the difficulty
of doing this is increased by the fact that I have still to
pay out of it some debts contracted here, from the time
of my flight and settling down. It is quite impossible

to think of accepting such a bill of exchange.—If, on the other hand, I could only learn what state my business is in ; there *must* be already some profit from it ? This is really my only hope, for otherwise I do not at all know how I shall satisfy the sudden importunity of the man.

Please be good enough to have my letter sent to Henniger ; I do not know the address.—

I suppose I must have patience with Wölfel : it is really a tiresome piece of work. I do hope he will be ready in the course of November—say by the middle ; then there will still be time, and by that date I shall have money to pay him.

(Have you anything more of mine ?)

I hear the Heines are really thinking about America. I also am invited there now, but for the present I have had to decline. Yet America floats before me as a possible money-source, if indeed one's sole aim were the making of a small fortune. In two years I shall have completed my *Nibelungen*, then I shall look around for a whole year to see whether it is possible to bring to pass a performance according to my ideas. If I see that possibility, then I'll move heaven and earth to carry it out. If, however, I am convinced to the contrary, I will have my scores beautifully bound, put them away in my chest, and go off to America—as I said above—to make a small fortune. Whether there or here, I shall then become a Philistine, and say to the world henceforth : . . . *Here*, I would then play the Philistine in your company : *there*, after all with the Heines. It would indeed be funny if *we all* played the Philistine there together !—Tell that to the *Heinerei*,

and assure them that, even if I do not write, everything remains as of old. I am delighted to hear of the
fellow's tough health.

Farewell! Hearty greetings to yours : study your
choruses, lead the life of a saint, and do not go in for
too much management! .

Ever your

RICHARD WAGNER.

Would you be so kind as to send a book of words of
the *Flying Dutchman* to H. Michaelson (Leipzigerstrasse
42, Berlin) ?

47.

MY DEAR OLD FRIEND!

I was still on my sick couch when what you
sent yesterday arrived, and there I have been ever
since I wrote my last letter to you.

I say nothing more !—

To-day I got up from bed for an hour, in order to
write to X., because the recent news about him left me
no rest. I prefer to have the letter sent through you :
first of all that X. may not be able to deny the receipt
of it, and secondly, that you may read it over first ;
you need then only to close it. It is really a pitiable
business ! ! !—

Many thanks for the copy ; it has turned out remarkably well. Tell that to Wölfel from me !

Then I have still a great request. Be so kind and
ask Fürstenau to send *at once* (by post) half a ream of
the *same paper* which Wölfel got from him. He could
receive the amount through the post-office ; or—if that

won't do—you could perhaps settle it ; or, if even that won't do, Fürstenau might perhaps draw a bill on me. Otherwise I would send him the trifling sum at once.

I can't keep up, and must go back to bed : I already feel bad.—

Greet me Heines, and hold in kind remembrance
Your thankful
RICHARD WAGNER.

48.

AH, YOU DEAR, GOOD, OLD FISCHER !

I have had " roses " on my face again ; but still my humour will not turn very rosy.   During such an illness letter-stuff always accumulates, and now to pay off my debts I must manage as sparingly as possible, so as not to impoverish my treasury of writing-inclination too markedly to the advantage of one creditor.—I thank you very much for thinking of me immediately on the news of X.'s death ; but what can *I* do from here in this case ?   I should much like to know what has taken place, and with what result.   I fear, however, that I can only consider that that copyright business has again taken an ominous turn, in direct consequence of X.'s death ! !   Ah ! how pleasant all that is ! !   At last one makes a success with an opera to which so much has been sacrificed, and then— ! !   It's a real joy !—

Also your news about *Lohengrin* at Bremen surprised me very much, since the management there has not yet troubled itself about me the least bit in the world : it gave the opera without saying a word to me on the subject.   I at once wrote, complained of such unloyal

behaviour, and demanded an immediate honorarium.
A fortnight has passed, and still I have no answer.
That is really the first time a theatre has played me
such a trick!—Tichatschek might do something in the
matter. Or shall I make a public scandal? That
again is not very pleasant. That T. has at last sung
the *Lohengrin* gave me great joy! I certainly was not
mistaken when, in writing that part, I foresaw that it
would be one of his best! Only, what a pity that I
could not give a performance of the opera with him,
and, instead, must leave it to bunglers to create the
part. I willingly believe, that even now Tichatschek
is the best in it, and again, willingly would I be present
when he sings it. If he had only employed his splendid
powers somewhere else! I would rather it had been
Hamburg or Breslau. Perhaps that will still be possible for him! Best greetings to him from me, and tell
him that in spirit here I stood upon my head, entirely
as he deserved!—

That I do not even manage to write to my good old
Heinemann is indeed dreadful: Heaven knows! I
would like to write many sheetsful of good sense to
him, and that's just what makes it so difficult that I
almost always can't help preferring to settle the matter
with a right honourable and cordial greeting.

For a long time I have been constantly dreaming that
I was back in Dresden, but secretly hidden in your
house; and just as secretly you brought me into the
theatre, and there I heard one of my operas, but all
wrong and out of tune, so that I became wild and
wanted to shout out loud, from which you, in great
alarm, were trying to stop me. Certainly, if ever I

were permitted to return to Germany, and could so far conquer my repugnance as to call at Dresden, it would for sure be only secretly and for the purpose of surprising you all one evening, and playing the fool with you. Mamma Heine would have to get ready the pickled herring, as on the *Rienzi* evening. Then indeed would we see who had altered!! A thousand hearty greetings for to-day!

At last the *Walküre* is finished: it has turned out remarkably beautiful: I lately had a performance of the First Act in my own house. I sang the *Siegmund and Hunding*, and Frau Heine, an excellent amateur, the *Sieglinde*: a friend accompanied.

Now, I shall soon set to work at *Junge Siegfried*. In 1857 I shall perform the whole thing here: seats are reserved for you. Get me a good tenor!—And till then hold me always in kind remembrance, and be thanked a thousand times for your faithful friendship, which always gives me the highest comfort. Live well and soundly.

Your
R. W.

ZURICH, *April 29th*, '56.

49.

DEAREST OLD FRIEND!

Do not be angry with me, if, after a lengthy silence, I only send you to-day a hurried request. Liszt, who is still with me, is pressing me for my arrangement of Palestrina's *Stabat Mater*. I once asked you to send it here with some other things. Would you be kind enough to send me a parcel right quickly, and, beside the *Stabat*, put in the Bach

Motets and *Passion* music, the Ninth Symphony, etc. ? The score of the *Iphigenia in Aulis* that I asked for, I would also much like to have : you said, you know, that Lüttichau had consented to let me have a copy.

So—let me have the said things at once.—I am more and more satisfied with my health : my last cure was highly beneficial to me, and I am well rid of the wretched erysipelas. Also I have again commenced working with great eagerness. Liszt's visit is now engrossing my time.—Whenever shall I see you again ? And how are you ? Always active and jolly ? That, etc., Tichatschek has not written me a word since his visit : tell him he is a ——

And greet Heine, and hold me dear, as you always are and will be to your

R. W.

ZURICH, *November 7th*, '56.

50.

Kindest greetings for the New Year, my dear good old Fischer !

Say, are you still angry with me on account of that letter to L., that you always keep on grumbling about it in spite of my detailed and (I think) satisfactory explanation ? And ever again, as though I consider you—*i.e.*, thee (?)—incapable of giving the *Lohengrin ?* If you happen—a thing I certainly do not expect—to preserve my letters, do read through again what I have already said to you in explanation on this point ; and do not be unfair with me, as though you did not know what I had meant in my former letter to L. You know that the countermanding of the scenery for *Lohengrin*

so embittered me, that I lost all desire to see this very
opera performed at Dresden, which I had specially
calculated for that place, and that in consequence I had
still to get rid of a feeling of revenge against L.   Now,
however, since I have discovered that L. did not of his
own impulse set aside my opera, but only did this in
obedience to a hint from *above*, I look at the matter
in quite a different light, and can no longer bear L.
a grudge about it.   This I have requested Tichatschek
to tell him : if he has not done it that is his affair.
But, you wicked old friend, you should not always be
worrying about a mistake that has been cleared up.
Still I must tell you again that the performance of
Lohengrin under the direction of R. or K. is for me an
unpleasant and painful thought, however high may be
your opinion of these gentlemen.

—So for the New Year I have now told you what
you astonished and vexed me with in the Old.—

Best thanks for what you have sent.   I have again
got a lot of silly stuff into my house !   How you really
manage to have so many worries with the rubbish, and
especially with me, is certainly a serious matter, and I
am sure any other but you would long ago have lost
all patience.   Heaven grant that I may be able one
day so to thank you for your faithful, touching, and
helpful friendship, as is so often my heart's desire
when I am with you in my thoughts.   How often do we
speak, Minna and I, of our good old friends *Fischer* and
Heine, and especially do we go back to the early days
of our arrival in Dresden, where we so suddenly found
these good, these best of friends !   That, too, is my most
refreshing remembrance of the *Rienzi* days.   That this

love has now maintained itself so long, and far beyond our separation, is certainly one of the most beautiful experiences of my life.   Most heartfelt greetings to you and Heine.—Do not be angry with me for taking advantage once more of your kindness, with regard to the sending of *Tannhäuser* to Basle.   *Tannhäuser* will probably soon have ended its fortunate course!—

Of Tichatschek you may hear somewhat further from me, though it be but little.   Farewell, and hold me dear!   *Auf Wiedersehen.*

Your
R. W.

ZURICH, *January 2nd,* '57.

51.

DEAR OLD FELLOW!

Do please send at once a revised score of the *Flying Dutchman* for the Carlsruhe Court Theatre, to E. D.   Give me an account of what you have laid out, for you have certainly advanced money, and tell me how much I shall send you, so that you may have something in hand to go on with.

You are already accustomed to these flying notes, so that I need not apologize.

With deep thanks, always

Your faithful
R. W.

ZURICH, *February 12th,* '57,

52.

MY DEAR GOOD FISCHER!

How are you, then, and how is Heine?   Did he give you my greetings last summer?—I live now in the greatest retirement from the world, even from Zurich,—*i.e.*, I seldom go into the town, but instead live quietly in my pleasant little country house, watch my wife attending to the garden, work, and go for walks in a pleasant valley : that is my whole life.   Yet I have had German visitors : Ed. Devrient, Präger, and Röckel (from England), Robert Franz, etc., etc., were this summer with me for a longer or shorter period, and we had a lot of music, *Rheingold*, *Walküre*, and the two finished acts of *Junge Siegfried*.   I am now composing *Tristan und Isolde*, about which Heine has probably told you something.   I hope to finish it next summer, and with this work to offer the theatres a task easy to master.   But I must first produce it somewhere *myself :* otherwise I do not give it forth.   I will wait and see how it succeeds, and what the possibilities are.

I have really little hopes of Dresden : the King is personally averse to me.   For the rest, I should think my stupid Dresden game of nine years back has been forgotten now ?

—Meanwhile, as Heaven wills : if I should never receive an amnesty, I must console myself with the thought that I should never have got much joy from the German theatres.

Greetings to Tichatschek from me.   I do not really know what to think of him.   About Easter he wrote to me that he was then leaving Dresden for several months, and would be glad to see me again.   Well, I kept on waiting for his visit : I would have written to him again about it, if I had only known where to. For he went, in fact, on his travels.   Now that he has not come, and has written nothing further to me thereon, I am as much surprised as grieved at heart.

Well, our Prague enthusiast, Apt, has also been here. I was glad to get news of you through him. He wished absolutely to buy a score of *Rienzi*, and I promised to write to you about it. But I think I shall do better to keep back the few scores still remaining ; the opera cannot, after all, be smothered, and I will do nothing to injure it, just out of consideration for K. and P., who, by the circulation of *Rienzi*, may be able to make profit. I therefore ask you to *lend* a score to Apt ; he can keep it for awhile, and have copied out of it what he wants.—

You gave me hopes of a visit from the music-publisher M. ; now, unfortunately, he has not come, and, on the other hand, I hear of nothing but fresh confusion and lack of energy in the management of the business. The pianoforte arrangement without words of *Tannhäuser* (so profitable for the market) is still not out ! Do persuade M. to write categorically to me about the whole matter.—

As regards *Tristan*, that must remain between ourselves. I will not let anything leak out concerning it.—

And now, you good, bad old friend ! when shall I at last see you again ? ? You and *Heine must* visit me next summer and stay with me ; if you don't do that I will never in my life write to you again !—But now, last of all, a thousand greetings to yourself, and greet Wilhelm, and let all of you hold me dear.

Adieu, good old fellow !   Your

R. W.

ZURICH, *October 29th,* '57.

53.

MY DEAR OLD FRIEND!

Hearty thanks for your last letter; your wonderful activity has rejoiced me uncommonly, and the promise of your visit next year gives me a hope that warms my heart, and which you must not reduce to nothingness.—

But it is characteristic and touching, above all else, that it should be left for an old fellow—like yourself—to introduce *Liszt* to Dresden! In this one sees what youth and old age are, and whether it is a question of years, or of heart and right understanding! In this you have again proved your metal, as once upon a time with me: for without you I should never have made my way with *Rienzi*. Honour to you, dear good old fellow!—

About Heine's activity with a *Conservatorium* I know nothing at all? But that is altogether grand, for therein I see that he also keeps himself fresh and active; still there is a good strong blend of my own egoism in it, for thus I may venture all the more to hope to see you both again, as the old fellows of former times. May it only be soon—at latest next summer, for then you will both come to me!—

I am very glad that you have not yet communicated to L. the last propositions I sent you, and I hope also that nothing has been done since then. For should you think—as you hinted to me—that that old debt may be regarded as cancelled, and that—in the case of an amnesty—they would not think of causing me any further unpleasantness on account of it: in that case I should be most thankful, and let the matter drop.   For —this I say honestly—the only thing that made me think of offering myself again to the Dresden Court in any capacity was the perplexity in which I was placed by the idea that they might still expect from me a satisfaction of that debt.

But apart from that, there is nothing I long for more than to remain—free, and never again to accept any kind of engagement whatever.   Dresden—the theatre —L., etc., awake in me such a train of tormenting remembrances, that I would like to be for ever considered there as dead.   Only yourself and Heine would I take from out of the place !   That you will see !—So, let that be kept to yourself, and—should the occasion arise—mention nothing of my propositions, unless you perceive that they are going to demand such a compensation from me.

Lately the Grand Duke of Baden sent me a message that he had just written to the King of Saxony, in order to obtain permission for me to visit Carlsruhe. I am now waiting to see if he has in any way succeeded, but naturally doubt it very much !—Yet I presume that my affair is likely now to be taken up again ; hence the above hint.

For the rest, I do not believe that anywhere in the world are there such muddled-headed men as in Dresden. You will easily guess that I refer again to the business successors of the late X. !   If you should see the music-publisher M., please tell him that, if his intentions are friendly, he ought not to refrain from writing me, and to some extent explaining the state of things.   As far back as last Easter the lawyer of Fraülein X. sent me the inventory, with the notice that the publishing business had been handed over to M.   But, as I have transferred all my rights in the business, it was my duty to hand over the whole matter to the attorney of these two persons, and at the same time to express to him my astonishment that he should look so badly after the interests of his clients that the attorney of the opposite party, in spite of the surrender, still thought it necessary to apply to me and not to him! Now for a long time I have heard nothing at all—until at last M. returns me, through you, this unheard-of, unexpected answer.   It is enough to make one mad! But tell M. that all I want from him is information about the technical part of the publishing ; because, though I have no longer any present right to the receipts, I still am anxious that the business should be conducted in such a way that my assignees may derive the utmost possible profit from it.—

Yes, considering that I can get no other news about the real state of affairs, I shall have to be prepared next for being summarily sued again, especially if people are always hearing such silly nonsense about my income as appears from time to time !—O—you divinely practical men !—

Well, that is the old story over again—much the same as it has been told for the last six years !   Do not be angry that I give it you to hear.   But you appear to me—alas ! the only clear and intelligent head amongst these stupid creatures.

Otherwise, dearest old fellow, I am well : I live alone, work, read, and make good music.   You may take my word for it : *Tristan* will please even you,

although there are not many choruses in it! A
thousand greetings to you and Heine from me and
Minna.

Good-bye! Remain what you are.

Your
R. W.

ZURICH, *December 2nd,* '57.

I herewith commission Herr Chorus-master Fischer,
Sen., of Dresden, to send off at once a copy of the
score and of the libretto of my opera *Rienzi* to the
High Intendant of the Royal Court Theatre in
Hanover.

RICHARD WAGNER.

PARIS, *January 18th,* '58.

54.

DEAREST FRIEND,

I beg you *this moment* to get sent here—to
Paris—the *two copies* I requested of the pianoforte
arrangements of my three operas that X. published.
I wrote about them last week, but on this point have
received no answer. The securing of the French copyright for these operas depends upon this step, and I
wish to ensure this result—for selling to publishers
here—should it come to that. If the things have not yet
gone (for with your people dawdling of all kinds is possible), they should be sent—**by post**—to the following
address: Monsieur E. Ollivier, Avocat au barreau de
Paris et membre du corps législatif, 29, Rue St.
Guillaume, Fbg. St. Germain à Paris.

You could perhaps have this seen to by the present
publisher himself.

Do not be angry with me.   But you are the only one on whom I can depend.

More shortly from Zurich.   Here I am always in horrible haste.

By the way, I read in the newspapers that my *Tannhäuser* is accepted for the Grand Opera here, and that I have come hither for the rehearsals.   Do contradict this.   Up to now no word of truth in it.   I am here to prevent its being used at other theatres (without asking my permission): but what is not, may be. Adieu!   In haste!

Your
RICH. WAGNER.

PARIS, *January 27th,* '58.

55.

Ha! I may as well write again to Fischer!—thought I to myself yesterday.—So listen!

DEAR OLD PARTNER!

I have just learnt, as the final result of my inquiries, that according to the agreement between France and Saxony of the year 1856, nothing more is necessary to establish the copyright even of musical works, than that the author or his publisher should deposit for this purpose *two copies* in *Leipzig* itself, I believe in the Booksellers' Exchange; they will there be registered under the terms of the treaty, and a *certificate to that effect* will be sent to Paris; which certificate, once deposited in the proper quarter, the right of publication is guaranteed for France.   Perhaps Herr M., the present agent for our publications, knew of this, and therefore did not send the pianoforte arrangements to Paris.

Now, I beg you (it is truly a shame that I should always yoke an old and worried man like you to such a heap of rubbish!—but it is because you are my only refuge), so I beg you to tell M., with all speed, that if the pianoforte arrangements have not yet been sent, he need not do so now: but, if this has been done, I will see about sending them back to Dresden. For the present we have only to see at once about *two* other copies for Leipzig, then to proceed in the manner indicated above. I suppose M. has his agent in Leipzig who attends to these matters: if not, he must have it arranged by *Breitkopf und Härtel*, to whom I will write to-morrow about taking over this commission.

But the *certificate* of registration should be sent to me in Paris immediately it is executed, and, mind you, to the address which I already gave in my last letter :

"*Monsieur E. Ollivier,*

Avocat au barreau de Paris, et membre du corps législatif, 29, *Rue St. Guillaume, Fbg. St. Germain à Paris.*"

This gentleman—Liszt's new son-in-law—is my lawyer, attends to everything for me, and is specially commissioned by me to look after this copyright ; while I, on the other hand, assign it to my creditors in such a way that I undertake that all future proceeds of sale or honoraria, which Parisian publishers shall pay for issuing one or other of these three operas, shall be handed over in their entirety, until the demands on me are fully satisfied.

Now, I am only curious as to whether I shall at last hear anything from you, and whether the matter will be set straight.

Yesterday evening I found in my room your last packet, the *Rienzi* text-book, which I asked for. You cannot think how delighted I am when I see your hand-writing, you dear, good old fellow !

Beyond that, there is not much to say about this text. Merely this, that a translator has offered himself to me who is said to be a good hand at his work. For the rest, I have come here simply to *prevent* a possible murdering of any of my operas at the subordinate theatres without my being asked. I could only be safe from this if the rights of ownership provided by the International Treaty were secured for these operas. On that basis I then gain this much, that I can also prevent performances ; and that was what I wanted. Moreover, all here think that overtures will very soon be made me on the part of the management of the Grand Opera ; but I must quietly wait for this, for if *I* offer myself, I tie my own hands. I will only allow *Tannhäuser* to be performed if it can be given in its entirety, without mutilations. It is possible, nay pro-bable, that that will come off next winter. So stand matters !

I travel back next week. Let me know soon what is being done about *Rienzi*. Greetings to Heine and Tichatschek, and remain good and kind to me !

Your fussy

RICHARD W.

PARIS, *January 29th*, '58.

56.

DEAREST FRIEND, BROTHER, AND *Regisseur*,

To your noble Latin hand-writing I must reply with my bad one as quickly as possible.

I am back, and thinking again of serious work. In Paris I had nothing further to attend to than the recognition of my copyright in my own operas. I was sorry to supply a fresh occasion of confusion to my Dresden confusion-counsellors. At the last moment I was obliged to countermand my first request to send two copies of my pianoforte editions, because it was only then that I received definite information as to what had to be done in conformity with the treaties. When I was informed, however, that the music had, after all, been sent off, I further wrote that the Dresden agent, Herr M., must now arrange whether it should be sent back again, or perhaps remain in Paris for other purposes. Anyhow, I am now waiting for the news that the required certificate regarding the deposition in Leipzig has arrived in Paris; for on that depends all further movements. Do be so good, and sharpen up the wits of Herr Musikhändler M. a little on this point. In general, too, I should very much like to enter into direct communication with this gentleman. I want nothing but that my advice respecting the fructification of the vested capital should be asked for and followed; and this I can only bring about by communicating directly with Herr M. But he still puts off writing to me. Meanwhile time is passing, and the pianoforte edition without words still does not appear. In Paris, on the other hand, I found in French families many copies of the full pianoforte score of *Tannhäuser*. They must be selling wonderfully well. So—please once more earnestly pray Herr M. to write to me ; he can, indeed, have all my proposals scrutinized by the lawyer. If they delay longer with the pianoforte score without words, I shall straightway fix a term within which I then give myself the right to hand over this important arrangement to another publisher ; for I can no longer bear to see the object of publication so carelessly exploited.

Besides this, I have lately wanted to impart to you a wish, the fulfilment of which is now, however, rendered more difficult by the unfortunate fact that, as you tell me, the *Rienzi* in Dresden has been again put off, until the summer. For I should like to make money out of this opera as rapidly as possible, before my latest work appears. In the hope that *Rienzi* might still come out in February at Dresden, I had already invited Hanover, Breslau, and Frankfort to produce it quickly. As *Rienzi* is now practically a dead letter, these theatres will naturally wait for the Dresden revival ; so my plan has fallen through. According to it, I had intended to seek out an agent to attend to the sale of the score to the theatres. The present stock of scores was to be given to him, with the right of making copies as soon as it should be exhausted ; I also proposed to give him an exact table of the charges to the different theatres, which I should have appraised according to the scale of payments made for *Tannhäuser*. Then the agent was to sell the opera, according to the prescribed terms for honoraria, and send me a quarterly account. In order to secure myself (and because I am very much in need of money !) he was to pay me at once 1,000-1,500 thalers in advance, in return for which I would not only pay him interest on this advance until the honoraria came in, but moreover (on condition of the advance), would adjudge him twenty-five per cent. of the profits as commission. This would certainly be a most advantageous business for an agent ; but as I should have to insist upon the advance, naturally the only person who could be found ready to undertake the matter would be one who was certain of the success of *Rienzi*, and placed full faith in it. Now, as things have gone hitherto with the opera, this could therefore only be a Dresdener, because every Dresdener knows what there is in *Rienzi*, and can be sure of his affair. Do you perhaps know some one on whom one could rely ? The best person would appear to me to be Herr M. Naturally, as this concerns my reserved right of sale to the theatres, it would remain a private matter of business between myself and M. ; and, if he undertook it, it would be wise to keep the affair, for the present, to ourselves, at least as regards the advance ; the advertisements and applications to the theatres he could issue nevertheless, simply in a private way. If you think he can scrape up the advance, do speak soon with him. Will you be so kind ?

For the rest, I may inform you that I possess my original score of *Rienzi* ; so it has not got lost. But the library of the Dresden theatre certainly possesses the first copy of the original score ; why did you not let Apt of Prague have the information he wanted out of that ?

Concerning Paris, I deem it possible that *Rienzi* may

be given next winter in the *Théatre Lyrique*, yet nothing
is settled.   I am waiting about *Tannhäuser*.

What, then, is your Heine doing with the Dresden
Conservatorium ?   Cannot I learn some more particulars
about it ?

And why have you not brought out *Rienzi* yet ?   This
has put me very much out, and also is a hindrance to
my Paris prospects !   Oh, you dawdlers !   Well, about
this, as about so many other things, I must learn to be
patient.   Good heavens ! who would have believed that
after nine years there would be no prospect for me of an
amnesty !—

Instead of that *you* must, in any case, pay me a visit
in the spring, however busy you may be as *Manager !*

Greet Heine !   Farewell, and remain good to your

RICH. WAGNER.

ZURICH, *February 7th,* '58.

57.

DEAREST OLD FELLOW !

To-day I come to you with a good strong pinch
of snuff.   I beg you, right quickly—either in person or
through Heine, but best of all through a well-disposed
and influential intermediate personage—to have the
letter to Prince Albert, in which I make a last attempt
for my pardon through his intercession, delivered into
the hands of the addressee.

Turn and twist it as I may, without a speedy
prospect of an amnesty, it is all up with me : I *must*
have the refreshment of performing my works—or I
must finally throw up the sponge.—

I say nothing more to you, and ever count on your kindness and love!

Cordial thanks for everything.

Your

RICHARD WAGNER.

(The address has not turned out very grand : if you think so too, you might have a fresh one written.)

ZURICH, *February 19th,* '58.

58.

O, YOU GOOD, FATHERLY BROTHER!

Best thanks for the news and the sign of life. But how can you say that I would not wait for you in Zurich? I did not even know that you would really come; I only heard a little whisper, but then again, on the top of that, that you had given it up and gone to take the waters!—Besides, you would have come to Zurich too late : I had waited nine years, and at last lost patience. Solely for that reason did I go away.— That you warn me to rest at last is not to the point. Heavens! how I love rest—for other people to take! To be serious : my poor wife is suffering very much; she has heart-disease, and one must have experienced that to know what it means! There is no more rest for the sufferer, nor for the persons in attendance. I hope that she is improving now, in comfort among her relatives at Zwickau.

In November she will—I think—go to Dresden, there to dispose herself and our chattels for the present. Where we shall finally settle down together after that must still be uncertain ; but, in any case, I long for a definitive stay in a large town with many art facilities, in order from time to time to be able to hear, and especially to conduct, a thing which has been wanting to me so long.

For to-day, I have to thank you for your continued friendly zeal in my behalf. I have written at once to Darmstadt (Schindelmeisser) and to Munich, and insisted that you should be paid for the pianoforte arrangements. For the future I would advise you to have nothing to do with pianoforte arrangements : how the devil do they concern us ? Let people go to the music-shops, and get their arrangements made from their own notes according to the score.—Concerning the honorarium I have written to Munich.

Now, Heaven grant that *Rienzi* may bring me in something ; I need it, and I shall have no new opera ready before next year. Keep scores in readiness ; I will settle with Tichatschek about the expenses. I have written to all the good theatres, and hope you will soon receive orders. I was delighted at your bringing *Rienzi* out again in such a grand way, and the fact awakened some of the pleasantest remembrances of my life. I thank your Wilhelm heartily for the choruses, which, as I hear, went so well. Concerning Tichatschek, one must say that the fellow is a living wonder. But above all, I rejoice that he is such an excellent fellow ! A thousand greetings to him !

What are Mamma and Papa doing in Little Oberseer Street ? If I could only see you all soon again : I much need such a cordial !

Hearty greeting, dear old fellow. With sincere thanks,

Your

VENICE, *October 9th,* '58.   R. W.

59.

DEAR FRIEND!

I beg you to confer at once in my name with Herr Musikhändler M. on the following subject.

Some time ago the musician Mehnert discovered, after a personal search, that there was still a supply of forty-two copies of my score of *Tannhäuser* in X.'s ware-house. Of these he revised thirty-two. Herr M. should now explain what has become of the other ten. At that time I gave him instructions that *no* copy should be sold any more through the music traders to private individuals, as these copies were my private property, and did not belong to the general body of publications I had surrendered. I learnt also that my instructions were carried out, since I received repeated proof that private individuals had wished to buy the score from the business, but had been there refused. Relying on this, and firmly believing that my instructions had been followed to the letter, I asked Härtels to engrave a new edition of the score, because *all* the copies were ex-hausted ; all the same I was bound, in return for their great sacrifice, to show them that the score was still, to some extent, a source of profit, and I therefore men-tioned that for the last five years no copies had been delivered to private individuals through the music trade, although there had been repeated inquiries for them. Hereupon Härtels assure me, however, that I must certainly be misinformed, as only last year they them-selves obtained a score through the music business. Herr M. might give me some explanation of this. If he has been forced by the other side to go on selling my scores, he ought at least to have given me notice of it; and if he has sold all the ten copies at present missing, that is a point about which we must have a settlement. Anyhow, I want—in this case—at least and first, a *formal declaration in writing* from Herr M. that he really possesses *no* more copies of the score, and thus will not sell any more. I want this declaration in order to induce Härtels to undertake the great cost of the new edition of the score which has now become necessary. I beg you to deliver the declaration to my wife, for her to forward to Härtels.

Hearty greetings from your

RICH. WAGNER.

VENICE, *March 10th,* '59.

LETTERS

TO

FERDINAND HEINE,

1841—1868.

LETTERS

TO

FERDINAND HEINE,

1841—1868.

I.

MOST ESTEEMED HERR HEINE!

You cannot believe how much you have rejoiced my hope-sick heart when, from time to time, in your letters to my brave friend Kietz, you made mention of me and of my affairs. They were hard times, and at moments there was need of some upward impulse; however vague and indeterminate your communications might be, yet they were of the greatest importance to me—firstly, because they came from a sympathetic man; and secondly, because they were the only ones. Since then I have certainly received a letter from Councillor W., but as he referred to an official answer which ought already to have been communicated to me, in reply to my writing—an answer, however, which I have never received—his letter contains nothing

definite, and allows of little in the way of anticipation.
Only lately have I become acquainted, through my
friend Laube in Leipzig, with certain expressions of Mad.
Devrient, which mainly confirmed what was already
known to me through your last letter to Kietz, namely,
that she was exerting herself with the most amiable
sympathy in my behalf, but which showed me still
more decidedly that the religious-catholic part of my
libretto was a chief stumbling-block. On this hint, I
lost no time in communicating to Councillor W. all
the changes which I had already long prepared with
regard to this point. First of all, I called his attention
to the fact that this was more a question of the catholic
costume than of the catholic idea : I pointed out to him
that the Pope—who, moreover, stands at a distance
from the scene of action—appears in my book, not as
a spiritual power that sets up or casts down theses
and dogmas, but simply as a temporal prince who is
busied in protecting his earthly possessions against rob-
bery and anarchy, and only as such at last makes use of
his dreaded power in order to get rid of the *too* bold
defender of his worldly interests. That *Rome*, is, in
reality, the seat of action of the drama, makes it of
course historically impossible to substitute another
sovereign for the Pope ; but as he is only represented
by his Legate, his interference is already somewhat
toned down,—and if I now leave it optional to change
this Legate and a Cardinal into one plain temporal
Envoy, then there would only remain the ban of
excommunication to which exception could be taken.
But was not the ban, though notably shortened in
form, still preserved in its essence and significance in

the performance of *La Juive* at Dresden ? Then why
not here also, where from the very first I considered it
advisable to make its proclamation as short as possible ?
There are, indeed, excellent means of substantially
allowing everything to be represented, if only certain
éclatant externals and symbols be omitted. *Les Hugue-*
nots has been given—what more would one have ?—for
in it, however much disguised the costume, the religious-
dogmatic tendency could now and never be expunged.
—But if in my *Rienzi* the word *Church* is not allowed
to stand, well—I suppose one must then have recourse
to the German Emperor, and beseech him to let one
thrust the whole affair into his satchel, and to himself
pronounce the excommunication as an Imperial ban.—
Surely priests and clerics have before now passed in
solemn procession across the Dresden stage ? I should
be glad if you would confirm this for me. Moreover,
there is no man fitter than you, most worthy sir, to
give a certain medley to the costume, so that it will be
impossible for the Censor, for instance, to definitely
point out the Cardinal, although every one else will
recognize him.

Well, I will not trouble you any further with my
explanations ; so I will only add that I have expressed
myself fully on this matter to Councillor W. (and,
indeed, with the request to bring my remarks to bear
upon the right quarter). But of what avail is all this,
if these gentlemen do not send me a single word of
direct reply ? If they will only challenge me, I both
can and certainly will remove each stumbling-block.
But why, in the name of fortune, is this not done ? In
order to come to this decision, do they require a period

of three months ? or is it true—as I almost fear—is it
true that the man who alone can be deputed to pass
judgment on my musical composition is a hindrance to
my cause ?—

It is certainly of unmeasurable importance that Mad.
Devrient is interested in my opera, for on this circumstance alone rests the most favourable *Chance* for the
success of my project.   Should she persist, and yield
herself with sympathy to my feeble inspirations, I shall
have to thank this grand woman for my All.   How the
pygmies here disgust me, when I reflect on *her* creative
genius !—

I found an opportunity to respond to an invitation of
Councillor W., and to write some Correspondence for
his *Abend Zeitung*.   In it you will find, among other
things, a notice, certainly only fugitive and superficial, on
Vieuxtemps—but I promise you to send more elaborate
accounts to the Brockhaus paper shortly.—Vieuxtemps
as well as friend Kietz greet you cordially, and will soon
write to you.   The latter has lately been so engrossed
in a large oil-portrait, that he could not yet discharge
his duty of writing to you.   He had sent to the exhibition a charming crayon-drawing, the portrait of my
wife, and has now the triumph of hearing that it is
accepted.—

In conclusion : a request for your kind forgiveness, if
I presume herewith to send you such a hasty—almost
slovenly, letter ; I hope you will forgive me, in remembrance of the "amusement" which I afforded you in
my youth, when in a certain "situation" I ran along by
the side of a certain carriage.   If you will manifest your
forgiveness by a few lines, it only remains for me to

beseech you to be assured of my most cordial thanks for your interest in me.

With sincere respect,

Your servant,

RICHARD WAGNER.

PARIS, 25, RUE DU HELDER, *March* 18*th*, '41.

2.

MY MOST ESTEEMED HERR HEINE,

It would indeed have given me immeasurable pleasure to have been fortunate enough to receive a few lines from your valued hand, informing me whether you justify me or not in presupposing your sympathy for me and my interests. But, on the other hand, I know through our friend *Kietz* that at first you had very great hindrances, and often, unfortunately, not of the pleasantest, so that you could only bestow scanty communications even upon him ; and as Kietz moreover assures me that he observes how kindly and sympathetically disposed you always are towards me, I therefore, counting on this your favourable inclination, forbear to woo afresh your friendship, and only wish most ardently that I may not outweary it.—

More than a month ago I received the desired formal acceptation of my opera, on the part of the general management of the Dresden Court Theatre. For the hastening on of this decision I am certainly indebted chiefly to the instigation of Councillor W., whom, by an unimportant counter-service, I have been enabled to win over to my interests. It is, however, obvious tha even W. could not have given so fortunate a turn to this decision had not the votes of Reissiger and other authorities concerned in the musical question been given in my favour. Reissiger, who had already expressed to me by letter his honest intentions towards me, has put me under endless obligation to him. What deep apologies have I to make to him, to you, and even to myself, for the doubt which I expressed about his unselfish and liberal intentions, a doubt which could only arise in me through my complete ignorance of what it was proposed to do in Dresden with my opera! Heaven be praised! Everything hitherto has shaped itself according to my wishes; for only in the past few days I received the consent to my last desire, namely, the wish that my opera should be put on the stage immediately, after the appearance of the new opera by Reissiger. Thus I have reason to hope that *Rienzi* will appear on the Dresden boards the end of this or beginning of next year; at length a long-awaited, gracious prospect!—

The most important thing which now remains to be kept alert is, without doubt, the good-feeling of the noble Schröder-Devrient; of what nameless weight is this to me! I have just written to *her*, as well as to *Herr Tichatschek*. May my good angel make and maintain both these persons well disposed towards me! Everything depends upon this; and if you, my dear Herr Heine, hold me worthy of some effort, you would render me a priceless service if you would exert your utmost friendly influence with these two celebrities in my favour.

I am now most eager to know whether the management will soon think of making preparations for the scenic equipment of my opera. As Herr von Lüttichau

wrote me, that only after most careful previous examination of the book and score had he given his consent
to the production of my opera, so I cannot entertain
a doubt but what he is fully acquainted with the heavy
expenditure which its equipment essentially demands.
Moreover, as I have never omitted to draw his special
attention to this point, I therefore feel confident that it
has already been decided that it shall want for nothing.
In this, my best Herr Heine, you are the most important man, and with all insistence I therefore beg you to
bestow on me your whole good-will.   As soon then as
the time of production of Reissiger's opera approaches,
I shall send you a detailed memorandum, containing
all my ideas and wishes with regard to decoration,
costume, and arrangement, as well as what concerns
the musical *mise en scène.*—Meanwhile *Kietz* has already
offered, should you approve, to jot down here and there
a sketch and send it to you.   Ah! if I could only get
to hear something, and that right soon.

Kietz, as you know, is about leaving Paris.   He is
always complaining—but has certainly no right to do so;
if he will only give himself the trouble, he can quite easily
maintain himself for some time yet by work—he has
some orders now.   Besides, if he must leave Paris, he
can do it with the consoling conviction that he carries
away with him a good slice of what he has learnt here;
even though the proof of this should consist in nothing
beyond the oil-portrait of *Anna Zecher*, to which he
can certainly point with pride.   In this painting, I was
less struck at finding Kietz' unrestrained conception
of a subject again displayed, in a sphere as yet so little
trodden by him; but the thing that most surprised me

was that he could so quickly become familiar with colour and the brush, that in the matter of execution it is scarcely possible to detect the novice.—He has a delightful talent and a splendid sensibility—I should like to write much more to you about him, if my space had not unfortunately come to an end ; for I confess that, purely out of consideration for yourself, I had no intention this time of writing you a long letter. Let me therefore with a brief sigh return to myself, and beg you from the bottom of my heart never to withdraw from me your friendly sympathy. In return I may assure you, that it is my greatest pleasure to be thankful ! With the best wishes for your prosperity, I commend myself most thankfully and respectfully as

Your most obliged

RICHARD WAGNER.

MEUDON, *September 7th,* '41.

P.S.—Would you have the great kindness to forward the enclosed letter to its address ?   R. W.

3.

ESTEEMED HERR HEINE !

There is nothing else for it—I must be as great a burden as possible to you ! About a month ago I took again the liberty to write you, and to load you with various requests ; and without waiting to see how you receive that letter, I feel constrained to take your forbearance once more by storm. Will you be able to forgive me ?—I seek and seek for any possible pretext that might give me even a shadow of right to lay *such* claim to you and to your kindness, as in a certain measure I feel compelled to do !   I find nothing, unless perchance it be the right of old family friendship, which I here might seek to bring into force. You were the friend of my family, of my departed father. You are entwined in the earliest recollections of my youth, and friend *Heine* appears to me so intimate, so long familiar a name, that it seems to me at times as though I needed no far-fetched excuses to lay claim to a friendship on which—as I, alas! must tell myself in sober moments—I cannot have the slightest right to count by reason of my own deserts.

In such moments, however, my friend *Kietz* consoles me; for without ceasing he assures me that all considerations for and against go for nothing with you —that wherever your powers permit you to be useful you gladly offer your assistance, without any great questioning " for whom ? "—and, further, that he himself has often written you about me, petitioning you on my behalf, so that I may well venture to throw myself directly on your kindness and good-nature, confident at the least of not meeting with a bad reception. Therefore, as I have often ventured much before, neither will I now lose courage, but act as though I were really turning to a *Friend*. I hope one day to yet acquire the right to call you by this name.

This, my dear Herr Heine, is what I so need at the present time in Dresden—a *friend* personally disinterested in my affair. In spite of my relations with Councillor W., which (thanks to the existence of the *Abend Zeitung !*) are pretty frequent, I still lack news about the state of my Dresden project. Winkler's news, of course, is always of so official a character that the chief matter itself is only given me in a short and cursory way, while many incidental things, often of great importance, are scarcely ever mentioned. Thus, the last letter of W. certainly gives me the good piece of news that Herr v. Lüttichau has definitely consented to my opera being put on the stage after Reissiger's. That is all very good; but how many questions does not this answer suggest! For instance: does the general management propose to place my work upon the stage with the outlay indispensable to a brilliant effect? On this point W. writes me: " The general management will leave nothing undone to equip your opera in a suitable manner." You will understand how terribly terse this seems to me! I am not greatly surprised at receiving no letter from Reissiger since last March: he has *worked* for me,—that is the best and most honourable answer; besides, it would be foolish on my part to expect that Reissiger, now that his own opera must be fairly engrossing his attention, should be much occupied about me.—But what alarms me is the absolute silence of our *Devrient!* I think I have already written a dozen letters to her : I am not exactly surprised at her sending me no single line in answer, because one knows how terrible a thing letter-writing is to many people. But that she has never even indirectly sent me a word, nor let me have a hint, makes me downright uneasy. Good heavens! So much depends upon her—it would really be a mere humanity on her part if she, perhaps through her lady's-maid, had sent me a message to this effect: " Make your mind easy! I am taking an interest in your affair!"—Certainly everything which I have learnt here and there about her behaviour with regard to me gives me every reason to feel comfortable; for instance, she is said to have declared some while ago in Leipzig that she hoped my opera would be brought out in Dresden. This token would have fully quieted me, if it had only come directly to my ears or eyes : hearsay, however, is far too uncertain a thing.—

A month ago I likewise wrote to her, and earnestly begged her to let me have *only a line* with the name of the lady singer whom she would like to be cast for the part of *Irene,* so that I might make a formal list to propose to the management. No answer !—Oh, my best Herr Heine, if your kindness would only allow you a few words in which to make me acquainted with the intentions of the adored Devrient ! Does she really *wish* to sing in my opera ?—That is the question.—

Good heavens ! only to know how all this stands ! I have written to Herr Tichatschek, and commended myself to his amiability : shall I be able to count on this gentleman ?

I have written to Herr Fischer,—to-day I send off a second, more circumstantial, letter to him. Can I count upon his kindness, on his so exceptionally weighty help ?

And lastly—is my opera being seriously thought of ? Have the preparations, the costs of its equipment, been pondered over ? I do not indeed yet know whether Reissiger's opera has already appeared ; should this still not have happened, I see right well that, for the moment, there can be no material thought of preparing for my opera. Meanwhile, unless they look on *Rienzi* as an easy burden, they must already have pretty well made up their minds in advance as to how they intend to deal with it. And that's the very point

I am so anxious to see cleared up. If they merely treat *Rienzi* as an opera about which one asks, a few days before the performance, " What shall we get put together for this ? " I should consider it a grave misfortune. On the contrary, I have counted on the probability that the direction would regard an opera which is calculated throughout for the grandest and most sumptuous proportions as an appropriate opportunity to show off the new theatre in all its splendour. As you, dear Herr Heine, will take a principal part in the solution of this question, I herewith apply to the man best fitted to give me information on the point. I therefore pray you most earnestly for an answer.—

Concerning the cast of the chief characters in the tragic pantomime in the second Act of my opera, I am writing too to-day to Herr Fischer : to correspond to my intention they must be represented by members of the comedy-troupe who are accustomed to play similar parts in spoken drama. It will be a troublesome matter to carry this through, and yet it must be done if the pantomime is to produce the desired imposing effect.—

Enough ! What should I not have to call to mind, and what to ask, were I to pour out all that I have at heart ! If you are willing, dear Herr Heine, to put my thankfulness to the venture, you will have the infinite kindness to give me the longed-for answer to the questions I here ask, and to tell me whatever else you may consider of importance. If you would only put yourself a little in my situation, you could easily picture to yourself how greatly you would oblige me by satisfying my request. If your certainly overloaded occupations

allow you before long to dispose of a free hour, I
beseech you to devote that hour to *me :* right willingly
shall I be ready to give you up whole days of my own
life, if ever I could be persuaded that they would be of
any value to you !

My humble regards to Mad. Devrient. I hesitate as
to whether I should write to her again to-day. Good
heavens ! what could I write to her, except the same
thing as ever—ever the same thing ! Must I not be
afraid of seriously wearying her ?—

Kietz is very soon coming to you. He is an excellent fellow, and very dear to me ; he will certainly
always get on well, for no one can help being kind
to him.

By this letter I have indeed loaded myself with a
fresh debt : so please have confidence in me and my
integrity !

With the most heartfelt respect and devotion,

Your most thankful and obliged servant,

RICHARD WAGNER.

MEUDON, *October* 14*th*, '41.

P.S.—If you should find time, or feel inclined, to
honour me with a letter before the 25th of this month,
it will reach me at *No.* 3, *Avenue de Meudon, à Meudon,
près Paris.* After that time you must please be kind
enough to address as follows : *No.* 14, *Rue Jacob, à Paris.*

4.

MY MOST HONOURED SIR AND FRIEND,

You are silent, *Herr Fischer* is silent—and I
almost fear that silence would reign everywhere, if I
did not write notices in the *Abend Zeitung,* and report

French comedies! What you would have had to announce to me is, however, as I now perceive (thanks to the *Abend Zeitung* and Councillor W.), so far from pleasant, that I can easily understand that you are silent out of *consideration* for me. I, fool that I am, was only anxious as to how Herr Fischer would receive my last letter with all its propositions, and about the trouble and care which I was occasioning to him and to my friends; but now I must learn that there is no present question of trouble and care, that not a breath of thought is given to my opera, and that for this I have to thank—a whim of my high patroness Mad. Schröder-Devrient, who yet had only lately assured me, through you and through my Leipzig relatives, that she had at heart the ultimate performance of my opera, and that she would joyfully do for it all she could! I confess that this came upon me like a thunderbolt;—I had accustomed myself to await the performance of *Guitarrero*, to watch the "star" of Pixis; but that it should suddenly occur to *Devrient* to wish to sing *Armida*, and forsooth before my opera—that, in truth, I had not expected. Herr W. merely writes me that it is decided, for the sake of Mad. Devrient, to put *Armida* on the stage early in *February;* but after that would come my *Rienzi*, so that it could still be given before Easter. Now, if everything goes off well and quickly, I might not have much to say against it; but if it should occur to any "star" or other to come across my path, or if one thing succeeds another with the customary slow progression, so that my opera does not come out before Easter,—I see beforehand, with sad certainty, that the word will then be: "It is too late now! Next winter!" But if you or any other person exactly realized how my *whole situation*, all *my plans*, and all *my resolutions* were destroyed by *such* procrastination, some pity would be surely shown me.

Should it really come to this, that my opera must be laid aside for the whole winter, I should indeed be **inconsolable**; and *he* or *she* who might be to blame for this delay would have incurred a grave responsibility —perhaps for causing me untold sufferings. I cannot write to Mad. Devrient; for that I am much too excited, and I know too well that my letters make no impression upon her. But if I have not yet worn out your friendly feeling toward me, and if I can be assured that you rely upon my fullest gratitude, I earnestly beg of you to go to Mad. Devrient. Tell her of my astonishment at the news that it is *she* who hinders my opera from at length appearing; and that I am in the highest degree disturbed to learn that she by no means feels that pleasure in and sympathy for my work which so many flattering assurances had led me to believe. Give her an inkling of the misery she would prepare for me, if (as I now have good reason to fear) a performance of *Rienzi* could not after all take place this year!—But, what am I saying? Though you may be the most *approved* friend of Mad. Devrient, even you will not have much influence over her. Therefore, I do not know at all what I should say, what I must do, or what advise! My one great hope I place in you, most valued friend!—I have written to Herr v. Lüttichau, and herewith turn to *Reissiger*. If Devrient cannot give up her *Armida*, if she cannot accord me the sacrifice of a *whim*, then all my welfare rests only on the **promptness** with which this opera is brought out, and my own is taken up. I therefore fervently pray *Reissiger* to hurry: and you—I beseech you—do the same with *Devrient*.—By *punctuality* and *diligence* everything can still be set right for me; for the chief thing is—only that my opera should come out before Easter (that is to say, in the first half of March). I am truly quite exhausted! Alas! I meet with so little that is encouraging, that it would really be of untold import to me, if at least in Dresden things should go according to my wish!

Only write to me—*yes*, at once—my honoured friend, and in your generosity do not again go so far as to frank your letter: by that you put me to cruel shame! On the contrary, if you found matter to devote a few lines to me every week, I would willingly pay for them in their weight of gold—however poor I am.—

A thousand cordial greetings to Herr Fischer! How has he received my letter and proposals? Please give him my warmest thanks!—

And thanks, thanks to you! Remain kind and friendly to me, and God grant that I may some day give you gladness. From my whole heart
Your faithfully devoted
RICHARD WAGNER.

PARIS, 14, RUE JACOB, *January 4th*, '42.

Kindly transmit enclosed note through the town-post.

5.

Your kind letter I received six days ago through Herr Lewy: so you will understand why it remained unanswered. After all that has now taken place, I have *to-day* only to answer the point concerning *Frau von Weber*. What I have learnt concerning W., by this occasion, shows me afresh how these ambiguous people are often more honourable and better than one sometimes feels tempted to consider them. Immediately upon the first news of the performance of *Der Freischütz* here, he inquired of me whether anything could be done for *Weber's widow?* At first I did not see much hope, but I went to Pillet (the Director of the Opera) and explained the state of affairs : he was surprised, and gave me the hope that he would not be unwilling to give a benefit performance in favour of Weber's heirs. I announced this to W. in all haste, and pressed him to urge Mad. Weber to write to Pillet. Then I remained—I think quite six weeks—without news, and so in astonishment wrote to W. He answered me, that he perceived from my letter how for the first time in his life a letter of his must have gone astray : that he and Frau v. Weber had written at once. Thereupon I begged him, as that letter had certainly not reached me, to write once more ; which he accordingly did by return. The enclosed letter from Frau v. Weber I at once forwarded through Berlioz to Pillet, pressing the former into the service as a suitable and useful confederate. Then Pillet answered that *he had already received a similar letter.* (How that fits in, I cannot conceive!) He added that he was ready to give the benefit, only for the moment had to struggle with pecuniary difficulties, etc. In order to put more fire into the matter, I got W. to invite Frau v. Weber to write to *Schlesinger;*—that also was done at once, and the letter was quickly

attended to by me. *Schlesinger* was highly flattered
by the confidence of Frau v. Weber, and promised
zealously to urge on the matter; so it is not his fault if
up to now no step has been taken.   The new opera
by *Halévy* stops the way.   Schlesinger has, however,
promised to make use of the first pause to bring his
energy to bear—for which he is the very man : he has
influence, and **gives up nothing** which he has once
begun.—But, to speak frankly, I nevertheless see no
prospect of the desired result :—*the best moment has
been missed*, and this was in the first month after the
first performance of *Der Freischütz*.   The fourth to
the ninth representations were those that enlisted the
sympathy of the public here : *after* these the performances became **villainous**, and were, moreover, but few
in number.   For that reason I anxiously waited *then*
for a letter : as this got lost (as I certainly do not doubt)
and the second came so late—after the favourable
moment—it was really already too late for the whole
affair.   Meanwhile, we do not despair : wonders happen
in Paris, and the *immortal Freischütz*, after so many
mortal apparitions, may easily be recalled to life, and
for *this contingency* all measures are taken.—My most
respectful greetings to Frau v. Weber !

Herr Lewy will himself shortly give you news of his
journey :—*here* he has only blown his horn at the *Court*,
in the concert of the *Duc d'Orléans*.—Unfortunately
we have not often seen each other.   Also I have not
been able to show him any particularly great service :
however, we have made friends with one another, and
appear to be mutually satisfied.

In order not to commence a fresh page, and to compel

myself at last to bring this long letter to a close, I write
on the margin ; your patience will also have got already
to the edge. Therefore only this—so far as it can be
done with words and strokes of the pen—my *thanks* !
How quickly this word is said, and yet how much it
takes to worthily fulfil it ! Shall I ever get so far ?
Ah ! if only a deep, strong will sufficed ! My dear
friend, you show your kindness to me, not surely to
gain thanks, still less reward—for could the *first*
flatter, the *second* satisfy you, you should certainly have
bestowed your friendship on another !—Yet, I hope
from the future ! May it be favourable to you, and
preserve your dear family in wellbeing—then has it been
a powerful help to me ! Farewell, and be assured of
the most faithful heart of

Your devoted
RICHARD WAGNER.

PARIS, 14, RUE JACOB, *January* 18*th*, '42.

6.

MOST HONOURED FRIEND,

I hope Herr Fischer has shown you my last
letter to him : for the chief part of it was at the same
time addressed to *you*, and I therefore considered it
unnecessary, and perhaps wearisome, to write also to
you in particular. You will have perceived from that
letter my state of mind with regard to the fresh great
adjournment of the performance of my opera. The
manner in which Herr Fischer informed me of this
excessively unpleasant decision was so convincing to
me, and at the same time it so clearly expressed a warm
interest for the success of my work, that I must have

been more than a fool if I had chosen to reject the reasons assigned.   On the contrary, I owe my fullest thanks to all who under *such* circumstances pressed for a delay ; and for this fresh proof of friendly intention, I should like to be able right soon to manifest my deepest gratitude.—

In any case, my worthy friend, I hope to see you shortly : I cannot endure Paris any more, and I pant for German soil.   At the same time, the not altogether satisfactory state of my wife's health makes it my duty to conduct her this summer to the Teplitz baths, which have been so universally recommended to her.   Thus, all things taken together, I am anxious to stay somewhere more in the neighbourhood of Dresden ; for however little weight I may ascribe to my personal influence in my affair, yet it will be a great comfort to me to be nearer to the whole thing.   I hope, however, that the last resolve, to put my opera into rehearsal immediately after the return of Devrient, will be adhered to !   And on this supposition I venture to assume that many things will now be quietly attended to, which may render the work easier later on ?—Meanwhile, there is no necessity for me to touch further on all these matters—before the proper time approaches, I shall have seen you, and discussed everything with you by word of mouth.

How is your valued family, dear Herr Heine ?   We take for granted that the evil demon of sickness has vanished from your hearth, and that little *Marie* is fully restored to health.—Friend Kietz, whose voluminous letter I have to thank for the enclosure of these lines, will probably give you much and sundry news about himself : Delaroche's portrait shines at the exhibition since yesterday—may it only prove of some use to the poor fellow! We must have a good talk about him and his interests, when we sit together in Dresden: his position is none of the best; and, considering how hard he is now put to it, it would be far better for him to be in Germany again. However, he does not wish to return until he has somewhat perfected himself in this and that—in which he is right; but without money he can accomplish neither the one thing nor the other.—

I am very uneasy about *Reissiger :* I have sent him a number of letters, but he has not answered a single word.—I sent to him and Herr Lewy a copy of the *Gazette Musicale*, in which I had managed to get in a *réclame* about them both;—I presumed that would not displease Reissiger, and would perhaps force him to show a sign of life. However, he remains stone-dead!

As to yourself, only remain alive and warm to me, and Heaven grant you some little rest for your refreshment; perhaps near you I too might then partake thereof. Councillor W. wrote me lately: "Every one is rushing away from here—*Devrient* goes to St. Petersburg, Frau *Schröder* to Berlin, etc. *Would that one could take flight too! I think of taking mine to Upper Italy* next May!" (The Flying Councillor strikes me as very comical.)—

So I will fly to Saxony, and—selfishly enough!—I only hope that *you* may not fly away from there before me.—

Cordial greeting to Herr Fischer, and a thousand good wishes for your prosperity from your grateful friend,

PARIS, *March* 16*th*, '42.   RICHARD WAGNER.

7.

My Most Esteemed Friend,

For Heaven's sake do not be angry with me, if I torture you with these lines ! But you will readily understand the uneasiness which drives me to this step ; and therefore, relying on your indulgent forgiveness, I burst on you with a question and a request that come from my very heart.—More than a week ago I wrote to our excellent friend Herr Fischer, and begged him to send me a few brief lines to let me know if Mad. Devrient and Tichatschek were already back, and whether, in consequence, the parts of my opera were given out ? I could have received an answer as early as last Monday, and as up to to-day I have waited in vain for one, you can easily imagine that I am not a little disquieted by it ; for I must necessarily conclude from Herr Fischer's silence that he has nothing consoling to announce to me. Notwithstanding this, and as there is nothing more painful than uncertainty, I am most anxious to learn definitely how matters stand with my opera ; for if everything is in a fair way, I do not see why I should cause desolation to my Dresden friends, by burdening them with my tormenting self before the end of this month ;—but should I learn that through my personal presence I could in any way be of advantage to my cause in Dresden, I would, nevertheless, not stop a day longer here. Therefore I entreat you, my most excellent friend, to have the great kindness to write me *this moment* how matters stand. No doubt I cause you some expense (which I beg you at any rate to charge to me) by writing on this letter,

" To be delivered immediately ; " but please do the same, and *very large and clear*, on the letter which I am awaiting ; for to my horror I have observed that otherwise a letter lies for more than twelve hours at the post, so that I only receive letters here the *third* day after they have been posted at Dresden. You see how I am tormented by unrest, and of your philanthropy I therefore hope that you will not leave me long to pine. Here I neither see nor hear the smallest atom of what is going on in the world, whereby I am certainly becoming somewhat fanciful. So listen to my prayer !

Please give right hearty greetings from me and my wife—who commends herself in the most devoted manner to you—to the most esteemed Mad. Heine, and assure her how much we rejoice at the thought of sitting again with you in your garden ;—give my thankful greetings to Herr Fischer, and remain well disposed to

Your ever-devoted
RICHARD WAGNER.

" ZUR EICHE," SCHÖNAU, NEAR TEPLITZ.

8.

FRAGMENT.

[From this letter forward, Heine is addressed in the second person singular.—Tr.]

DEAR HEINE,

When I wrote my *Flying Dutchman*, it was in the firm conviction that I could not write otherwise than I did write. The raw material—already long known to me from the work of your namesake— acquired for me on my famous sea-voyage, and amid

the Norwegian crags, a quite peculiar colour and individuality, gloomy no doubt, but borrowed from the
whispers of the Nature to which we all belong, and not
from the speculations of a gloom-sick enthusiast. But
the vast wild ocean, with its broadcast fables, is an
element that does not willingly and obediently permit
itself to be polished down to fit a modern opera; and
the whole sea-blown *Saga* of the *Flying Dutchman*—
which now seized my fancy so completely that it cla-
moured to me for artistic reproduction—appeared to
need an utterly dreadful maiming and mutilation, if
it were to be forced to meet the requirements of a
modern opera-text, with its piquant suspenses and
surprises. I therefore preferred to modify the material
which lay to my hand of itself, in *no* way other than
the progress of a dramatic plot requires, but to leave
the full fragrance of the old tale to spread itself undisturbed over the whole. Thus only did I believe that I
could chain the audience to that rare mood in which—
if only gifted with but a modicum of poetry—one
even wins affection for the gloomiest of Sagas. It was
thus, too, that I fared in the creation of my music: in
order to attain my object, I needed not to look around
on my left hand and my right, nor to make the slightest
concession to modern taste; for otherwise I should have
acted not only inartistically, but also unwisely. The
modern division into Arias, Duets, Finales, and so on I
had at once to give up; and in their stead narrate the Saga
in one breath, just as should be done in a good poem. In
this wise I brought forth an opera, of which, now that
it has been performed, I cannot conceive how it could
have pleased. For in its every external feature it is so

completely unlike that which one now calls opera, that I see indeed how much I demanded of the public, namely, that they should with one blow dissever themselves from all that which had hitherto entertained and appealed to them in the theatre. Yet that this opera, not only in Dresden, but especially in Cassel and in Riga, has gained for itself so many friends, and even won the favour of the larger public, appears to me a finger-sign pointing to show us that we must only write just as the poetic sense inborn in our German hearts dictates, never making the least concession to foreign modes, and simply choosing out our stuff and handling it as it appeals to ourselves, in order to be surest to win the pleasure of our fellow-countrymen. In this way may we win for ourselves once more a German School of Original Opera; and all who despair of this, and import foreign models, may take an example from this *Dutchman*, which certainly is so conceived as never a Frenchman nor Italian would have dreamt of conceiving it.

Your
RICHARD WAGNER.

9.

Well, my good Heine! how are you then? I have received some news of you; Müller—who has been visiting me—had heard a great deal of good about your performance, and I have also read your lines to my sister-in-law. You are going to recoup yourself— that is capital—and I have no doubt you mean it. I shall now stay in the country until the end of *July*, and am therefore counting much on the fulfilment of your

promise to spend a week with me.   Believe me, that I
heartily rejoice at the thought of being together with you
so long as that under God's free sky ; and that I now
write to you is only with the view to impress upon you
your promise, and strengthen you in your purpose.

Well, I have actually managed for the last few weeks
to abide undisturbed in the country—not counting *the*
interruption which my visit to *Spohr* in Leipzig necessarily caused :—I was delighted with the honourable,
genuine old man ; and *he* was evidently pleased that I
had accepted his invitation.   More by word of mouth !—

The aim of these lines is fully attained if I soon see
you with me !   And Heaven grant that they find you
in good health !

Best greetings to your folk from myself and Minna !
Fare you well, and come soon !

Your
RICHARD WAGNER.

GROSS-GRAUPEN, *July 6th,* '46.

10.

DEAREST FRIEND !

Now at last to you !   News from you comes in
but seldom : Koch brought the last, and this was, to
our comfort, fairly good ; are you really unable to write ?
I have still not given up the idea of paying you a visit,
but see less chance than ever of carrying it out, as I
shall have to take a little *congé* this month, in order,
at Küstner's request, to view by eye and ear the two
Berlin tenors.   According to Koch's latest information,
it appears that—reckoning from then—you would need
six weeks longer to thoroughly establish the cure, but

that your brother-in-law was perfectly certain that you would now recover. I cannot judge how far this will influence your future position as actor : but if it lengthens your acting career, I should always mournfully deplore the cause—though certainly not the effect. If we all can be sure that in the event of a declaration of your unfitness for active work, your income—owing to the Royal favour, on which we may certainly count, and to the retention of your position as *Costumier*—would not be materially reduced, then I can only wish you from the bottom of my heart the good-fortune to have nothing more to do with the actual theatre from this time forth, but to look forward to a long and cheerful evening of your life, spent in the enjoyment of science and true art. I have such deep contempt for the ruling spirit of our Modern Stage, that—since I now feel I cannot improve it—I have no more ardent wish than to be in a position to cry off from the whole thing ; and I consider it a real curse that my whole productive impulse should have directed itself to the dramatic form, for in the wretched condition of all our theatres I can but see the thorough mockery of my endeavours. —Perhaps you have already heard something of my having definitely broken off with X. about three weeks ago, so that, on my side at least, there is no hope whatever of a reconciliation : G. was the occasion of it. The details are really quite a matter of indifference : it is the old, old strife of knowledge and conviction, as against ignorance. Agreement is not to be thought of ; but when the conflict has reached such a pitch as this last, even a *modus vivendi* is out of the question, and so I adhere to my fixed resolve to put an end to the matter. However, I took counsel of prudence, and recognized that if I could only put a great Berlin success into my side of the scale, this must but tell in my favour. If therefore I can keep X. at arm's-length until I have won that advantage, so as only *then* to approach the King, I should much prefer it ; but if before that he will not leave me in peace—well, this step must be taken sooner. Naturally, I have no inclination to make a great sacrifice of my pay ; but if there's no other way I must put up with even that.—(Are you not filled with envy to play a part in this long comedy also ?)

Now to more satisfactory news! My life at Marcolini's suits me well :—still sound in health, I have now finished the two Acts of my *Lohengrin*, thus ending the composition of this opera ; and am glad and happy over it, for I am pleased with my work. If *Rienzi* goes off in Berlin as well as I hope, *Lohengrin* will follow there immediately afterwards. The King of Prussia was a week in Pillnitz (an opportunity of which L. unfortunately made no use !). The former, however, must have spoken much about me to the latter, and probably to the whole Court—for on the day after a great banquet, L. rushed into town, and ordered everything else to be laid aside, and *Rienzi* at once put again on the stage (mind you, all this *after* my catastrophe). Last Sunday we had *Tannhäuser* to an *overflowing* house ; the new ending went well, for even the foreigners, who on such occasions always gape, but do not stir their hands, were quite lively.

Rienzi will come out at Berlin in November ; the hlegel, who is to sing *Adriano*, is engaged there from the 1st of October.—

There is my news for you, you poor *Heinemännel!* Let me, in exchange, soon hear something definite from you, for till then I really cannot carry on a proper conversation with you.—Minna, who has thought it necessary to keep on reminding me about writing, most heartily wishes you speedy recovery, and showers kind greetings all round :—*I* follow her example.

Farewell, and soon send good news to

Your

RICHARD WAGNER.

DRESDEN, *August 6th,* '47.

II.

MY DEAR OLD FRIEND!

A line at last to you, of whom I have so often thought, at once in joy and suffering. You poor, good fellow, who gave yourself such endless trouble to become a right-down Philistine, and yet now feel compelled to the most un-Philistine resolves! Could one conceive that a life is so quickly outlived! You dear, good people—you and your wife, the pair of you, what are you living through now, joy or pain? Both together! But that is right; *Life* is the principal thing, and life means to be joyful and sorrowful, to perceive, to feel, to act, to do and strive; and all this is not thinkable apart from joy and pain. How is it with your hearts, when you think of your Wilhelm? Are you bemoaning? Not so—for the dead alone should be lamented—and when one has a son so full of life as yours, one laughs with him and rejoices over him. Go, and leave the old mud, mud to remain; is it so great a misfortune not to stay glued to it?

I live through a whole world-history, each time I realize that the *Heinerei* is about to migrate to America ; and truly, the whole history of the world is at the bottom of it ! Yet how simple and natural such an event seems to us at times. When, at the end of June, I had returned to Paris from the country, Wilhelm came to visit me, an hour before my departure for Zurich. I found the healthy, brave young fellow more to my liking than ever, and was delighted with him. When he bluntly told me that there was nothing more to be done with Europe, that he was off to America, and father, mother, brothers, and sisters would follow him within two years, I thought it so natural and reasonable that I calmly took a pinch of snuff and said, " That's sensible ! " Look you, that was a moment of world-history ! Then all personal, petty, miserable consciousness of man stood still ; and great, naked, and open lay at our feet the earth-ball which we call the world, while with one glance we understood the whole carpentry of this globe. But now too often this world-historical consciousness passes from me, and an unspeakable heartache seizes me at the thought, " The dear old Heines are going also—to America ! " Then I clench my fists and gnash my teeth, and even an unearthly curse escapes my lips ! Still, before you go away, let us see one another once more ; we will make a *rendezvous*, and I will keep it !—that I promise you ! !—Enough of this !

My better half has reached me safe and sound. I went as far as Rohrschach, on the Lake of Constance, to meet her. The bird and dog have also come, and we are just settling down in a little abode. The magnificent Swiss air, the grand fresh Alpine scenery, a few staunch friends whom I have won here, the feeling of freedom, uncribbed activity, hearty pleasure in my work,—all these things together make me and my good wife gay, and I think that this merry mood may bring forth much that is worthy and good. Should we be in bad humour ? No, even my wife cannot, after the recent proofs that we have had of human nobleness ; if they be few in number, yet they are of the right sort, and we have learnt them at the right time ; and thus it is, that the worst time is often the best. Devil take it ! we shall not starve,—if it comes to the worst, I shall write to my patron, your Wilhelm in America, and tell him to get me some kind of post, as the last of the German Mohicans,—then you shall pack us up with you, and we will all sail off together. If I still hold on with all my roots to Europe, it is because I have work to do here, and with all my mind's weapons ; but I cannot yet bring my heart to agree that a portion of these weapons should be forged in the French tongue, and it is at bottom a mad suggestion that I, of all people, should compose a French opera-book. Every one who indulges me with his intimate sympathy, must understand that. My repugnance is boundless, for it is really nothing but a question of gaining fame ; and at whose hands this fame ? Great heavens ! only of good-for-nothings, not of honest, sensible folk !—Well, we shall see !

At the moment, I look upon it as my duty to satisfy an inner necessity, which impels to speak out once for all, clearly and definitely, about our whole practice of Art. There is already in the press in Paris and Leipzig a short treatise of mine: *Art and Revolution.*—Presently a second essay will follow this : *The Art-work of the Future*, which will finally be concluded by a third: *The Art-workers of the Future.*   When you make their acquaintance, dear friend, you will understand, I hope, that, not from outside influence, but from deepest inner need, I have evolved to what I am, and now proclaim the views I hold.   It seems to be the fancy of you all, that everything which has failed to please you in myself, and that, owing to the tendencies of the age in general and to my nature in particular, you have not been able to explain at once, must be set down to the evil influence of another.   The premisses of my creed, as you had known them from my works and from my views, you admitted to be right, but drew back in terror from the logically necessary conclusions from these premisses.   In this you all were wrong, just as our whole so-called cultured world is wrong, when it will not allow B, after it has admitted A.   But this B demands both courage and conviction firm-set as a rock ; and these two have nowhere a sure seat,—hence we may explain the present sorry outcome of great inceptions.   Do you think that my conviction will part me from my artistic production ?   Quite the opposite.   For since I have clearly seen that our whole public art is no Art, but only art-journeymanship,—that it, with all the foundations on which it is built, must go unpitied to the devil,—only since then have I at last found true joy in art-work, in that art-work which shall spring of itself, by natural laws, from the Future ; and at which, for my own part, recognizing its conditionments, I now can and will toil with liking and with love.   This process, dear friend,

comes not about by eating of oysters and delicacies, in
comfortable sofa-corners ; but on the broadest market-
place of life, must one first sharpen his teeth by biting
stones, ere the eye shall become as clear as the inner
nature of this eye permits. For this reason, brother
Fischer, to whom I now write through you, inasmuch
as I pray you in my name to greet him with a fervent
brother-kiss—for he has given me the great joy of at
last, and of his own accord, proffering me his brothership,—brother·Fischer whom, as he is now my brother,
and this is permitted among brethren, I ought properly
to call an old fool for refusing brothership before on no
other ground than because our " position " (! !) did not
allow it,—brother Fischer, then, will shake his head
violently and suspiciously, when he hears of these my
latest views on Art. Yet, do you assure him, the dear,
good, honest *brother Fischer*, that these latest views are
throughout but the old ones, only that they are clearer,
less bedizened, and therefore more humanized. He
can't help being glad when he once more sees something of my thoughts, how clear, precise, comprehensible, and reasonable the whole thing shall look,—for
my public of the Future cannot be composed of the
clever and would-be-clever *ennuyés* of our privileged
art-world of the day, but of all sound, uncrippled men,
who have as valiant a heart in their body as brother
Fischer himself has—(I don't, of course, refer to you,
with my " uncrippled " ; I hope you will credit me with
sufficient delicacy of feeling not to have wished to play
upon your one-toned chime of bells).

Look now, good little Heinemann, we have fallen
upon our old ways, as though nothing had happened,

and it seems to me as if we were our same old incorrigible selves ! So shall it be, and so remain ! If the new comes forth from myself, yet, at the bottom, it is ever the old, only made young again and beautified ; but if the new comes from without to disturb us, we thrust it one side as well as we can ; and if nothing else is possible, at least we reach our hands to one another across the ocean, even if you must needs stand a wee bit on tiptoe. When you go to America, who knows but that I may meet you from Kamtschatka, through which country I may have got myself smuggled from Siberia, as soon as the Russians have opened up the route. You must then welcome me, and not, as an American Republican, disown me because, forsooth, I come to you in the ragged uniform of the Saxon Court !—

But meanwhile, so long as we yet remain so near to one another in Europe, we must hear one another reasonably often, if only by letter. So, send me a right good letter, and tell brother Fischer that he must also write me,—a hotch-potch of everything that occurs to him,—just as though we were chumming together in the evening over our herring-pickle. That is the right thing, and has the genuine homely scent.

One thing more ; greet Krieten for me, and give him a good hand-grip ; do you hear ? He belongs to those who in these latter times have taught me more and more to love mankind.

Greet also X. ; I understand and value him, although he may think his love of me a fault.—

And you good wife, and Marie—greet them from me and my good wife, to the best of all your might ;

for I mean it all and heartily. Greet Müller too, and tell him all about me.—And now farewell ; keep a stout heart ; you have good reason to, for many are worse off than you, and they have no Wilhelm, to whom I pray you commend my most obedient service, by letter. Fare you well, and hold me dear.

Your
RICHARD.

ZURICH, *September*, '49.

12.

DEAREST, BEST FRIEND,

I do not really write a letter to-day, but only wished a short notice to reach Uhlig with regard to a Wigand matter, about which he wrote to me lately.— Now that I have at last got into a quiet home here, my fingers are absolutely burning to write my pamphlet, *Das Kunstwerk der Zukunft*, the composing and issuing of which have become for me a veritable heart-need. The work is instinctively expanding itself under my hands to the full—and as I now see, to its necessary— proportions ; and—I think you know me—when I have anything of this kind on my mind, I curse the time which I must spend on eating, sleeping, and necessary recreation, and for which I must twitch off a corner from my appetite for work. For nothing in the world, then, could I constrain myself to devote a morning to letter-writing ; but I merely give up a few moments to the settlement of other matters. That is why you receive no letter from me to-day, but only a couple of very hasty lines, as I cannot possibly post a letter to Dresden without at least saying good-day or good-night to you !

Do not be vexed with me for preferring to write direct to Wigand in the "*Nibelungen*" matter, and not, as you wished, through you ; for I could settle it in a few words with Wigand—but to you I should have had to write quite a treatise, in order to quiet your scrupulous soul. But when I am occupied with anything so engrossing as my present work, I like to be kept from it for as short a time as possible. So do not be vexed with me for this ! For, after so nice a letter as the one I have just received from you, you would have no right to be so. Be assured, I could wish for nothing pleasanter than to receive such a letter every day, not perchance on account of the flattery in it, but because of the true heart-and-soul interest which it caused or excited in me.

However, I did not mean to write you a letter at all, and so you shall not even get so much as half a one !

As soon as my work—which is turning into quite a book—is finished, which I hope—with the copy—will be the middle of November, I will write nothing but letters for a whole week—letters—immense letters— and you shall receive an extra-special pleasant one : also brother Fischer's letter shall not be so bad. Give him one hundred thousand greetings, the good, excellent soul, and tell him how I am impaled on the Work-of-the-Future.

If meanwhile you receive any news from Wilhelm, I beg you, in the most pressing manner, to write to me at once. Yet, apart from that, you would rejoice me above everything if you would soon let me hear a trifle again.

Best and heartiest greetings to wife and child from

myself and my wife ! Keep in good health, and do not be such a cursed egoist as to complain about future decrease of ability to work, etc. What the devil have you got your son for ? How we always look upon our own powers as our only ones, while the glorious extension of our being through that of others, especially of our own children, we contemptuously overlook : " We all know nothing as yet of love ! "—

More of this another time ! Farewell, and make yourself familiar with the idea that we shall soon see each other again—certainly before the two years are over !—Adieu !

Your
RICHARD.

October 26th, '49.

And was I not delighted with your family picture, and Wilhelm's portrait in plaster, which both arrived here safe and sound ? ! In thinking of what is far off, one often forgets what is close at hand,—so it was in my last letter !—The best of thanks, and the assurance that your emigration *in effigie* to Switzerland—and under my roof—has made me ever so happy. You are all hanging at full length on our walls,—better, however, than the Hungarian generals in Pesth and Arad !— Kind thanks, old fellow !

13.

DEAR LITTLE HEINEMÄNNEL !

Here you have a living letter : a faithful, good soul, who will give you news from myself and Minna, a thousand times better than my poor pen could do.

Moreover, this letter will not strain your eyes. If you can send me nothing of this living sort, be assured that with immense delight I would accept, by way of compensation, a pen-ink-and-paper-letter instead. Do not keep me waiting for it, and believe me I ever and ever think of you with faithful affection.

Your
RICHARD.

14.

MY GOOD HEINE,

You will be more than surprised to have had no letter from me for so long. The debt weighs heavily on my mind, and for a long time I have thought of paying it off. Latterly I really was uncertain as to whether you were still in Dresden, or already in Berlin : I waited therefore to receive news, and so the matter got delayed.

I will be honest, and tell you that for some time I *would* not write to you, because I knew not what I *could* write. The great infatuation of a section of my friends—however easily explained—is what has brought me into this state of deepest distraction and melancholy : it was that unfortunate urging of me to Paris. In the last months of the past year, I had already firmly resolved to give up the Paris plan entirely : but such a letter as yours, in which you suddenly painted so black a picture of my past and future, was quite enough to induce me—half in despair—to overthrow my resolution. You, Fischer, and all of you had only one thing before your eyes : the glories of Paris,—of which you all knew absolutely nothing. Well, I looked at my wife, and

saw that she also had the Parisian bee in her bonnet,—
so I then resolved—ill, very ill, as I was—to go to
Paris in the devil's name, and indeed in the most
excellent temper in the world.   My stay in Paris is one
of the most villainous things that I have ever experienced.   Everything which I foretold and foresaw
came literally to pass.   My sketch for an opera-poem
appeared ridiculous, and with good reason, to everybody who knew anything of the French language and
the French Opera.   The condition of this Opera itself,
the *Prophet*, No. 5, and all impressions connected
therewith, made me seem mad even to myself: and,
finally, the impossibility of getting so much as an overture performed—my frightful disgust at the banker's-
music, from which every decent person in Paris itself
turns away,—all this brought me, suffering as I was
from terrible relaxation of the nerves, into a state of
mind not quite the best fitted for my turning with
apologetic explanations to those of my friends who
were now probably expecting nothing but news of
Parisian triumphs and successes.   On the contrary, I
had got so far that I held it fitter to break with heaven
and earth; to which I saw myself more pressed each
day.   It was as though everything with which I had
any closer ties were now conspiring to drive me to
extremes.—And I had really come to an extreme, for
anything was preferable to continuing this life, to continuing with those who held that the very thing most
repulsive to my nature was the best thing for me—who
were all agreed, that in theory one should be an honest
fellow, but in practice a scoundrel!—

   Enough; that heavy time is over for me,—the

mephitic clouds of Paris have dispersed before me, and since the last two or three months I have been back again in my friendly, healthy Zurich, from which neither god nor devil shall drive me any more. So now once more I can look at you with the requisite cheerfulness, and say in peace that I heartily and willingly forgive you, if you laboured under a mistake with regard to me ; while, on the other hand, I beg you to pardon me for so long withholding from your sympathy its corresponding nourishment. I was truly beside myself, and have now returned to myself—and this is the chief thing I wished to point out to you.—

For the rest, I have nothing particular to tell you about myself. You know that Liszt has given my *Lohengrin* at Weimar. The performance is said to have been excellent in all secondary matters, but the principal thing—the actors on the stage—feeble and altogether unsatisfactory. Well, that explains itself ; Providence will not work private miracles for me, neither will it make actors—such as I want—grow on every tree !—Nevertheless, I am now thinking of writing the music to my *Siegfried*. In order one day to be able to produce it properly, I am cherishing all sorts of bold and out-of-the-way plans ; to the realization of which nothing further is necessary than that some old uncle or other should take it into his head to die. Later on you shall hear more about it !—If you feel inclined once again to read something of mine, get the last numbers of the *Neue Zeitschrift für Musik* (Leipzig) : the article "Das Judenthum in der Musik," by R. Freigedank, is mine.

From certain preparations which have been made for

the purpose, it is possible that here in Zurich I may
from time to time do a little active work for art.   Also
more of this later.

First of all, I am anxious for news about you, yours,
and my old Fischer !   May it be good news !   In order
that we may get into step once more, write to me soon,
tell me much, greet your folk and Fischer in a prcper
manner,—and keep me in kind remembrance.

Your
RICHARD W.

ZURICH, *September* 14*th*, '50 (ABENDSTERN, IN ENGE).

15.

DEAR OLD FRIEND,

It is certainly right wrong of me not yet to have
answered your January letter.   I will not excuse myself
by saying that I have been too deeply engrossed in my
work, but I must confess that for me—in my own
peculiar mood—it was most difficult to write to you ;
for your news of yourself was of a kind to fill me with
sighing and heaviness, but not with the strength to
console you.—By chance I learn now that you are still
in Berlin, that your connection with the theatre will
not be definitely fixed until the new management starts,
and a report gives me reason to hope that you are in
better spirits than at first.

Now I should so much like to know how things
are with you, and I say this chiefly in the hopes of
hearing something more favourable than was the case
with your last letter.   That is the real occasion of these
lines.   May I not be deceived in my hope—of at least

tolerable news.—I cannot trust myself to say more concerning your state—at last described by you : I could—as I said—only sigh, so mournful was everything, and so powerless did I feel to help you !—

With me it fares both well and ill : it is only a matter of the moods into which I am thrown, which with me naturally fluctuate violently—like ebb and flow. My own courage I never completely lose ; I am so far at one with myself and the moods of the world, that I can explain to myself *why* everything is just as it is ; and as it never occurs to me to wish to reverse the nature of things, so I wait where I recognize my own powers of activity avail not ; but where I see that my activity might have any success, I grapple with all my available force, and content myself with the smallest result. I have thus the conscious knowledge of doing what I *can*, and, on the other hand, of calmly giving up that which I *must* give up. Thus I maintain myself now in sounder health than, for example, was the case last year. That I often have bad times is easily understood ; but I am in all respects candid beyond measure ; I complain when I have occasion to complain, and rejoice when I have reason for joy. Our dear little *Papo* died this winter ; I put no restraint on my heartfelt, bitter mourning for the sad loss of our little whistling, chattering, household fairy, that clung to me with such endless love.—With this open-heartedness, I have at least won this much, that I am no longer surprised at any outward misfortune ; a dash of irony also helps me over all such things— for I know that it cannot be otherwise.—

As for money, it so happens with me that whenever my purse is dry and Minna already begins to look

black, straightway a fresh supply comes in. This is
how it comes about: I have few friends, but these
few *love* me ; any one of them who *can*, always does
help me. The most active in this respect is Frau
R. in Dresden ; from time to time Liszt also does his
share. I live in completely communistic fashion, but
only with those who fully know me, and are heartily
devoted to me. From no one else would I take a penny.
So—understand me well : only one who respects and
loves me would I permit to help support me. Now
and then, too, I earn a trifle. This winter I have
written a fairly large book : *Oper und Drama.* J. J.
Weber was willing to pay 100 thalers ; A. offered 75
thalers more after the sale of 400 copies,—so it will
shortly be published by the latter. You have probably
heard, and especially read, something about *Lohengrin*
recently—Breithopf & Härtel are now engraving the
pianoforte score of it ; and probably will publish the
full score later. This will bring me no money, but merely
wipe off a c——d old debt to that firm. Do you see ?
I am even paying off debts : what more do you want ?
During the winter I practised here a few of Beethoven's
Symphonies, with a mixed orchestra of amateurs and
professionals. The thing got talked about : now they
are about to engage for me a good standing orchestra.
I declined to have anything to do with the theatre.
But shortly a pamphlet of mine will appear under the
title, *Ein Theater in Zürich*—in which I shall open
people's eyes a bit, and show them what they should
do, if they wish to have anything of value. You shall
soon receive the pamphlet.—

In May I set to the composition of *Siegfried.* For a

change I shall sometimes climb the Alps.—Ah! if no one would pity me any more on account of my loss of my Dresden position! How little they know me, who look upon this loss as my misfortune! Were I amnestied to-day, and were I again appointed Chief Court Capellmeister at Dresden, you would see how calmly I should remain in my Switzerland, and perhaps scarcely even put my feet on the blessed soil of the German confederacy!—Yes, that is how I feel!—Herewith I give you good news of myself: as to my gloomy days, I can the rather keep silence, as they mostly come from overwork and nervous exhaustion ; for then I certainly look with an eye of despair on the wretchedness of the present order of things. But is one not lucky enough if able from time to time to conquer these moods?—So now give yourself the trouble to write something good about yourself, and let your *Wilhelm* serve as theme : your living, moving work, far better than my paper works. Give me good news then: greet wife and child, and keep me in kind remembrance.

Your

RICHARD W.

ENGE, NEAR ZURICH, *April* '51.

Peps is still alive, but fearfully lazy whenever he is not barking.

16.

BEST HEINEMANN!

Hearty thanks for your kind letter! But unfortunately the big one, promised to me through a certain lady—I have not received. I waited until to-day in the hopes of getting it. Still, above all, I express to you my very great joy in that you (and others also) tell me of your good state of health : certainly that was the pleasantest thing which you could write to me !

Now, as I cannot answer you anything about your own affairs—as I have not received the letter in question—and as everything which I could tell you about myself has already been put into my letter to Fischer, I limit myself for to-day to a cordial greeting to you and yours, while I beg Fischer to let you have my letter to him. What I write to him is nearly all for you as well.—So let me know more about yourself and Wilhelm, and thus I shall have better occasion for a special answer ! Once again, best and most heartfelt thanks for your friendship, and for the continued proofs of the same ! Farewell, and let me soon have further particulars.

Your
RICHARD WAGNER.

September '51.

From the 15th onwards, at *Albisbrunn,* near Hausen, in the Canton of Zurich.

Müller is going with me to the hydropathic establishment ; your old and faithful doctor has got him into a nice state. O you unhappy men, with your poison-dosing doctors ! You are all wretched, and no one believes it ! It's terrible !

17.

DEAREST HEINEMANN,

I have kept on thinking it was your turn to write to me, as you owe me news about yourself and family,

since—as you know—the letter *per* the famous Fräulein
E. (or somehow) has not reached me. So I only write
to-day to remind *you* about writing. Especially do I
beg for news about Wilhelm ; I should also particularly
like to have his address.

Before I know from yourself how you are, I will just
tell you this about my doings : that I have become a
complete water-man. This time I was ten weeks in
the hydropathic establishment ; only on account of the
winter setting in early and with great severity, have I
given up the cure for the present. However, it was
sufficient to give me the clearest foretaste of perfect
health, a new and indescribable feeling of comfort,
of which not one of us has any idea until he has
experienced it : (for it is well known that we are made
ill from youth upwards, so that we have absolutely no
consciousness of health !)—and this complete health I
will win for myself next spring, when I shall go again
to the hydropathic establishment.—I shall pass the
winter in comfortably lounging about as much as
possible—the only thing which I find somewhat irk-
some—in order when summer comes to set to the
greatest work of my life in full harness and restored to
health. Concerning that work I tell you nothing here,
because you will shortly read more about it in an
" Address to my Friends," which I shall put as " Preface " to the edition of my Three Opera-poems (*Flying
Dutchman, Tannhäuser,* and *Lohengrin*).—So enough
for the present !—

Do you know where the Frommanns live ? If so,
please send them the enclosed lines !—

So, *Nante,* write ! To your wife and child heartiest

greetings from myself and Minna, who is quite well and
cheerful!—Farewell, old fellow!

Your
R. W.

Zurich (Zeltweg), *December 20th*, '51.

18.

Dear Nante!

Do not take it amiss that I only to-day send you
news! But even to-day I merely write you briefly, to
tell you that to-day I shall not write you at length,
because I can only do this after some little time.
Why?—you shall learn that at once. You know what
an obstinate beast I am; well, I have just finished my
great *Nibelungen* poem, and I mean to make a clean
copy of the stuff, so that my friends, too, may be able
to taste as much as possible of it. This will take a full
month of my time away, for at present I can at most
spend three hours on such work: but it must be done
before I go to anything else; otherwise I shall have no
rest. Now, I cannot write as I ought to you, without
thoroughly acknowledging your amiable care about
Lohengrin. But I see again, especially from your
letter, that I must express myself very clearly and in
detail with regard to my wishes for the staging of
Lohengrin, before I can be certain not to be misunderstood on any point. For this purpose I shall have to
bring my—unfortunately somewhat neglected—painting
talent into service; but in any case I see a work before
me that cannot be dashed off in a moment: I therefore
save it until I have finished what I have immediately in
hand. Fortunately this matter does not press: I have

withdrawn *Lohengrin* everywhere for this winter, and shall not open the doors for it until the next. The *Flying Dutchman* is being given in place of it at Schwerin and Breslau. I rejoice at the thought of the work which we shall *both* do presently: something "orderly" will come out of it. You have already given me most "disorderly" joy by your ready consent, as well as by your preliminary designs. You will receive the *pianoforte score* at the same time as my sketches : I have a copy for you. I doubt whether we can persuade Härtels to publish the *scenarium :* I shall probably have to pay the costs myself, but sha'n't make anything by it.

The visit of yourself and Fischer to Weimar surprised me very much : how the deuce do you old-young fellows come to take such a jaunt ? There must be some witchcraft in it !—Your notes about the Weimar performance were of the highest interest to me : I saw everything vividly before me, and, so far as I can conjecture, agree with you as to the character of the performance.—Hearty thanks ! The small attention which G. paid to all my hints and directions appears to have made your hair stand on end ! And yet Papa *Fischer* blames me so much for my Guide to *Tannhäuser* —he always imagines it to be my sole concern to see my operas performed, and that it is *therefore* " unwise " to make so many out-of-the-way demands ! ! I have indeed good ground for shame, to have been misunderstood on the most important points even by you and him. I care **absolutely nothing** about my things **being given :** I am only anxious that they should be **so given** as I intended ; he who will not and cannot do that, let him leave them alone.   That is my whole meaning—and has Fischer not *yet* found that out ?   O you hardened sinner ! !—*Na*, greet him heartily.   Best thanks for his letter : answer *anno* 1853 !

Give greetings to good Aunt Heine and Marie : in his sail round the world I hope Wilhelm will meet *you* again in Japan, and, to be sure, stuttering.   Many hearty greetings and good wishes from myself and Minna : to-morrow we give our Christmas-boxes.   Farewell !

Your soon forty-year-old
RICHARD

December '52.

P.S.—As to the *Flying Dutchman*, I have referred Breslau and Schwerin to Berlin for the *scenarium* (it was not at all bad there !) : perhaps with your acquaintances you could help them ?

19.

DEAR NANTE !

Would it be possible to *lend* the costume-pictures for *Tannhäuser* to the very *small* (but well-disposed) theatre at Freiburg (Baden) ; or—if not—to let it have them as cheaply as possible ?   The people there have arranged the rest as well as they could.—If you can, then do it quickly ; for they have been doddering, and are now in a desperate hurry.—I shall soon set to the *Lohengrin* work, which I shall then send you at the same time as the pianoforte score.

Hearty greeting from

Your
R. WAGNER.

February 3rd, '53.

31

20.

DEAREST BROTHER,

It was very kind of you to take such interest in the Freiburg people : it has borne very good fruit. From all reports I learn that in this small nest—through the uncommon zeal of all, and particularly of the young but extremely talented musical director—an exceptionally good performance of *Tannhäuser* has taken place. The singer of the principal *rôle*, a young man of twenty-two, so interests me that I have made an appointment with him, in order to make his acquaintance. Eduard Devrient was also there (at the third performance). —I tell you this in reward for your friendliness toward these people.

The long letter which I owe you I cannot write to-day. I have for the present knocked myself up with many and various things : especially have I a wretched lot of letters to answer, and indeed to persons who are not so indulgent as you and Fischer. But I shall soon settle to the *Lohengrin* work : Härtels will publish it—provided the matter is made easy for them. With the pianoforte score I will then send you also my recently finished great poem (*Der Ring des Nibelungen*). In the course of the next few days I hope, too, to manage to write to P : kind greetings to him for to-day, and announce my letter to him, which certainly will contain much business-stuff (for we must take X. by the nape of the neck !).

For to-day, only one further question and request. The *Leipziger Illustrirte* again wishes to make a fuss about me (in connection with *Tannhäuser*) : for that purpose they wished to give my portrait, and from a

new photograph. I tried it, but the weather was so
bad that it turned out a failure. So at last—with my
great dislike to a sitting—I yielded to the request of a
lady portrait-painter here, who is really a most intelligent and practised water-colourist, and am now having
my portrait taken : the *Illustrirte* will receive a photo-
graphic copy of it. But the picture, in the opinion of
all who have watched its growth, has turned out so
exceptionally good, that we have now come upon the
idea of having a portrait so like my present self at
last—and indeed for that very reason—lithographed
for my friends in Germany. The artist is not satisfied
with the lithographers here ; and she would only permit
it to be lithographed abroad, provided there were some
one in the place who was well acquainted with me, and
who could therefore supervise the copy in the interest
of the likeness. So I thought of Hanfstängl—as lithographer—and you as supervisor. Please then speak
soon to Hanfstängl, and see if he will undertake the
stone-drawing : any one who cares may see about
publishing it. I should think no one would do badly
with it ; but if there is any difficulty, Härtels will take
it up at once. If you agree, I will send you the portrait
next week ; but the lithographing must be first-rate !—

Well, as this is not to be a proper letter, you've had
enough for to-day ; besides, I am rather more in the
dumps than usual. Yesterday I worried the members
of our orchestra out of their lives, and into quite a magnificent performance of the *Eroica :* I feel some of the
effects of it now.—

You appear to be going on fairly well ! Heaven
knows ! you will come out of it in grand style at the

finish! Excuse me this superficial scribbling — but greet wife and child, with Uncle Fischer, most heartily from both of us!

Farewell! Soon more from your
Veery gude
RICHARD W.

ZURICH, *March 9th*, '53.

(Do not frank letters to me! I get quite enough now to pay for that, although in my other money-matters I shall always be a good-for-nothing.)

21.

DEAREST OLD FELLOW!

Many thanks for your letter, to which I at once answer in the briefest way just what is absolutely necessary!—About the portrait you have made a silly mistake : the *water-colour drawing* is the original, and the *phototype* is taken from the *water-colour drawing*. This by way of rectification. It would be only fair to the lady artist, if she were named on the lithograph : her name is—Clementine Stockar-Escher.

I know Härtels are slow, and wish first to *see* the original : you ought certainly to have been able to manage that at once. But now in a word : let *Hanfstängl* commence **immediately,** and for the present directly to *my order* and *at my cost.* If the plates are ready, send Härtels an impression, and ask if they will publish it, provided the costs be made good. If they will not, *I* will pay, and you must think of some one to whom you could give the sale on commission : perhaps one could try again with the—good—M. The principal thing is for the plate to be ready: the caricatures of me, which are now bought, annoy me much. (*Apropos!* Let the R.'s see the original at once.)

For your willingness to attend to the *Lohengrin* work, in spite of your suffering, I heartily thank you; if you soon get it done—well and good; but one must not flog a willing horse.

Good heavens! if only there were an end to these misunderstandings of Fischer's! What you again reproach me with is really absolute nonsense; I *never* said anything of the sort. Leave the whole bother alone; there's nothing in it but empty straw. We know, I think, how we stand with each other!—

I was very sorry to hear you had been bad again for three months: I hope you are better now.

You are probably quite clear now about the copy of my new poem: in ordering the number, I certainly thought of *you* and *Fischer*, but not exactly about P.; so that came—casually—betwixt and between. You old discontented doubters, you!!

I was quite astonished about Wilhelm's route to Japan: I always thought it went from North America round Cape Horn. Well, that's all right! but it's a capital joke after all. Dearest friend, in future we shall bring up our sons by first sending them on a journey round the world. What miserable toads are we! for we spend our dear lives in dreaming of heaven, and never get the least glimpse of earth!—

M.'s sisters grow younger every day.—Minna is quite pleased with our lovely new home. Greetings to your household and to our friends! Take care of yourself, and cure your stomach for the sake of your eyes ! Again, many thanks for your letter !

Farewell !

Your

R. W.

ZURICH, *April* 30*th*, '53.

The phototypist who made the copy was stupid enough to leave the water-colour drawing exposed to the sun, and it became quite faded, etc. Hence, the *Stockar's* request to take more care of it.

I am now up to my ears in muddle, on account of my musical performances. I am getting my orchestra from Switzerland, France, and Germany : it makes a lot of correspondence! So—forgive this hasty scrawl ! !

22.

GOOD NANTE !

The story of the portrait is becoming quite tedious. If only you had not been so conscientious, and had sent the portrait at once to Härtels, in the devil's name ! If they wish to have it lithographed in Berlin, it's all the same to me in the end ; only I request that a proof-print be sent *to you*, so that you may keep a control over the likeness, which no one, I should say, can do as well as you. But if, in accordance with my last letter, you have given over the matter to Hanf-stängl, then he may keep it, and we will stick to what I settled in that letter : I pay Hanfstängl, and X. receives the commission. Why do Härtels drag on so long ?—So you are now provided with instructions for every event ! Do as you like, only take care that the phiz soon comes out. You have not yet sent us the

lithograph of yourself! Do't!—I have terrible work
with my music sheets!

Excuse haste! Good-bye!

Your
R. W.

ZURICH, *May 3rd,* '53.

I can write no more to Härtels about the portrait
affair.

23.

DEAR FELLOW!

Many thanks for your letter! I can't see any
good reason why I should not send you just a scrap
of answer!—You are right, quite right! Yet I must
excuse Schindelmeisser somewhat: for months back
he had repeatedly begged me for designs for the *mise
en scène;* I always put him off, and at last left him quite
in the lurch. The fault was with me: I naturally
thought nothing of the whole tale. So you ought to
have devoted a good part of your reproaches really
to me, and not to him. Moreover, I am convinced
that Sch., ever since he undertook the *Tannhäuser,*
has meant honourably with me; that notwithstanding
this he has so carried out his task that I should probably shake my head considerably at the results, I can
also well imagine; still, it is not ill-will and intentional
superficiality, but insufficient knowledge of the matter,
combined with the depravity into which nowadays
every *routinier* falls, after long practice in the ordinary
rut of our operas. The light would only break in
upon him and such as him, if they were once to see
the opera given under my direction: with them, their
blindness is their ruin!!

Do you then think after all, dear Heine (and dear Fischer, to whom I also address these lines ?), that I set any value on the present performances in Germany ? that I persuade myself that they answer in any way to my demands?　Ah ! great heavens !—I certainly thought I might do some good by my Guide ; but—as I have already told you both—only in the sense that, at least, something of it would catch hold.　But that this Guide could only be an *embalming* of my own intentions, that it could thus be only a protest uttered in advance against the bad performances that we might expect,— I felt all this quite clearly when I wrote it ; and that gave me, too, the despairing mood in which I became so inconsiderate toward friends.　It was a true cry of anguish, was "*this guide.*"　Well, well ! the thing is taking its own course, in my despite ; but I can only say that I am glad to see nothing of these performances. Now, when I am in a better humour toward this or that success, toward this or that conductor, it is merely because I fancy I see at least a little good-will displayed (as, for instance, was *not* the case with R. of Leipzig, for which reason I have no intention of giving him the *Lohengrin !*).　Then, also, I am more indifferent toward smaller places : with more important places, such as Berlin, I am (as you have seen) more outspoken.

There is *one* young conductor who gives me great pleasure : that is *Schöneck*, formerly of Freiburg, now of Posen.　I have learnt to know him thoroughly here in Zurich, and have trained him in my method ; he has a very good young tenor with him, about whom I have heard wonderful things.　I am naturally anxious that he, who has given at Posen the *Tannhäuser* five

times within nine days, should let his light shine elsewhere than under these bushels; and therefore *I*, as
well as *Liszt*, have agreed that he and his company
shall give *Tannhäuser* for a couple of months at *Kroll's*
Theatre in Berlin.   The only thing I had to find fault
with was the smallness of the theatre ; but during the
coming summer it is to be rebuilt, enlarged, and specially arranged for the *Tannhäuser*.   Even should *Liszt*
manage to get called to Berlin later on, through the
Princess of Prussia, for the conducting of our two
operas,—this forerunner does not the least harm, and
puts a lot of money into my pocket.—

Talking of much money, brings Fischer to my mind,
who wanted an advance from me : I thought then that
matters would be arranged through Genée in Dantzig.
Up to now nothing has come of it, and I have already
been mean enough to refer a couple of new orders to
myself for payment, as for the moment I am cleaned
out.   The Theatre-Jew M. in Berlin will make an
advance for Genée, so as to get the score at once from
Fischer, to whom he will send as quittance the postal
slip recording the payment, whereupon the score is to
be sent to him.   Again, director *Hein* of Stettin applies
to me ; I have also directed him to send the honorarium
to me, and only to deliver the postal slip to Fischer,
by way of receipt.   Now Uncle Tom—I meant to say,
brother Fischer—will make an astonished grimace,
because nothing falls to him ; in return I assure him,
that within the space of a month he shall be with me
in Paradise, *i.e.*, he shall have money, *notwithstanding*.   But he must keep scores in readiness ; Königsberg
threatens, and Darmstadt likewise (for Schindelmeisser

will enter upon his duties as Capellmeister there on
the 1st of August).—It would be as well if you, too,
could have *scenarium* and sketches ready for *Tannhäuser;*
for that purpose I think to be able to provide you with
money for expenses, likewise within the space of a
month ; so don't let the little painter stop making his
little figures.—

Härtels wrote to me lately about the portrait, and
thereupon I wrote to them about the sixty copies.
They also advised me that their pianoforte arrangement (without words) of *Lohengrin,* for two and four
hands, had now appeared.   However absurd are such
pianoforte arrangements without words of my operas,
yet I must confess that for the publisher they have a
great value.   The regular herd of pianoforte-playing
diletantti naturally wants nothing but this sort of score,
which, after all, suits their silly purpose better than
the vocal score.   Here, for example, there are endless
demands for the pianoforte score without words of the
Dutchman and *Tannhäuser.*   Of the latter, at least, X.
really ought to get such a score made and published ;
it is a real treachery to the business if this is not
done, and I cannot help my creditors if they neglect
such a source.   X. ought to ask *Liszt* as to who
should arrange the pianoforte score.   Ah me ! if men
only knew how to help themselves !—

Once more : my musical festival was splendid, and
gave me great hopes of accomplishing wonderful things
here in the future.   One day I shall certainly myself
give performances here of my operas, and also of the
Nibelungen ; but naturally only under quite exceptional
circumstances.   For that I shall require (*ut semper*)

the services of Wilhelm. Within three or four years Wilm must really come to Switzerland : write him that to Japan !

Now, enough chattering for to-day ; more another time ! Greetings right and left from

Your
R. W.

June 10th, '53.

Lately I received an engagement proposal from Bremen: ah ! how pleased I was !—How have things gone off at Cassel ? I fancy wretchedly ! No one sends news. Does F-ff-fischer know nothing ? Is his Wilhelm already in Drrresden ?

(Veronika—Amerika !)

"Als zullendes Kind zog ich Dich auf" ; *Mime.*

If you could only succeed in bringing T. some common sense ! Good gracious ! there was no intention of any slight on him ; when he begins to be sensible, I will write to him. He is really the man I should like best for *Lohengrin.*

So K-k-kietz has become an irreclaimable *Plastiker ?* I am glad of it ! but he must really write to me : gr-r-reet him heartily ! (I am thinking too much about Japan, and that's why I st-st-stutter !)

Here the selections from *Lohengrin* pleased best. The Prelude impresses me very much.

24.

Your silence, dear Heinemännel, almost makes me melancholy. Either you are very ill, or you are angry with me. Say, have you taken anything amiss ?

Perhaps my last remarks on your communication respecting the *scenarium* for *Lohengrin?* This I must almost believe, especially as the scenic indications have been entirely omitted from the little work that has appeared. Certainly that annoyed you with me, and you thought, "If he knows better, let him do it himself." If I were right? Then you were wrong!—Well, I will say no more about it, for perhaps I am altogether in the wrong with regard to the whole suspicion, so truly painful as it is to me!—Please inform me soon!—

I have now received the *scenarium :* you have done your work well—yes, in many ways too well! I owe you so many thanks for it, that I should feel quite inconsolable if I had to think that—in reward for your friendly trouble—I had hurt your feelings on this occasion! Do set my mind at rest about it!—

Everything—as I said—answers perfectly to my wish : where you have differed somewhat from me in the scenery—as in the lay of the river in the First Act —I fully acknowledge that your corrections are right. I should only have liked, in the Castle courtyard, the balcony and stairs from the Kemenate down to the Palace brought somewhat more into view, which could have been very well done by shifting the palace-tower more to one side—to the right. But perhaps that could not be easily arranged otherwise—especially on small stages.—In short, the whole is so good, that I must offer you my heartiest thanks for it in every respect !!—

I need scarcely tell you, moreover, how unhappy I now feel at not being able to produce the work myself. To bring me into this deep discontent about the whole thing, it hardly needed the latest Leipzig outrage on

my *Lohengrin*.   As far as that goes, Fischer will laugh
his fill at me, and will contrast my scruples regarding
Dresden with my Leipzig levity.   I must just put up
with it, if he does not understand the state of matters.
I only consented to the performance in Leipzig on
condition that Liszt should represent me—if not as conductor, still as superintendent of the whole production;
and he was to have the right to stop it, if he saw there
was no reasonable expectation of a favourable result.
Now, first do I learn that R. quite set up his back against
this, and that the whole thing would long ago have
come to a rupture had it not been that Härtels effected
a prudent compromise through Liszt's complaisance,
whereby the latter was only to come occasionally to
the general rehearsals, and perhaps give a few friendly
hints to R.   Now, no single notice seems to have been
given to Liszt of the rehearsals, and he has had the
somewhat too diplomatic weakness of leaving the affair
to take its own course—for good or bad.

But that was certainly not my intention, and so the
performance has taken place entirely against my will.
I shall take other precautions for the future.—Fischer,
besides, is quite out of temper with me : I have corre-
sponded with him all the summer on mere matters of
business, and it were high time to let him have some
little news as friend.   But I tell *him* and *you*, that of
late I have written to almost no one, so up to my
ears was I with composition.   Since I returned from
Paris—beginning of November—I have written the
music to *Rheingold ;* I got so enthusiastic over it, that
until it was finished I had neither ears nor eyes for
anything else.—Give heartiest greetings to my dear

old friend, and make my excuses also to his Wilhelm ;
in the matter of letters one must not be too hard on me
just now, when I have really a fearful amount of correspondence.   But this very month I will write to our
plump friend : if he wishes meanwhile to heap coals
of fire upon my head, let him revise a score of the
Flying Dutchman, and send it to the management at
Wiesbaden.   *Tannhäuser* must also be kept ready :
orders are again drawing on.—I shall not begin a fresh
sheet until I get news again from thee and you.   Very
soon ! And now best greetings to yours, and keep
in kind remembrance

Your

R. W.

Zurich, *January* 19*th,* '54.

25.

My Dear, Good Heine !

If I were not really driven to it, I certainly
should not get so far as writing to you ! Excuse me
all protestations about being so continually plagued
with letter-writing and bothers of the kind, that I
absolutely find no time for anything else.

I really believe that I shall soon be able to see you
and Mamma Heine again : then we will set everything
properly to rights.

Meanwhile, for to-day a piece of business, for which
I must take refuge in you.—Our *Tannhäuser* costume-
and scenery-sketches are wanted.   Desplechin no longer
possesses the latter, and for the former we wish to have
recourse to your work.   So be good enough to see to
the French sketches (if only in copy) being sent here
again : if things were really more successful in Berlin

than in Dresden, you might perhaps manage to get the sketches from there. The Tournament-hall is said to have turned out very fine in Berlin : I certainly do not believe it answers to my scenic demands (for I cannot consent to give up the open arch with the stairway and tower)—still it probably contains interesting suggestions of which we could make use.—The costume-pictures you have entirely in your power. So send everything as soon as possible, for *Tannhäuser* is to be taken in hand at once. Make an account of the whole expenses, and draw a bill for the amount, or simply charge it to the management : it will be sent you by return. Address the whole to

Mr. Alphonse Royer,
Directeur de l'Académie Impériale de Musique,
3, *Rue Drouot, Paris.*

Now, do this very nicely, right quickly, and let me know beforehand when you hope to send it off.

It must surely seem a good joke to you, that your costume-designs should be wanted in Paris as models !

I regret not to be able to do anything for my health this summer : I cannot get away from Paris for a single day. Heaven knows how I shall feel this winter ! My wife has gone off to the baths at Soden, as P. wished. Altogether, she feels fairly well, although my recent life-adventures have not been exactly of a kind to make me good-tempered and patient. I am now heavy, very heavy at heart, and the only thing which at all enlivens me is, that from a distance I am always looked upon as one who does not know which way to turn for good-fortune and prosperity.

Now, let me have good news from you : greetings to Mamma and Maria, and the Emperor of Japan into the bargain !

Farewell, dear old friend !

Your

RICHARD WAGNER.

PARIS, *July* 10*th*, '60 (16, RUE NEWTON, BARRIÈRE DE L'ÉTOILE).

26.

MY DEAR OLD HEINEMÄNNEL !

Thanks for the friendly sign of life, and be forbearing if I only reply to you with a like sign of life. I still intend to pay a more agreeable visit soon to my old home, friends, and connections ; but for that I must wait until a time when many things shall have been definitely, publicly settled, and till I no longer have reason to fear exhaustion through constant narration and answering of questions. My future and final welfare depends upon whether I can bring my manner of life, and consequently my whole disposition, to a state of greater quietude and freedom from excitement. Talking, letter-writing, business complications—these are my life-foes : undisturbed, peaceful creation and work are, on the contrary, my life's preservers. As a matter of fact, I have only wrested to myself this benefit under the escort of unspeakable torments : my settling in Lucerne, where I find a home in the most absolute stillness and retirement, has this for aim. Here I always am only " *en visite*," and I run off the moment the " entertainment " and "distraction" become too much for me.

It would be fine if you came here for the *Meister-singer ;* I would willingly pay the cost of this expedition. Within the next few days it will, at all events, be definitely settled whether we are to have the performance in May, or not till the autumn : this depends upon the hitherto very clumsily negotiated acquisition of the Dresden tenor, Bachmann, who is certainly not my ideal ; but, when all is said and done, is still the most promising substitute for the singer I should wish for *Walther.*

You are altogether in the wrong to write me so many details about a lady singer whom you wish to recommend to me : you assume on my side an interest in these affairs which certainly shows your good opinion of my tenacity. I have nothing whatever to do with the theatre, and this is the fundamental basis of the peace which I have conquered. So long as my nerves hold out, I am present at important rehearsals of my works ; but I never attend a performance, and by the time it occurs I am already back among my mountains. In order, however, to appear a wee bit mannerly to you, you good old fellow, I may tell you, with regard to Frln. Blume, that we here have also heard nothing but good of her. But really the more she answers to your description of her the less do we need her ; for we already possess in a certain Frln. Mallinger an artist endowed with great talent, while a general utility hack, with staying power, would be a most desirable acquisition.—

Greetings to Mamma Heine, and thank her for

3 2

the delicate herrings and potatoes in *Campo vac-chino !*—

Good-bye ! dear old fellow ! Come to the *Meister-singer*. In any case, I will come soon and visit the one-chime-of-bells coasts.*

Your true friend,
RICH. WAGNER.

MUNICH, *March* 28*th*, '68.

---

* Küster = also "Sacristans."

THE END.

INDEX.

In this index an attempt has been made to classify the more important passages, to trace some of the bare initials by following the clue afforded through the occasional appearance of corresponding proper names in full, and also to group the indefinite allusions to "X." under different headings suggested by the subject-matter. For this endeavour to throw a little light on obscure hints, recourse has been made to nothing beyond internal evidence and that offered by the *Wagner-Liszt Correspondence* and C. F. Glasenapp's *Richard Wagner's Leben u. Wirken*.

In consequence of the large number of references noted, the following plan has been adopted in cases of more frequent occurrence—viz., the cyphers denoting tens and hundreds are not reiterated each time those numerals recur under the same heading, excepting where the indexed numbers run into a fresh line of type ; thus 12, 16, 81, 84, 105, 110, 154, 231, 276, are printed : 12, 6, 81, 4, 105, 10, 54, 231, 76.—W. A. E.